AP®
U.S. Government & Politics
Prep Plus
2019–2020

AP® is a registered trademark of the College Board, which was not involved in the production of, and does not endorse, this product.

Special thanks to the following for their contributions to this text: Steve Bartley, Matt Belinkie, Leslie Buchanan, Sterling Davenport, M. Dominic Eggert, Tim Eich, Chris Elmore, Mark Feery, Chris Gage, Joanna Graham, Adam Grey, Allison Harm, Katy Haynicz-Smith, Peter Haynicz-Smith, Samee Kirk, Rebecca Knauer, Liz Laub, Mandy Luk, Melissa McLaughlin, Maureen McMahon, Jenn Moore, Iain Morton, Kristin Murner, Monica Ostolaza, Caroline Sykes, Rebecca Truong, Oscar Velazquez, Robert Verini, Shayna Webb-Dray, Ethan Weber, Lee Weiss, Jessica Yee, Amy Zarkos, and Nina Zhang.

AP® is a registered trademark of the College Board, which was not involved in the production of, and does not endorse, this product.

This publication is designed to provide accurate information in regard to the subject matter covered as of its publication date, with the understanding that knowledge and best practice constantly evolve. The publisher is not engaged in rendering medical, legal, accounting, or other professional service. If medical or legal advice or other expert assistance is required, the services of a competent professional should be sought. To the fullest extent of the law, neither the Publisher nor the Editors assume any liability for any injury and/or damage to persons or property arising out of or related to any use of the material contained in this book.

"View of Political Concepts" graph adapted from "Americans' Views of Socialism, Capitalism Are Little Changed." Frank Newport, Gallup, May 2016; permission conveyed through Copyright Clearance Center, Inc. Republished with permission of Gallup.

"Public Opinion on Overturning *Roe v. Wade*" table adapted from "Wide differences in views of *Roe v. Wade* by education, religion, party." Pew Research Center, Washington, D.C. (2016) http://www.pewresearch.org/fact-tank/

10 9 8 7 6 5 4 3 2 1

Retail ISBN-13: 978-1-5062-0338-6
Course ISBN: 978-1-5062-4936-0

Kaplan Publishing print books are available at special quantity discounts to use for sales promotions, employee premiums, or educational purposes. For more information or to purchase books, please call the Simon & Schuster special sales department at 866-506-1949.

TABLE OF CONTENTS

Table of Contents

PART 1

Getting Started

CHAPTER 1

What You Need to Know About the AP U.S. Government and Politics Exam

Congratulations—you have chosen Kaplan to help you get a top score on your AP U.S. Government and Politics exam. Kaplan understands your goals and what you're up against: conquering a tough exam while participating in everything else that high school has to offer.

You expect realistic practice, authoritative advice, and accurate, up-to-the-minute information on the exam. And that's exactly what you'll find in this book. To help you reach your goals, we have conducted extensive research and have incorporated insights from an AP Expert who has 20 years of experience with AP U.S Government and Politics.

ABOUT THE AP EXPERT

Chris Elmore is a political scientist and professional educator with over 20 years of experience working with the AP U.S. Government and Politics exam. Throughout his career, he has written curriculum for and taught AP Comparative Politics, AP European History, AP World History, and AP U.S. History, in addition to AP U.S. Government and Politics. Chris has also taught American National Government, Introduction to Political Science, and Comparative Politics as an adjunct faculty member at several local colleges and universities.

Chris is currently employed as a freelance writer, editor, and subject matter expert (SME). He has worked on several projects involving the newly revised AP U.S. Government curriculum framework that serves as the foundation for the 2018–2019 school year and the 2019 redesigned exam. He has also participated in scoring for the AP European History exam.

Chris lives in Westwood, Kansas, and enjoys spending time with his 15- and 12-year-old daughters. In his spare time, Chris enjoys reading, listening to music, and following sports.

ABOUT THIS BOOK

In preparing for the AP exam, you certainly will have built a solid foundation of knowledge about political trends and the way the U.S. government operates, both past and present. While this knowledge is critical to your learning, keep in mind that just being able to recall isolated facts does not ensure success on the exam. Memorizing information, like constitutional amendments and court cases, builds general knowledge but does little for understanding what government looks like when applied to real-life situations.

U.S. Government and Politics is about big ideas. It's about the interconnections between how the American political system is structured, how people interact with the government every day, and how major concepts and ideals have evolved over time. The College Board (the maker of the AP exam) asks you to consider all of these topics and the ways they intersect. On the official exam, you'll need to apply the knowledge you've learned at a higher level in order to show evidence of college-level abilities.

That's where this book comes in. This guide offers much more than a review of basic content. We'll show you how to put your knowledge to brilliant use on the AP exam through structured practice and efficient review of the areas you need to work on most. We'll explain the ins and outs of the exam structure and question formats so you won't experience any surprises. We'll even give you test-taking strategies that successful students use to earn high scores.

Are you ready for your adventure in the study and mastery of everything AP U.S. Government and Politics? Good luck!

EXAM STRUCTURE

The AP U.S. Government and Politics exam is divided into two sections, with a 10-minute break in between. Section I gives you 1 hour 20 minutes to answer 55 multiple-choice questions spanning a variety of topics. Each question contains four possible answer choices, with only one correct response. The topics covered are as follows. You'll notice that our book is organized by these same topics.

1. **Foundations of American Democracy:** The historical and philosophical ideas underpinning the U.S. Constitution, and the compromises and conflicts that have continued to this day.

2. **Interactions Among Branches of Government:** The distribution of power, and the checks and balances that keep each branch under control.

3. **Civil Liberties and Civil Rights:** The freedoms and protections granted through the Constitution, specifically the Bill of Rights and the Fourteenth Amendment, and the balance between liberty and social order.

4. **American Political Ideologies and Beliefs:** The values and ideas held by both individuals and groups, the factors that influence these beliefs, and the ways in which these beliefs impact public policy.

5. **Political Participation:** The ways in which citizens and institutions influence government and public policy.

Section II gives you 1 hour 40 minutes to answer four free-response questions. These questions can involve any of the content tested in the multiple-choice section, but will require you to make connections across a variety of ideas that relate to each question's theme. To receive full credit on each of these questions, you'll need to write an organized, thought-out response that addresses all parts of the prompt.

EXAM SCORING

Student answer sheets for the multiple-choice section (Section I) are scored by machine. Scores are based on the number of questions answered correctly. No points are deducted for wrong answers, and no points are awarded for unanswered questions.

The free-response section (Section II) is evaluated and scored by hand by trained AP readers. Rubrics based on each specific free-response prompt are released on the AP central website after the exams are administered. Readers do not see the rubrics until the official reading has commenced. The rubrics have specific point values, assigned by the chief reader.

The score from the multiple-choice section of the exam counts for 50 percent of your total exam score. The other 50 percent is the combined score from the four free-response questions (which each count for 12.5 percent of your score).

After your total scores from Sections I and II are calculated, your results are converted to a scaled score from 1 to 5. The range of points for each scaled score varies depending on the difficulty of the exam in a particular year, but the significance of each value is constant from year to year. According to the College Board, AP scores should be interpreted as follows:

5 = Extremely well qualified

4 = Well qualified

3 = Qualified

2 = Possibly qualified

1 = No recommendation

Colleges will generally not award course credit for any score below a 3, with more selective schools requiring a 4 or 5. Note that some schools will not award college credit regardless of your score. Be sure to research schools that you plan to apply to so you can determine the score you need to aim for on the AP exam.

Registration and Fees

To register for the exam, contact your school guidance counselor or AP Coordinator. If your school does not administer the AP exam, contact the College Board for a listing of schools that do.

There is a fee for taking AP exams. The current cost can be found at the official exam website listed below. For students with acute financial need, the College Board offers a fee reduction equal to about one third of the cost of the exam. In addition, most states offer exam subsidies to cover all or part of the remaining cost for eligible students. To learn about other sources of financial aid, contact your AP Coordinator.

For more information on all things AP, contact the Advanced Placement Program:

Phone: (888) 225-5427 or (212) 632-1780

Email: apstudents@info.collegeboard.org

Website: https://apstudent.collegeboard.org/home

CHAPTER 2

How to Get the Score You Need

HOW TO GET THE MOST OUT OF THIS BOOK

Kaplan's *AP U.S. Government & Politics Prep Plus* contains precisely what you'll need to get the score you want in the time you have to study. The unique format of this book allows you to customize your prep experience to make the most of your time.

Start by going to kaptest.com/moreonline to register your book and get a glimpse of the additional online resources available to you.

Book Features

Specific Strategies

This chapter features both general test-taking strategies and strategies tailored specifically to the AP U.S. Government and Politics exam. You'll learn about the types of questions you'll see on the official exam and how to best approach them to achieve a top score.

Customizable Study Plans

We recognize that every student is a unique individual, and there is no single recipe for success that works for everyone. To give you the best chance to succeed, we have developed three customizable study plans. Each offers guidance on how to make the most of your available study time. In addition, we have split this book into "Rapid Review and Practice" and "Comprehensive Review" sections for each major topic. There is guidance in both the study plans and the Rapid Review and Practice assessments to help you determine how to best move through this book and optimize your study time.

Rapid Review and Practice

The Rapid Review and Practice chapters (3–7) aim to cover the most high-yield content in the shortest amount of time. They will guide you in figuring out exactly how much you need to study each topic and precisely what to do to study that topic effectively.

After introducing the Learning Objectives, each Rapid Review and Practice chapter begins with a "Test What You Already Know" section containing a quiz and a checklist of key terms; this combination allows you to see where you stand with the topic at hand before you even begin studying the content. In the middle, the section entitled "Essential Content" contains a summary of key takeaways and a complete list of definitions for all of the key terms. Finally, the "Test What You Learned" section contains another quiz and checklist, so you can see how you're doing after some focused studying. For both the pre-quiz and the post-quiz, there are recommended "Next Steps" that contain prep advice and instructions based on your performance.

Comprehensive Review

The Comprehensive Review chapters cover everything you need to know for the exam, with key terms in bold. In fact, these bold terms are the very same ones that appear in the Rapid Review and Practice chapters; those checklists are in the same order the terms appear in the Comprehensive Review chapters. Chapters 8–12 are like an abbreviated version of a textbook you would use in class. Chapter 13 is an in-depth review of the free-response section of the exam, including practice questions, sample essays, and grading rubrics.

The most commonly tested content in the Comprehensive Review chapters is denoted with High-Yield icons. This helps you recognize when information is absolutely essential to know. AP Expert Notes also appear throughout the Comprehensive Review chapters, highlighting important connections between topics and providing tips about how to better apply your knowledge on the official exam.

Full-Length Practice Exams

In addition to all of the exam-like practice questions featured in the chapter quizzes, this book contains three practice exams. These full-length exams mimic the multiple-choice and free-response questions on the real AP exam. Taking a practice exam gives you an idea of what it's like to answer exam-like questions for about three hours. Granted, that's not exactly a fun experience, but it is a helpful one. And the best part is that it doesn't count! Mistakes you make on our practice exams are mistakes you won't make on your real exam.

After taking each practice exam, you'll score your multiple-choice and free-response sections using the answers and explanations in the back of this book. Then, you'll navigate to the scoring section in your online resources and input your raw scores to see what your overall score would be with a similar performance on the official exam. See the study plans for guidance on when to take the practice exams.

Online Quizzes

While this book contains hundreds of exam-like multiple-choice questions, distributed across the pre-quizzes, post-quizzes, and full-length exams, you may still find yourself wanting additional practice on particular topics. That's what the online quizzes are for! Your online resources contain one additional quiz for each of the topic areas. Go to kaptest.com/moreonline to find them all.

CHOOSING THE BEST STUDY PLAN FOR YOU

The tear-out sheet in the front of the book consists of three separable bookmarks, each of which covers a specific, customizable study plan. You can use one of these bookmarks both to hold your place in the book and to keep track of your progress in completing one of these study plans. But how do you choose the study plan that's right for you?

Fortunately, all you need to know to make this decision is how much time you have to prep. If you have two months or more with plenty of time to study, then we recommend using the Two Months Plan. If you only have about a month, or if you have more than a month but your time will be split among competing priorities, you should probably choose the One Month Plan. Finally, if you have less than a month to prep, your best bet is the Two Weeks Plan.

Regardless of your chosen plan, you have flexibility in how you follow the instructions. You can stick to the order and timing that the plan recommends or tailor those recommendations to fit your particular study schedule. For example, if you have six weeks before your exam, you could use the One Month Plan but spread out the recommended activities for Week 1 across the first two weeks of your studying.

Don't forget to use the guidelines in the Rapid Review and Practice chapters, and your performance on those quizzes and key term identifications, to further customize how you study.

STRATEGIES FOR EACH QUESTION TYPE

The AP U.S. Government and Politics exam can be challenging, but with the right strategic mindset, you can get yourself on track for earning the 3, 4, or 5 that you need to qualify for college credit or advanced placement. Below are strategies to aid you on each section of the exam. These strategies, along with the information reviewed in the following chapters, will set you up for success on the official exam.

Multiple-Choice Questions

Overview

The multiple-choice section is worth 50 percent of your total score, with the other 50 percent coming from the free-response section. The multiple-choice section is scored electronically. Each correct question is awarded one point, and no points are deducted for incorrect or unanswered questions.

Multiple-choice questions will ask about a variety of topics, ranging from more straightforward to more complex. One question might ask you to identify an example of the separation of powers, while the next question might ask you to apply a constitutional principle to a hypothetical scenario, and the question after that might ask you to analyze relevant trends based on a table of election data.

Question Sets

There are several question formats you will see on the AP exam. One is the question set, typically containing between two and four questions that all pertain to a visual or textual stimulus. Question sets test the following skills.

- **Quantitative Analysis:** You must interpret data from an information graphic, such as a bar graph or a data table.

- **Qualitative Analysis:** You must interpret a text passage.

- **Visual Analysis:** You must interpret a political cartoon, map, or historical image.

The following question set is similar to one you would see on an official exam. (It is from Kaplan's Practice Exam 3, Questions 1 and 2, and the answers and explanations are available at the back of this book.)

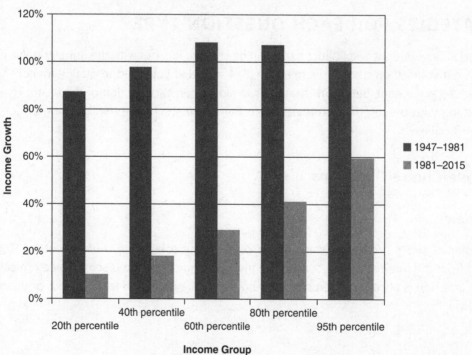

1. Which of the following is an accurate statement about the information presented in the bar graph?

    (A) Between 1981 and 2015, the 95th and 20th percentile saw approximately equal increases in their income growth.

    (B) The 95th percentile consistently saw the greatest income growth over the entire timespan depicted.

    (C) Growth was more evenly distributed across all income groups in the 1947–1981 time period.

    (D) The growth of the American middle class after World War II is most strongly reflected in the 1981–2015 period.

2. A liberal response to the data from the 1981–2015 period most likely would include

    (A) increasing taxes on at least the 95th percentile paired with increasing the national minimum wage

    (B) redistributing wealth across society through the nationalization of major industries

    (C) cutting taxes in order to increase the income of all groups across the socioeconomic spectrum

    (D) removing all government regulations in order to allow the economy to develop freely

Comparison Tables

This is a unique question type that puts political concepts side by side in a table format. The skill you will need to demonstrate is part of the name itself.

- **Comparison:** You must identify the similarities and differences between political concepts.

Take a look at the following sample question to get an idea of how comparison-table questions work. (It is from Kaplan's Practice Exam 2, Question 44, and the answer and explanation is available in the back of this book.)

44. Which of the following is an accurate comparison of judicial philosophies?

	Judicial Restraint	Judicial Activism
(A)	Courts are not constrained by political popularity and must act as a safeguard against the whims of the electoral process	Courts should defer to the judgment of the legislative and executive branches unless laws are clearly unconstitutional
(B)	Courts must be limited to the Constitution's text and read it as commonly understood at its adoption	Courts must consider contemporary notions of fairness and equality to inform its decisions
(C)	The court system is best positioned to safeguard liberty and equality	The democratically elected branches of government can best safeguard liberty and equality
(D)	Generally associated with the political philosophy of liberalism	Generally associated with the political philosophy of conservatism

Stand-Alone Questions

These are individual, one-off questions. They typically test the following skills.

- **Concept Application:** You must explain the application of political concepts in various contexts.

- **Knowledge:** You must define and identify political principles, processes, institutions, policies, and behaviors.

The following two questions are examples of how stand-alone questions might look on the official exam. (They are from Kaplan's Practice Exam 3, Question 41, and Practice Exam 2, Question 42, respectively, and the answers and explanations are available in the back of this book.)

41. One month before the 2018 U.S. Senate election, a major business corporation purchases TV airtime to broadcast a film, which it spent $15 million to produce, that negatively portrays an incumbent senator's policies and directly opposes her reelection. Supporters of the criticized senator claim the film will unfairly impact the election. Which of the following is most relevant in determining whether the corporation's actions were legal?

    (A) *New York Times Co. v. United States* (1971), which determined that, due to the First Amendment's protection of freedom of speech, the government has a "heavy burden" for justifying its use of prior restraint

    (B) *Citizens United v. Federal Election Commission* (2010), which determined that the right of groups, such as corporations and labor unions, to spend money on political messages is protected by the First Amendment

    (C) Article I of the Constitution, which specifies that the states have the power to determine most of the logistics of federal congressional elections

    (D) The Bipartisan Campaign Reform Act of 2002, which implemented the regulation of soft money contributions in federal elections

42. Which of the following is the primary function of a congressional whip?

    (A) Effectively enforcing inter-party discipline

    (B) Organizing fellow party members to vote uniformly

    (C) Making committee assignments

    (D) Breaking a vote in the event of a tie

Pacing

You have 1 hour 20 minutes to answer 55 multiple-choice questions. Some questions, such as stimulus-based question sets, may naturally take longer to answer, while other questions may take less time. As you move through the exam, gauge your time accordingly. Check your time periodically (but not obsessively); in order to stay on pace, you should complete about 10–12 questions every 15 minutes.

Answer questions as efficiently as you can in order to bank extra time for the questions that need it. Don't rush, though, or you'll open yourself up to making silly mistakes. Save yourself a little time at the end to fill in guesses on any questions you skipped over or didn't have time to answer. If you finish early, you can go back to spend some extra time on any questions you skipped.

Terminology

There are many important key terms in the study of U.S. Government and Politics, and multiple-choice questions will fold these terms into both the question stem and the answer choices. Therefore, in order to answer the questions, you'll need to have a solid foundation of terminology. Free-response questions (as you'll see in the following section) also rely on knowledge of terminology, so learning these terms and practicing with them in the multiple-choice section will help prepare you for the AP exam as a whole.

When studying terminology, it's crucial to learn both the definitions of terms and the connections they have to other terms and topics. For example, to answer a question about the Supreme Court case *Wisconsin v. Yoder* (1972), you need to know about jurisprudence, the free exercise clause, and the rights granted in the First Amendment. Furthermore, you need to know how this case could potentially impact future decisions and legislation.

Stimulus Analysis

The AP exam now has more stimulus-based questions than ever. These are questions based on some type of chart, map, graph, or other visual element, and they almost always come in sets of two or more questions.

Before you spend too much time studying the stimulus, make sure you carefully read the relevant question stems and understand what they are asking. For example, the first question about a stimulus typically is straightforward analysis of the information presented, such as identifying trends in a data table. The second question often deals with applying stimulus data to your knowledge of government and politics. Questions involving a stimulus can be narrowly focused. One question may only deal with a certain part of a table or section of a chart. Generalized questions are also possible, such as identifying the theme of an image stimulus.

For any stimulus, focusing on just a few main aspects will often yield what you need to answer the question at hand.

- **Titles or captions:** Students are often tempted to skip these seemingly simple features, but a lot of information can be gleaned from them. Read any titles or captions carefully, noting the subject as well as any years, sources, or other pertinent details.

- **Keys or labels:** There might be color coding in a map, or bars in a graph, that you need to understand in order to answer the question. The AP exam will always provide a key or label to help you decode this information.

- **Trends:** Think about what trends or patterns this stimulus is depicting, where they are occurring, and where they are *not* occurring. It may help to think about why people would have created the image. What were they trying to convey? Why did they choose to include certain information? After all, maps, charts, and other visuals are ways we organize information to better understand it.

With stimulus-based questions, keep in mind that you'll need to both analyze the given stimulus *and* activate your prior knowledge.

Process of Elimination and Educated Guessing

Never leave a multiple-choice question unanswered! A blind guess gives you a 1 in 4 (25 percent) chance of getting the correct answer. Even better, every incorrect answer you can confidently eliminate increases those odds: eliminate one answer choice and your chances improve to 33 percent, two and you're at 50 percent. Eliminate all three incorrect answer choices, and you just got the question right!

Whenever the correct answer isn't immediately clear, start eliminating and see where it gets you. One approach for elimination is to identify answer choices that address a topic other than the one being discussed in the question stem. For example, you may not know what a congressional whip does, but you might know that one of the answer choices, casting a tie-breaking vote, is actually a duty of the vice president. Therefore, you can at least get rid of that choice. If you end up guessing on that question, at least you have now improved your odds.

General background knowledge can be helpful for eliminating answer choices as well. For example, when dealing with Supreme Court cases, dates are a good tool. Between the 1950s and the 1980s, the Supreme Court issued many landmark rulings that dealt with civil rights and civil liberties. Beginning in the 1990s, the Supreme Court became increasingly skeptical of federal power. Thus, rulings that deal with either of those themes can typically be sorted by those respective date ranges. Throughout the multiple-choice section, remember: there's no penalty for wrong answers, so answering every question can't hurt. It might even help your score.

Focus on Your Strengths

The questions on the AP exam are numbered, but that doesn't mean you have to answer them in the order presented. Every question, regardless of how hard or easy it seems, is worth the same amount. That means you should feel free to answer the questions in an order that plays to your strengths and minimizes your weaknesses. You don't want to spend precious minutes puzzling over a question that has you stumped. Always be willing to skip over a tough question and come back to it later.

When using this approach, it's important to be extra careful filling in your answer grid. If you decide to skip a particular multiple-choice question, do not leave it blank! Instead, make a mark next to that question so you know where to come back to in your next pass. (Just make sure to remove all extra marks from your grid before time is up.)

Free-Response Questions

Overview

The free-response section is 1 hour 40 minutes long and consists of four questions, which are each worth 12.5 percent of your total score. You must answer all four; you do not have the option, as in some other AP exams, to choose the questions that you would like to answer. AP readers, hired by the College Board, score the free-response section by hand. (More details about scoring, question types, and free-response strategies can be found in Chapter 13.)

Each free-response question (FRQ) will be distinct and will address different topics of AP U.S. Government and Politics. The four types of FRQs are:

1. **Concept Application:** You must apply government and politics concepts to a given scenario.

2. **Quantitative Analysis:** You must interpret data from an information graphic and apply that data to government and politics concepts.

3. **SCOTUS Comparison:** You must compare a description of a non-required Supreme Court case to one of the College Board's required Supreme Court cases.

4. **Argument Essay:** You must construct a full essay with a thesis, provide specific evidence, and respond to a view that opposes your thesis.

Every exam will feature these four question types, in this order. Across the four FRQs on every exam, you will encounter a range of U.S. Government and Politics topics from all five units. Most prompts will ask you to integrate multiple ideas, and each will contain three or four tasks (labeled A, B, C, D).

Pacing

For the first three types of free-response questions, you should write organized paragraphs that clearly address all parts of the question. Do everything you can to make it straightforward for the readers to follow your responses and easily locate your quality content. For the fourth type of FRQ, the Argument Essay, you will need to write a longer essay with a central argument or thesis statement. With this in mind, you should aim to spend 20 minutes each on the Concept Application, Quantitative Analysis, and SCOTUS Comparison prompts and 40 minutes on the Argument Essay prompt.

Writing Strategies

The following are some general writing strategies and guidelines to keep in mind for every style of FRQ.

- Attempt to answer every part of every prompt. But what if you're unsure of the answer?
    - Still try to make a plan. Brainstorm ideas that you think are at least related to the topic, and you might just stumble onto information that will earn you some or all of the points.
    - Err on the side of including a little extra information or writing your best educated guess. You generally don't lose points for including incorrect information in the AP U.S. Government and Politics free-response section, unless the details you write are clearly contradictory (such as saying both "the court ruled the law unconstitutional" and "the court ruled the law constitutional").
    - Consider providing two answers for this same reason, especially for prompts asking for an example or explanation that have multiple possible correct responses. If one of your answers is correct (and doesn't contradict other information you've written), you will earn the point(s). However, any additional information you provide must be explicitly related to the question.
- Make sure you intentionally address each task. Although you won't be penalized for extra information, don't waste time unnecessarily writing too much. Make sure you clearly answer each specific part of each prompt. Remember, the only way to earn points is to complete the assigned tasks.
- Similarly, avoid "filler" and "fluff." The length of your response has nothing to do with your score; the quality of the content and how well it addresses the prompt is what counts. Time is limited, so every word you write should help you earn points.
- Don't include your opinion on political issues or political parties. No free-response prompt, even the Argument Essay, will ask for your personal political views. Rather, you should make confident assertions backed by specific evidence. Aim for neutral language and impartial analysis.
- Make sure you write neatly. Readers can't award points if they can't read what you wrote. Keep in mind that actual people will be reading every word you write, so make them happy by making it as easy as possible to read.
- Make your responses clear for a reader to follow by keeping them organized.
    - For FRQs 1, 2, and 3, respond to the parts in order, typically devoting one paragraph to each part and beginning each paragraph with a topic sentence.
    - For FRQ 4, write multiple full paragraphs that clearly establish your thesis, discuss each piece of evidence, and address an alternate view.

For even more detailed information about how to successfully address AP U.S. Government and Politics free-response questions, be sure to check out Chapter 13.

Focus on Your Strengths

You must respond to all four FRQs to earn a high score, but the order in which you answer the prompts doesn't matter. Therefore, begin with the prompt(s) that you feel you can write about most confidently, using the strongest supporting information. Just be sure to write each response in the correct designated area for that answer.

Practice, Practice, Practice

Now you've learned about the structure of the exam sections and the types of questions you'll encounter. This knowledge will help you confidently approach the official AP exam, but to maximize your scoring potential, you'll need to practice these question types. The pre-quizzes and post-quizzes in the Rapid Review and Practice chapters, the free-response chapter, the full-length exams, and the additional quizzes in your online resources provide the perfect opportunity to practice your skills with hundreds of exam-like questions!

COUNTDOWN TO THE EXAM

This book contains detailed review, guidance, and practice for you to utilize in the weeks leading up to your AP exam. In the final few days before your exam, we recommend the following steps.

Three Days Before the Exam

Take a full-length practice exam under timed conditions. Use the techniques and strategies you've learned in this book. Approach the exam strategically, actively, and confidently. (Note that you should *not* take a full-length practice exam with fewer than 48 hours left before your real exam. Doing so will probably exhaust you and hurt your score.)

Two Days Before the Exam

Go over the results of your latest practice exam. Don't worry too much about your score or whether you got a specific question right or wrong. Instead, examine your overall performance on the different topics, choose a few of the topics where you struggled the most, and brush up on them one final time.

Know exactly where you're going to take the official exam, how you're getting there, and how long it takes to get there. It's probably a good idea to visit your testing center sometime before the day of your exam so that you know what to expect: what the rooms are like, how the desks are set up, and so on.

The Night Before the Exam

Do not study! You cannot cram for a test as extensive as the AP Exam. Worse, pulling an all-nighter will simply deplete your stamina ahead of the exam. If you feel you must review some AP material, only do so for a little while and stick to broad review (such as the Essential Content sections of this book). The best, most effective way to prepare for the AP Exam at this point is to rest the night beforehand.

Get together an "AP Exam Kit" containing the following items:

- A few No. 2 pencils (Pencils with slightly dull points fill the ovals better; mechanical pencils are NOT permitted.)
- A few pens with black or dark blue ink (for the free-response questions)
- Erasers
- A watch (as long as it doesn't have Internet access, have an alarm, or make noise)
- Your 6-digit school code (Home-schooled students will be provided with their state's or country's home-school code at the time of the exam.)
- Photo ID card
- Your AP Student Pack
- If applicable, your Student Accommodation Letter verifying that you have been approved for a testing accommodation such as braille or large-type exams

Make sure that you don't bring anything that is *not* allowed in the exam room. You can find a complete list at the College Board's website (https://apstudent.collegeboard.org/home). Your school may have additional restrictions, so make sure you get this information from your school's AP Coordinator prior to the exam.

Again, try to relax. Read a good book, take a hot shower, watch something you enjoy. Go to bed early and get a good night's sleep.

The Morning of the Exam

Wake up early, leaving yourself plenty of time to get ready without rushing. Dress in layers so that you can adjust to the temperature of the testing room. Eat a solid breakfast: something substantial, but nothing too heavy or greasy. Don't drink a lot of coffee, especially if you're not used to it; bathroom breaks cut into your time, and too much caffeine is a bad idea. Read something as you eat breakfast, such as a newspaper or a magazine; you shouldn't let the exam be the first thing you read that day.

Leave extra early so that you can ensure you are on time to the testing location. Allow yourself extra time for any traffic, mass transit delays, and/or detours.

During the Exam

Breathe. Don't get shaken up. If you find your confidence slipping, remind yourself how well you've prepared. You know the structure of the exam; you know the material covered on it; you've had practice with every question type.

If something goes really wrong, do not panic! If you accidentally misgrid your answer page or put the answers in the wrong section, raise your hand and tell the proctor. He or she may be able to arrange for you to regrid your exam after it's over, when it won't cost you any time.

After the Exam

You might walk out of the AP exam thinking that you blew it. This is a normal reaction. Lots of people—even the highest scorers—feel that way. You tend to remember the questions that stumped you, not the ones that you knew. Keep in mind that almost nobody gets everything correct. You can still score a 4 or 5 even if you get some multiple-choice questions incorrect or miss several points on a free-response question.

We're positive that you will have performed well and scored your best on the exam because you followed the Kaplan strategies outlined in this chapter and reviewed all the content provided in the rest of this book. Be confident and celebrate the fact that, after many hours of hard work and preparation, you have just completed the AP U.S. Government and Politics exam!

PART 2

Rapid Review and Practice

CHAPTER 3

Foundations of American Democracy

LEARNING OBJECTIVES

- List the underlying ideals and purposes of the Constitution and Declaration of Independence.

- Compare and contrast the influences of the three principal models of representative democracy on U.S. political life.

- Summarize the Federalist and Anti-Federalist positions on how a centralized government should be organized.

- List and explain the provisions in the Articles of Confederation that reflect the centralized power debate.

- Connect Constitutional Convention compromises to subsequent ideas and events in U.S. history.

- Explain how separation of powers, and checks and balances, limit the U.S. government.

- Detail the effects of separation of powers, and checks and balances, on U.S. politics.

- Demonstrate how federalism reflects society's needs.

- Track changes in the balance between federal and state governments over time.

- List factors that facilitate and constrain the flow of power within and among U.S. governments.

TEST WHAT YOU ALREADY KNOW

Part A: Quiz

3

Questions 1–3 refer to the passage below.

"The smaller the society, the fewer probably will be the distinct parties and interests composing it; the fewer the distinct parties and interests, the more frequently will a majority be found of the same party; and the smaller the number of individuals composing a majority, and the smaller the compass within which they are placed, the more easily will they concert and execute their plans of oppression. Extend the sphere, and you take in a greater variety of parties and interests; you make it less probable that a majority of the whole will have a common motive to invade the rights of other citizens; or if such a common motive exists, it will be more difficult for all who feel it to discover their own strength, and to act in unison with each other. . . . Hence, it clearly appears, that the same advantage which a Republic has over a Democracy, in controlling the effects of faction, is enjoyed by a large over a small Republic—is enjoyed by the Union over the States composing it."

—James Madison, *Federalist* 10

1. Which of the following is the best summary of Madison's position?

   (A) In a republic covering a larger area, it is less likely that a majority group would be able to oppress a minority one.

   (B) A government covering a smaller area is preferential because it is easier to execute political plans.

   (C) In a republic covering a larger area, the government is more likely to violate the civil rights of its citizens.

   (D) In a republic covering a smaller area, there are likely to be a greater variety of political factions.

2. Based on the text, Madison is advocating for which model of democracy?

   (A) Participatory model

   (B) Pluralist model

   (C) Elite model

   (D) Direct democracy

3. Based on the text, with which of the following statements would the author most likely agree?

   (A) A purely democratic form of government would be possible in a country the size of the United States.

   (B) Under a democracy, it is less likely that a majority will find common motive to act.

   (C) A central government is more effective at controlling the effects of faction than individual state governments.

   (D) A two-party system cannot adequately represent the political spectrum of the United States.

Questions 4 and 5 refer to the passage below.

"It may be a reflection on human nature, that such devices should be necessary to control the abuses of government. But what is government itself, but the greatest of all reflections on human nature? If men were angels, no government would be necessary. If angels were to govern men, neither external nor internal controls on government would be necessary. In framing a government which is to be administered by men over men, the great difficulty lies in this: you must first enable the government to control the governed; and in the next place oblige it to control itself. A dependence on the people is, no doubt, the primary control on the government; but experience has taught mankind the necessity of auxiliary precautions."

—James Madison, *Federalist* 51

4. Which of the following is another term that could be used to describe the "auxiliary precautions" referred to by Madison in this excerpt?

(A) Checks and balances

(B) State sovereignty

(C) The elastic clause

(D) A system of state and federal taxation

5. The holding from which of the following Supreme Court cases reflects the main point made by Madison in the above passage?

(A) *McCulloch v. Maryland* (1803)

(B) *Schenck v. United States* (1919)

(C) *Marbury v. Madison* (1819)

(D) *Gideon v. Wainwright* (1963)

3

6. If the executive branch of the federal government wishes to exercise a power not explicitly granted to it in the Constitution, what does the Constitution require it to do?

    (A) It must get approval from the House of Representatives.

    (B) It must get approval from the Senate.

    (C) It must get approval from two-thirds of the states.

    (D) It must not exercise that power.

7. Which of the following is enumerated in Article III of the Constitution?

    (A) The number of justices on the Supreme Court

    (B) The structure of the lower federal courts

    (C) The term of service of a Supreme Court justice

    (D) The power of the Supreme Court to declare a statute unconstitutional

8. Which of the following is an example of a concurrent power?

    (A) The power to declare war

    (B) The power to negotiate treaties with foreign governments

    (C) The power to tax imported goods

    (D) The power to levy income taxes

9. Which of the following federal laws would most likely be found an unconstitutional use of the commerce clause under the holding of *United States v. Lopez* (1995)?

    (A) A law regulating the use of a toxic pesticide by a farm that sells its produce nationwide

    (B) A law banning the sale of children's clothing manufactured from flammable materials

    (C) A law increasing the minimum sentence for assaults using certain kinds of knives

    (D) A law banning the import of certain minerals from a country with a record of human rights violations

10. The author of *Brutus* 1 would be less likely to oppose the ratification of the Constitution if he had assurance that it included the

    (A) Electoral College

    (B) Connecticut Compromise

    (C) Three-Fifths Compromise

    (D) Bill of Rights

11. The framers created the federal system in order to

    (A) prevent the Articles of Confederation from establishing a monarch-style presidency

    (B) provide the original 13 states with equal representation in the U.S. Congress

    (C) allow for stronger state governments than existed under the Articles of Confederation

    (D) maintain a level of state sovereignty while allowing for a stronger central government

12. Which of the following is an accurate comparison of the roles of the House of Representatives and the Senate in impeachment proceedings?

	House of Representatives	Senate
(A)	Brings impeachment charges and adopts them with a simple majority vote	Conducts a trial in which conviction requires a two-thirds majority vote
(B)	Conducts a trial in which conviction requires a two-thirds majority vote	Brings impeachment charges and adopts them with a simple majority vote
(C)	Brings impeachment charges and adopts them with a simple majority vote	Conducts a trial in which conviction requires a simple majority vote
(D)	Conducts a trial in which conviction requires a two-thirds majority vote	Brings impeachment charges and adopts them with a two-thirds majority vote

3

Part B: Key Terms

The following is a list of the major ideas, events, and people for the AP U.S. Government and Politics topic, Foundations of American Democracy. You will likely see many of these on the official AP exam.

For each key term, ask yourself the following questions:

- Can I define this key term and use it in a sentence?
- Can I provide an example related to this key term?
- Could I correctly answer a multiple-choice question about this key term?
- Could I correctly answer a free-response question about this key term?

Check off the key terms if you can answer "yes" to at least three of these questions.

Democratic Ideals

- ☐ The Declaration of Independence
- ☐ Popular sovereignty
- ☐ Federalism

- ☐ Bill of Rights
- ☐ Republic
- ☐ Participatory model
- ☐ Pluralist model

- ☐ *Federalist* 10
- ☐ Factions
- ☐ Elite model
- ☐ Direct democracy

The Birth of the Constitution

- ☐ Articles of Confederation
- ☐ Confederal government
- ☐ Unicameral
- ☐ Shays' Rebellion
- ☐ Constitutional Convention
- ☐ U.S. Constitution

- ☐ Virginia Plan
- ☐ Bicameral
- ☐ New Jersey Plan
- ☐ Great Compromise (Connecticut Compromise)
- ☐ Three-Fifths Compromise
- ☐ Electoral College

- ☐ Federalists
- ☐ Anti-Federalists
- ☐ *Brutus* 1
- ☐ *The Federalist Papers*
- ☐ Ratification
- ☐ Mandates

Limits on Power

- ☐ Separation of powers
- ☐ Checks and balances

- ☐ *Federalist* 51
- ☐ Legislative branch

- ☐ Executive branch
- ☐ Judicial branch

Federalism

- ☐ Enumerated powers
- ☐ Implied powers
- ☐ Elastic clause/ necessary and proper clause
- ☐ Inherent powers
- ☐ Reserved powers
- ☐ Concurrent powers

- ☐ Prohibited powers
- ☐ Tenth Amendment
- ☐ Supremacy clause
- ☐ Dual federalism
- ☐ Cooperative federalism
- ☐ Revenue sharing

- ☐ Fiscal federalism
- ☐ Categorical grant
- ☐ Block grant
- ☐ *McCulloch v. Maryland* (1819)
- ☐ Commerce clause
- ☐ *United States v. Lopez* (1995)

3

Next Steps

Step 1: Tally your correct answers from Part A and review the quiz explanations at the end of this chapter.

1.	A	7.	C
2.	B	8.	D
3.	C	9.	C
4.	A	10.	D
5.	C	11.	D
6.	D	12.	A

_____ out of 12 questions

Step 2: Count the number of key terms you checked off in Part B.

_____ out of 53 key terms

Step 3: Read the Key Takeaways in this chapter.

Step 4: Consult the table below and follow the instructions based on your performance.

If You Got...	Do This
80% or more of the Test What You Already Know assessment correct (10 or more questions from Part A and 42 or more key terms from Part B)	• Read definitions in this chapter for all the key terms you didn't check off. • Complete the Test What You Learned assessment in this chapter.
50% or less of the Test What You Already Know assessment correct (6 or fewer questions from Part A and 26 or fewer key terms from Part B)	• Read the comprehensive review for this topic in Chapter 8. ◦ If you are short on time, read only the High-Yield sections. • Read through all of the key term definitions in this chapter. • Complete the Test What You Learned assessment in this chapter.
Any other result	• Read the High-Yield sections in the comprehensive review of this topic in Chapter 8. • Read definitions in this chapter for all the key terms you didn't check off. • Complete the Test What You Learned assessment in this chapter.

ESSENTIAL CONTENT

Key Takeaways: Foundations of American Democracy

1. Democratic ideals are reflected in early American documents. The Declaration of Independence provided a foundation for popular sovereignty. The Articles of Confederation provided an early structure for national government, ultimately proving too weak. The Constitution provided the structure and foundations for a unique form of political democracy and a republican form of government. The Bill of Rights was designed to protect the rights of the citizens from governmental abuse.

2. The Federalists, proponents of a strong national government, believed that a large republic would help control the potential issues with factions by spreading governing authority to elected representatives as well as by dividing power between the national and state governments. Anti-Federalists feared that a strong central national government would diminish or violate the rights of individual citizens; instead, they preferred to delegate more authority to the state governments.

3. The Great Compromise (the Connecticut Compromise), the Electoral College, and the Three-Fifths Compromise were direct results of the political negotiation that took place at the Constitutional Convention.

4. Key constitutional principles, such as the separation of powers and checks and balances, help prevent one branch of government from becoming too powerful or subject to corruption. The three branches (the legislative, executive, and judicial branches) are allocated distinct powers and duties, and each branch has certain "checks," or controls, on the other two. These ideas were advocated for in *Federalist* 51, in which James Madison expressed concerns about potential abuses by majorities.

5. Federalism is one of the basic principles of American government, dividing powers between national and state governments. The Constitution's supremacy clause states that the Constitution is "the supreme Law of the Land." All public officials of the country must give oaths to support the Constitution, and states cannot override the national powers.

6. The exact balance between state and national power has long been the subject of debate; the balance has changed over time, partly based on U.S. Supreme Court interpretation in certain landmark cases, such as *McCulloch v. Maryland* (1819) and *United States v. Lopez* (1995).

3

Key Terms: Foundations of American Democracy

Democratic Ideals

The Declaration of Independence: Formal statement written by Thomas Jefferson in 1776 declaring the freedom of the thirteen American colonies from Great Britain.

Popular sovereignty: The principle that a government derives its power from the consent of the people, primarily through their elected representatives.

Federalism: A key constitutional principle that calls for the division or separation of power across local, state, and national levels of government.

Bill of Rights: The first 10 amendments to the Constitution, which were added in 1789; protected rights include freedom of speech, freedom of religion, and the right to be free from unreasonable searches and seizures.

Republic: A form of government in which the power to govern comes not directly from the citizens but rather through representation by elected officials.

Participatory model: A model of democracy that emphasizes broad citizen participation in government and politics.

Pluralist model: A model of democracy that emphasizes the need for different organized groups to compete against each other in order to influence policy.

***Federalist* 10:** Essay in which James Madison argues that the power of factions is best controlled through a republican form of government.

Factions: Groups of like-minded people who try to influence the government and public policy.

Elite model: A model of democracy that emphasizes limited participation in politics and civil society.

Direct democracy: A form of democracy in which the citizens are able to decide on policy and governmental action directly.

The Birth of the Constitution

Articles of Confederation: The first governing document that attempted to establish a national government. The Articles called for the individual states to maintain supreme power over a national government with restricted governing authority. A form of government in which states hold power over a limited national government.

Confederal government: A form of government in which states hold power over a limited national government.

Unicameral: A one-house (or chamber) legislative body.

Shays' Rebellion: An armed revolt that lasted for six months in January 1787; more than a thousand armed soldiers, led by Daniel Shays, seized an arsenal in Massachusetts to protest high taxes and the loss of their farms due to debt.

Constitutional Convention: An assembly that convened in 1787 to revise the Articles of Confederation but that ultimately proposed an entirely new framework for the federal government.

The Birth of the Constitution (cont.)

U.S. Constitution: Ratified in 1788, the Constitution established a federal form of government that distributed powers between a strong central government and the individual states.

Virginia Plan: A proposal made by Constitutional Convention delegates from large states, favoring congressional representation based on population size.

Bicameral: A legislative body that consists of two houses, or chambers; the U.S. Congress consists of both the House of Representatives and Senate.

New Jersey Plan: A proposal made by the Constitutional Convention delegates from small states, favoring a Congress with equal representation among all the states.

Great Compromise (Connecticut Compromise): An agreement by the framers that the House of Representatives would be the larger house of Congress and include members that were directly elected by the citizens to serve two-year terms and that the Senate would be the smaller house of Congress and include members who were appointed by state legislatures for six-year terms.

Three-Fifths Compromise: A decision made during the Constitutional Convention to count each slave as three-fifths of a person in a state's population for the purposes of determining the number of House of Representatives members and the distribution of taxes.

Electoral College: A system for electing the president in which each state is provided a certain number of electoral votes equal to the number of its representatives plus the number of its senators.

Federalists: Favored a strong central government that could manage the nation's debt, foreign policy, and other political affairs.

Anti-Federalists: Opposed the development of a strong central government, preferring instead for power to remain in the hands of state and local governments.

***Brutus* 1:** A document that sets forth the Anti-Federalist concern and fear that the central government would gain too much power, violating the individual rights and liberties of the citizens.

***The Federalist Papers*:** A set of essays written by James Madison, Alexander Hamilton, and John Jay that contains arguments in favor of a strong national government.

Ratification: An official authorization of a constitutional amendment, treaty, or other piece of legislation.

Mandates: Official legal orders for the states to comply with federal laws.

Limits on Power

Separation of powers: The division of government power across the executive, legislative, and judicial branches.

Checks and balances: A system in which each branch of government has some power over the others in order to limit the abuse or accumulation of power by one branch.

***Federalist* 51:** Essay written by James Madison to address concerns raised by the Anti-Federalists, who feared that the national government would grow too powerful. Promoted the ratification of the Constitution; argued that the federal system and the separation of powers would prevent any one part of the government from becoming too powerful.

3

Limits on Power (cont.)

Legislative branch: Branch of government that makes laws, regulates interstate and foreign commerce, controls taxation, creates spending policies, and oversees the other branches of government.

Executive branch: Branch of government that carries out and enforces the laws. It consists of the president, vice president, Cabinet, executive departments, independent agencies, and other boards, commissions, and committees.

Judicial branch: Branch of government, consisting of the U.S. Supreme Court and the federal judicial system, that provides judicial interpretation and review of laws.

Federalism

Enumerated powers: Powers that are expressly written in the Constitution.

Implied powers: Powers supported by the Constitution that are not expressly stated in it.

Elastic clause/necessary and proper clause: A statement in Article I of the Constitution giving Congress the implied power to expand the scope of its enumerated powers.

Inherent powers: Powers that do not rely on specific clauses of the Constitution; usually these powers are in the area of foreign affairs and grow out of the very existence of the national government (e.g., the power to recognize foreign states).

Reserved powers: Powers that are neither delegated to the federal government nor denied to the states. These powers are not expressly listed in the Constitution but are rather guaranteed to the states by the Tenth Amendment.

Concurrent powers: Powers that are those held by both the federal and state governments.

Prohibited powers: Also known as restricted powers, these are powers that are denied to the federal government, the state governments, or both.

Tenth Amendment: Gives state governments any powers that are neither delegated to the federal government nor denied to the states by the Constitution.

Supremacy clause: Found in Article VI of the Constitution, this clause states that the Constitution and the laws and treaties made through it are "the supreme Law of the Land."

Dual federalism: A concept of federalism in which national and state governments are seen as distinct entities providing separate services, thereby limiting the power of the national government.

Cooperative federalism: A concept of federal and state governmental units working together equally to make policy and to provide goods and services to citizens.

Revenue sharing: The distribution of tax dollars or other revenue from one level of government to another, such as from the federal government to a state government.

Federalism (cont.)

Fiscal federalism: A concept of federalism in which funding is appropriated by the federal government to the states with specific conditions attached.

Categorical grant: Money from the federal government that comes with rules and restrictions on how it is used; the money must be used for a very specific purpose, such as improving public transportation.

Block grant: Federal money given to states to achieve a general policy goal; states are given discretion on how to specifically allocate the money.

McCulloch v. Maryland **(1819):** Landmark Supreme Court decision that affirmed the constitutionality of implied legislative powers by holding that the necessary and proper clause authorizes Congress to create a national bank; also established the supremacy of the U.S. Constitution and federal laws over state laws.

Commerce clause: Found in Article I, Section 8 of the Constitution; gives Congress power to regulate international and interstate trade and commerce.

United States v. Lopez **(1995):** The Supreme Court ruled that the Gun-Free School Zones Act of 1990 was unconstitutional because Congress had exceeded its authority under the commerce clause.

TEST WHAT YOU LEARNED

Part A: Quiz

Questions 1 and 2 refer to the cartoon below.

BORN TO COMMAND.

OF VETO MEMORY.

HAD I BEEN CONSULTED.

KING ANDREW THE FIRST.

Source: Library of Congress

1. What is the primary purpose of this political cartoon?

   (A) To document the evolution of the president's power

   (B) To contend that Congress has not fulfilled its constitutional responsibilities

   (C) To demonstrate that the president should have increased powers

   (D) To criticize the president for overstepping the bounds of his authority

2. Which of the following documents would the subject of this cartoon most likely use to defend his use of presidential power?

   (A) *Federalist* 51

   (B) *Federalist* 70

   (C) *Federalist* 78

   (D) *Brutus* 1

Questions 3–5 refer to the chart below.

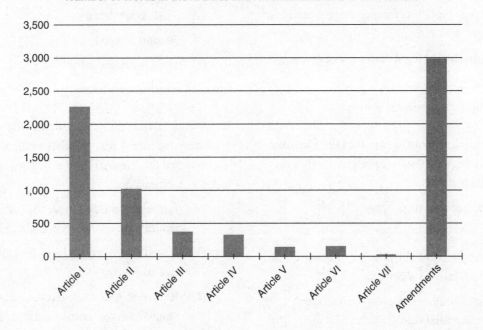

Number of Words in the Articles and Amendments of the Constitution

3. Based on the information in this chart, which of the following did the framers most likely believe was the most important institution in the new government created by the U.S. Constitution?

(A) The executive branch

(B) The legislative branch

(C) The judicial branch

(D) The Electoral College

4. Which of the following Supreme Court cases addressed an ambiguity in the Constitution that was due, in part, to the brevity of Article III?

(A) *United States v. Lopez* (1995)

(B) *McCulloch v. Maryland* (1819)

(C) *Schenck v. United States* (1919)

(D) *Marbury v. Madison* (1803)

5. In *Federalist* 86, Alexander Hamilton states, "It has been urged that the persons delegated to the administration of the national government will always be disinclined to yield up any portion of the authority of which they were once possessed." Which of the following columns in the chart above provides evidence that could be used to counter Hamilton's argument?

(A) Article I

(B) Article II

(C) Article III

(D) Amendments

6. Which of the following accurately lists powers granted by the Constitution to the Senate but not the House of Representatives?

    (A) Passing articles of impeachment against the president

    (B) Introducing legislation to raise revenue

    (C) Ratifying treaties

    (D) Passing revenue legislation

7. Which of the following is part of the system of checks and balances in the original text of the Constitution?

    (A) Presidential term limits

    (B) The Electoral College

    (C) The power of either house of Congress to expel its own members

    (D) The ability of Congress to override a presidential veto

8. Which of the following would likely be considered an implied power of Congress, under the ruling in *McCulloch v. Maryland* (1819)?

    (A) Passing a law requiring local police departments to equip their officers with body cameras

    (B) Passing a law requiring that public school teachers participate in continuing education courses to maintain their state certifications

    (C) Passing a law requiring stringent background checks for federal employees who handle currency

    (D) Passing a law requiring that city governments provide mandatory retirement benefits for firefighters

9. Which of the following amendments most directly addresses the main concerns expressed by the author of *Brutus* 1?

    (A) First Amendment

    (B) Second Amendment

    (C) Fourth Amendment

    (D) Tenth Amendment

10. Which of the following explains why a representative from a less populated state would have rejected the Virginia Plan at the Constitutional Convention?

    (A) It made it less likely that the state's residents would have a voice in presidential elections.

    (B) It would have created a bicameral legislative structure.

    (C) It did not guarantee that the state's residents would be represented equally in the legislature.

    (D) It did nothing to assure the representative that a Bill of Rights would be passed.

11. Which of the following is the best explanation of why the commerce clause provides more power today than when it was drafted?

    (A) As society has evolved, economic activity that crosses state lines has become more common.

    (B) Court cases such as *United States v. Lopez* (1995) have altered the modern conception of the commerce clause.

    (C) Constitutional amendments have increased the power of Congress.

    (D) The executive order has become a more common method of implementing policies.

12. Which of the following is an accurate comparison of the Federalist and Anti-Federalist opinions on the necessity of the Bill of Rights?

	Federalist	Anti-Federalist
(A)	Not needed, since the national government is limited to enumerated powers	Needed as protection against the national government, which erodes state sovereignty
(B)	Needed as protection against strong state governments	Needed as protection against the national government, which erodes state sovereignty
(C)	Needed as protection against a strong national government	Not needed, since stronger state governments will protect citizens' rights
(D)	Not needed, since the national government is limited to enumerated powers	Not needed, since stronger state governments will protect citizens' rights

3

Part B: Key Terms

This key terms list is the same as the list in the Test What You Already Know section earlier in this chapter. Based on what you have now learned, again ask yourself the following questions:

- Can I define this key term and use it in a sentence?
- Can I provide an example related to this key term?
- Could I correctly answer a multiple-choice question about this key term?
- Could I correctly answer a free-response question about this key term?

Check off the key terms if you can answer "yes" to at least three of these questions.

Democratic Ideals

- ☐ The Declaration of Independence
- ☐ Popular sovereignty
- ☐ Federalism
- ☐ Bill of Rights
- ☐ Republic
- ☐ Participatory model
- ☐ Pluralist model
- ☐ *Federalist* 10
- ☐ Factions
- ☐ Elite model
- ☐ Direct democracy

The Birth of the Constitution

- ☐ Articles of Confederation
- ☐ Confederal government
- ☐ Unicameral
- ☐ Shays' Rebellion
- ☐ Constitutional Convention
- ☐ U.S. Constitution
- ☐ Virginia Plan
- ☐ Bicameral
- ☐ New Jersey Plan
- ☐ Great Compromise (Connecticut Compromise)
- ☐ Three-Fifths Compromise
- ☐ Electoral College
- ☐ Federalists
- ☐ Anti-Federalists
- ☐ *Brutus* 1
- ☐ *The Federalist Papers*
- ☐ Ratification
- ☐ Mandates

Limits on Power

- ☐ Separation of powers
- ☐ Checks and balances
- ☐ *Federalist* 51
- ☐ Legislative branch
- ☐ Executive branch
- ☐ Judicial branch

Federalism

- [ ] Enumerated powers
- [ ] Implied powers
- [ ] Elastic clause/ necessary and proper clause
- [ ] Inherent powers
- [ ] Reserved powers
- [ ] Concurrent powers

- [ ] Prohibited powers
- [ ] Tenth Amendment
- [ ] Supremacy clause
- [ ] Dual federalism
- [ ] Cooperative federalism
- [ ] Revenue sharing

- [ ] Fiscal federalism
- [ ] Categorical grant
- [ ] Block grant
- [ ] *McCulloch v. Maryland* (1819)
- [ ] Commerce clause
- [ ] *United States v. Lopez* (1995)

3

Next Steps

Tally your correct answers from Part A and review the quiz explanations at the end of this chapter.

1.	D	7.	D
2.	B	8.	C
3.	B	9.	D
4.	D	10.	C
5.	D	11.	A
6.	C	12.	A

_____ out of 12 questions

Count the number of key terms you checked off in Part B.

_____ out of 53 key terms

Compare your Test What You Already Know results to these Test What You Learned results to see how exam-ready you are for this topic.

- Read (or reread) the comprehensive review for this topic in Chapter 8.
- Go to kaptest.com to complete the online quiz questions for Foundations of American Democracy.
  - Haven't registered your book yet? Go to kaptest.com/moreonline to begin.

CHAPTER 3 ANSWERS AND EXPLANATIONS

Test What You Already Know

1. A

Topic: 8.1 Democratic Ideals

In *Federalist* 10, Madison discusses the causes and effects of faction, and in this excerpt he primarily discusses how the size of a governed area affects the ability of a faction to gain control. In a larger country, there will be more parties, and thus it will be harder for a group with bad intentions to put their plans into effect. **(A)** is correct because it summarizes this purpose nicely. While it is easier to execute political plans in a smaller country, Madison views this as a disadvantage, not an advantage, making (B) incorrect. (C) and (D) are both the opposite of what Madison is arguing. He thinks that a large country is less, not more, likely to violate its citizen's rights, and he argues that a small country would have fewer political factions.

2. B

Topic: 8.1 Democratic Ideals

In this excerpt, Madison discusses how the size of a country affects how easily a faction can gain a majority. The pluralist model is about how organized groups can have an effect on government, so **(B)** is correct. The participatory model focuses on how individuals can participate directly in policy making, while the elite model focuses on how the wealthy or powerful can have an outsized effect on government. Because neither of these models are discussed in this excerpt, (A) and (C) are incorrect. (D) is incorrect because a direct democracy is a government in which citizens act as legislators, voting directly on policies without representatives.

3. C

Topic: 8.1 Democratic Ideals

While most of the excerpt focuses on the size of the area being governed, the final line says that the federal government, in comparison to the states, shares the same advantage in controlling factions; thus, **(C)** is correct. (A) is incorrect because the passage describes one particular flaw of democracy; therefore, it's unlikely that the author would argue in favor of a democracy. Madison argues that when there are fewer interests, it is more likely that a majority will be able to act, and the final sentence shows that democracies share this flaw, so (B) is incorrect. While

the passage does discuss a problem that can happen when there are fewer parties (one faction can more easily gain control), (D) is incorrect because it mentions a different downside of a two-party system.

4. A

Topic: 8.3 Limits on Power

In *Federalist* 51, Madison mentions "auxiliary precautions" in the context of restraining the government. He states that one important aspect of a government is that it must be able to control itself, and these precautions are what's needed to do so. The system of checks and balances between branches of government in the Constitution is designed to do precisely this, so **(A)** is correct. The fact that states are sovereign might mean that a strong state or local government may be able to provide a check against a strong federal government; however, (B) is incorrect because it does not mention the federal government; additionally, even if it did, this would be an example of one level of government restraining another, not a government restraining itself. (C) can be eliminated because the elastic clause grants to Congress the ability to make laws that are necessary and proper to its enumerated powers; in other words, rather than restricting its power, it expands it. Finally, (D) is incorrect because the issue of taxation does not pertain directly to how a government might be able to control itself.

5. C

Topic: 8.3 Limits on Power

Madison's main point in the passage is that there must be means by which the federal government can control itself; this could be accomplished through one part of the government restraining another part. *Marbury v. Madison* held that the Supreme Court has the power to declare an act of Congress unconstitutional; thus, **(C)** is correct. (A) is incorrect because *McCulloch v. Maryland* did not limit the federal government's powers; it affirmed the ability of Congress to charter a national bank. (B) is incorrect because *Schenck v. United States* established that speech that constitutes a "clear and present danger" is not protected by the First Amendment. *Gideon v. Wainwright* guaranteed the right to be represented by an attorney even to those who could not afford one, so (D) is incorrect.

6. D

Topic: 8.4 Federalism

In order to perform any action, the federal government must be explicitly permitted to do so by the Constitution. If not, it can't perform that action, as the Tenth Amendment reserves all powers not given to the federal government to the states and the people. Thus, **(D)** is correct. While there are many situations in which the powers of the executive and legislative branches intersect (the president can sign or veto legislation, for instance), Congress cannot empower the executive branch to do something not allowed by the Constitution; (A) and (B) are incorrect. (C) may be reminiscent of the amendment process, in which the states can ratify amendments that may give the federal government more powers. However, that requires ratification by three-fourths of the states, not just two-thirds, making (C) incorrect.

7. C

Topic: 8.3 Limits on Power

Article III defines the judicial branch of the federal government. However, of the choices here, only the term of service for a justice is defined in the Constitution itself; a justice will serve "during good behaviour." This means that a justice's term will end only due to retirement, death, or impeachment. Thus, **(C)** is correct. Both (A) and (B) are incorrect because the number of justices and the structure of the lower courts are defined by statute rather than the Constitution. (D) is incorrect because the Court's power to declare a statute unconstitutional (also known as judicial review) is not enumerated in the Constitution; it was established in *Marbury v. Madison*, an early Supreme Court case.

8. D

Topic: 8.4 Federalism

A concurrent power is one that can be exercised by either the federal government or a state government. The Sixteenth Amendment allows the federal government to collect an income tax, and since it is not explicitly prohibited, the states may do so as well; **(D)** is correct. Article I, Section 10 specifically prohibits the states from engaging in war (unless invaded), making (A) incorrect. The same section also prohibits states from entering into treaties with foreign powers and from taxing imports without the approval of Congress, so (B) and (C) are incorrect.

9. C

Topic: 8.4 Federalism

In *United States v. Lopez*, the Supreme Court held that Congress could not ban the possession of guns in a school zone under the commerce clause because the purported effect on interstate commerce was too tenuous. **(C)** is correct because it presents an analogous situation; because there does not seem to be an evident link between criminal assault and interstate commerce, the Court would likely find this to be an invalid use of the commerce clause. (A) and (B) are incorrect because both refer to activities involving the sale of goods, making it likely that the Court would find these laws to be valid uses of the power to regulate interstate commerce. (D) is incorrect because it does not implicate interstate commerce at all; instead, it involves the importation of foreign goods.

10. D

Topic: 8.2 The Birth of the Constitution

The author of *Brutus* 1 was worried that a central government would gain too much power, which it could use to violate the rights of its citizens. He was worried that there was nothing in the Constitution that could restrain the actions of the federal government and that the federal government would eventually overshadow the state governments. Thus, he would support the Bill of Rights, which puts specific restraints on what the federal government can do; **(D)** is correct. The Electoral College was a compromise that ensured both small and large states would have a voice in presidential elections; *Brutus* 1 expressed no concerns about such elections, so (A) is incorrect. The Connecticut Compromise also dealt with the issue of equal representations for states; under this compromise, a bicameral legislature was created, with the number of representatives for each state depending on population but with an equal number of senators for each state. The Three-Fifths Compromise similarly concerned issues of representation in the federal legislature. It was an agreement to count slaves in state populations for legislative representation purposes, but with each counting as only three-fifths of a person. While *Brutus* 1 did express concerns that the national legislature would be too powerful, the author's issues did not involve the specifics of how the number of congresspeople would be determined, so (B) and (C) are incorrect.

11. D

Topic: 8.4 Federalism

Federalism is the sharing of power between state and federal governments, and establishing a power-sharing arrangement was one of the framers' primary objectives; one of the faults they found with the Articles of Confederation was the lack of a strong central government. Therefore, **(D)** is correct. (A) is incorrect because it features distorted facts about the Articles of Confederation. The Articles did not feature a strong executive branch; it was the Constitution's definition of the role of president that inspired a fear, in some of its opponents, of establishing a monarch-style presidency. (B) is incorrect because equal state representation was not the goal of federalism; instead, this was the concern behind the different forms of state representation in the House of Representatives and Senate. (C) is incorrect because, again, the issue with the Articles of Confederation was not that the states were too strong but that the central government was too weak.

12. A

Topic: 8.3 Limits on Power

In an impeachment proceeding, the charges originate in the House of Representatives and must be adopted by a majority vote. A trial is then held in the Senate, and there must be a two-thirds majority vote for conviction. Only **(A)** correctly describes this process. (B) is incorrect because it reverses these roles. (C) describes the general concept of the roles correctly but misstates the number of votes required in the Senate. (D) both reverses the roles and misstates the number of votes required to adopt charges.

Test What You Learned

1. D

Topic: 8.3 Limits on Power

The cartoon shows President Andrew Jackson dressed as a monarch, standing on a shredded Constitution. This shows that, in the cartoonist's opinion, President Jackson has abused his presidential powers. Thus, **(D)** is correct. (A) is incorrect because the cartoon does not show how the president's power has changed over time; it merely shows that the president has abused his powers. (B) is incorrect because, even though the cartoonist thinks the actions of the president should have been restrained, the cartoon does not suggest that Congress should have restrained him. (C) is incorrect in that it reverses the meaning of the cartoon. This is not an admiring portrait of a strong president, as it shows him stepping on the Constitution.

2. B

Topic: 8.3 Limits on Power

This cartoon criticizes President Jackson for abusing his presidential powers. *Federalist* 70 argued in favor of a strong executive power vested in a single person. Thus, President Jackson (the subject of the cartoon) would likely argue that this essay supported his actions; **(B)** is correct. *Federalist* 51 describes the system of checks and balances in the Constitution; if anything, this artist would be in favor of these checks on the authority of a strong executive, so (A) is incorrect. *Federalist* 78 deals with the judicial branch, not the executive branch, making (C) incorrect. *Brutus* 1 argues against the idea of a strong central government, so the artist of the cartoon would likely support that argument; (D) is also incorrect.

3. B

Topic: 8.2 The Birth of the Constitution

According to the chart, Article I has by far the most number of words of any of the articles in the Constitution. Article I defines the powers of Congress; the level of detail implied by the length of the description of these powers shows that the framers thought the legislative branch was the preeminent part of the government; **(B)** is correct. The executive branch (defined in Article II) and the judicial branch (Article III) are both described in fewer words, implying that the framers thought they were less important and needed less detail; therefore, (A) and (C) are incorrect. (D) is incorrect because the Electoral College is described in just a portion of Article II, which has far fewer words than Article I.

4. D

Topic: 8.3 Limits on Power

Article III defines the judicial branch of the government, but it does so in relatively few words. Thus, in the early days of the republic, there was some uncertainty about how extensive judicial powers were. The ruling in *Marbury v. Madison* clarified Article III and established that the Supreme Court had the power of judicial review, the ability to declare acts by the legislative or executive branches unconstitutional. **(D)** is correct. *United States v. Lopez* and *McCulloch v. Maryland* were both rulings on the powers of Congress, which is discussed in Article I, not III; (A) and (B) are therefore incorrect. *Schenck v. United States* ruled on the extent to which speech is protected under the First Amendment, so (C) is incorrect.

5. D

Topic: 8.2 The Birth of the Constitution

Articles I, II, and III all grant powers to the various branches of the government rather than limit them, so (A), (B), and (C) do not challenge Hamilton's position. Nearly all of the amendments, however, limit the power of the federal government in some way. The fact that the combined text of the amendments is longer than any of the individual articles of the Constitution, and nearly as long as the entire original document itself, shows that, at least in some circumstances, the national government may give up some powers. **(D)** is correct.

6. C

Topic: 8.3 Limits on Power

While the two houses of Congress have, for the most part, similar powers, the Constitution does differentiate them somewhat. Only the Senate can approve treaties, so **(C)** is correct. (A) and (B) are incorrect because the House of Representatives has the exclusive power to pass articles of impeachment and to introduce revenue legislation. (D) is incorrect because both houses of Congress have the ability to pass revenue legislation.

7. D

Topic: 8.3 Limits on Power

The system of checks and balances refers to the ways in which one branch of government may be able to restrain another branch. The ability to override a veto is a way in which Congress can provide a check against presidential action; thus, **(D)** is correct. (A) is incorrect because, even though term limits do limit the office of the president, they are not at the discretion of another branch of government; furthermore, they were not enacted until the Twenty-Second Amendment was ratified in 1951. (B) is incorrect because the Electoral College is merely the manner in which the president is elected, not a check on his or her power. (C) is incorrect because it is a way for Congress to provide a check on its own members, rather than on a separate branch of government.

8. C

Topic: 8.4 Federalism

McCulloch v. Maryland affirmed that Congress has the authority to pass laws that are "necessary and proper" to carrying out its specifically enumerated duties; this allows it to pass laws that are connected to its enumerated powers but that may not be explicitly permitted under the Constitution. **(C)** is correct. While the Constitution does not explicitly mention background checks, they would likely be considered "necessary and proper" to Congress's enumerated powers involving currency: for instance, coining money, borrowing money, and military appropriations. If untrustworthy people are handling this money, this could impede the ability of Congress to carry out these duties. (A), (B), and (D) are incorrect because the Constitution does not provide the federal government any powers in relation to local police departments, state-certified teachers, or firefighters, so these laws would not be considered "necessary and proper" to any enumerated power.

9. D

Topic: 8.1 Democratic Ideals

The author of *Brutus* 1 expressed concern that the federal government would become too powerful under the Constitution and, in so doing, would erode the boundaries between the state and federal governments. Thus, the Tenth Amendment, which reserves those rights to the states that are not explicitly granted to the federal government, is the most direct safeguard against this danger, and **(D)** is correct. While the author would likely have been supportive of the entire Bill of Rights, including the First Amendment (freedom of speech, religion, and the press), Second Amendment (gun ownership), and Fourth Amendment (freedom from unreasonable search and seizure), these amendments do not address his concerns directly; therefore, (A), (B), and (C) are incorrect.

10. C

Topic: 8.2 The Birth of the Constitution

The Virginia Plan would have created a bicameral legislature in which representation was based on a state's population. Thus, a representative from a small state would likely have rejected this plan because they would not have an equal voice in the legislature, so **(C)** is correct. (A) is incorrect because, although there was a concern that small states would be ignored in presidential elections, this was not the subject of the Virginia Plan. (B) is incorrect because it was not the bicameral structure of the proposed legislature that the smaller states objected to; indeed, some of the smaller states later supported the Connecticut Compromise, which set up a bicameral legislature with more balanced representation. (D) is incorrect for similar reasons to (A); the lack of a Bill of Rights was a concern many states had with the proposed Constitution, but this concern was not connected to the Virginia Plan.

11. A

Topic: 8.4 Federalism

When the Constitution was drafted, interstate commerce was much less common than it is in the modern world. Thus, Congress now has more power because the commerce clause covers more activity; **(A)** is correct. (B) is incorrect because *United States v. Lopez* actually limited Congress's power under the commerce clause by ruling that it could not be used to ban guns in school. (C) is incorrect because nearly every amendment to the Constitution has limited the power of the government, rather than increase it. One exception is the Sixteenth Amendment, which grants Congress the power to collect income taxes; however, this is an independent basis for power rather than an expansion of the commerce clause. (D) is incorrect because the executive order is a tool of the presidency, while the commerce clause establishes a power of Congress.

12. A

Topic: 8.2 The Birth of the Constitution

The Federalists thought the Bill of Rights was not needed because the enumerated powers of the national government would provide protection against oppression, while the Anti-Federalists thought it was needed given that the weaker state governments would be less able to protect the rights of citizens. **(A)** is therefore correct because it accurately compares the views of these two groups. While (B) accurately states the Anti-Federalist opinion, it misstates that of the Federalists, making (B) incorrect. Federalists did not believe that a Bill of Rights was necessary at all. (C) is incorrect because it makes this same error with the Federalist opinion and also misstates the Anti-Federalist opinion. While Anti-Federalists would have been in favor of stronger state governments, this had no bearing on their position that the Bill of Rights was necessary. (D) states the right Federalist position but makes the same mistake as (C) with regard to the Anti-Federalists; thus, (D) is also incorrect.

CHAPTER 4

Interactions Among Branches of Government

LEARNING OBJECTIVES

- Discriminate among the structures and functions of the two houses of Congress.

- Cite factors that influence the policy-making process in Congress.

- Detail historical and current influences on congressional effectiveness.

- Summarize the president's formal and informal powers.

- Identify reasons for tensions between the executive and legislative branches.

- Demonstrate how the president's role has changed throughout history.

- Cite technological advances that presidents use to communicate.

- Summarize the constitutional and legal basis for the development of judicial review.

- State past and present challenges to SCOTUS legitimacy.

- Explain checks on SCOTUS power.

- Detail the primary characteristics of the federal bureaucracy.

- Explain ways in which federal bureaus use discretionary and rule-making authority.

- Identify methods through which Congress may exercise oversight of the federal bureaucracy.

- Define specific ways in which the president can influence, and ways the president is limited by, the federal bureaucracy.

TEST WHAT YOU ALREADY KNOW

Part A: Quiz

Questions 1 and 2 refer to the passage below.

THERE is an idea, which is not without its advocates, that a vigorous Executive is inconsistent with the genius of republican government. The enlightened well-wishers to this species of government must at least hope that the supposition is destitute of foundation; since they can never admit its truth, without at the same time admitting the condemnation of their own principles. Energy in the Executive is a leading character in the definition of good government. It is essential to the protection of the community against foreign attacks; it is not less essential to the steady administration of the laws; to the protection of property against those irregular and high-handed combinations which sometimes interrupt the ordinary course of justice; to the security of liberty against the enterprises and assaults of ambition, of faction, and of anarchy. Every man the least conversant in Roman story, knows how often that republic was obliged to take refuge in the absolute power of a single man, under the formidable title of Dictator, as well against the intrigues of ambitious individuals who aspired to the tyranny, and the seditions of whole classes of the community whose conduct threatened the existence of all government, as against the invasions of external enemies who menaced the conquest and destruction of Rome.

—Alexander Hamilton, *Federalist* 70

1. Which of the following statements best summarizes Hamilton's argument?

   (A) A strong executive leader is needed to ensure a strong government.

   (B) The idea of a republican government will be challenging to implement without more support from the people.

   (C) The new nation needs a weaker executive leader due to the fear of dictatorship.

   (D) A strong executive leader is more likely to lead to a poorly run government.

2. Which of the following would supporters of Hamilton's view most likely endorse?

   (A) The Articles of Confederation's provision for an executive branch

   (B) The Articles of Confederation's provision for a president of Congress

   (C) The Constitution's provision for a leader with absolute power

   (D) The Constitution's provision for a separate executive branch

Questions 3 and 4 refer to the passage below.

This exercise of judicial discretion, in determining between two contradictory laws, is exemplified in a familiar instance. It not uncommonly happens, that there are two statutes existing at one time, clashing in whole or in part with each other, and neither of them containing any repealing clause or expression. In such a case, it is the province of the courts to liquidate and fix their meaning and operation. So far as they can, by any fair construction, be reconciled to each other, reason and law conspire to dictate that this should be done; where this is impracticable, it becomes a matter of necessity to give effect to one, in exclusion of the other. The rule which has obtained in the courts for determining their relative validity is, that the last in order of time shall be preferred to the first. But this is a mere rule of construction, not derived from any positive law, but from the nature and reason of the thing. It is a rule not enjoined upon the courts by legislative provision, but adopted by themselves, as consonant to truth and propriety, for the direction of their conduct as interpreters of the law. . .

—Alexander Hamilton, *Federalist* 78

3. Which of the following statements best summarizes Hamilton's argument?

   (A) The Supreme Court must identify contradictory laws before they go into effect.

   (B) If there are two contradictory laws, the most recent should be considered valid and will remain in effect.

   (C) If there are two contradictory laws, the first law should be considered valid and will remain in effect.

   (D) It is the Supreme Court's responsibility to interpret the Constitution and reconcile contradictory laws.

4. Supporters of Hamilton's view that federal courts are responsible for determining the constitutionality of acts of Congress could point to which of the following cases?

   (A) *McDonald v. Chicago* (2010)

   (B) *Marbury v. Madison* (1803)

   (C) *McCulloch v. Maryland* (1819)

   (D) *Schenck v. United States* (1933)

5. During a Senate debate over proposed legislation, the minority party would like to postpone a final vote on a bill in order to prevent its passage. Which of the following would be the most effective strategy to achieve this goal?

   (A) Engage in a filibuster

   (B) Motion for cloture

   (C) File a discharge petition

   (D) Appeal to the Speaker of the House

6. Which of the following statements best illustrates the impact of the House Committee on Rules?

   (A) This committee typically considers bills since the quorum requirement is lower.

   (B) This committee makes it possible for individual members to circumvent the majority when a bill is stalled.

   (C) This committee's membership evens the playing field by balancing the ratio of majority to minority members.

   (D) This committee can establish rules for a bill that affect its likelihood of passage.

7. A bill passed by both the House and the Senate is vetoed by the president. Which of the following actions can Congress take if it wishes to pass the bill despite the president's opposition?

   (A) Vote to pass the bill again with a simple majority vote in each house

   (B) Override the veto by a two-thirds vote in each house

   (C) Revise and pass the bill again within 10 days of a veto

   (D) Receive a supermajority vote from the House

8. The president wishes to make an arrangement with a foreign country but knows that a clear majority of the Senate opposes her intended goals in negotiating this treaty. How might the president achieve her goals while bypassing the Senate?

   (A) Discussing the treaty further with the Senate

   (B) Making an executive agreement

   (C) Obtaining the House of Representatives's approval

   (D) Signing an executive order

9. A new president disagrees with the Supreme Court's constitutional interpretation in a series of high-profile cases. Which of the following tactics could he use to change the direction of the Court?

   (A) Dismissing justices who have ruled differently than he would have liked

   (B) Appointing new justices who share his views on constitutional interpretation when vacancies arise

   (C) Confirming judicial nominees appointed by the Senate

   (D) Invoking his constitutional right to preside over important cases

10. Congress has passed legislation to create a new program and is attempting to implement this policy. Which of the following actions can be taken by the federal bureaucracy to ensure compliance with this policy?

    (A) Grant additional funding to implement the policy

    (B) Schedule hearings to hold the departments accountable

    (C) Issue fines to those not in compliance

    (D) Select a new bureaucratic executive who supports the program

11. Which of the following is an accurate comparison of the House of Representatives and the Senate?

	House of Representatives	Senate
(A)	Decisions require agreement from three-fifths of members	Decisions require a simple majority vote
(B)	Debate is unlimited	Debate is heavily structured
(C)	Number of seats is prescribed by Constitution	Number of seats is determined by federal law
(D)	Members serve two-year terms	Members serve six-year terms

12. Which of the following is an accurate comparison of the executive and legislative branches?

	Executive branch	Legislative branch
(A)	Is responsible for appointing judges	Confirms the president's selections of public officials
(B)	Offers confirmation for new judges	Has the ability to declare war
(C)	Has the power to veto any bills from Congress	Has the power to make treaties with foreign countries
(D)	Has the power to overturn Supreme Court rulings	Is responsible for regulating interstate commerce

Part B: Key Terms

The following is a list of the major ideas, events, and people for the AP U.S. Government and Politics topic, Interactions Among Branches of Government. You will likely see many of these on the official AP exam.

For each key term, ask yourself the following questions:

- Can I define this key term and use it in a sentence?
- Can I provide an example related to this key term?
- Could I correctly answer a multiple-choice question about this key term?
- Could I correctly answer a free-response question about this key term?

Check off the key terms if you can answer "yes" to at least three of these questions.

The Congress

- ☐ U.S. Congress
- ☐ Senate
- ☐ House of Representatives
- ☐ Bicameral legislature
- ☐ Enumerated powers
- ☐ Necessary and proper clause
- ☐ Implied powers
- ☐ *McCulloch v. Maryland* (1819)
- ☐ Speaker of the House
- ☐ Majority leader
- ☐ Majority whip
- ☐ Minority leader

- ☐ Minority whip
- ☐ President of the Senate
- ☐ President pro tempore
- ☐ Standing committees
- ☐ Select committees
- ☐ Joint committees
- ☐ Conference committees
- ☐ Rules Committee
- ☐ Committee of the Whole
- ☐ Quorum
- ☐ Discharge petition
- ☐ Cloture

- ☐ Filibustering
- ☐ Unanimous consent
- ☐ Hold
- ☐ Mandatory spending
- ☐ Discretionary spending
- ☐ Earmarking
- ☐ Pork barrel
- ☐ Log rolling
- ☐ Trustee model
- ☐ Delegate model
- ☐ Politico model
- ☐ Gerrymandering
- ☐ *Baker v. Carr* (1962)
- ☐ *Shaw v. Reno* (1993)

The Presidency

- [ ] President of the United States (POTUS)
- [ ] Veto
- [ ] Pocket veto
- [ ] Commander-in-Chief
- [ ] Executive agreements
- [ ] Executive order
- [ ] Signing statement
- [ ] Articles of Confederation
- [ ] *Federalist* 70
- [ ] Term limits
- [ ] Twenty-Second Amendment
- [ ] Line-item veto
- [ ] Bully pulpit

The Courts

- [ ] Supreme Court of the United States (SCOTUS)
- [ ] Judicial review
- [ ] *Federalist* 78
- [ ] *Marbury v. Madison* (1803)
- [ ] Jurisdiction
- [ ] *Stare decisis*
- [ ] Precedent
- [ ] Judicial activism
- [ ] Judicial restraint
- [ ] *Lopez v. United States* (1995)
- [ ] Original jurisdiction
- [ ] Appellate jurisdiction

The Bureaucracy

- [ ] Bureaucracy
- [ ] Civil servants
- [ ] Patronage
- [ ] Merit-based system
- [ ] Federal regulations
- [ ] Rule-making process
- [ ] Rule-making authority
- [ ] Discretionary authority
- [ ] Delegation
- [ ] Enabling legislation
- [ ] Power of the purse

Next Steps

Step 1: Tally your correct answers from Part A and review the quiz explanations at the end of this chapter.

1.	A	7.	B
2.	D	8.	B
3.	D	9.	B
4.	B	10.	C
5.	A	11.	D
6.	D	12.	A

_____ out of 12 questions

Step 2: Count the number of key terms you checked off in Part B.

_____ out of 74 key terms

Step 3: Read the Key Takeaways in this chapter.

Step 4: Consult the table below and follow the instructions based on your performance.

If You Got...	Do This
80% or more of the Test What You Already Know assessment correct (10 or more questions from Part A and 60 or more key terms from Part B)	• Read definitions in this chapter for all the key terms you didn't check off. • Complete the Test What You Learned assessment in this chapter.
50% or less of the Test What You Already Know assessment correct (6 or fewer questions from Part A and 37 or fewer key terms from Part B)	• Read the comprehensive review for this topic in Chapter 9. ○ If you are short on time, read only the High-Yield sections. • Read through all of the key term definitions in this chapter. • Complete the Test What You Learned assessment in this chapter.
Any other result	• Read the High-Yield sections in the comprehensive review of this topic in Chapter 9. • Read definitions in this chapter for all the key terms you didn't check off. • Complete the Test What You Learned assessment in this chapter.

ESSENTIAL CONTENT

Key Takeaways: Interactions Among Branches of Government

1. The U.S. Congress is divided into two chambers: the Senate and the House of Representatives. The Senate was designed to represent the interest of state governments, while the House of Representatives was designed to represent the people; the functions and procedures of each house reflect these different constituencies.

2. The primary function of Congress is to enact legislation that is necessary and proper to carry out the powers it was granted by the Constitution. To handle the large volume of legislation it considers, Congress utilizes a complex committee system.

3. The president's ability to veto legislation is an important check on congressional power. The president also performs other formal and informal roles, such as civilian Commander-in-Chief of the military, diplomatic head of state, and de facto leader of his or her political party.

4. The nature of the president's role has changed over time, with the scope of the president's power gradually expanding despite efforts by Congress and the Supreme Court to limit the president's authority.

5. The purpose of the federal court system is to resolve disputes that arise under federal law. When the federal courts resolve a conflict between a statute and the Constitution, they engage in a process known as judicial review; judicial review empowers the court system to void laws that violate the Constitution, giving the judiciary an important check against the legislative and executive branches.

6. The courts are self-limited by the principle of *stare decisis*, which requires them to adhere to previous decisions when making new rulings. The court system is also subject to being overruled by Congress through legislation or constitutional amendment, and the president exercises preemptive oversight of the judiciary through the nomination process.

7. The bureaucracy consists of the numerous departments, agencies, commissions, and government corporations that make up the administrative arm of the federal government. The bureaucracy employs millions of workers known as civil servants, who are hired and promoted under a merit-based system; the most senior officials within the bureaucracy are appointed by the president.

8. As an extension of the executive branch, the primary purpose of the bureaucracy is to create regulations that govern the implementation and enforcement of federal law. The work of the bureaucracy is checked by various forms of presidential, congressional, and judicial oversight.

Key Terms: Interactions Among Branches of Government

The Congress

U.S. Congress: The legislature of the federal government, divided into a Senate and a House of Representatives.

Senate: Upper house of Congress, designed to represent state interests; this chamber consists of 100 members, two from each state.

House of Representatives: Lower house of Congress, designed to represent the people; this chamber consists of 435 members, with each state allotted a number of seats based on its population.

Bicameral legislature: A lawmaking body that is divided into two houses, such as the U.S. Congress.

Enumerated powers: Powers that are explicitly granted to Congress within the text of the Constitution.

Necessary and proper clause: A statement in Article I of the Constitution giving Congress the implied power to expand the scope of its enumerated powers.

Implied powers: Powers belonging to a government entity that are not expressly stated in the Constitution; powers that are derived from explicit or enumerated powers.

McCulloch v. Maryland (1819): Landmark Supreme Court decision that held that Congress has implied powers necessary to implement its enumerated powers and that established the supremacy of the U.S. Constitution and federal laws over state laws.

Speaker of the House: Formal presiding officer of the House of Representatives; a position established by Article I of the Constitution and elected by the entire House.

Majority leader: Member of Congress elected by the majority party in each house to promote its legislative agenda, primarily by speaking with leaders of both parties of both houses, and the public.

Majority whip: Member of Congress elected by the majority party of each house to encourage fellow party members to support the majority party's legislative agenda.

Minority leader: Member of Congress elected by the minority party of each house to promote its legislative agenda; analogous to the majority leader.

Minority whip: Member of Congress elected by the minority party of each house to encourage fellow party members to support the minority party's legislative agenda; analogous to the majority whip.

President of the Senate: The title used by the vice president of the United States in his or her role as the presiding officer of the Senate; a position established by Article I of the Constitution.

President pro tempore: The senator elected by the Senate to serve as its presiding officer in the absence of the vice president; a position established by Article I of the Constitution.

Standing committees: Permanent legislative panels within the House and Senate, each with a dedicated policy focus and the authority to review proposed legislation and conduct oversight of the executive branch within its legislative jurisdiction.

Select committees: Special legislative panels that are created for a specific purpose, such as to review legislation that does not fall within the jurisdiction of an existing standing committee.

Joint committees: Permanent legislative panels with a dedicated policy focus or administrative purpose that consist of members from both the House and Senate.

The Congress (cont.)

Conference committees: Temporary legislative panels with members from both the House and Senate that are established to reconcile different versions of the same bill following its passage by both houses.

Rules Committee: The committee in the House that determines the procedures for debating a specific bill; formally known as the House Committee on Rules.

Committee of the Whole: A committee consisting of all the members of the House; a parliamentary mechanism with fewer procedural requirements that is often used to expedite the legislative process.

Quorum: Minimum number of legislators that must be present in order for a legislative body such as the House or Senate to hold votes or conduct other business.

Discharge petition: Procedural mechanism in the House that can be used to move a bill that has stalled in committee to the floor of the House for a full vote.

Cloture: Process by which the Senate ends debate.

Filibustering: Act of blocking a vote in the Senate by speaking for an excessive length of time during debate or otherwise preventing cloture.

Unanimous consent: Parliamentary procedure used by the Senate in which it is assumed that all senators approve of an action unless an objection is raised.

Hold: Informal process by which a senator can prevent legislation from being considered by the full Senate.

Mandatory spending: Government expenditures that are mandated by preexisting law; primarily includes funding for entitlement programs like Social Security and Medicaid.

Discretionary spending: Government expenditures that are considered optional and can be added, modified, or eliminated each year during the annual budget process.

Earmarking: The act of inserting a provision into a spending bill that allocates funding for a specific program.

Pork barrel: Funding earmarked for a localized program that primarily benefits the home district of the legislator who proposed the earmark; commonly referred to as "pork."

Log rolling: Informal bargaining that occurs between legislators who agree to trade votes on each other's legislation or amendments.

Trustee model: A model of political representation in which an elected representative is entrusted by the voters to use his or her own judgment, even when it conflicts with the voters' interests or preferences.

Delegate model: A model of political representation in which an elected representative is obligated to vote according to the interests or preferences of his or her constituents.

Politico model: A model of political representation that combines elements of the trustee and delegate models and that seeks to describe how elected representatives actually operate in practice.

Gerrymandering: Act of drawing the geographic boundaries for legislative districts in such a way that the party controlling the process gains a political advantage.

***Baker v. Carr* (1962):** Landmark Supreme Court decision that held that the Constitution implies a "one person, one vote" standard that requires legislative districts to have roughly equal populations.

***Shaw v. Reno* (1993):** Landmark Supreme Court decision that held that race cannot be used as a factor when drawing the boundary lines for legislative districts.

The Presidency

President of the United States (POTUS): The head of the executive branch of the federal government.

Veto: Ability of the president to reject a bill passed by Congress.

Pocket veto: Passive veto that occurs when the president does not formally sign or veto a bill and Congress is no longer in session when the president's deadline to do so expires.

Commander-in-Chief: Title used to describe the president's role as the head of the military.

Executive agreements: Formal international agreements between the president and foreign leaders that do not require ratification by the Senate; can be rescinded by future presidents.

Executive order: Formal directive issued by the president outside of the legislative process pursuant to the president's power to execute and enforce the laws; can be rescinded by future presidents.

Signing statement: Informal declaration issued by the president when he or she signs a bill into law that indicates the president's reasons for signing the bill or plans for implementing it.

Articles of Confederation: Document that first established the federal government of the United States; in effect from 1781 to 1789, prior to the ratification of the current Constitution.

Federalist 70: An article defending the decision to grant the executive power to a single official by creating the office of the presidency; published as part of *The Federalist Papers*, a collection of essays written in support of the Constitution.

Term limits: Limitations on the maximum number of terms, or sometimes years, that an elected official may hold the same office.

Twenty-Second Amendment: Constitutional amendment that imposes a two-term limit on the office of the presidency; ratified in 1951.

Line-item veto: Ability of the president to reject specific provisions of a bill while signing others into law; currently not a recognized power.

Bully pulpit: Term coined by Theodore Roosevelt to describe the president's ability to advocate for his or her policy agenda as a result of his or her unique position as the sole executive officer at the head of the federal government.

The Courts

Supreme Court of the United States (SCOTUS): The highest court in the federal court system; established by Article III of the Constitution.

Judicial review: Process by which courts are empowered to invalidate legislative and executive actions that violate the Constitution.

Federalist 78: Article defending judicial review; published as part of *The Federalist Papers*, a collection of essays written in support of the Constitution.

***Marbury v. Madison* (1803):** Landmark Supreme Court decision that formally established the federal court system's authority to engage in judicial review.

Jurisdiction: Authority of a court to hear or decide a certain type of case.

Stare decisis: Judicial doctrine that requires judges to follow previous rulings; synonymous with adherence to precedent.

Precedent: Prior rulings that make an established body of case law.

The Courts (cont.)

Judicial activism: Judicial philosophy that holds judges are not required to defer to elected officials or adhere to established precedent when engaging in judicial review; tendency is to find laws unconstitutional.

Judicial restraint: Judicial philosophy that holds judges should defer to elected officials and/or established precedent when engaging in judicial review; tendency is to uphold laws.

***Lopez v. United States* (1995):** Landmark Supreme Court decision that invalidated the Gun-Free School Zones Act on the grounds that it was not sufficiently connected to interstate commerce and therefore exceeded the scope of congressional authority under the commerce clause.

Original jurisdiction: Authority of a court to hear cases that are being tried for the first time; for the Supreme Court, its scope is fixed by the Constitution.

Appellate jurisdiction: Authority of a court to hear cases on appeal (i.e., to review the decision of another court); for the Supreme Court, its scope is determined by federal law.

The Bureaucracy

Bureaucracy: Umbrella term for the departments, agencies, commissions, government corporations, and other organizations that make up the administrative arm of the federal government; an extension of the executive branch.

Civil servants: Bureaucratic employees who are hired and promoted pursuant to a merit-based system.

Patronage: Practice of rewarding the president's political supporters with bureaucratic appointments; also known as spoils system.

Merit-based system: Practice of hiring and promoting federal employees based on their objective qualifications rather than their support of the president or their other political affiliations.

Federal regulations: Legally binding rules generated by bureaucratic entities that govern the implementation and enforcement of federal law.

Rule-making process: Formal procedure used by bureaucratic entities to produce federal regulations.

Rule-making authority: Constitutional authority of the bureaucracy to create binding federal regulations.

Discretionary authority: Constitutional authority of the bureaucracy to resolve disputes that arise under federal regulations via administrative adjudication.

Delegation: The act of assigning one's duty or responsibility to another person or entity (e.g., when Congress assigns its rule-making authority to the bureaucracy).

Enabling legislation: A law or a provision within a law that authorizes the bureaucracy to take a specific action (e.g., to make regulations to guide the implementation of a federal statute).

Power of the purse: Informal term referring to the ability of Congress to influence the bureaucracy through the budget process.

TEST WHAT YOU LEARNED

Part A: Quiz

Questions 1–3 refer to the passage below.

The Government of the Union, though limited in its powers, is supreme within its sphere of action, and its laws, when made in pursuance of the Constitution, form the supreme law of the land.

There is nothing in the Constitution of the United States similar to the Articles of Confederation, which exclude incidental or implied powers.

If the end be legitimate, and within the scope of the Constitution, all the means which are appropriate, which are plainly adapted to that end, and which are not prohibited, may constitutionally be employed to carry it into effect.

—Chief Justice Marshall, *McCulloch v. Maryland* (1819)

1. Which of the following statements is most consistent with the author's argument in the passage?

   (A) The Articles of Confederation are supreme over any other laws.

   (B) States can make laws that are within the Constitution's scope.

   (C) The states take priority over the federal government.

   (D) The federal government is supreme over the states.

2. Which of the following governmental actions would the author most likely support?

   (A) Authorizing Congress to make any laws necessary to exercise its enumerated powers

   (B) Allowing the states to interpret the Constitution and create laws accordingly

   (C) Combining parts of the Articles of Confederation and the Constitution to create a new U.S. founding document

   (D) Excluding incidental and implied powers from the Constitution

3. Based on the passage, which of the following statements would the author most likely agree with?

   (A) The federal government and its laws should be considered supreme over the Constitution.

   (B) The government has the power to pass and implement laws that are outside the scope of the Constitution.

   (C) The government's limited powers prevent it from creating effective laws for future generations.

   (D) Laws created by Congress that are consistent with its constitutional powers should be considered the law of the land.

Questions 4 and 5 refer to the cartoon below.

1902 Finds the Helm in Safe Hands

Source: Library of Congress

4. Which of the following best describes the message of this political cartoon depicting President Theodore Roosevelt?

(A) The president must offer creative approaches to governance.

(B) The president represents a powerful executive.

(C) The president is easily swayed depending on the conditions.

(D) The president must remain focused in order to succeed.

5. Which of the following documents is most relevant to the way the presidency is portrayed in the cartoon?

(A) The Constitution

(B) The Articles of Confederation

(C) The Bill of Rights

(D) The Declaration of Independence

4

6. The minority party in the Senate has prolonged debate over a healthcare bill for the last few weeks, and the majority party is prepared to move to a vote. Which of the following actions must the majority party take to achieve this goal?

   (A) Engage in a filibuster

   (B) Gain approval from half of the Senate

   (C) Call a motion for cloture

   (D) Request a vote from the Senate's president

7. The president would like to promote a new domestic policy agenda. Which of the following actions can the president take to influence the legislative process?

   (A) Enlist the support of a senator

   (B) Introduce legislation in Congress

   (C) Issue an executive agreement

   (D) Create new legislation to pass through the Senate

8. If Congress were not satisfied with a recent Supreme Court ruling on immigration, which of the following would be the most effective strategy Congress could use to check the Supreme Court's power?

   (A) Appoint new justices who align with Congress's views

   (B) Ignore the most recent Supreme Court decision

   (C) Pass new legislation to override the Supreme Court ruling

   (D) Create a new agency to issue immigration regulations

9. Which of the following best describes the concept of *stare decisis*?

   (A) A confirmation process in which justices are appointed by the president and approved by the Senate

   (B) A legal doctrine holding that precedent should not be reversed except in the most extraordinary circumstances

   (C) A process allowing similar court cases to yield inconsistent rulings

   (D) A guiding principle enabling justices to decide cases based on their philosophical beliefs

10. Within the next 90 days, a regulation proposed by the Department of Veterans Affairs will take effect, mandating that veterans must submit an estimate of any necessary medical care they will require at the beginning of each calendar year. Which of the following is the most effective course of action Congress could take to stop the regulation?

    (A) Create new budgetary incentives that will reward the department for ending its pursuit of the policy

    (B) Schedule a committee hearing to review the department's reasoning

    (C) Vote the regulation down within the next couple of months to prevent it from taking effect

    (D) Decrease the department's funding to limit its ability to enforce the policy

11. Which of the following is an accurate comparison of the Judiciary Act of 1789 and *Marbury v. Madison* (1803)?

	Judiciary Act of 1789	Marbury v. Madison
(A)	Granted the Supreme Court authority to issue writs of mandamus	Established judicial review and ruled the Judiciary Act of 1789 unconstitutional
(B)	Expanded the original jurisdiction of the Supreme Court beyond the scope of Article III	Strengthened the Judiciary Act of 1789 in establishing judicial review
(C)	Established that the Supreme Court is the sole interpreter of the Constitution	Ruled that the Supreme Court can void laws passed by Congress
(D)	Strengthened the role of the courts by allowing them to void certain acts passed by Congress	Allowed the Supreme Court to expand its powers by issuing writs of mandamus

12. Which of the following is an accurate comparison of the authority of the president and the authority of Congress over the federal bureaucracy?

	President	Congress
(A)	Adjusts the scope of bureaucratic organizations' powers	Reviews decisions made by the federal bureaucracy
(B)	Appropriates more funds to favored bureaucratic organizations	Selects and confirms those nominated to become bureaucratic executives
(C)	Holds committee hearings to review the federal bureaucracy's work	Influences actions through budgetary incentives
(D)	Selects bureaucratic executives to lead organizations	Sets the budget for individual agencies

Part B: Key Terms

This key terms list is the same as the list in the Test What You Already Know section earlier in this chapter. Based on what you have now learned, again ask yourself the following questions:

- Can I define this key term and use it in a sentence?
- Can I provide an example related to this key term?
- Could I correctly answer a multiple-choice question about this key term?
- Could I correctly answer a free-response question about this key term?

Check off the key terms if you can answer "yes" to at least three of these questions.

The Congress

- ☐ U.S. Congress
- ☐ Senate
- ☐ House of Representatives
- ☐ Bicameral legislature
- ☐ Enumerated powers
- ☐ Necessary and proper clause
- ☐ Implied powers
- ☐ *McCulloch v. Maryland* (1819)
- ☐ Speaker of the House
- ☐ Majority leader
- ☐ Majority whip
- ☐ Minority leader

- ☐ Minority whip
- ☐ President of the Senate
- ☐ President pro tempore
- ☐ Standing committees
- ☐ Select committees
- ☐ Joint committees
- ☐ Conference committees
- ☐ Rules Committee
- ☐ Committee of the Whole
- ☐ Quorum
- ☐ Discharge petition
- ☐ Cloture

- ☐ Filibustering
- ☐ Unanimous consent
- ☐ Hold
- ☐ Mandatory spending
- ☐ Discretionary spending
- ☐ Earmarking
- ☐ Pork barrel
- ☐ Log rolling
- ☐ Trustee model
- ☐ Delegate model
- ☐ Politico model
- ☐ Gerrymandering
- ☐ *Baker v. Carr* (1962)
- ☐ *Shaw v. Reno* (1993)

The Presidency

- [ ] President of the United States (POTUS)
- [ ] Veto
- [ ] Pocket veto
- [ ] Commander-in-Chief

- [ ] Executive agreements
- [ ] Executive order
- [ ] Signing statement
- [ ] Articles of Confederation

- [ ] *Federalist* 70
- [ ] Term limits
- [ ] Twenty-Second Amendment
- [ ] Line-item veto
- [ ] Bully pulpit

The Courts

- [ ] Supreme Court of the United States (SCOTUS)
- [ ] Judicial review
- [ ] *Federalist* 78
- [ ] *Marbury v. Madison* (1803)

- [ ] Jurisdiction
- [ ] *Stare decisis*
- [ ] Precedent
- [ ] Judicial activism
- [ ] Judicial restraint

- [ ] *Lopez v. United States* (1995)
- [ ] Original jurisdiction
- [ ] Appellate jurisdiction

The Bureaucracy

- [ ] Bureaucracy
- [ ] Civil servants
- [ ] Patronage
- [ ] Merit-based system
- [ ] Federal regulations

- [ ] Rule-making process
- [ ] Rule-making authority
- [ ] Discretionary authority

- [ ] Delegation
- [ ] Enabling legislation
- [ ] Power of the purse

4

NEXT STEPS

Tally your correct answers from Part A and review the quiz explanations at the end of this chapter.

1.	D	7.	A
2.	A	8.	C
3.	D	9.	B
4.	B	10.	C
5.	A	11.	A
6.	C	12.	D

_____ out of 12 questions

Count the number of key terms you checked off in Part B.

_____ out of 74 key terms

Compare your Test What You Already Know results to these Test What You Learned results to see how exam-ready you are for this topic.

- Read (or reread) the comprehensive review for this topic in Chapter 9.
- Go to kaptest.com to complete the online quiz questions for Interactions Among Branches of Government.
  - Haven't registered your book yet? Go to kaptest.com/moreonline to begin.

CHAPTER 4 ANSWERS AND EXPLANATIONS

Test What You Already Know

1. A
Topic: 9.2 The Presidency

In the excerpt, Hamilton states, "Energy in the Executive is a leading character in the definition of good government…" before explaining why having a strong executive leader is essential; **(A)** is correct. (B) is incorrect because the topic of the excerpt concerns a strong leader versus a weak leader, not whether a republican government will be difficult to execute without additional support. While Hamilton mentions that many believe "that a vigorous Executive is inconsistent with the genius of republican government," he actually rejects this idea; (C) is incorrect. (D) is incorrect because Hamilton explains that even a casual study of Roman history will show the repeated need for a strong executive figure.

2. D
Topic: 9.2 The Presidency

Since Hamilton explains the benefits of an "energetic executive" in the excerpt, supporters of Hamilton would likely endorse the idea of a separate executive branch as provided for by the Constitution; **(D)** is correct. (A) is incorrect because the Articles of Confederation did not establish a separate executive branch. (B) is incorrect because the president of Congress established in the Articles was a weak executive, contrary to what Hamilton preferred. (C) is incorrect because the Constitution does not provide for a leader to have absolute power.

3. D
Topic: 9.3 The Courts

In the passage, Hamilton states that "it is the province of the courts to liquidate and fix [the] meaning and operation" of contradictory laws; additionally, he refers to the courts as "interpreters of the law." Thus, **(D)** is correct. Hamilton does not mention that the Supreme Court needs to identify contradictory laws before they go into effect, making (A) incorrect. (B) and (C) are incorrect because these do not relate to the Supreme Court's ability to reconcile laws and are considered to be "a mere rule of construction."

4. B
Topic: 9.3 The Courts

In the excerpt, Hamilton explains that the federal courts are responsible for determining whether acts of Congress are constitutional, which matches the establishment of judicial review in *Marbury v. Madison*; **(B)** is correct. (A), (C), and (D) are incorrect because these cases did not impact the Court's ability to void acts of Congress as unconstitutional. In *McDonald v. Chicago*, the Supreme Court ruled that the right to keep and bear arms for self-defense is applicable to the states; in *McCulloch v. Maryland*, the Court established the federal government as supreme over the states; and in *Schenck v. United States*, the Court ruled that speech may be restricted if it poses a "clear and present danger" to national security.

5. A
Topic: 9.1 The Congress

Once an up-or-down vote is called, the Senate's minority party can invoke its right to continue debate, thereby postponing the voting process and blocking passage of the bill. This prolonged debate is called a filibuster; therefore, **(A)** is correct and (D) is incorrect. (B) is incorrect because a motion for cloture is the only way to end debate and call for a final up-or-down vote. Successfully filing a discharge petition will discharge the bill from the jurisdiction of the standing committee and bring it to the floor for a vote in the House of Representatives, not the Senate; (C) is incorrect.

6. D
Topic: 9.1 The Congress

The limitations chosen by the Rules Committee can significantly affect the likelihood that a bill will pass the House; **(D)** is correct. (A) is incorrect because this describes the Committee of the Whole, not the House Committee on Rules. Filing a discharge petition allows individual members to circumvent the majority when a bill is stalled in any committee; (B) is incorrect. The membership of the Rules Committee tilts heavily in favor of the majority party; (C) is incorrect.

7. B

Topic: 9.2 The Presidency

If the president chooses to veto a bill, Congress has the opportunity to override the president's veto by a two-thirds vote in each house; **(B)** is correct. Since passing a vetoed bill requires a supermajority vote in each house, (A) and (D) are incorrect. (C) is incorrect because revising and passing a bill within 10 days of a veto does not ensure that the bill will pass.

8. B

Topic: 9.2 The Presidency

Although treaties must be ratified by the Senate, the Supreme Court has held that the president can enter into executive agreements, which are agreements between the leaders of countries (but are not necessarily binding on later leaders), without the Senate's approval; thus, **(B)** is correct. Returning to the Senate for further discussion would not guarantee the Senate's support; (A) is incorrect. (C) is incorrect because the president is not required to obtain approval from the House of Representatives to make treaties and pacts with other countries. (D) is incorrect because executive orders impact how a federal law is implemented and are not related to treaties with foreign governments.

9. B

Topic: 9.3 The Courts

As a check on the Supreme Court, the president may appoint new justices; **(B)** is correct. (A) is incorrect because justices are appointed to serve for life unless they resign, retire, or are impeached by Congress. It is the Senate's duty to confirm new justices, making (C) incorrect. (D) is incorrect because overseeing trials is not within the president's power.

10. C

Topic: 9.4 The Bureaucracy

When implementing a new law or policy, the federal bureaucracy can write and enforce regulations, issue fines, and testify before Congress; **(C)** is correct. (A) and (B) are incorrect since setting the budget and holding hearings are within Congress's, not the federal bureaucracy's, power. Only the president can select new bureaucratic executives; (D) is incorrect.

11. D

Topic: 9.1 The Congress

Members of the House of Representatives must seek reelection every two years, while members of the Senate must seek reelection every six years; **(D)** is correct. (A) is incorrect because it is the House of Representatives that requires a simple majority for decisions, while the Senate must reach an agreement among three-fifths of its members. (B) and (C) are incorrect because these also confuse the characteristics of the House and the Senate.

12. A

Topics: 9.1 The Congress & 9.2 The Presidency

The president is able to appoint new judges, while the Senate confirms the president's selection of public officials; **(A)** is correct. (B) is incorrect because the Senate, not the president, confirms new judges. The Senate can only ratify, not create, a treaty with another country, making (C) incorrect. Only a new law or a new Supreme Court decision can overturn a Supreme Court ruling, neither of which the executive branch can perform; (D) is incorrect.

Test What You Learned

1. D

Topic: 9.1 The Congress

In this Supreme Court decision, Chief Justice Marshall explains that "the Government of the Union, though limited in its powers, is supreme within its sphere of action." Thus, **(D)** is correct and (C) is incorrect. (A) is incorrect because Marshall states that "laws, when made in pursuance of the Constitution, form the supreme law of the land." Marshall argues that the federal government, not the states, is able to make laws within the scope of the Constitution, making (B) incorrect.

2. A

Topic: 9.1 The Congress

In the last paragraph of the excerpt, Marshall argues that "all...means...are appropriate" for Congress to carry out its powers listed in the Constitution; **(A)** is correct. Marshall asserts that the federal government is supreme and may make laws within the scope of the Constitution; he does not mention the states' ability to interpret either the Constitution or laws, making (B) incorrect. (C) and (D) are incorrect because the passage does not indicate that Marshall believes that the Articles of Confederation and the Constitution should be combined or that incidental and implied powers should be excluded from the Constitution.

3. D

Topic: 9.1 The Congress

Chief Justice Marshall explains that the government's "laws, when made in pursuance of the Constitution, form the supreme law of the land"; therefore, **(D)** is correct and (B) is incorrect. The passage does not argue that the federal government should be considered supreme over the Constitution. Instead, Marshall states that laws created by the federal government that are constitutional should be considered "the supreme law of the land," making (A) incorrect. While the passage does read that "the Government of the Union, though limited in its powers, is supreme within its sphere of action," Marshall does not imply that this limited power may prevent it from creating effective laws. Thus, (C) is incorrect.

4. B

Topic: 9.2 The Presidency

The political cartoon depicts President Theodore Roosevelt as the strong-handed captain of the "ship of state." The ship represents the nation as a whole, and the way in which Roosevelt handily steers the ship solo symbolizes the president's power to govern the nation; **(B)** is correct. The cartoon illustrates the strength of the presidency, not the creativity needed for governance; (A) is incorrect. While the image shows a ship moving through treacherous weather and waters, Roosevelt is pictured as being strong enough to continue steering the ship, which is a metaphor for the nation; (C) is incorrect. Roosevelt appears to have intense focus on the path ahead; however, this is not the main idea of the illustration, making (D) incorrect.

5. A

Topic: 9.2 The Presidency

The political cartoon shows the president as a powerful and stable executive guiding the "ship of state"; the Constitution established the executive branch while also creating a strong federal government, so **(A)** is correct. The Articles of Confederation purposefully created a weak executive, which is not in line with the political cartoon, making (B) incorrect. (C) is incorrect because the Bill of Rights represents the first 10 amendments to the Constitution and does not speak to the strength of the presidency. (D) is incorrect because the Declaration of Independence signals America's beginnings as a nation separate from Great Britain's rule and does not specifically discuss the executive branch.

6. C

Topic: 9.1 The Congress

In order to end debate and move to a final up-or-down vote, the Senate's majority party must motion for cloture, which requires three-fifths approval from the senators; thus, **(C)** is correct and (B) is incorrect. A filibuster is a way to extend debate, not end it; (A) is incorrect. (D) is incorrect because the President of the Senate cannot vote unless there is a tie.

7. A

Topic: 9.2 The Presidency

A president can influence the legislative process by enlisting the support of a senator or representative who agrees to introduce legislation consistent with the president's policy vision; **(A)** is correct. Only senators and representatives can introduce legislation in Congress, and only Congress can create new legislation; (B) and (D) are incorrect. (C) is incorrect because executive agreements are foreign pacts with foreign governments, which do not have a direct influence on the legislative process for domestic policy issues.

8. C

Topic: 9.3 The Courts

As a check on the Supreme Court, Congress can pass new legislation that impacts court jurisdiction or modifies the impact of prior Supreme Court decisions, and it can propose constitutional amendments; **(C)** is correct. (A) is incorrect because only the president can appoint new justices. (B) is incorrect because Congress is not authorized to ignore Supreme Court decisions. While the federal bureaucracy indeed issues regulations and Congress creates new agencies, the Department of Homeland Security already focuses on immigration, and it would not make sense for Congress to create an additional agency with this same focus; (D) is incorrect.

9. B

Topic: 9.3 The Courts

Stare decisis is a legal doctrine that holds that precedent, once established, should not be reversed except in the most extraordinary circumstances. Therefore, **(B)** is correct and (D) is incorrect. (A) is incorrect because this describes the checks and balances of the executive, legislative, and judicial branches, not *stare decisis*. *Stare decisis* ensures that decisions made are almost always consistent with precedent; thus, (C) is also incorrect.

10. C

Topic: 9.4 The Bureaucracy

In this example, the best course of action Congress could take to prevent the regulation from taking effect would be to vote the regulation down; **(C)** is correct. While budgetary incentives, committee hearings, and decreasing funding are indeed oversight powers of Congress, these actions could hurt future regulations by this department or others as much or more than they impact this regulation; thus, (A), (B), and (D) are incorrect.

11. A

Topic: 9.3 The Courts

The Judiciary Act of 1789 allowed the Supreme Court to issue writs of mandamus. However, this was ruled unconstitutional with the Supreme Court's decision in *Marbury v. Madison*, the case that established judicial review; thus, **(A)** is correct and (D) is incorrect. *Marbury v. Madison* struck down, not strengthened, the Judiciary Act of 1789, making (B) incorrect. (C) is incorrect because the Judiciary Act of 1789 did not establish the Supreme Court as the sole interpreter of the Constitution; it was the ruling in *Marbury v. Madison* that did this.

12. D

Topic: 9.4 The Bureaucracy

The president can select executives to lead bureaucratic organizations, and Congress sets the budget for individual agencies within the federal government. This budgetary authority allows Congress to appropriate more money to bureaucratic entities that it favors and less money to those that it disfavors. Therefore, **(D)** is correct and (B) is incorrect. It is within the authority of Congress, not the president, to adjust the scope of bureaucratic organizations' powers; (A) is incorrect. (C) is incorrect because Congress, not the president, has the ability to hold committee hearings.

CHAPTER 5

Civil Liberties and Civil Rights

LEARNING OBJECTIVES

- Distinguish between civil liberties and civil rights in the United States.

- Identify the protections in the Bill of Rights.

- Cite specific SCOTUS decisions that affected how the First and Second Amendments have been interpreted.

- Detail tensions between civil liberties and public safety.

- Summarize the legal basis of selective incorporation.

- List and explain specific legal consequences of the due process clause.

- List and explain specific U.S. social movements that opposed discrimination.

- Cite laws and SCOTUS decisions that directly responded to social movements.

- Compare the different ways in which SCOTUS has either expanded or restricted civil rights.

TEST WHAT YOU ALREADY KNOW

Part A: Quiz

Questions 1 and 2 refer to the passage below.

As to the *Times*, we similarly conclude that the facts do not support a finding of actual malice. The statement by the *Times*' Secretary that, apart from the padlocking allegation, he thought the advertisement was "substantially correct," affords no constitutional warrant for the Alabama Supreme Court's conclusion that it was a "cavalier ignoring of the falsity of the advertisement [from which] the jury could not have but been impressed with the bad faith of the *Times*, and its maliciousness inferable therefrom."

The statement does not indicate malice at the time of the publication; even if the advertisement was not "substantially correct"—although respondent's own proofs tend to show that it was—that opinion was at least a reasonable one, and there was no evidence to impeach the witness' good faith in holding it. The *Times*' failure to retract upon respondent's demand, although it later retracted upon the demand of Governor Patterson, is likewise not adequate evidence of malice for constitutional purposes.

—Supreme Court, *New York Times Co. v. Sullivan* (1964)

1. Which of the following statements is most consistent with the Supreme Court's argument in the passage?

   (A) A newspaper publishing content that is partially truthful would indicate actual malice.

   (B) The freedom to publish is considered free speech unless there are indications of actual malice.

   (C) A publication retracting content that was mostly truthful indicates actual malice by the press.

   (D) The publishing of advertisements that portray public officials negatively is considered illegal.

2. Based on the passage, which of the following actions would the Supreme Court most likely support?

   (A) A national magazine's publishing any material it chooses, including stories that contain classified security information

   (B) The government's censoring a newspaper because it had run stories that decreased the public's faith in public officials

   (C) A regional newspaper's running damaging information, which is mostly accurate, about the mayor

   (D) A newspaper's losing a lawsuit because it unknowingly ran false information about the governor

Questions 3 and 4 refer to the passage below.

If for instance, there was a law, which imposed imprisonment or a fine upon me if I manumitted a slave, I would on no account resist that law, I would set the slave free, and then go to prison or pay the fine. If a law commands me to sin I will break it; if it calls me to suffer, I will let it take its course unresistingly. The doctrine of blind obedience and unqualified submission to any human power, whether civil or ecclesiastical, is the doctrine of despotism, and ought to have no place among Republicans and Christians.

—Angelina Emily Grimké, "Appeal to the Christian Women of the South" (1836)

3. Which of the following statements is most consistent with the author's argument in the passage?

   (A) Social movements should obey the law as written.

   (B) Social movements must sometimes use illegal tactics that come at a personal cost.

   (C) Social movements must renounce violent means in order to act conscientiously.

   (D) Social movements should use violent means to achieve nonviolent ends.

4. Which of the following forms of political participation is the author defending in this passage?

   (A) Participation in civil disobedience

   (B) Adherence to the law

   (C) Publishing of open letters

   (D) Organized violent resistance

5

5. Which of the following scenarios would violate the Nineteenth Amendment?

   (A) A district's allowing only men the right to vote on election day

   (B) A city's preventing African Americans from voting at the polls

   (C) A state's making the sale of wine in liquor stores illegal

   (D) A local government's denying citizenship to a U.S.-born African American woman

6. Which of the following actions would be deemed unconstitutional using the Supreme Court's reasoning in *Shaw v. Reno* (1993)?

   (A) A district in California denying an African American man the right to vote

   (B) A private company opening two Italian restaurants: one for African Americans and another for whites

   (C) A public school in Texas turning away African American students

   (D) Massachusetts redrawing its voting districts to include one district with African Americans in the majority

7. The right to an attorney is found in which amendment?

   (A) Fourth Amendment

   (B) Fifth Amendment

   (C) Sixth Amendment

   (D) Seventh Amendment

8. Which of the following constitutional clauses was cited by the Supreme Court to justify its ruling in *Roe v. Wade* (1973)?

   (A) The citizenship clause

   (B) The privileges and immunities clause

   (C) The equal protection clause

   (D) The due process clause

9. Which of the following policies would a supporter of the women's rights movement be most likely to endorse?

   (A) Restrictions on access to contraception

   (B) Equal opportunity in employment

   (C) The abolition of slavery

   (D) The prohibition of alcoholic beverages

10. Which First Amendment clause was cited in *Wisconsin v. Yoder* (1972)?

    (A) The free exercise clause

    (B) The commerce clause

    (C) The establishment clause

    (D) The due process clause

11. The Supreme Court has changed over time since the mid-nineteenth century. Based on previous rulings, which of the following best describes the Supreme Court in its interactions with civil rights?

    (A) From 1850 to 1900, the Supreme Court took a more expansive view of civil rights.

    (B) In the mid-1900s, the Supreme Court became more divided on the issue of civil rights.

    (C) Since the 1950s, the Supreme Court has reversed many of its earlier decisions as culture and perspectives shift.

    (D) In the 1850s, the Supreme Court pushed for greater government protection of individual rights.

12. Which of the following is an accurate pairing of the exclusionary rule and the establishment clause?

	Exclusionary Rule	Establishment Clause
(A)	An attorney cannot be barred from an interrogation.	The citizens' right to religious belief is protected.
(B)	Improperly seized evidence cannot be used at trial.	The government cannot favor one religion over another.
(C)	Police cannot search a car without a warrant.	The government must view each religion, including non-religion, equally.
(D)	The government must be inclusive of all religions and non-religion.	Lawyers must establish that any evidence used in a trial was obtained legally.

Part B: Key Terms

The following is a list of the major ideas, events, and people for the AP U.S. Government and Politics topic of Civil Liberties and Civil Rights. You will likely see many of these on the official AP exam.

For each key term, ask yourself the following questions:

- Can I define this key term and use it in a sentence?
- Can I provide an example related to this key term?
- Could I correctly answer a multiple-choice question about this key term?
- Could I correctly answer a free-response question about this key term?

The Bill of Rights

- ☐ Bill of Rights
- ☐ Civil liberty
- ☐ Civil right
- ☐ Civil Rights Act of 1964
- ☐ Voting Rights Act of 1965
- ☐ Title IX
- ☐ Jurisprudence

- ☐ Establishment clause
- ☐ Free exercise clause
- ☐ *Engel v. Vitale* (1962)
- ☐ *Wisconsin v. Yoder* (1972)
- ☐ *Schenck v. United States* (1919)

- ☐ *Tinker v. Des Moines Independent Community School District* (1969)
- ☐ Prior restraint
- ☐ *New York Times Co. v. United States* (1971)
- ☐ Libel
- ☐ *McDonald v. City of Chicago* (2010)

The Fourteenth Amendment

- ☐ Incorporation
- ☐ Selective incorporation

- ☐ Due process clause
- ☐ *Gideon v. Wainwright* (1963)

- ☐ *Roe v. Wade* (1973)

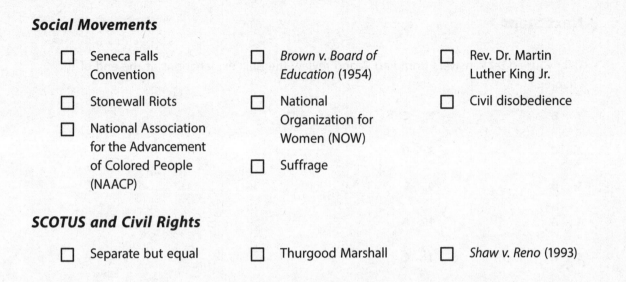

Social Movements

- ☐ Seneca Falls Convention
- ☐ Stonewall Riots
- ☐ National Association for the Advancement of Colored People (NAACP)

- ☐ *Brown v. Board of Education* (1954)
- ☐ National Organization for Women (NOW)
- ☐ Suffrage

- ☐ Rev. Dr. Martin Luther King Jr.
- ☐ Civil disobedience

SCOTUS and Civil Rights

- ☐ Separate but equal
- ☐ Thurgood Marshall
- ☐ *Shaw v. Reno* (1993)

5

Next Steps

Tally your correct answers from Part A and review the quiz explanations at the end of this chapter.

1.	B	7.	C
2.	C	8.	D
3.	B	9.	B
4.	A	10.	A
5.	A	11.	C
6.	D	12.	B

_____ out of 12 questions

Step 2: Count the number of key terms you checked off in Part B.

_____ out of 33 key terms

Step 3: Read the Key Takeaways in this chapter.

Step 4: Consult the table below and follow the instructions based on your performance.

If You Got...	Do This
80% or more of the Test What You Already Know assessment correct (9 or more questions from Part A and 27 or more key terms from Part B)	• Read definitions in this chapter for all the key terms you didn't check off. • Complete the Test What You Learned assessment in this chapter.
50% or less of the Test What You Already Know assessment correct (6 or fewer questions from Part A and 17 or fewer key terms from Part B)	• Read the comprehensive review for this topic in Chapter 10. ◦ If you are short on time, read only the High-Yield sections. • Read through all of the key term definitions in this chapter. • Complete the Test What You Learned assessment in this chapter.
Any other result	• Read the High-Yield sections in the comprehensive review of this topic in Chapter 10. • Read definitions in this chapter for all the key terms you didn't check off. • Complete the Test What You Learned assessment in this chapter.

ESSENTIAL CONTENT

Key Takeaways: Civil Liberties and Civil Rights

1. The Constitution protects the rights and privileges of people in the United States. Some rights, such as voting, require citizenship; others, such as the right to counsel, apply to any person in U.S. jurisdiction. Rights are not absolute and may be limited for a legitimate governmental reason.

2. Civil liberties and civil rights are two distinct categories. A civil liberty is typically freedom to do something, usually to exercise a right; a civil right is typically freedom from something, such as discrimination. The boundaries of civil rights and civil liberties have shifted over the history of the United States as courts have applied the laws in different ways at different times.

3. The Bill of Rights is the formal name for the first 10 amendments to the Constitution. Most of the rights within the Bill of Rights have been applied to the states through incorporation via the Fourteenth Amendment.

4. Due process is the legal concept that prohibits random or arbitrary governmental action; it is one of the rationales for applying the Bill of Rights to the states, along with the equal protection clause.

5. Social movements need clear goals and frameworks to successfully advance their causes. Notable movements include the civil rights movement, the women's rights movement, and the LGBTQ rights movement.

6. Successful movements engage in community building within their core constituency and work in coalition with allied groups to effect desired changes. Movements must also navigate challenges between compromise and idealism. Social change is a slow process that requires work on legal, cultural, and moral fronts.

7. The Supreme Court has gone back and forth on civil liberties since its founding, producing rulings that expanded liberties from the 1950s through the 1970s and rulings that have slowly narrowed them since then.

Key Terms: Civil Liberties and Civil Rights

The Bill of Rights

Bill of Rights: The first 10 amendments to the U.S. Constitution.

Civil liberty: Freedom to do something, usually to exercise a right.

Civil right: Freedom from something, such as discrimination.

Civil Rights Act of 1964: Law signed by President Johnson that prohibited discrimination in public accommodations on the basis of race or sex.

Voting Rights Act of 1965: Law signed by President Johnson that guaranteed federal enforcement of voting rights in states with histories of racial bias.

Title IX: Part of the Education Amendments of 1972 signed by President Nixon that prohibited discrimination based on sex in any federally funded education programs.

Jurisprudence: The study of law and legal interpretation; sometimes used to refer to a set of established legal precedents (e.g., First Amendment jurisprudence would be about cases involving the freedoms in the First Amendment).

Establishment clause: The first of the two religion clauses in the First Amendment, this clause prevents the government from supporting a single religion, or religion over non-religion.

Free exercise clause: The second of the two religion clauses in the First Amendment, this clause prevents the government from limiting religious exercise of citizens; free exercise is limited, not absolute, and may be constrained for a compelling reason.

Engel v. Vitale (1962): Supreme Court case that struck down public payments to parochial schools; cited the establishment clause.

Wisconsin v. Yoder (1972): Supreme Court case that upheld religious exemption for Amish parents and students; cited the free exercise clause.

Schenck v. United States (1919): Supreme Court case that set limits on permissible speech; established the "clear and present danger" test.

Tinker v. Des Moines Independent Community School District (1969): Supreme Court case that upheld for students the free speech right to protest.

Prior restraint: A governmental body telling a publisher what it can and cannot publish.

New York Times Co. v. United States (1971): Supreme Court case that allowed the *New York Times* and the *Washington Post* to publish the Pentagon Papers; effectively abolished prior restraint.

Libel: A published, false defamatory statement.

McDonald v. City of Chicago (2010): Supreme Court case that incorporated the Second Amendment to the states.

The Fourteenth Amendment

Incorporation: The legal mechanism by which the Supreme Court applies the Bill of Rights to the states.

Selective incorporation: The method used in the United States of applying the protections in the Bill of Rights on a case-by-case basis.

Due process clause: A clause in both the Fifth and Fourteenth Amendments guaranteeing the right to due process in any action depriving people of life, liberty, or property.

Gideon v. Wainwright **(1963):** Supreme Court case that incorporated the right to an attorney found in the Sixth Amendment.

Roe v. Wade **(1973):** Supreme Court case that upheld the right of women to have access to abortion with some mandated limits; example of the use of substantive due process.

Social Movements

Seneca Falls Convention: First organized gathering of the American women's rights movement, in 1848.

Stonewall Riots: Riots at the Stonewall Inn from June 28 to July 1 in 1969; commonly accepted as the beginning of the gay liberation movement.

National Association for the Advancement of Colored People (NAACP): Organized group involved with the civil rights movement; litigated most civil rights cases, including *Brown v. Board of Education* (1954), argued by Thurgood Marshall.

Brown v. Board of Education **(1954):** Supreme Court case that overturned the "separate but equal" holding from *Plessy v. Ferguson* (1896) and declared segregated schools unconstitutional.

National Organization for Women (NOW): Women's rights organization founded in 1966 and run by feminist leaders such as Betty Friedan, Shirley Chisholm, Pauli Murray, and Gloria Steinem.

Suffrage: The right to vote; sometimes described as women's suffrage in the American context.

Rev. Dr. Martin Luther King Jr.: Leader of the civil rights movement; Baptist minister known for his advocacy of nonviolent direct action and civil disobedience.

Civil disobedience: Knowingly disobeying a law that an individual considers to be unjust to bring the issue to the attention of a wider audience.

SCOTUS and Civil Rights

Separate but equal: The holding from *Plessy v. Ferguson* (1896) that allowed discrimination in public accommodations as long as they were theoretically equal; overturned by *Brown v. Board of Education* (1954).

Thurgood Marshall: Lead attorney in *Brown v. Board of Education* (1954) and the first African American Supreme Court justice.

Shaw v. Reno **(1993):** Supreme Court case that mandated districts drawn along racial lines must be considered under strict scrutiny and be consistent with the Voting Rights Act of 1965.

TEST WHAT YOU LEARNED

Part A: Quiz

Questions 1–3 refer to the passage below.

We admit that, in many places and in ordinary times, the defendants, in saying all that was said in the circular, would have been within their constitutional rights. But the character of every act depends upon the circumstances in which it is done. The most stringent protection of free speech would not protect a man in falsely shouting fire in a theatre and causing a panic. It does not even protect a man from an injunction against uttering words that may have all the effect of force. The question in every case is whether the words used are used in such circumstances and are of such a nature as to create a clear and present danger that they will bring about the substantive evils that Congress has a right to prevent. It is a question of proximity and degree. When a nation is at war, many things that might be said in time of peace are such a hindrance to its effort that their utterance will not be endured so long as men fight, and that no Court could regard them as protected by any constitutional right.

—Justice Oliver Wendell Holmes, majority opinion, *Schenck v. United States* (1919)

1. Which of the following statements is most consistent with the author's argument?

   (A) The entire Constitution should remain in force even if the nation is at war.

   (B) Persons in the United States have an unlimited right to free speech.

   (C) Rights can be limited if necessary for the government to achieve an essential function.

   (D) Speech should be censored only if it can be proven false.

2. Which of the following would the author argue is the most important distinction regarding the speech discussed in *Schenck*?

   (A) The advocating of "substantive evils"

   (B) The United States being at war

   (C) The nationality of the speaker

   (D) The truth or falsity of the content

3. Which of the following actions would the author most likely argue should be censored according to the "clear and present danger" test?

   (A) A member of a peace organization calling for the end of a war in which the United States is not involved

   (B) A member of a domestic political organization calling for the overthrow of a foreign government during a war

   (C) A member of an international peace organization calling for the overthrow of a foreign government during a war

   (D) A member of a domestic political organization calling for the overthrow of the American government during a war

Questions 4 and 5 refer to the table below.

Year	Segregated Public Schools (%)	Integrated Public Schools (%)
1925	92	8
1935	87	13
1945	86	14
1955	78	22
1965	7	93

4. Based on the information in the table, which of the following statements would be most accurate regarding education in the twentieth century?

    (A) Between 1925 and 1965, public schools desegregated at a steady rate.

    (B) Between 1925 and 1965, public schools viewed desegregation as a way to increase the quality of education.

    (C) Between 1935 and 1955, public schools were varied in their approaches to desegregation.

    (D) Between 1955 and 1965, public schools were encouraged to desegregate.

5. Which of the following Supreme Court cases is most relevant to the information in the table?

    (A) *Brown v. Board of Education* (1954)

    (B) *Engel v. Vitale* (1962)

    (C) *Wisconsin v. Yoder* (1972)

    (D) *Tinker v. Des Moines Independent Community School District* (1969)

5

5

6. Which of the following scenarios would likely be considered a violation of Title IX of the Education Amendments of 1972?

(A) A private college granting a white man admission over an African American man with the same credentials

(B) A public university refusing admission to a white woman who has better test scores and grades than other male applicants

(C) A southern university giving priority to in-state and regional students

(D) An all-male private high school refusing admission to a female student

7. A German citizen is arrested at a major theme park in Orlando, Florida after complaining about the poor quality of the beer and causing significant property damage to a resort bar. Having spent all his money at the bar before he destroyed it, he is unable to pay for his own attorney and is thus classified as an indigent defendant. In which case did the Supreme Court establish the principle that the Bill of Rights requires the court to appoint an attorney to represent the defendant?

(A) *McDonald v. City of Chicago* (2010)

(B) *Shaw v. Reno* (1993)

(C) *Gideon v. Wainwright* (1963)

(D) *Roe v. Wade* (1973)

8. Based on his "Letter from a Birmingham Jail," which of the following would Martin Luther King Jr. most likely oppose?

(A) Delaying direct action until the timing is right

(B) Organizing a demonstration to disrupt an establishment

(C) Disobeying laws as a form of protest

(D) Accepting punishment for disobeying unjust laws

9. The Supreme Court has extended the Bill of Rights over time to apply to state and local governments on a case-by-case basis. This process is called

(A) piecemeal incorporation

(B) selective incorporation

(C) partial incorporation

(D) individual incorporation

10. A police department has a pattern of pulling over only sports cars for speeding in excess of five miles per hour over the limit, while pulling over all other vehicles if they are speeding at least 15 miles per hour over the limit. This is a violation of

   (A) the right to free speech, because the drivers of sports cars view vehicles as an expression of themselves

   (B) the right to fair and proper counsel, because the drivers of sports cars are not able to appeal their speeding tickets

   (C) the right to due process, because the police are arbitrarily choosing when to give speeding tickets

   (D) the right to equal protection, because the police are treating drivers differently based on the type of car they drive

11. In a certain town, when an African American is found loitering, police officers take this person into custody immediately. However, when an Asian or white citizen is caught trespassing, the police issue only a verbal warning. For which of the following reasons would the Supreme Court likely find these practices unconstitutional?

   (A) This situation violates the right to free speech, as the African Americans are protesting discrimination when arrested.

   (B) This situation violates the right to counsel, as the African Americans are not given the chance to hire a lawyer prior to arrest.

   (C) This situation fails the strict scrutiny test and violates the right to due process.

   (D) This situation is considered suspect classification and violates the right to equal protection.

12. Which of the following is an accurate comparison of the two Supreme Court rulings?

	Tinker v. Des Moines Independent Community School District (1969)	_Wisconsin v. Yoder_ (1972)
(A)	Advocated that speech calling for rebellion can be restricted	Bolstered the freedom of the press, even in cases involving national security
(B)	Decided that school sponsorship of religious activities violates the establishment clause	Allowed students to wear armbands at school in protest of war
(C)	Required that speech must advocate felony conduct before it can be censored	Applied to speech during wartime and did not address peacetime speech
(D)	Stated that students can legally wear armbands in school as a protest against war	Ruled that forcing students to attend high school against their religious beliefs violates the free exercise clause

Part B: Key Terms

This key terms list is the same as the list in the Test What You Already Know section earlier in this chapter. Based on what you have now learned, again ask yourself the following questions:

- Can I define this key term and use it in a sentence?
- Can I provide an example related to this key term?
- Could I correctly answer a multiple-choice question about this key term?
- Could I correctly answer a free-response question about this key term?

Check off the key terms if you can answer "yes" to at least three of these questions.

The Bill of Rights

- ☐ Bill of Rights
- ☐ Civil liberty
- ☐ Civil right
- ☐ Civil Rights Act of 1964
- ☐ Voting Rights Act of 1965
- ☐ Title IX
- ☐ Jurisprudence

- ☐ Establishment clause
- ☐ Free exercise clause
- ☐ *Engel v. Vitale* (1962)
- ☐ *Wisconsin v. Yoder* (1972)
- ☐ *Schenck v. United States* (1919)

- ☐ *Tinker v. Des Moines Independent Community School District* (1969)
- ☐ Prior restraint
- ☐ *New York Times Co. v. United States* (1971)
- ☐ Libel
- ☐ *McDonald v. City of Chicago* (2010)

The Fourteenth Amendment

- ☐ Incorporation
- ☐ Selective incorporation

- ☐ Due process clause
- ☐ *Gideon v. Wainwright* (1963)

- ☐ *Roe v. Wade* (1973)

Social Movements

- [ ] Seneca Falls Convention
- [ ] Stonewall Riots
- [ ] National Association for the Advancement of Colored People (NAACP)
- [ ] *Brown v. Board of Education* (1954)
- [ ] National Organization for Women (NOW)
- [ ] Suffrage
- [ ] Rev. Dr. Martin Luther King Jr.
- [ ] Civil disobedience

SCOTUS and Civil Rights

- [ ] Separate but equal
- [ ] Thurgood Marshall
- [ ] *Shaw v. Reno* (1993)

5

Next Steps

Tally your correct answers from Part A and review the quiz explanations at the end of this chapter.

1.	C	7.	C
2.	B	8.	A
3.	D	9.	B
4.	D	10.	C
5.	A	11.	D
6.	B	12.	D

_____ out of 12 questions

Count the number of key terms you checked off in Part B.

_____ out of 33 key terms

Compare your Test What You Already Know results to these Test What You Learned results to see how exam-ready you are for this topic.

- Read (or reread) the comprehensive review for this topic in Chapter 10.

- Go to kaptest.com to complete the online quiz questions for Civil Liberties and Civil Rights.

  ◦ Haven't registered your book yet? Go to kaptest.com/moreonline to begin.

CHAPTER 5 ANSWERS AND EXPLANATIONS

Test What You Already Know

1. B
Topic: 10.1 The Bill of Rights

In the Supreme Court opinion the Court states, "As to the *Times*, we similarly conclude that the facts do not support a finding of actual malice"; therefore, the *New York Times* was legally able to publish the content, and **(B)** is correct. Because the opinion states that "even if the advertisement was not 'substantially correct' ... that opinion was at least a reasonable one, and there was no evidence to impeach the witness' good faith in holding it," (A) is incorrect. Later in the passage, the Court explains that "the *Times'* failure to retract upon respondent's demand, although it later retracted upon the demand of Governor Patterson, is likewise not adequate evidence of malice for constitutional purposes"; (C) is incorrect. (D) is incorrect because unless there is an indication of "malice at the time of the publication," it is within the *Times'* rights to publish freely.

2. C
Topic: 10.1 The Bill of Rights

In *New York Times Co. v. Sullivan*, the Supreme Court established the actual malice standard, which meant that a public figure or official must prove that a publication knowingly published falsehoods before a published story can be considered libel. Because the regional newspaper ran information that was "substantially correct," it would not have been seen as acting with disregard for the truth; **(C)** is correct. There is no absolute right to publish because material can be censored for legitimate security concerns (a common example being troop movements); (A) is incorrect. (B) and (D) are incorrect because the public official must prove that the newspaper acted with disregard for the truth.

3. B
Topic: 10.3 Social Movements

Grimké asserts in this excerpt that abolitionists must sometimes use illegal tactics that come at a personal cost, such as jail time or paying a fine for freeing slaves; **(B)** is correct. While Grimké says that one should accept punishment for breaking the law, she also states that a bad law should be broken as a matter of conscience. A person must simply accept the punishment for acting according to their conscience; (A) is incorrect. Although Grimké discusses morality as a sort of higher law, (C) is incorrect because it is too extreme; she never states that all illegal means, such as violence, should be renounced. Likewise, (D) is incorrect because Grimké advocates something closer to civil disobedience than violent resistance.

4. A
Topic: 10.3 Social Movements

Civil disobedience is knowingly disobeying a law that an individual considers to be unjust. The aim is to bring the issue to the attention of a wider audience, as well as to show that the individual peaceably objects to a certain law as a matter of conscience. This is what the passage advocates for; thus, **(A)** is correct and (B) is incorrect. Although the excerpt is an open letter that Grimké published about abolitionism, she does not explicitly advocate for this means of political participation in the letter itself; (C) is incorrect. While Grimké states that she would not resist "imposed imprisonment or a fine" if she illegally freed a slave, she never mentions using violence to combat unjust laws. In fact, she frames civil disobedience as respecting the punishment for violating even unjust laws. Therefore, (D) is incorrect.

5. A
Topic: 10.3 Social Movements

The Nineteenth Amendment grants women the right to vote; **(A)** is correct. (B), (C), and (D) are incorrect because each would violate other amendments: the Fifteenth, Twenty-First, and Fourteenth Amendments, respectively.

6. D

Topic: 10.1 The Bill of Rights

In *Shaw v. Reno*, the Supreme Court decided that race-conscious districting must meet the standard of strict scrutiny, making the creation of minority-majority districts more difficult; **(D)** is correct. (A) is incorrect because this would violate the Fifteenth Amendment, not the holding in *Shaw v. Reno*. (B) and (C) are incorrect because these would likely be considered unconstitutional based on a different case, *Brown v. Board of Education* (1954), which struck down the "separate but equal" doctrine.

7. C

Topic: 10.1 The Bill of Rights

The right to counsel is in the Sixth Amendment, so **(C)** is correct. (A), (B), and (D) are incorrect: the Fourth Amendment concerns unreasonable searches and seizures, the Fifth Amendment concerns self-incrimination, and the Seventh Amendment concerns the right of trial by jury and protection against double jeopardy.

8. D

Topic: 10.2 The Fourteenth Amendment

In *Roe v. Wade*, the Supreme Court expanded the right to personal privacy, which they located in the due process clause of the Fourteenth Amendment; **(D)** is correct. Birthright citizenship, the privileges and immunities clause, and the equal protection clause were not at issue in the *Roe* case, so (A), (B), and (C) are incorrect.

9. B

Topic: 10.3 Social Movements

One of the primary goals of the women's rights movement is to foster equality of opportunity, so that all people regardless of gender have a fair chance to succeed. Thus, a supporter of this movement would be most likely to endorse equal opportunity in employment, making **(B)** correct. (A) is incorrect because members of the women's movement typically advocated for increased access to contraception, not decreased. While many members of the early women's movement supported the abolition of slavery, the abolitionist cause was a distinct movement (and most of the history of the women's movement occurred after slavery had already been abolished), so (C) is incorrect. Similarly, (D) is incorrect because, even though many women were members of the temperance movement that led to prohibition, that was also a distinct movement.

10. A

Topic: 10.1 The Bill of Rights

Yoder established free exercise protections for Amish parents and students, specifically the right for Amish students not to attend public school; it is one of the few cases that the Court has upheld on free exercise grounds. **(A)** is correct. The commerce clause, found in Article I of the Constitution, was not cited in *Yoder*; (B) is incorrect. The establishment clause was central to other cases involving school and religion, such as *Lemon v. Kurtzman* (1971), but not to *Yoder*, making (C) incorrect. The due process clause, found in the Fifth and Fourteenth Amendments, was also not central to the *Yoder* decision; (D) is incorrect.

11. C

Topic: 10.4 SCOTUS and Civil Rights

By the 1950s, many ideas had changed, and the previously held theories of eugenics and biological racism had fallen from public favor. This resulted in many court cases reversing previous rulings, such as *Brown v. Board of Education* (1954) striking down the former *Plessy v. Ferguson* ruling of "separate but equal"; **(C)** is correct and (B) is incorrect. Between 1850 and 1900, the Supreme Court took a narrow view of civil rights, driven by theories of biological determinism and racial prejudice; (A) is incorrect. In the 1950s through the 1970s, movements pushed for greater government protection of individual rights, and the Court decided cases in favor of expanding those rights, as with *Roe v. Wade* (1973); (D) is incorrect.

12. B

Topics: 10.1 The Bill of Rights & 10.2 The Fourteenth Amendment

The exclusionary rule states that improperly seized evidence cannot be used in trial, while the establishment clause prohibits the government from favoring any religion; **(B)** is correct and (D) is incorrect. (A) is incorrect because it mistakenly defines the exclusionary rule and confuses the free exercise clause with the establishment clause. While searches without a warrant are generally prohibited by the Fourth Amendment, the exclusionary rule deals with evidence found during these searches, not with questioning the searches themselves; (C) is incorrect.

Test What You Learned

1. C

Topic: 10.1 The Bill of Rights

The central holding of *Schenck* is that the government can censor or punish speech during wartime if it meets the "clear and present danger" criterion (though the interpretation of this criterion has changed over time); thus, **(C)** is correct. Because some rights can be limited during times of crisis, (A) and (B) are incorrect. (D) is incorrect because the truth or falsity of the speech is not at question, only the timing.

2. B

Topic: 10.1 The Bill of Rights

The "clear and present danger" test depends on "proximity and degree," as stated by Justice Holmes; therefore, in a time of heightened tension such as a war, speech that would otherwise be permissible would be considered dangerous. Thus, **(B)** is correct. While (A) reflects part of the requirement for censored speech, it does not encompass all of it, making (A) incorrect. People of any nationality have the constitutional right to free speech in the United States, making (C) incorrect. Lastly, (D) is incorrect because, according to Justice Holmes, the truth of the content would not be a defense.

3. D

Topic: 10.1 The Bill of Rights

Someone calling for the overthrow of the American government during a time of heightened tensions, like a war, would likely breach the "clear and present danger" standard; **(D)** is correct. In the passage, Justice Holmes notes that free speech rights are more extensive in peacetime, so (A) is incorrect. American free speech law is broadly permissive of criticism of governments, especially foreign ones; (B) and (C) are incorrect.

4. D

Topic: 10.4 SCOTUS and Civil Rights

The table shows that schools slowly desegregated from 1925 to 1955 and then more quickly began to integrate between 1955 and 1965, which implies that public schools were either encouraged or mandated to desegregate in this decade; therefore, **(D)** is correct and (A) is incorrect. There is no indication in the table that public schools perceived desegregation as a way to increase the quality of education or that public schools approached desegregation in any given way; thus, (B) and (C) are incorrect.

5. A

Topic: 10.4 SCOTUS and Civil Rights

The infographic illustrates a decrease in segregated schools and an increase in desegregated schools; these trends are the direct result of *Brown v. Board of Education*, the landmark case that struck down the "separate but equal" doctrine of *Plessy v. Ferguson*. Thus, **(A)** is correct. While *Engel v. Vitale*, *Wisconsin v. Yoder*, and *Tinker v. Des Moines Independent Community School District* each relate to schools, the rulings declared that school sponsorship of religious activities violated the establishment clause, held that compelling Amish students to attend school beyond the eighth grade violates the free exercise clause, and decided that public school students could wear black armbands in school to protest the Vietnam War, respectively. Thus, (B), (C), and (D) are incorrect.

6. B

Topic: 10.3 Social Movements

Title IX of the Education Amendments of 1972 invalidated discrimination on the basis of sex in federally funded education; **(B)** is correct. (A) and (D) are incorrect because these describe private schools, which are not federally funded; additionally, (A) does not deal with discrimination based on sex. (C) is incorrect because Title IX does not prohibit a regional university from prioritizing in-state or regional students.

7. C

Topic: 10.2 The Fourteenth Amendment

In *Gideon*, the Court extended the right to legal representation, located in the Sixth Amendment, to every defendant in criminal trials; **(C)** is correct. *McDonald* deals with the Second Amendment, making (A) incorrect. In *Shaw*, the Supreme Court ruled that legislative redistricting must be conscious of race and ensure compliance with the Voting Rights Act of 1965; (B) is incorrect. Lastly, (D) is incorrect because *Roe* deals with the Fourteenth Amendment.

8. A

Topic: 10.3 Social Movements

In King's "Letter from a Birmingham Jail," he specifically opposes the moderate approach of waiting until the time is right to negotiate or take action; **(A)** is correct. (B) is incorrect because this would create "constructive tension," but not a violent situation. King encouraged disobeying unjust laws as a form of protest; (C) is incorrect. (D) is incorrect because King praised those who accepted the penalty for breaking unjust laws as a means of respecting the law and drawing attention to the movement.

9. B

Topic: 10.2 The Fourteenth Amendment

Selective incorporation is the process of applying amendments to the states on a case-by-case basis; thus, **(B)** is correct. (A), (C), and (D) are incorrect because these describe the way in which amendments are incorporated but do not properly identify the term.

10. C

Topic: 10.2 The Fourteenth Amendment

Arbitrary and inconsistent government actions violate the right to due process found in the Fifth and Fourteenth Amendments; **(C)** is correct. (A) and (B) are incorrect because neither is implicated by arbitrary enforcement. (D) is incorrect because there is no indication of a pattern of bias that would be required for an equal protection claim.

11. D

Topic: 10.2 The Fourteenth Amendment

The scenario in this question presents evidence of the pattern of bias required for an equal protection claim; therefore, **(D)** is correct. (A) is incorrect because the scenario states that African Americans are arrested for loitering and because people cannot protest on private property against the property owner's will. (B) is incorrect because the right to counsel has not been violated here; once arrested, those being held are still able to speak with an attorney if they choose. While the scenario may be a violation of due process, it would likely pass the strict scrutiny test; (C) is incorrect.

12. D

Topic: 10.1 The Bill of Rights

The Supreme Court ruled that students were allowed to wear armbands in school to protest the Vietnam War in *Tinker v. Des Moines Independent Community School District* and, in *Wisconsin v. Yoder*, that compelling Amish students to attend high school is in violation of the free exercise clause; **(D)** is correct. (A) is incorrect because the *Tinker* decision did not focus on restricting speech that calls for rebellion; in addition, (A) confuses the *New York Times v. United States* (1971) and the *Wisconsin v. Yoder* rulings. (B) is incorrect because it references *Engel v. Vitale* (1962) and confuses the rulings for *Tinker* with that of *Wisconsin v. Yoder*. (C) is incorrect because the *Tinker* decision did not distinguish speech in this way, and the *Wisconsin v. Yoder* did not address speech during wartime versus peacetime.

CHAPTER 6

American Political Ideologies and Beliefs

LEARNING OBJECTIVES

- Match particular core values with the specific political attitudes they typically accompany.

- List means by which people's political attitudes are formed.

- Define scientific polling's salient characteristics.

- Cite factors affecting the credibility of polls.

- Distinguish between traditional Democratic and Republican platforms.

- Track changes in U.S. political debates and public policies over time.

- Distinguish among conservative, liberal, and libertarian positions on market regulation.

- Distinguish between Keynesian and supply-side perspectives on fiscal and monetary policy.

- Distinguish among conservative, liberal, and libertarian views on government intervention.

- Distinguish between conservative and liberal perspectives on social issues.

TEST WHAT YOU ALREADY KNOW

Part A: Quiz

Questions 1 and 2 refer to the table below.

A nonpartisan research organization was paid to predict how a policy reducing taxes for businesses would fare if taken to a nationwide vote. It conducted an in-person poll across the United States to gather the results, which are listed below. The organization predicted that this policy would pass.

Political Party	Population Surveyed	Region Surveyed	Number of Votes in Favor
Democratic Party	1,541	West and Northwest	254
Republican Party	5,698	Southeast, Southwest, Northeast, and Midwest	4,979
Libertarian Party	4,234	Southeast, Northeast, and Midwest	2,348
Green Party	2,157	Southeast, Southwest, Northeast, and Midwest	1,042

1. Based on the results shown in the table, which political party was most in favor of the tax reduction policy?

   (A) Democratic Party

   (B) Libertarian Party

   (C) Republican Party

   (D) Green Party

2. Based on the information in the table, which of the following is an issue with the poll?

   (A) The poll neglected to poll a sample of each group relative to the actual size of the group in society.

   (B) The poll should have represented at least five political parties to produce a more accurate prediction.

   (C) The poll should have been available online instead of in person so that it could reach more people.

   (D) The poll reflects the research organization's bias, skewing the results and the prediction.

Questions 3 and 4 refer to the passage below.

One of the great problems of government is to determine to what extent the Government itself shall interfere with commerce and industry and how much it shall leave to individual exertion. It is just as important that business keep out of government as that government keep out of business. No system is perfect. We have had abuses in the conduct of business that every good citizen resents. But I insist that the results show our system better than any other and retains the essentials of freedom.

As a result of our distinctly American system, our country has become the land of opportunity to those born without inheritance not merely because of the wealth of its resources and industry but because of this freedom of initiative and enterprise.

—Herbert Hoover, *Rugged Individualism* (1928)

3. Which of the following statements is most consistent with Hoover's argument in the passage?

   (A) The separation of government and business in the United States has led to increased individualism and opportunity.

   (B) The U.S. economic system is imperfect; however, Americans continue to work toward the good of the collective society.

   (C) The U.S. government could be improved with additional guidance from businesses.

   (D) It is essential for the government to increase its commercial interactions.

4. Which of the following ideological perspectives is most consistent with the passage?

   (A) Liberal

   (B) Socialist

   (C) Collectivist

   (D) Conservative

6

5. A multi-billion dollar corporation has been cutting corners when paying state taxes. The governor has overlooked this action because the company donated a million dollars to the governor's recent election campaign. This scenario violates which of the following American core values?

   (A) Individualism

   (B) Equality of opportunity

   (C) Rule of law

   (D) Free enterprise

6. Which of the following describes an effect of polling on election campaigns?

   (A) Causes fewer voters to show up at the polls if they see that their candidate is either winning or losing by a large margin

   (B) Reflects the biases of the audience of the media outlet that conducted the poll

   (C) Indicates to candidates how a population's opinions have changed over time

   (D) Assists candidates in deciding where to focus their campaign resources to effectively persuade the electorate

7. Which of the following policies would an individual who identifies as a liberal most likely oppose?

   (A) Increasing fracking as a means to extract oil and gas from the earth

   (B) Legalizing the possession, production, and sale of marijuana

   (C) Raising taxes on the upper class in order to put entitlements on firmer financial footing

   (D) Regulating more strictly the sale and ownership of semi-automatic rifles and their ammunition

8. Which of the following best describes a tracking poll?

   (A) An informal, unscientific poll that can measure public opinion in a non-randomized population

   (B) A poll of likely voters conducted as they enter a polling station to cast their ballots

   (C) A poll that provides information on a particular candidate in hopes of leading participants to vote against that candidate

   (D) A running poll that regularly surveys the same respondents to measure changes in opinion over time

9. Which of the following is a policy that would be supported by a proponent of supply-side economics during an economic recession?

   (A) Lowering taxes for the entire population while increasing government spending

   (B) Granting increased tax cuts to investors and entrepreneurs to encourage them to save and invest more

   (C) Avoiding interference with the economy by maintaining the same level of taxes and government expenditures

   (D) Cutting taxes in half for the working lower class to encourage spending and reignite the economy

10. Which of the following best defines the concept of political socialization?

   (A) An element of polling that takes a person's background into account

   (B) The process of learning about a specific political party's platform and beliefs

   (C) A single event that encourages a person to switch from one political party to another

   (D) The process by which people shape their ideas about politics and their political values

6

11. Which of the following best describes American exceptionalism?

    (A) Belief that America holds a unique place in world history

    (B) Emphasis on unique states' rights

    (C) Support of changes in beliefs over time

    (D) Support for expanded government

12. Which of the following is an accurate comparison of positions liberals and conservatives would likely support?

	Liberals	Conservatives
(A)	Hold to a platform built around traditional American values	Encourage the use of affirmative action in college admissions
(B)	Consider social and economic equality a core tenet of their philosophy	Believe in the power of free-market capitalism
(C)	Believe in the power of free-market capitalism	Consider social and economic equality a core tenet of their philosophy
(D)	Believe that affirmative action is unnecessary	Hold to a platform built around traditional American values

6

Part B: Key Terms

The following is a list of the major ideas, events, and people for the AP U.S. Government and Politics topic of American Political Ideologies and Beliefs. You will likely see many of these on the official AP exam.

For each key term, ask yourself the following questions:

- Can I define this key term and use it in a sentence?
- Can I provide an example related to this key term?
- Could I correctly answer a multiple-choice question about this key term?
- Could I correctly answer a free-response question about this key term?

Check off the key terms if you can answer "yes" to at least three of these questions.

Political Attitude Formation

- ☐ Political attitudes
- ☐ Political culture
- ☐ Individualism
- ☐ Equality of opportunity
- ☐ Equality of outcome
- ☐ Free enterprise
- ☐ Rule of law
- ☐ Limited government
- ☐ Political socialization
- ☐ Social groups
- ☐ Generational effects
- ☐ Life-cycle effects

Polling

- ☐ Polling
- ☐ Benchmark poll
- ☐ Tracking poll
- ☐ Exit poll
- ☐ Scientific polling
- ☐ Sample
- ☐ Straw poll
- ☐ Pollster
- ☐ Margin of error

Ideology and Policy

- ☐ Democratic Party
- ☐ Liberalism
- ☐ Republican Party
- ☐ Conservatism
- ☐ American exceptionalism
- ☐ Libertarianism
- ☐ Fiscal conservatism
- ☐ Monetary policy
- ☐ Fiscal policy
- ☐ Keynesian economics
- ☐ Supply-side economics
- ☐ Social policy

Next Steps

Tally your correct answers from Part A and review the quiz explanations at the end of this chapter.

1.	C	7.	A
2.	A	8.	D
3.	A	9.	B
4.	D	10.	D
5.	C	11.	A
6.	D	12.	B

_____ out of 12 questions

Step 2: Count the number of key terms you checked off in Part B.

_____ out of 33 key terms

Step 3: Read the Key Takeaways in this chapter.

Step 4: Consult the table below and follow the instructions based on your performance.

If You Got...	Do This
80% or more of the Test What You Already Know assessment correct (10 or more questions from Part A and 26 or more key terms from Part B)	• Read definitions in this chapter for all the key terms you didn't check off. • Complete the Test What You Learned assessment in this chapter.
50% or less of the Test What You Already Know assessment correct (6 or fewer questions from Part A and 16 or fewer key terms from Part B)	• Read the comprehensive review for this topic in Chapter 11. ○ If you are short on time, read only the High-Yield sections. • Read through all of the key term definitions in this chapter. • Complete the Test What You Learned assessment in this chapter.
Any other result	• Read the High-Yield sections in the comprehensive review of this topic in Chapter 11. • Read definitions in this chapter for all the key terms you didn't check off. • Complete the Test What You Learned assessment in this chapter.

ESSENTIAL CONTENT

Key Takeaways: American Political Ideologies and Beliefs

1. The core American values of individualism, equality of opportunity, free enterprise, rule of law, and limited government play a key role in shaping the political attitudes and beliefs of individuals and American political culture as a whole.

2. Other factors that influence the development of political opinions include family, school, peer groups, media, social groups, historical events, and personal experience.

3. Polls are commonly used to gauge the public's opinion about an issue or candidate. Politicians use polls to make decisions about which policies to support and how to utilize their campaign resources.

4. To be useful, polls must be reliable. Various factors affect the reliability of polling, including the size of the sample, the way in which the sample was selected, and the format of the questions asked.

5. The three most common political ideologies in the United States are libertarianism, conservatism, and liberalism. Libertarianism and conservatism tend to advocate for individualism and limited government intervention in the private sphere, while liberalism envisions an important role for government in promoting equality and injustice.

6. The Republican Party is the more conservative of the two major parties and tends to favor limited government and protections for civil liberties and economic freedom. The Democratic Party is the more liberal of the two major parties and tends to emphasize civil rights and the role of government in improving the lives of the American people.

6

Key Terms: American Political Ideologies and Beliefs

Political Attitude Formation

Political attitudes: The opinions people hold about the role of government and the specific programs and policies that their government should implement.

Political culture: The combined set of political attitudes held by individuals within the same culture.

Individualism: A social and political philosophy that promotes individual well-being over the well-being of society as a whole.

Equality of opportunity: The belief that each person should have an equal chance at success and that no person should be limited by circumstances outside of her control.

Equality of outcome: Having similar or equal results among individuals within a society; often contrasted with equality of opportunity.

Free enterprise: The ability of individual people and businesses to make money with minimal interference by the government.

Rule of law: The notion that everyone within a country, including government officials, are subject to its laws.

Limited government: The belief that political officials and institutions should have significant constraints on their power.

Political socialization: The process by which people form their political attitudes and beliefs.

Social groups: Formal or informal groups of people who share similar characteristics and a common sense of identity.

Generational effects: Significant historical or cultural events that can permanently affect the political attitudes of the people who lived through them.

Life-cycle effects: Fluctuations in political beliefs that can occur as a result of life events that commonly occur at particular points in a typical lifespan.

Polling

Polling: The monitoring of public opinion.

Benchmark poll: A poll taken at the beginning of an election cycle.

Tracking poll: A series of polls given repeatedly in several consecutive time periods to assess how opinions are changing over time.

Exit poll: A poll given to people on election day as they are leaving their voting station.

Scientific polling: Any polling conducted using commonly accepted guidelines for gathering reliable statistical results; at a minimum, requires a randomly selected sample from a relevant population and clear, unbiased questions.

Sample: For any type of poll, the subset of the population that is actually surveyed.

Straw poll: An unofficial survey taken from a group of people who have already assembled for a different purpose.

Pollster: A person or group of persons who conduct a poll.

Margin of error: The maximum expected difference between the results of a poll and the opinions actually held by the population as a whole.

Ideology and Policy

Democratic Party: One of the two major political parties in the United States; the more liberal party of the American two-party system.

Liberalism: A political philosophy characterized by the belief that a primary purpose of government is to promote equality and justice.

Republican Party: One of the two major political parties in the United States; the more conservative party of the American two-party system.

Conservatism: A political philosophy characterized by an emphasis on personal liberty and limited government.

American exceptionalism: The view that the United States plays a unique role in human history as a global leader, and that, accordingly, it cannot be held to the same standards as other nations.

Libertarianism: A political philosophy that advocates for minimal government involvement in personal and business decisions.

Fiscal conservatism: A political and economic theory that advocates for lower taxes and a balanced budget.

Monetary policy: The set of actions taken by a central bank to control the money supply by measures such as raising or lowering interest rates.

Fiscal policy: The set of actions taken by the government to use its tax and spending power to influence the economy.

Keynesian economics: An economic theory characterized by the belief that government should manage the economy by regulating demand.

Supply-side economics: An economic theory characterized by the belief that government should manage the economy by regulating supply.

Social policy: The programs and other actions that a government implements to promote the social welfare of its citizens.

6

TEST WHAT YOU LEARNED

Part A: Quiz

Questions 1–3 refer to the passage below.

I believe we can embark on a new age of reform in this country and an era of national renewal. An era that will reorder the relationship between citizen and government, that will make government again responsive to people, that will revitalize the values of family, work, and neighborhood and that will restore our private and independent social institutions...

That's why I've said throughout this campaign that we must control and limit the growth of federal spending, that we must reduce tax rates to stimulate work and savings and investment. That's why I've said we can relieve labor and business of burdensome, unnecessary regulations and still maintain high standards of environmental and occupational safety. That's why I've said we can reduce the cost of government by eliminating billions lost to waste and fraud in the federal bureaucracy, a problem that is now an unrelenting national scandal...

—Ronald Reagan, "A Vision for America" (1980)

1. Which of the following statements is most consistent with Reagan's argument in the passage?

    (A) Fraud in the federal bureaucracy is to blame for the United States' current economic condition.

    (B) To resolve the current economic crisis, the U.S. government should reduce its spending and cut taxes.

    (C) Labor and business must create their own regulations as a means to decrease government spending.

    (D) U.S. private and social institutions are at risk of being eliminated if the government does not take action.

2. Which of the following economic theories is most consistent with the passage?

    (A) Laissez-faire economics

    (B) Keynesian economics

    (C) Supply-side economics

    (D) Demand-side economics

3. Which of the following actions would the author most likely support?

    (A) Relieving businesses from adhering to strict marketing regulations

    (B) Increasing income taxes for the middle and upper classes

    (C) Increasing the Department of Transportation's budget by 50 percent

    (D) Rolling back anti-retaliation regulations in the workplace

Questions 4 and 5 refer to the cartoon below.

"The trouble, my friends, with socialism is that it would destroy initiative" (1910)

"THE TROUBLE, MY FRIENDS, WITH SOCIALISM IS THAT IT WOULD DESTROY INITIATIVE."
Puck Is Not an Advocate of Socialism, but He Finds Some Grim Humor in Monopoly's Argument Against It.

Source: Library of Congress

4. Given the rise of the Socialist Party in the early twentieth century, which of the following best describes the message of this political cartoon?

   (A) The United States must focus on eliminating monopolies, not adopting socialism.

   (B) If the U.S. government were to adopt socialism, the government would become too large for citizens to thrive.

   (C) The U.S. government must level the playing field for workers to avoid the negative effects of socialism.

   (D) The best way for the United States to increase initiative and productivity is to value the individual.

5. Which of the following American core values is most aligned with the cartoon's message?

   (A) Individualism

   (B) Collectivism

   (C) Equality of opportunity

   (D) Rule of law

6. An individual donor would be most likely to contribute less money to a candidate's election campaign when

   (A) the candidate is a few points behind in the polls

   (B) the candidate is significantly behind in the polls

   (C) the candidate is a few points ahead in the polls

   (D) the candidate is significantly ahead in the polls

7. Which of the following best illustrates the concept of free enterprise?

   (A) A major grocery store chain buys out its competitors to dominate the market.

   (B) A state government rules that the price of gasoline may not exceed five dollars per gallon.

   (C) An entrepreneur opens a new fruit stand and sets produce prices based on the season.

   (D) Congress votes that any new business must request approval for its inventory and prices.

8. A candidate announced her run for governor last week and is deciding how to best distribute campaign resources. Which of the following polls should her campaign conduct?

   (A) Benchmark poll

   (B) Tracking poll

   (C) Entrance poll

   (D) Exit poll

9. A political pollster is conducting a poll online to determine whether public opinion leans significantly toward a certain candidate. The pollster plans to include a representative sample of voters by political party, and experts will analyze and produce a prediction once the results are in. Which of the following challenges is the pollster most likely to face in conducting this opinion poll?

   (A) Polling enough people to make the results significant

   (B) Misinterpreting the poll's results

   (C) Eliminating bias from the questions

   (D) Gathering participants from every region of the country

10. A recent poll shows that 72 percent of U.S. residents approve of increasing health insurance premiums for those who use insurance the most. Which of the following, if true, would undermine the credibility of the poll results?

   (A) The sample population included only those who have not gone to the doctor in the last 12 months.

   (B) The poll was conducted across multiple regions and included thousands of participants.

   (C) The sample population included a mix of those who use health insurance often and those who rarely use their health benefits.

   (D) The poll was administered using the same wording each time its questions were asked.

6

11. Which of the following policies would an individual who identifies as a Republican be most likely to support?

    (A) Decreasing use of fossil fuels in favor of renewable energy

    (B) Allowing women to receive an abortion in most cases

    (C) Reducing corporate income taxes

    (D) Setting strict governmental restrictions on gun sales

12. Which of the following is an accurate comparison of conservative and libertarian ideologies?

	Conservative	Libertarian
(A)	Prefers greater government regulation	Believes that minimum wage should be protected from the free market
(B)	Considers environmental laws to be a top priority	Values strong private property rights
(C)	Supports very little to no government regulation	Values traditions as the basis for society and, as such, views them as important
(D)	Prefers a small, fiscally responsible government that rarely interferes with social and economic liberty	Prefers no government intervention beyond what is needed to protect private property and individual liberty

Part B: Key Terms

This key terms list is the same as the list in the Test What You Already Know section earlier in this chapter. Based on what you have now learned, again ask yourself the following questions:

- Can I define this key term and use it in a sentence?
- Can I provide an example related to this key term?
- Could I correctly answer a multiple-choice question about this key term?
- Could I correctly answer a free-response question about this key term?

Check off the key terms if you can answer "yes" to at least three of these questions.

Political Attitude Formation

- ☐ Political attitudes
- ☐ Political culture
- ☐ Individualism
- ☐ Equality of opportunity
- ☐ Equality of outcome
- ☐ Free enterprise
- ☐ Rule of law
- ☐ Limited government
- ☐ Political socialization
- ☐ Social groups
- ☐ Generational effects
- ☐ Life-cycle effects

Polling

- ☐ Polling
- ☐ Benchmark poll
- ☐ Tracking poll
- ☐ Exit poll
- ☐ Scientific polling
- ☐ Sample
- ☐ Straw poll
- ☐ Pollster
- ☐ Margin of error

Ideology and Policy

- ☐ Democratic Party
- ☐ Liberalism
- ☐ Republican Party
- ☐ Conservatism
- ☐ American exceptionalism
- ☐ Libertarianism
- ☐ Fiscal conservatism
- ☐ Monetary policy
- ☐ Fiscal policy
- ☐ Keynesian economics
- ☐ Supply-side economics
- ☐ Social policy

Next Steps

Tally your correct answers from Part A and review the quiz explanations at the end of this chapter.

1.	B	7. C
2.	C	8. A
3.	A	9. D
4.	D	10. A
5.	A	11. C
6.	B	12. D

_____ out of 12 questions

Count the number of key terms you checked off in Part B.

_____ out of 33 key terms

Compare your Test What You Already Know results to these Test What You Learned results to see how exam-ready you are for this topic.

- Read (or reread) the comprehensive review for this topic in Chapter 11.
- Go to kaptest.com to complete the online quiz questions for American Political Ideologies and Beliefs.
    - Haven't registered your book yet? Go to kaptest.com/moreonline to begin.

CHAPTER 6 ANSWERS AND EXPLANATIONS

Test What You Already Know

1. C

Topic: 11.2 Polling

According to the table, 87 percent of Republicans polled were in favor of the tax-cutting policy to benefit businesses, accounting for the largest percentage among the specified political affiliations; **(C)** is correct. Only 16 percent of Democrats polled, 55 percent of Libertarians polled, and 48 percent of Green Party voters polled were in favor; (A), (B), and (D) are incorrect.

2. A

Topic: 11.2 Polling

Because the organization polled mostly Republicans and Libertarians, and because it polled Republicans in more regions than it did other groups, it skewed the results toward these parties' platforms, which generally support tax cuts for businesses; **(A)** is correct. (B) is incorrect because the number of political parties included does not necessarily pose an issue with the poll's results. (C) is incorrect because expanding the overall sample size is not the issue; the issue is that the organization did not poll a sample relative to the actual size of the group in society. Because the poll was conducted by a nonpartisan organization, there is no reason to think the pollster biased the results; (D) is incorrect.

3. A

Topic: 11.1 Political Attitude Formation

In the passage, Hoover explains, "It is just as important that business keep out of government as that government keep out of business." He advocates for a system that maintains "individual exertion" and "retains the essentials of freedom," reflecting the American core belief of individualism. This matches **(A)**. While Hoover states that the U.S. system is not perfect, he highlights the benefits to individuals, not the collective; (B) is incorrect. (C) and (D) are incorrect because Hoover promotes minimal governmental interference in business and minimal business interference in government.

4. D

Topic: 11.1 Political Attitude Formation

Conservatives advocate for very little government regulation, which matches Hoover's perspective; **(D)** is correct. Liberals tend to promote more government regulations because of their belief that people should be protected from adverse effects of the free market; (A) is incorrect. (B) and (C) are incorrect because socialism and collectivism focus on society as a whole rather than on the individual.

5. C

Topic: 11.1 Political Attitude Formation

The rule of law is the principle that everyone—including corporations, organizations, and government leaders—is held accountable to the same legal standards. In allowing the corporation to operate above the law, the governor in this scenario is violating the American core value of rule of law; **(C)** is correct. (A), (B), and (D) are incorrect because the scenario does not violate these core values. Equality of opportunity refers to the belief that each person should be given an equal chance to succeed; individualism is a social and political philosophy that assigns greater importance to individuals than to society as a whole; and free enterprise refers to the ability of people and businesses to make money with minimal interference from the government.

6. D

Topic: 11.2 Polling

A benchmark poll is taken at the beginning of a particular election cycle to give the candidate an idea of where she stands with the voting public and where to focus her campaign resources to effectively persuade the electorate; **(D)** is correct. (A) and (C) are incorrect because these describe effects on the voters themselves, rather than campaigns. (B) is incorrect because this is an effect of the sample that is chosen for polling.

7. A

Topic: 11.3 Ideology and Policy

Most Democrats agree with the evidence that carbon emissions, such as those from fossil fuels, are causing global warming. Thus, **(A)** is correct because Democrats would likely oppose any policy that could exacerbate climate change, such as fracking (also known as hydraulic fracturing, a process that uses chemical-treated water at high pressures to extract hydrocarbons). (B), (C), and (D) are incorrect since these are policies that Democrats would likely support.

8. D

Topic: 11.2 Polling

A tracking poll is a regular survey of the same respondents to measure changes in their opinions over time; **(D)** is correct. (A), (B), and (C) are incorrect because these describe other types of polls: a straw poll, an entrance poll, and a push poll, respectively.

9. B

Topic: 11.3 Ideology and Policy

Supply-side economics promotes the theory that allowing investors and entrepreneurs to save and invest more will produce economic benefits that will eventually impact the overall economy; **(B)** is correct and (D) is incorrect. (A) and (C) are incorrect because these describe Keynesian and laissez-faire economics, respectively.

10. D

Topic: 11.1 Political Attitude Formation

Political socialization is the lifelong process through which an individual develops political values and beliefs. An individual's family, school, peers, media, and social environment can influence this development; **(D)** is correct. (A) is incorrect because political socialization is not a polling element. (B) is incorrect because political socialization focuses on the development of an individual's political stance, not on a particular party's platform or beliefs. While factors in a person's life could influence his political party, political socialization represents a lifelong process, not a single event; (C) is incorrect.

11. A

Topic: 11.3 Ideology and Policy

American exceptionalism is the notion that the United States occupies a unique place in world history as a long-standing democratic republic committed to personal liberty; **(A)** is correct. The remaining choices are incorrect because they do not describe American exceptionalism specifically.

12. B

Topic: 11.3 Ideology and Policy

Liberals hope to promote social and economic equality, and free-market capitalism is a major component of conservatism; **(B)** is correct and (C) is incorrect. (A) and (D) are incorrect because liberals, not conservatives, are typically in favor of affirmative action policies, and conservatives, not liberals, hold to a platform built around traditional American values.

Test What You Learned

1. B

Topic: 11.3 Ideology and Policy

In his speech, Reagan argues that "we must control and limit the growth of federal spending...we must reduce tax rates to stimulate work and savings and investment" as a way to revitalize the nation; **(B)** is correct. While Reagan mentions that "we can reduce the cost of government by eliminating billions lost to waste and fraud in the federal bureaucracy," this is not the main argument of the passage; (A) is incorrect. (C) is incorrect because Reagan only mentions removing "unnecessary regulations"; he does not propose that labor and business must create their own. (D) is incorrect because Reagan only states that private and social institutions can be restored, not necessarily that they are at risk of being eliminated.

2. C

Topic: 11.3 Ideology and Policy

In the passage, Reagan explains that "we must control and limit the growth of federal spending...we must reduce tax rates to stimulate work and savings and investment." Supply-side economics is a theory that argues for lowering taxes and decreasing government regulation as a way to increase economic growth; **(C)** is correct and (D) is incorrect. Laissez-faire economics supposes that the economy will correct itself over time with no government action, while Reagan calls for the government to limit its spending and reduce taxes; (A) is incorrect. The Keynesian theory proposes that increasing government spending and lowering taxes will produce economic growth; (B) is incorrect.

3. A

Topic: 11.3 Ideology and Policy

Reagan argues that he would like to "relieve labor and business of burdensome, unnecessary regulations," but insists on maintaining "high standards of environmental and occupational safety." Removing strict marketing regulations would continue to maintain this standard of safety and would likely be a regulation Reagan would end; **(A)** is correct. With this same line of thinking, anti-retaliation regulations would qualify as a standard that he would likely retain since this would endanger "occupational safety"; (D) is incorrect. According to the excerpt, one of Reagan's key campaign promises is to "reduce tax rates to stimulate work and savings and investment"; (B) is incorrect. (C) is incorrect because Reagan stresses the importance of limiting "the growth of federal spending."

4. D

Topic: 11.1 Political Attitude Formation

The cartoon equates socialism with a large animal that sweeps up individual citizens, squashing initiative. Responding to the presence of socialism globally and the rise of the Socialist Party in the United States, the cartoon emphasizes the core value of individualism, not the collective values of socialism; **(D)** is correct. (A) and (B) are incorrect because the cartoon focuses on the lack of initiative that socialism causes, rather than on the need to eliminate monopolies or the size of the U.S. government. Leveling the playing field refers to equality of opportunity, which the cartoon does not refer to; (C) is incorrect.

5. A

Topic: 11.1 Political Attitude Formation

Individualism is an American core value that emphasizes the individual over the collective. Individualistic cultures value independence, autonomy, assertiveness, and self-reliance. The cartoon demonstrates the need for the preservation of initiative; thus, **(A)** is correct. (B) is incorrect because collectivism is a core value of socialism, which the political cartoon rejects. Equality of opportunity refers to the belief that each person should be given an equal chance to succeed and should not be limited by circumstances outside of that person's control; this is not relevant to the cartoon, making (C) incorrect. The rule of law is the principle that everyone—including corporations, organizations, and government leaders—is held accountable to the same legal standards, which does not directly relate to a citizen's initiative or lack thereof; (D) is incorrect.

6. B

Topic: 11.2 Polling

Donors are unlikely to spend a large amount of money on a candidate who is seen as having little or no chance of winning, while candidates who are leading the race according to polls have greater access to campaign funding; **(B)** is correct. (A) is incorrect because an individual donor might be more inclined to give additional money to a candidate who is behind but close to winning, especially since this money could affect the outcome of the race. (C) is incorrect for a similar reason as (A); additional donations are likely in close elections. (D) is incorrect because, even though a donor is less likely to have an impact on the outcome, people like to back a winner, and may hope to gain influence by monetarily supporting a future political official.

7. C

Topic: 11.1 Political Attitude Formation

Free enterprise allows private businesses to set their own prices based on supply and demand, with little government regulation; **(C)** is correct. (A) is incorrect because it illustrates a monopoly rather than the competitive system created by free enterprise. (B) and (D) are incorrect because both situations suggest that the state or federal government is either approving or setting prices.

8. A

Topic: 11.2 Polling

Candidates conduct benchmark polls at the beginning of an election cycle to get an idea of where they stand with the voting public and where to focus their campaign resources to effectively persuade the electorate; **(A)** is correct. (B) is incorrect because tracking polls are conducted repeatedly and indicate how opinions change over time. Entrance and exit polls are both taken on election day, when it would be too late for a candidate to redistribute campaign resources accordingly; (C) and (D) are incorrect.

9. D

Topic: 11.2 Polling

Since the pollster is only planning to make the poll available online, he or she runs the risk that the poll will not draw participants from every region of the country; **(D)** is correct. (A) is incorrect because the pollster plans to poll a representative sample size, which could then be weighted accordingly. (B) is incorrect because political experts will analyze the results, reducing the chance that the poll results will be misinterpreted. The political pollster is not representing a biased organization, reducing the risk of introducing bias within the questions; (C) is incorrect.

10. A

Topic: 11.2 Polling

A sample restricted to only those individuals who have not visited a doctor in the last 12 months would not be representative of the population at large, likely leading to biased results and undermining the credibility of the poll results; **(A)** is correct. (B), (C), and (D) are incorrect because these factors would not directly undermine the poll's results.

11. C

Topic: 11.3 Ideology and Policy

A Republican would most likely support the reduction of corporate income taxes in an effort to encourage entrepreneurs and other business leaders to start and invest in companies, creating jobs; **(C)** is correct. (A), (B), and (D) are incorrect because a Republican would likely oppose each.

12. D

Topic: 11.3 Ideology and Policy

Both conservatives and libertarians are in favor of a small government and the free market, but libertarians are not in favor of any government intervention beyond that required to protect property and individual liberty. Thus, **(D)** is correct. (A) is incorrect because liberals advocate for more government regulations and believe that certain standards, such as the minimum wage, should be enforced to protect people from some of the negative consequences of the free market. (B) is incorrect because liberals, not conservatives, consider environmental laws a top priority. Conservatives, not libertarians, view traditions as the basis for society; (C) is incorrect.

CHAPTER 7

Political Participation

LEARNING OBJECTIVES

- Detail significant U.S. voting rights protections.

- Distinguish among rational-choice, retrospective, prospective, and party-line voting models.

- List major factors affecting election turnout.

- Cite examples of linkage institutions.

- Identify processes that political parties use to influence U.S. political life.

- List factors that influence political parties to change over time.

- Detail U.S. political structures that impede third-party candidate success.

- Identify positive and potentially negative effects of interest-group politics.

- Detail major influences on public policy outcomes.

- Identify the impact of presidential elections' discrete components.

- Provide prominent arguments for and against the Electoral College.

- Identify the impact of congressional elections' discrete components.

- List the pros and cons of the manner in which political campaigns are currently conducted.

- Detail U.S. legal constraints on campaign finance.

- List specific influences of mass media on politics.

- Track recent trends altering the media's effect on U.S. political life.

TEST WHAT YOU ALREADY KNOW

Part A: Quiz

Questions 1 and 2 refer to the passage below.

All speakers, including individuals and the media, use money amassed from the economic marketplace to fund their speech. The First Amendment protects the resulting speech, even if it was enabled by economic transactions with persons or entities who disagree with the speaker's ideas . . .

If the First Amendment has any force, it prohibits Congress from fining or jailing citizens, or associations of citizens, for simply engaging in political speech.

—Anthony Kennedy, majority opinion in *Citizens United v. Federal Election Commission* (2010)

1. The 2010 U.S. Supreme Court case *Citizens United v. FEC* established what campaign finance practice?

   (A) The ability of individuals to donate an unlimited amount of money to a political candidate

   (B) The ability of super PACs to coordinate fundraising activities with political campaigns

   (C) The replacement of private campaign financing with public campaign financing

   (D) The ability for unlimited sums of union and corporate money to be used for "election-related" activities

2. A supporter of the majority opinion in *Citizens United* would most likely be against which of the following?

   (A) Hard-money donations to political campaigns

   (B) The Supreme Court's ruling in *Schenck v. United States*

   (C) The Bipartisan Campaign Reform Act of 2002

   (D) Individual contributions to political action committees

Questions 3–5 refer to the table below.

	George Bush (Republican)	Al Gore (Democrat)	Ralph Nader (Green)	Patrick Buchanan (Reform)
Total Popular Votes	50,456,062	50,996,582	2,858,843	438,760
% of Popular Vote	47.87	48.38	2.74	0.43
Total Electoral Votes	271	266	0	0

3. Which of the following statements is most accurately supported by the data in the table?

   (A) Fewer than 100 million people voted in the 2000 election for both of the major-party candidates combined.

   (B) To become president, a candidate does not need to receive a majority of the popular votes.

   (C) The number of popular votes received by the candidates has no impact on the election outcome.

   (D) Third-party candidates collected approximately 3 percent of the electoral votes in the 2000 election.

4. Based on the data, what conclusion can be drawn concerning the impact third-party candidates have in presidential elections?

   (A) A third-party candidate who collects a large number of popular votes may change the electoral vote outcome.

   (B) A third-party candidate could never have a significant impact on either the national popular vote or electoral vote totals.

   (C) Third-party candidates benefit from the winner-take-all method of counting electoral votes.

   (D) Third-party candidates have less experience running for public office.

5. Which of the following reflects a reason that the Founding Fathers favored electoral votes over popular votes in presidential elections?

   (A) They wanted small states to be included because they would be underrepresented in the popular vote.

   (B) They intended the Electoral College to be a short-term arrangement until the U.S. population could increase.

   (C) They wanted to encourage politicians to campaign primarily in smaller states.

   (D) They believed that conducting a popular vote would be too costly.

6. Which of the following would a proponent of the Electoral College most likely cite as a reason to keep the Electoral College as the method for electing U.S. presidents?

    (A) From 2000 to 2016, two U.S. presidents were elected without winning the national popular vote.

    (B) The Electoral College is established in the U.S. Constitution, which cannot be changed.

    (C) All 50 states and the District of Columbia have the same number of electoral votes, making the outcome of the election fair.

    (D) Together, the 10 most populous U.S. states have more than half of the total U.S. population.

7. Which of the following is a barrier for third-party presidential candidates?

    (A) Inability to purchase television advertisements

    (B) Exclusion from presidential prime-time debates

    (C) Inability to distinguish themselves ideologically

    (D) Departure from the policy platforms of major parties

8. Which of the following most accurately describes voter turnout in U.S. elections?

    (A) Voter turnout is approximately the same for midterm and presidential elections.

    (B) Voter turnout is consistently higher in primaries than it is in general elections.

    (C) Voter turnout tends to be higher in federal elections than in state and local elections.

    (D) A higher level of education has not been shown to correlate with voter turnout.

9. Which of the following is most advantageous for a congressional candidate?

    (A) Lack of experience in politics, business, or the military

    (B) Running as an outsider attacking the party establishment

    (C) Incumbency and name recognition

    (D) A voting record that spans several terms in office

10. Which of the following describes the potential impact on the electorate when daily media coverage presents the election as a "horse race" between the two major-party candidates?

    (A) The electorate will enjoy in-depth investigative journalism that digs into the substance of both candidates.

    (B) The electorate will learn little about the qualifications and platforms of the two candidates.

    (C) The electorate will have an informed understanding of how well their preferred candidate is performing.

    (D) The electorate will understand that the outcome of an election that is not very competitive is probably not in doubt.

7

Questions 11 and 12 refer to the map below.

2016 U.S. Presidential Primary & Caucus Schedule

February | March | April | May | June

Source: U.S. Presidential Election News, Tribune News Service

Note: The map shows which month each state held its 2016 U.S. presidential primary or caucus. Some states hold the GOP and Democratic primaries on different days. In these states, Democratic primary months are indicated on the left, Republican primary months on the right.

11. Which of the following statements best describes the information in the map?

    (A) The majority of southern states hold late primaries.

    (B) The majority of the February primaries are in the Midwest.

    (C) The majority of all states hold April primaries.

    (D) The majority of the April primaries are in the Northeast.

12. States that have recently moved their primaries from May to March most likely hope to

    (A) reduce the amount of negative political advertising on local television channels

    (B) avoid having third-party candidates campaign in their states

    (C) narrow the number of candidates on their primary ballot

    (D) encourage candidates to spend more campaign time in their state

Part B: Key Terms

The following is a list of the major ideas, events, and people for the AP U.S. Government and Politics topic of Political Participation. You will likely see many of these on the official AP exam.

For each key term, ask yourself the following questions:

- Can I define this key term and use it in a sentence?
- Can I provide an example related to this key term?
- Could I correctly answer a multiple-choice question about this key term?
- Could I correctly answer a free-response question about this key term?

Check off the key terms if you can answer "yes" to at least three of these questions.

Voting

- ☐ Universal suffrage
- ☐ Thirteenth Amendment
- ☐ Fourteenth Amendment
- ☐ Fifteenth Amendment
- ☐ Jim Crow laws
- ☐ Twenty-Fourth Amendment
- ☐ Voter registration

- ☐ Nineteenth Amendment
- ☐ Twenty-Sixth Amendment
- ☐ Voter eligibility
- ☐ Seventeenth Amendment
- ☐ Retrospective voting
- ☐ Prospective voting
- ☐ Rational-choice voting

- ☐ Party-line voting
- ☐ Voter turnout
- ☐ Political efficacy
- ☐ Primary election
- ☐ Open primaries
- ☐ Closed primaries
- ☐ General elections
- ☐ Midterm elections
- ☐ Voter identification laws
- ☐ Motor-voter law

Linkage institutions

- ☐ Linkage institution
- ☐ Media
- ☐ Political party
- ☐ Party convention
- ☐ Realignment

- ☐ Critical election
- ☐ Party coalition
- ☐ Third party
- ☐ Winner-take-all
- ☐ Interest group

- ☐ Lobbying
- ☐ Electioneering
- ☐ Single-issue group
- ☐ Iron triangle
- ☐ Free-rider problem

7

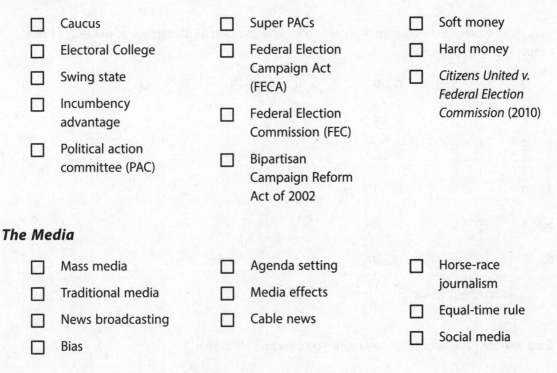
Elections

- ☐ Caucus
- ☐ Electoral College
- ☐ Swing state
- ☐ Incumbency advantage
- ☐ Political action committee (PAC)

- ☐ Super PACs
- ☐ Federal Election Campaign Act (FECA)
- ☐ Federal Election Commission (FEC)
- ☐ Bipartisan Campaign Reform Act of 2002

- ☐ Soft money
- ☐ Hard money
- ☐ *Citizens United v. Federal Election Commission* (2010)

The Media

- ☐ Mass media
- ☐ Traditional media
- ☐ News broadcasting
- ☐ Bias

- ☐ Agenda setting
- ☐ Media effects
- ☐ Cable news

- ☐ Horse-race journalism
- ☐ Equal-time rule
- ☐ Social media

7

Next Steps

Tally your correct answers from Part A and review the quiz explanations at the end of this chapter.

1.	D	7.	B
2.	C	8.	C
3.	B	9.	C
4.	A	10.	B
5.	A	11.	D
6.	D	12.	D

_____ out of 12 questions

Step 2: Count the number of key terms you checked off in Part B.

_____ out of 61 key terms

Step 3: Read the Key Takeaways in this chapter.

Step 4: Consult the table below and follow the instructions based on your performance.

If You Got...	Do This
80% or more of the Test What You Already Know assessment correct (10 or more questions from Part A and 48 or more key terms from Part B)	• Read definitions in this chapter for all the key terms you didn't check off. • Complete the Test What You Learned assessment in this chapter.
50% or less of the Test What You Already Know assessment correct (6 or fewer questions from Part A and 31 or fewer key terms from Part B)	• Read the comprehensive review for this topic in Chapter 12. ○ If you are short on time, read only the High-Yield sections. • Read through all of the key term definitions in this chapter. • Complete the Test What You Learned assessment in this chapter.
Any other result	• Read the High-Yield sections in the comprehensive review of this topic in Chapter 12. • Read definitions in this chapter for all the key terms you didn't check off. • Complete the Test What You Learned assessment in this chapter.

ESSENTIAL CONTENT

Key Takeaways: Political Participation

1. When the Constitution was ratified in 1788, only white, landowning men could vote, and U.S. senators were not directly elected by the citizens. Over time, various amendments extended voting rights, including the Fifteenth, Seventeenth, Nineteenth, Twenty-Fourth, and Twenty-Sixth Amendments.

2. Political scientists study demographics to understand and predict voter turnout. Generally, citizens older than 65, those with higher incomes, and those with more education tend to have the highest turnout; conversely, citizens under 30 years old, those lacking college education, and those earning lower incomes tend to have much lower turnout. Voting laws and registration requirements are also major drivers of voting turnout.

3. Linkage institutions are groups that connect people to the government and assist in turning the citizens' concerns into political issues that prompt governmental action. The media, political parties, and interest groups are examples of linkage institutions.

4. A political party is an organization of people with similar political ideologies that seeks to influence public policy and control the government through electing its candidates. American politics has been dominated by the two-party system, which today is made up of the Democratic and Republican parties. While interest groups focus primarily on policy outcomes, political parties seek to win elections.

5. Several third parties, such as the Libertarian, Reform, and Green parties, have emerged over time. Major barriers have prevented them from electing national candidates, including the winner-take-all system and the incorporation of third-party ideas into Democratic and Republican platforms.

6. The president and vice president are elected by the Electoral College following the general election. With very few exceptions, electors from each state plus Washington, D.C., vote for the candidate who won their statewide popular vote. This winner-take-all approach of distributing electors has raised questions about the extent to which the Electoral College facilitates or impedes democracy.

7. In *Citizens United v. FEC* (2010), the Supreme Court held that political spending by corporations and other groups is a form of free speech that is protected by the First Amendment. This ruling has sparked the creation of super PACs and ignited debate over the role that money can and should play in elections.

8. The media influences how the public learns about political issues and events. Mass-media coverage raises awareness of certain topics, thereby increasing the public demand for government action. Social media and the changing nature of media are significantly changing the way campaigns are run and political issues are communicated.

Key Terms: Political Participation

Voting

Universal suffrage: The extension of the right to vote to all adult citizens, with no qualifications based on race, sex, or property ownership.

Thirteenth Amendment: An amendment to the U.S. Constitution abolishing slavery; ratified in 1865.

Fourteenth Amendment: An amendment to the U.S. Constitution defining national citizenship and forbidding the states to restrict the basic rights of citizens or other persons; ratified in 1868.

Fifteenth Amendment: An amendment to the U.S. Constitution prohibiting the restriction of voting rights on account of race, color, or previous condition of servitude (e.g., slavery); ratified in 1870.

Jim Crow laws: Any of the laws that enforced racial segregation in the South between the end of Reconstruction in 1877 and the civil rights movement in the mid-twentieth century.

Twenty-Fourth Amendment: An amendment to the U.S. Constitution forbidding the use of the poll tax as a requirement for voting in national elections; ratified in 1964.

Voter registration: A system in which citizens must register to vote in advance of election day; some states allow election-day registration.

Nineteenth Amendment: An amendment to the U.S. Constitution guaranteeing women the right to vote; ratified in 1920.

Twenty-Sixth Amendment: An amendment to the U.S. Constitution lowering the voting age to 18; ratified in 1971.

Voter eligibility: Any U.S. citizen who is at least eighteen years old on election day and not disqualified due to a felony conviction; some states add additional criteria that trigger disqualification, such as being declared mentally incompetent by a court.

Seventeenth Amendment: An amendment to the U.S. Constitution providing for the election of two U.S. senators from each state by popular vote and for a term of six years; ratified in 1913.

Retrospective voting: A theory that voting decisions are made after taking into consideration factors such as the performance of a political party, an officeholder, and/or the current administration.

Prospective voting: A theory that voting decisions are based on predictions of how candidates or parties will act once they are elected.

Rational-choice voting: A theory that voting decisions are made on the basis of a series of judgments about which candidate will benefit the voter the most.

Party-line voting: The practice of voting based strictly on political party identification.

Voter turnout: The percentage of eligible voters who cast a ballot in an election.

Political efficacy: Citizens' faith and trust in government and their belief that they can understand and influence political affairs through voting and other forms of political participation.

Primary election: A nominating election in which the field of candidates who will run in the general election is chosen.

7

Voting (cont.)

Open primaries: Primaries in which voters are allowed to vote for candidates from any party.

Closed primaries: Primaries in which voters must be registered with a political party to vote for one of its candidates.

General elections: Occur every November to choose among the candidates nominated by the various political parties or running as independents to fill local, state, and national offices.

Midterm elections: Occur in even-numbered years between presidential election years.

Linkage Institutions

Linkage institution: a structure or channel within a society that connects the people to the national, state, and local levels of government. Linkage institutions include elections, the media, political parties, and interest groups.

Media: A linkage institution that communicates to the general public; newspapers, television, radio, and the Internet are the most common forms of media.

Political party: Organized group of people that seeks to gain governmental control through winning elections.

Party convention: Political party meeting held to select candidates, set priorities, and develop the party's political platform.

Realignment: When a large proportion of voters that traditionally votes for one party shifts its support to another political party (e.g., southern Democrats realigning with the Republican Party after the 1960s).

Critical election: An election that signals a party realignment.

Voter identification laws: Also known as voter ID laws, they require a person to show official identification before being allowed to register to vote or actually vote on election day.

Motor-voter law: Officially known as the National Voter Registration Act of 1993, this law enables people to register to vote when they apply for driver's licenses, through the mail, and at some state offices.

Party coalition: Occurs when different political parties cooperate on a common political agenda.

Third party: Any political party in American politics that competes against the two main parties: the Democratic and Republican parties.

Winner-take-all: The basis on which most states (except Nebraska and Maine) award electoral votes in a presidential election. The candidate who gets the most votes receives all of that state's electoral votes.

Interest group: Any association of individuals or organizations that is based on one or more shared concerns or issues and attempts to influence public policy in its favor; also referred to as a special-interest group.

Lobbying: The act of representing an interest group or organization before government to influence public policy.

Electioneering: Direct involvement in the electoral process, especially communication that refers to a candidate for federal office.

Linkage Institutions (cont.)

Single-issue group: An interest group that focuses on a particular issue.

Iron triangle: The close three-way relationship among congressional committees, interest groups, and executive branch bureaucracy.

Elections

Caucus: A private meeting run by a political party in which members of the party vote for candidates, dividing themselves into groups according to the candidate they support.

Electoral College: A group of state electors who indirectly elect the president and vice president based on the popular vote in each state.

Swing state: A state where the Democrats and Republicans have similar levels of support among voters; viewed as important in determining the overall result of a presidential election.

Incumbency advantage: The edge, or advantage, that current officeholders (i.e., incumbents) possess when they run for reelection.

Political action committee (PAC): An organization set up by an interest group to raise money to contribute to campaigns or to spend on advertising in support of candidates. The amount a PAC can receive from each of its donors and the amount it can spend on federal electioneering are regulated by the Federal Election Commission.

Super PACs: Groups that may raise and spend unlimited amounts of money from corporations and other associations to advocate for or against candidates and issues; unlike traditional PACs, super PACs are prohibited from donating money directly to political candidates, and they cannot coordinate directly with candidates.

Free-rider problem: A challenge faced by interest groups when citizens can reap the benefits of interest-group action without actually joining and contributing to the group.

Federal Election Campaign Act (FECA): 1971 law that regulates the reporting of campaign contributions and expenditures and outlines contribution rules for corporations and organizations to follow.

Federal Election Commission (FEC): An independent regulatory agency that administers and enforces election laws and campaign finance rules for national elections.

Bipartisan Campaign Reform Act of 2002: Banned soft money until it was overruled by the Supreme Court in *Citizens United v. FEC* (2010); commonly known as the McCain-Feingold Act.

Soft money: Political contributions that are not limited by federal campaign laws. Currently, soft money can be spent in support of a candidate but cannot be given directly to a candidate.

Hard money: Political contributions that are limited and regulated by federal campaign laws; hard money can be given directly to a party or candidate.

***Citizens United v. Federal Election Commission* (2010):** A Supreme Court case that decided that corporations, nonprofits, and labor unions have the same political speech rights as individuals under the First Amendment and can therefore donate unlimited amounts of campaign money.

7

The Media

Mass media: Media sources such as newspapers, television networks, radio stations, and websites that provide information to the average citizen.

Traditional media: Media sources that predate the Internet, such as newspapers, radio, and television.

News broadcasting: The media's communication of various news events and other information via television, radio, or the Internet.

Bias: Occurs when journalists and news media favor one political view, candidate, or story, influencing their reporting and coverage.

Agenda setting: The media's ability to influence the importance placed on the topics of the public agenda.

Media effects: The influence that the media has on its consumers; those who study media effects analyze how much people's political attitudes and opinions are affected by exposure to media coverage.

Cable news: Traditional media providers devoted to television news broadcasts; the name derives from the proliferation of such networks in the 1980s during the development of cable television.

Horse-race journalism: a practice in which journalists and media providers almost exclusively focus on which candidate is winning or losing in the polls and on candidate personalities and differences.

Equal-time rule: A federal requirement that television and radio broadcast stations must treat qualified political candidates equally with regard to selling or giving away air time.

Social media: Online media platforms such as Facebook, YouTube, and Twitter that enable users and political candidates to create and share content or participate in social and political networking.

TEST WHAT YOU LEARNED

Part A: Quiz

Questions 1 and 2 refer to the passage below.

In summary, there are three simple points that were raised by the [Supreme] Court's consideration of the Citizens United case. First . . . . Congress is the most democratically elected branch of government and should be able to make laws that do not stand in the face of the Constitution whether or not the members of the Court would themselves support such legislation if they served in the elected branches of government. . . . Secondly, the principle enshrined in law for many years was that corporations, because of their artificial legal nature and special privileges, including perpetual existence, pose a unique threat to our democracy. . . . Lastly, I stress again to my colleagues . . . [the] Court is considering a question that may lead to corporations being treated as "persons" under the Constitution, would allow a corporation to assert a Fifth Amendment right to . . . to keep documents from lawful investigations, and would allow corporations to be subject to individual tax brackets. Are my colleagues prepared to provide such rights to corporations? Are my colleagues prepared to pass legislation that taxes corporations and persons at the same rate? If the Court provides full First Amendment rights to corporations, there is no reason that corporations could not receive the benefits as well as the responsibilities of "being a person."

—Senator John McCain, speech regarding *Citizens United v. Federal Election Commission*
(October 21, 2009)

1. Which of the following is the most accurate interpretation of the speech?

   (A) The Bipartisan Campaign Reform Act of 2002 is inherently unconstitutional.

   (B) Corporations will lobby against legislative efforts to regulate corporate influence in federal elections.

   (C) Extending free speech rights to corporations will lead to further problems.

   (D) The Supreme Court will refuse to overturn campaign finance law.

2. Based on the text, which of the following would Senator McCain most likely have supported?

   (A) A ban on gifts from lobbyists to members of Congress

   (B) A private agency that assists former members of Congress in becoming lobbyists

   (C) A formal relationship in which lobbyists and members of Congress collaborate on public policy

   (D) A constitutional amendment to revoke the Supreme Court's power of judicial review

7

3. Which of the following is an accurate description of interest groups?

   (A) Interest groups are required to provide accurate information about the issues they advocate for.

   (B) Interest groups focus on issues that affect the majority of the citizens of the United States.

   (C) Political parties rely on interest groups to pick Congressional candidates and to write the party platform.

   (D) Interest groups aim to gain influence over decision making on policies important to the group.

4. Which of the following scenarios would the Federal Election Commission most likely consider a violation of campaign finance rules?

   (A) A super PAC official assisting a candidate with campaign strategy

   (B) An individual donating $2,000 directly to a political candidate

   (C) A political candidate asking a private fundraiser for campaign contributions

   (D) A political candidate donating personal funds to her own campaign

5. Which of the following scenarios best illustrates the benefit of a closed primary?

   (A) The candidates can be assured of broad-based support for their campaign from the general public.

   (B) Only those dedicated enough to listen to speeches and attend for several hours will participate.

   (C) Voters are allowed to vote for candidates from any party and merely need to be registered to vote.

   (D) The candidates can be assured that the registered members of their own party support them.

6. Consumer-driven media has led to an increase in "attack journalism," which manifests itself in

   (A) talk radio and Internet news outlets that act as nonpartisan watchdogs for government misdeeds

   (B) mean-spirited coverage of rival media outlets in order to tarnish their brands and attract their audiences

   (C) politically affiliated outlets that provide a platform for allies while undermining political rivals

   (D) the avoidance of all controversial topics that may offend a mainstream audience

7. In which of the following types of elections would voters have to disclose the candidates for which they vote?

   (A) An open primary

   (B) A closed primary

   (C) A caucus

   (D) A general election

8. In its role as gatekeeper, the national news media performs what function?

   (A) Influences what political topics get covered

   (B) Decides which political candidates are shown on television

   (C) Investigates governmental corruption

   (D) Conducts public opinion polling

7

Questions 9 and 10 refer to the map below.

Women's Suffrage Prior to the Nineteenth Amendment

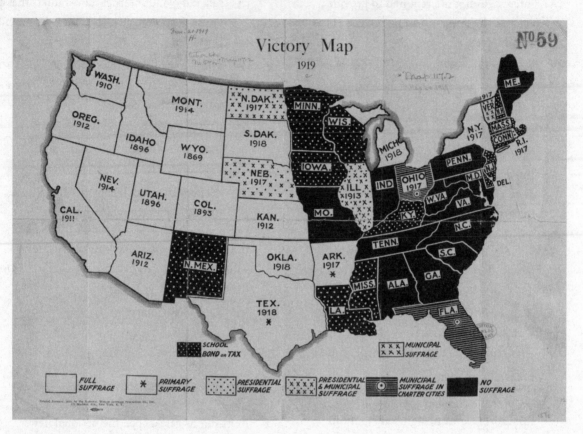

Source: Norman B. Leventhal Map Center Collection

9. Which of the following statements best describes the information in the map?

(A) Suffragists enjoyed their earliest successes in the Northeastern states.

(B) Most of the Midwestern states offered limited voting rights to women.

(C) Women had no voting rights in any of the Southern states.

(D) In the states that offered full suffrage, the majority did so in the year prior to the Nineteenth Amendment's ratification.

10. Based on the map, which of the following strategies would a group seeking to secure suffrage in 1919 likely pursue?

(A) Lobbying Congress to hold committee hearings on the issue

(B) Lobbying state legislatures to establish legal protections

(C) Using advertisements to raise public awareness nationwide

(D) Seeking a state supreme court ruling in their favor

Question 11 refers to the table below.

Percentage of Voting Participation in Two National Elections

	2012	2016
White	64.1	65.3
Black	66.6	59.6
Hispanic	48.0	47.6
Other race	49.9	49.3
18–29 years old	45.0	46.1
30–44 years old	59.5	58.7
45–64 years old	67.9	66.6
65 and over	72.0	70.9

11. Based on the information in the table, which of the following statements about voting patterns in national elections is most accurate?

    (A) The youth vote is a key voting bloc in presidential elections.

    (B) Black voters are more likely to vote than Hispanics.

    (C) White voters vote at approximately the same rate as all other races.

    (D) Elderly Hispanic voters would likely vote at a lower rate than middle-aged Hispanics.

12. Which of the following is an accurate comparison?

	Key Term	Example
(A)	Media Effects	framing, filtering, priming, and the equal-time rule
(B)	Suffrage	soft money, hard money, political action committee, and super PACs
(C)	Linkage Institution	motor-voter law, political efficacy, and party-line voting
(D)	Iron Triangle	Congress, an interest group, and the federal bureaucracy

7

Part B: Key Terms

This key terms list is the same as the list in the Test What You Already Know section earlier in this chapter. Based on what you have now learned, again ask yourself the following questions:

- Can I define this key term and use it in a sentence?
- Can I provide an example related to this key term?
- Could I correctly answer a multiple-choice question about this key term?
- Could I correctly answer a free-response question about this key term?

Check off the key terms if you can answer "yes" to at least three of these questions.

Voting

- ☐ Universal suffrage
- ☐ Thirteenth Amendment
- ☐ Fourteenth Amendment
- ☐ Fifteenth Amendment
- ☐ Jim Crow laws
- ☐ Twenty-Fourth Amendment
- ☐ Voter registration

- ☐ Nineteenth Amendment
- ☐ Twenty-Sixth Amendment
- ☐ Voter eligibility
- ☐ Seventeenth Amendment
- ☐ Retrospective voting
- ☐ Prospective voting
- ☐ Rational-choice voting
- ☐ Party-line voting

- ☐ Voter turnout
- ☐ Political efficacy
- ☐ Primary election
- ☐ Open primaries
- ☐ Closed primaries
- ☐ General elections
- ☐ Midterm elections
- ☐ Voter identification laws
- ☐ Motor-voter law

Linkage institutions

- ☐ Linkage institution
- ☐ Media
- ☐ Political party
- ☐ Party convention
- ☐ Realignment

- ☐ Critical election
- ☐ Party coalition
- ☐ Third party
- ☐ Winner-take-all
- ☐ Interest group

- ☐ Lobbying
- ☐ Electioneering
- ☐ Single-issue group
- ☐ Iron triangle
- ☐ Free-rider problem

7

Elections

- [ ] Caucus
- [ ] Electoral College
- [ ] Swing state
- [ ] Incumbency advantage
- [ ] Political action committee (PAC)

- [ ] Super PACs
- [ ] Federal Election Campaign Act (FECA)
- [ ] Federal Election Commission (FEC)
- [ ] Bipartisan Campaign Reform Act of 2002

- [ ] Soft money
- [ ] Hard money
- [ ] *Citizens United v. Federal Election Commission* (2010)

The Media

- [ ] Mass media
- [ ] Traditional media
- [ ] News broadcasting
- [ ] Bias

- [ ] Agenda setting
- [ ] Media effects
- [ ] Cable news

- [ ] Horse-race journalism
- [ ] Equal-time rule
- [ ] Social media

Next Steps

Tally your correct answers from Part A and review the quiz explanations at the end of this chapter.

1.	C	7.	C
2.	A	8.	A
3.	D	9.	B
4.	A	10.	B
5.	D	11.	B
6.	C	12.	D

_____ out of 12 questions

Count the number of key terms you checked off in Part B.

_____ out of 61 key terms

Compare your Test What You Already Know results to these Test What You Learned results to see how exam-ready you are for this topic.

- Read (or reread) the comprehensive review for this topic in Chapter 12.
- Go to kaptest.com to complete the online quiz questions for Political Participation.
  - Haven't registered your book yet? Go to kaptest.com/moreonline to begin.

7

CHAPTER 7 ANSWERS AND EXPLANATIONS

Test What You Already Know

1. D

Topic: 12.3 Elections

Following *Citizens United v. FEC*, super PACs were able to raise and spend unlimited amounts of money for the purpose of electing or defeating federal election candidates. **(D)** is correct. The Federal Election Campaign Act (FECA) limits the amount of money that individuals can contribute to support candidates for federal office, making (A) incorrect. (B) is incorrect because super PACs are prohibited from coordinating directly with candidates or political parties. (C) is incorrect because *Citizens United* concerns the ability to raise and spend more private money from entities such as corporations and associations, not public money from the government.

2. C

Topic: 12.3 Elections

Better known as the McCain-Feingold Act, the Bipartisan Campaign Reform Act of 2002 sought to regulate campaign contributions to national elections. This act prohibited national political parties from raising or spending any funds not subject to federal limits. *Citizens United*, however, overturned the Bipartisan Campaign Reform Act. Many supporters of the Court's decision in *Citizens United* have been critical of the Bipartisan Campaign Reform Act and similar efforts to limit campaign contributions. Thus, **(C)** correct. Because *Citizens United* protects campaign contributions as a form of free speech, the supporters of this case would likely also support the contributions of hard money (i.e., money from individuals to political campaigns) as well as contributions to political action committees; (A) and (D) are incorrect. In *Schenck v. United States* (1919), the Supreme Court ruled that speech may be restricted if it presents a "clear and present danger" to national security. This is not directly related to campaign finance, so (B) is also incorrect.

3. B

Topic: 12.3 Elections

In the 2000 presidential election, George W. Bush defeated Al Gore. While Gore received more popular votes, Bush received a majority of the electoral votes (271 to 266). The final result of a U.S. presidential election is determined by the number of electoral votes, so a candidate can win the presidency without necessarily winning a majority of the popular votes. Thus, **(B)** is correct. (A) is incorrect because over 100 million people voted for both the Democratic and Republican candidates. (C) is incorrect because the popular vote does have an important role in determining the winner, as a candidate must win a state's popular vote contest to get its electoral votes. While the data shows that the third-party candidates, Nader and Buchanan, collected approximately 3 percent of the popular vote, neither received any electoral votes; (D) is incorrect.

4. A

Topic: 12.2 Linkage Institutions

Given the winner-take-all system for awarding the states' electoral votes, third-party candidates could collect enough votes to change the outcome of an election. Many political scientists believe that in the 2000 election, Ralph Nader earned enough votes to change the outcome in the state of Florida. Had Nader not been in the race, Al Gore would likely have received enough popular votes to win Florida and its electoral votes. Had Gore won Florida, he would have won the general election. Therefore, **(A)** is correct, and (B) is incorrect. Given the fact that third-party candidates did not win any electoral votes in 2000 under the winner-take-all system, (C) is incorrect. (D) is incorrect because this conclusion cannot be drawn from the table data; third-party candidates may, in fact, have vast experience running for public office.

5. A

Topic: 12.3 Elections

The Founding Fathers feared that if the presidential election were decided on the basis of the popular vote, candidates would overlook smaller states. To ensure that smaller states would matter to the election outcome, the creators of the Constitution established the Electoral College. Even a few electoral votes from a small state such as New Hampshire or Maine can have a sizable impact on the election outcome. **(A)** is correct. The Founding Fathers wrote the Electoral College into the Constitution, thus intending it to be a permanent feature of the American political structure. Therefore, (B) is incorrect. The Founding Fathers did not suggest that politicians campaign *primarily* in smaller states. Instead, they hoped politicians would have a more balanced campaign in which both large and small states were important; (C) is incorrect. (D) is incorrect because the financial cost of an election was not a factor directly involved in creating the Electoral College.

6. D

Topic: 12.3 Elections

Because the 10 most populous states account for more than half of the population, candidates might focus only on those states if the Electoral College were not in effect; **(D)** is correct. While (A) is a true statement (referring to Presidents George W. Bush and Donald Trump), this would more likely be cited by a critic of the Electoral College. Though the Electoral College is established by the U.S. Constitution, (B) is incorrect because the Constitution can be amended, or changed. (C) is incorrect because the number of electoral votes per state is based on state population.

7. B

Topic: 12.2 Linkage Institutions

To be included in a presidential debate, a candidate typically needs to be polling at 15 percent; because third-party candidates rarely poll this high, they do not often have access to the debates. **(B)** is correct. The Federal Communications Commission (FCC), an independent regulatory agency of the federal government, prohibits television companies from charging different candidates different rates. Therefore, third-party candidates have equal access to purchasing TV ads; (A) is incorrect. One of the few benefits third-party candidates have is

ideological purity. They can run on unorthodox platforms and advance policies that are outside the mainstream of the two major parties; thus, both (C) and (D) are incorrect.

8. C

Topic: 12.1 Voting

Presidential and congressional candidates draw more media attention and are generally viewed by many voters as more important than candidates in state and local elections. Therefore, turnout is higher in federal elections than it is in state and local elections; **(C)** is correct. (A) is incorrect because voter turnout is higher for presidential elections than for midterm elections. Voter turnout is also higher in general elections than it is in primary elections; (B) is incorrect. College-educated voters typically turn out in higher percentages than do those without college degrees; (D) is incorrect.

9. C

Topic: 12.3 Elections

The most advantageous factors for running for the U.S. Congress are incumbency and name recognition. In fact, since 1982, incumbents running for reelection to the Senate have won more than 75 percent of the time. Name recognition is also a crucial factor. In the case of two otherwise equal candidates, voters tend to prefer the one who is better known. Thus, **(C)** is correct. While "outsider" candidates can enjoy success, they can typically point to experience in the business world or a military career to demonstrate that they can be trusted with high office. Victories by complete outsiders to politics, business, or the military are somewhat rare. (A) is incorrect. While attacking the establishment of one's party can garner attention, it is not the most advantageous strategy, since the establishment can strike back by supporting a rival in the primary or by not supporting the outsider in the general election. So, (B) is incorrect. A long voting record can leave a politician vulnerable, as he may have to explain a controversial vote or a vote in support of a position that is no longer popular with his party's base. (D) is incorrect.

10. B

Topic: 12.4 The Media

Horse-race journalism describes the media's use of polling results to turn elections into "horse races," which focus on which candidate is ahead or behind in polls rather than the candidates' qualifications or policy platforms. Thus, **(B)** is correct and (A) is incorrect. The ability of horse-race journalism to attract ratings, clicks, or other measures of popularity depends on the public's believing an election is "neck and neck," with the two candidates performing at roughly equal levels, leaving the final outcome in doubt. Thus, (C) and (D) are incorrect.

11. D

Topic: 12.3 Elections

The majority of the April primaries are held in the Northeastern states, with the two exceptions being Wisconsin and Wyoming, although the latter only holds the Democratic primary in April. Thus, **(D)** is correct. The majority of Southern states hold their primaries in March, which would be considered earlier as opposed to late; (A) is incorrect. No one region holds the majority of the earliest primaries in February. On the contrary, the first four primaries and caucuses are held in four distinct regions of the United States, making (B) incorrect. The majority of all states hold their primaries in March, not April, so (C) is incorrect.

12. D

Topic: 12.3 Elections

In recent years, many states have moved their primaries and caucuses earlier in the presidential election year. States do this in order to get more attention from the candidates and figure more prominently in the election outcome. States that have late primaries (e.g., in late May or June) may miss the opportunity to make a difference in the election if one candidate has already won enough of the earlier states to secure the nomination. **(D)** is correct. Changing the date of a state primary would not necessarily change the amount of negative advertising or the number of third-party candidates in the race, so (A) and (B) are incorrect. Early in the primary season, there are typically more candidates in the race; one of the benefits of having an earlier primary is having a larger number of candidates for the state's voters to choose from, so (C) is incorrect.

Test What You Learned

1. C

Topic: 12.3 Elections

In this Senate floor speech, John McCain mounts a defense of campaign finance law in the face of a looming Supreme Court decision. He also discusses how extending free speech rights to corporations may potentially lead to additional consequences, such as corporations gaining the Fifth Amendment protection against self-incrimination. Thus, **(C)** is correct. McCain actively supported the Bipartisan Campaign Reform Act of 2002 (also known as the McCain-Feingold Act); additionally, this excerpt does explicitly discuss that legislation. (A) is incorrect. (B) is incorrect because the speech deals with an existing law before the Supreme Court, not with a proposed law that could be lobbied against. (D) is incorrect because it reverses the message of the speech; McCain supports campaign finance law and is concerned that the Supreme Court will overturn it.

2. A

Topic: 12.3 Elections

The Bipartisan Campaign Reform Act of 2002, commonly known as the McCain-Feingold Act, dealt with the regulation of campaign financing. Senator McCain's support would indicate that he would likely also have supported a ban on gifts from lobbyists to members of Congress; **(A)** is correct. Given the McCain-Feingold Act's reformist bent, Senator McCain would likely have rejected any action or process that made it easier for public officials to become lobbyists; (B) is incorrect. Similarly, he would likely not have supported a formal collaborative relationship between lobbyists and Congress or private-sector input on presidential appointees, making (C) incorrect. (D) is incorrect because it is too extreme; while McCain casts doubt on the wisdom of the Supreme Court overturning a campaign finance law passed by the "most democratically elected branch of government," McCain does not call for the Supreme Court's powers to be limited.

7

3. D

Topic: 12.2 Linkage Institutions

Interest groups are associations of individuals or organizations that share one or more concerns and attempt to influence public policy in their favor. They often do this by putting pressure on the federal bureaucracy to direct public policy in a favorable manner to them; **(D)** is correct. One of the common criticisms of interest groups is that they can try to persuade public officials, the media, and the general public by using misleading or even inaccurate information. So, (A) is incorrect. While some interest groups do focus on a wide array of issues, many focus on a single issue. The issues that a group advocates may benefit only a small number of individuals rather than the general public, making (B) incorrect. While interest groups often try to influence political parties and their platforms, political parties do not outsource candidate recruitment to interest groups. (C) is incorrect.

4. A

Topic: 12.3 Elections

The Federal Election Commission (FEC) is an independent regulatory agency responsible for disclosing campaign finance information and enforcing contribution limits. The FEC regulates political action committees, including super PACs. Super PACs are not allowed to directly assist a candidate with campaign strategy. Thus, **(A)** is correct. Currently, individuals may give up to $2,700 to a candidate per election, making (B) incorrect. Nearly all political candidates attend private fundraisers to solicit campaign contributions, and some candidates donate their own personal funds to their campaigns; (C) and (D) are incorrect.

5. D

Topic: 12.1 Voting

During closed primaries, participants must be registered with a political party to vote for one of its candidates. Most state political parties favor closed primaries because they believe such primaries ensure that the winning nominee is truly backed by his party's members. Thus, **(D)** is correct. (A) and (C) are incorrect because they describe an open primary. (B) is incorrect because it describes a feature of caucuses.

6. C

Topic: 12.4 The Media

The creation of the Internet and explosion of talk radio have led to the prevalence of "attack journalism" and partisan political coverage. Conservative and liberal groups constantly try to attack each other in the media, and the media enjoys the higher ratings such attacks engender, while partisan media outlets provide platforms predominantly for views that they favor. Thus, **(C)** is correct. While "attack journalism" involves talk radio and Internet outlets, among others, the coverage is inherently partisan and focused on missteps of the rival party rather than any government misbehavior. So, (A) is incorrect. While (B) points out the nature of "attack journalism," it incorrectly says the point is to win over the rival outlets' audiences; In addition, these people would be ideologically different and thus not likely to begin following the attacking outlet. Although it is true that some consumer-driven media avoids controversial topics, "attack journalism" thrives on controversies. Also, it does not seek to appeal to a strictly mainstream audience but rather a passionately partisan one, so (D) is incorrect.

7. C

Topics: 12.1 Voting & 12.3 Elections

A caucus is a private meeting run by a political party in which members of the party vote for candidates. In most caucuses, voters divide into groups according to the candidate they support. As such, voters are unable to vote in secrecy. **(C)** is correct. In both open and closed primaries, as well as in general elections, voters are able to vote using a secret ballot, so (A), (B), and (D) are incorrect.

8. A

Topic: 12.4 The Media

Gatekeeping is the process through which the media filters information. The media decides whether certain stories and topics should be disseminated through broadcasting, print, the Internet, or some other mode of communication. **(A)** is correct. While certain news organizations may cover one candidate more than another, television media companies are not allowed to air ads for one candidate and deny airtime to another. This would violate federal election laws, making (B) incorrect. Many news media outlets do investigate governmental corruption and conduct public opinion polling, but these do not adequately describe the gatekeeping function, making (C) and (D) incorrect.

9. B
Topic: 12.1 Voting

Among the Midwestern states, only Michigan offered full suffrage, and only Indiana and Missouri extended no suffrage whatsoever to women. Most Midwestern states offered some form of limited voting rights to women. Thus, **(B)** is correct. While suffragists enjoyed some successes in the Northeast during the 1910s, (A) is incorrect because Wyoming offered full suffrage in 1869, and three other Western states did likewise in the nineteenth century. While it is true that women had few voting rights in the southern states, (C) is incorrect because the lack of suffrage was not absolute. For example, Florida offered municipal suffrage in some cities, and Arkansas offered suffrage in primary elections. The Nineteenth Amendment was ratified in 1920. Most states did not extend suffrage to women in 1919; (D) is incorrect.

10. B
Topic: 12.2 Linkage Institutions

The suffragists secured success by lobbying at the state level for bills that extended voting rights to women. Only later, with suffrage established in several states, was it possible to successfully lobby Congress for an amendment. Thus, **(B)** is correct and (A) is incorrect. While a nationwide ad campaign can be one tool of a lobbying effort, (C) is incorrect because it was not a core strategy of the suffragists, who initially operated at the state level. While operating first at the state level can be fruitful, (D) is incorrect because the suffragists mainly secured their civil rights through legislation rather than through judicial rulings.

11. B
Topic: 12.1 Voting

Historically, black Americans have voted at lower rates than whites. However, black voters have consistently out-voted Hispanic voters in national elections; **(B)** is correct. (A) is incorrect because young people typically vote at far lower rates than people in older age cohorts. Although blacks and whites vote at approximately the same rate, (C) is incorrect because Hispanics and people of other races vote at a lower rate. (D) is incorrect because, if race is a constant, older members of any racial demographic would be more likely to vote than younger members of that same group.

12. D
Topic: 12.2 Linkage Institutions

The iron triangle refers to the close three-pronged relationship among congressional committees, interest groups, and the executive branch bureaucracy. Thus, **(D)** is correct. Media effects are effects that the media has on its consumers, such as how much people's political attitudes and opinions are affected by exposure to media coverage. The four key media effects are framing, slant, filtering, and priming. The equal-time rule is not one of them. So, (A) is incorrect. Suffrage refers to the right to vote in political elections. It is typically used in discussions of expanding voting rights to new groups, such as African Americans and women. The examples given are for campaign financing; (B) is incorrect. A linkage institution is a structure or channel within a society that connects people to the national, state, and local levels of government; linkage institutions include elections, the media, political parties, and interest groups. So, (C) is incorrect.

PART 3

Comprehensive Review

CHAPTER 8

Foundations of American Democracy

8.1 DEMOCRATIC IDEALS

Foundational Documents

LEARNING OBJECTIVE

- List the underlying ideals and purposes of the Constitution and Declaration of Independence.

The Declaration of Independence

The Declaration of Independence of 1776 set forth the principles on which later the new American form of government would be established. Thomas Jefferson and a committee of delegates to the second Continental Congress agreed on a statement that explained the need for independence from Britain.

Crafted using the philosophical arguments of John Locke and others, the Declaration establishes a basic philosophy of what government should and should not be allowed to do. A cornerstone of the Declaration (and later, the Constitution) is the idea of **popular sovereignty**: that a government derives its power from the consent of the people it governs. Jefferson found inspiration in Locke's *Second Treatise of Civil Government* (1690), arguing that government is a form of social contract between citizens and leaders. Locke wrote that government exists to provide liberties and freedoms for those who agree to abide by its rules and limits and that people have natural rights that cannot be taken away by any government. Jefferson drew on Locke's ideas of the importance of life, liberty, and property to elucidate the fundamental goals of government. The Declaration of Independence remains a key philosophical guide to the rights promoted by American government.

The Constitution

While the Declaration of Independence establishes the ideals of government, the Constitution establishes the basic forms of political authority that are central to American government. Leadership through representatives that serve at the will of the voters is established in Article I, which delineates the powers of Congress, as well as specific limits on its powers. Articles II and III establish the power of the executive and judicial branches, respectively; however, they do so in much less detail than Article I, as the founders saw Congress as the most important branch of government. Together, the first three articles establish a separation of powers among the three branches of government by designating exclusive powers to each branch. For instance, the president is the commander of the military, but only Congress can declare war. The Constitution also provides for checks and balances, or ways in which one branch can restrain the action of another. One important example is the presidential veto; Congress can pass legislation with a majority vote, and the president can either sign it, in which case it becomes law, or veto it, in which case it will not become law unless Congress overrides the veto with a two-thirds majority vote.

As evidenced by the list of grievances in the Declaration of Independence, the founders were worried about what could happen when a country is ruled by an unrestrained central government. Thus, in addition to establishing separation of powers and checks and balances, the Constitution instituted an innovative form of government: **federalism**. Under this system, the national (federal) government can do only what it is explicitly permitted to do in the Constitution. In other words, when any part of the federal government wants to act, it must be able to point to a specific part of the Constitution that enables it to perform that action.

The Bill of Rights

The founders were committed to the protection of citizens' rights, but as originally drafted, the Constitution did not include a list of specific rights. This was because some founders argued that the enumeration of certain rights would lead some to conclude that these were the only rights the citizens had. In 1789, however, the first 10 amendments to the constitution were ratified as the **Bill of Rights**, which protected rights such as freedom of speech, freedom of religion, and the right to be free from unreasonable searches and seizures. The Ninth Amendment contained an important caveat: that this list of rights is not exclusive and does not deny the existence of other rights.

✔ **AP Expert Note**

Know the key points from all 9 foundational documents

The College Board (the maker of this exam) has decided that the following 9 foundational documents are central to the study of U.S. Government and Politics. Be sure to know the ins and outs of each of these documents, as they will appear in many ways on the exam. (A table containing key information about these documents is available in the back of this book.)

1. The Articles of Confederation

2. *Brutus* 1

3. The Constitution of the United States

4. The Declaration of Independence

5. *Federalist* 10

6. *Federalist* 51

7. *Federalist* 70

8. *Federalist* 78

9. Letter from a Birmingham Jail

Models of Representative Democracy

High-Yield

LEARNING OBJECTIVE

- Compare and contrast the influences of the three principal models of representative democracy on U.S. political life.

The framers of the Constitution created a democratic **republic** in which the power to govern comes not directly from the citizens but rather through representation by elected officials. In this system, the citizens can influence governmental actions primarily through elections. When creating the Constitution and debating what type of democracy the United States should have, the framers drew inspiration from three models of democracy: participatory, pluralist, and elite. Aspects of all three models can be found in our system of government today.

The **participatory model** of democracy emphasizes broad citizen participation in government and politics. Citizens should have the power to exert strong influence on the policy-making process as well as on the politicians responsible for implementing that policy. While the United States does not have a pure form of participatory democracy, there are instances in which U.S. citizens do broadly participate in government. For example, in state and local elections, citizens may have the chance to vote directly on legislative matters, such as whether to develop a local land area. Perhaps the most common examples of participatory democracy are town hall meetings, which give citizens the opportunity to meet directly with elected officials to discuss issues and proposed legislation. Citizens can ask their elected representatives questions and exchange ideas in a conversational format. The massive citizens' organizations that sprung up in support of the civil rights movement and women's suffrage movement are also examples of participatory democracy. Their members sought to participate more broadly and more directly in the governing process to achieve their objectives.

The **pluralist model** emphasizes the need for different organized groups to compete against each other in order to influence policy. This competition, according to the model, will prevent any one dominant group from exerting too much power over the minority. Later on, in the chapter about political participation, you will read about one very prominent argument for pluralist democracy. The argument is from James Madison. In **Federalist 10**, Madison expressed concern for the ability of **factions**, or groups, to gain too much control and to dominate the minority. He assumed that such factions formed naturally from society. He believed that if there were many groups, or factions, that they would compete against one another, holding each group in check. Today, we refer to one type of faction as an interest group. Interest groups are citizen groups that try to convince politicians and government officials to support their members' position on a common interest or issue. For example, the NRA (the National Rifle Association) is a well-known interest group that seeks to influence policy makers on certain gun-related issues. AARP (formerly the American Association of Retired Persons) is another example of an interest group; with over 35 million members, AARP represents the interests of Americans aged 50 and over.

The **elite model** emphasizes limited participation in politics and civil society. A small number of citizens—often the wealthy and powerful—influence government action. Some framers thought that governmental decision making should be left up to a small group of well-educated citizens (and not the mass of ordinary citizens). They believed that such an elite group would be better equipped and more informed to make the best decisions for the country. The Electoral College is a prime example of an elite democratic institution in the United States. The Electoral College consists of a small group of delegates who are put in charge of selecting the president and vice president every four years. Although the Electoral College delegates almost always follow the will of the popular vote in their respective states, this system was put in place to prevent the masses from electing an unqualified president who is unfit for office.

The framers of the Constitution debated and combined aspects of these models as they crafted the new government. For example, to prevent factions from abusing power, Madison did not believe the answer was to have a **direct democracy**, a prominent feature of the participatory model, in which the citizens would directly control the government and decision-making process. In a large country such as the United States, he believed that citizens could not possibly protect everyone's individual and property rights. Instead, Madison argued that the power of factions was best controlled through a republican form of government. In a republic, citizens elect representatives to make policy decisions and administer the government on the citizens' behalf. Madison believed that in a large country, there would be a sufficient pool of candidates from which to elect qualified officials. Because there were more citizens with diverse views in a large country, they would be more apt to control power abuses by factions.

8.2 THE BIRTH OF THE CONSTITUTION

The Articles of Confederation

LEARNING OBJECTIVE

- List and explain the provisions in the Articles of Confederation that reflect the centralized power debate.

Written in 1777 and ratified in 1781, the **Articles of Confederation** represented the first attempt to create a truly American form of government. The Articles called for a **confederal government** in which the states would retain sovereignty. Fearing that the new government would devolve into a monarchy, the authors of the Articles did not provide for a president or national executive to lead the government. Instead, the Articles gave all national power to the newly created **unicameral** (one-house) Congress. Each state had one vote, and any proposed congressional action required the approval of 9 of the 13 states. Unlike members of today's Congress, members of this early Congress were elected by state legislatures rather than directly by the people. The Articles also did not create a federal judiciary. Rather, all judicial and legal matters were left to the individual states. The Articles, however, did allow Congress to appoint special judges to resolve legal disputes between individual states. Finally, the framers made the Articles nearly impossible to amend. To change the Articles, all 13 states had to agree. By not sacrificing any significant power to the national government, the 13 states maintained nearly total autonomy under the Articles. The limited powers that were granted to the national government, such as making treaties and coining money, were also powers that the states possessed.

The Articles, however, proved inadequate for running the new country. Congress could not collect taxes, draft soldiers, control interstate commerce, or pay off its Revolutionary War debts. To fund the national government, Congress depended on unreliable payments by the 13 states. Without funds to support the military, Congress was powerless to deal with situations such as land intrusions by Great Britain and Spain, whose territories bordered the United States.

When the United States gained independence in 1783, the Articles of Confederation had already been ratified and accepted by the general population. Then, **Shays' Rebellion** occurred. For six months in January 1787, more than a thousand armed soldiers, led by Daniel Shays, seized an arsenal in Massachusetts to protest high taxes and the loss of their farms due to debt. This revolt alarmed many American leaders, including former revolutionary commander George Washington, who wrote, "Unless a remedy is soon applied, anarchy and confusion will inevitably ensue." The confederation established under the Articles of Confederation was too weak to deal with this and other internal problems. To maintain public order and enforce laws, Washington and others realized that they needed to revise their initial creation. Soon, a Constitutional Convention would undertake this task.

8

The Constitutional Convention

LEARNING OBJECTIVE

- Connect Constitutional Convention compromises to subsequent ideas and events in U.S. history.

The Articles of Confederation ultimately proved to be an inadequate form of government for the new country. To address this problem, the **Constitutional Convention** met in Philadelphia in 1787. Twelve of the 13 states sent delegates (55 in total) to participate in the convention, with Rhode Island choosing not to attend. The delegates, who included key figures such as Benjamin Franklin, James Madison, Alexander Hamilton, and George Washington, created the **U.S. Constitution** and established a federal form of government that distributed powers between a strong central government and the individual states.

The Great Compromise

High-Yield

In the convention debate, delegates from large states favored the **Virginia Plan**, a proposal offered by James Madison in which congressional representation would be based on population size. The Virginia Plan called for a **bicameral** (two-house) legislature in which representation was based on state population. Delegates from small states, on the other hand, favored the **New Jersey Plan**, in which representation would be equal among the states. While debating the Virginia Plan, delegates from the smaller states threatened to dissolve not only the convention but the union itself. As a compromise, Connecticut's Roger Sherman offered a proposal in which each state would have equal representation in one house, called the Senate, while population would determine the number of representatives in the other house, called the House of Representatives. This proposal became known as the **Great Compromise** or the **Connecticut Compromise**. After much debate, the framers agreed that the House of Representatives would be the larger house of Congress and include members who were directly elected by the citizens to serve two-year terms. They agreed that the Senate would be the smaller house of Congress and include members who were appointed in a manner determined by state legislatures for six-year terms. States could either directly elect the senators or authorize a direct popular vote election. State legislatures would control the election of senators until the Seventeenth Amendment was ratified in 1913, authorizing the direct election of senators by popular vote.

Debates over Slavery

The convention delegates agreed that every 10 years, a census of the national population would be conducted in order to adjust the distribution of members of the House of Representatives. The method for counting the population, however, proved highly controversial. Southern delegates argued that slaves should be counted in the population, because this method of counting would yield more representatives for Southern states than if only free persons were counted. Northern delegates objected, arguing that slaves should not be counted at all. The result was the **Three-Fifths Compromise** in which slaves were counted as three-fifths of a free person.

Another highly controversial issue at the convention involved the importation of slaves. The northern states wanted to permit Congress to control and possibly ban the importation of slaves in the future. The southern states strongly objected to this idea and wanted to allow slave importation to continue indefinitely. Reaching a compromise, the framers postponed the abolition of foreign slave importation until 1808 and allowed slave states to import as many slaves as they wanted in the meantime. Additionally, the Constitution placed no restrictions on domestic slave trade within the United States. Article IV of the Constitution required states to return runaway slaves to their owners' states and prevented slaves from gaining their freedom by escaping to non-slave states.

The Electoral College

High-Yield

The Constitutional Convention considered several methods of selecting the president. One proposal was to have the Congress choose the president. This idea was rejected, however, because some delegates believed that making such a choice would be too contentious and subject to corruption. A second proposal was to have the state legislatures choose the president. This idea was rejected out of a fear that the president would be too beholden to the states, which would diminish the president's federal authority. A third proposal was to have the president elected by a direct popular vote. This too was rejected because the framers feared people would vote without having adequate information about the candidates. In addition, if several candidates ran for the presidency, it was likely that no candidate would obtain a popular majority. Also, the framers believed that the choice of president would be decided by the most populous states, thereby ignoring the will of the smaller states.

Finally, a compromise was reached that protected the interests of both small and large states in presidential elections. This compromise created the **Electoral College**, a system in which each state is provided a certain number of electors equal to the number of its U.S. representatives plus the number of its U.S. senators. Because it allocated more weight to large states while ensuring that small states would not be ignored in presidential elections, the Electoral College was agreed to by delegates from both large and small states.

The Centralized Power Debate

LEARNING OBJECTIVE

- Summarize the Federalist and Anti-Federalist positions on how a centralized government should be organized.

A government in which the states have more power than the national government is called a confederal government. This is in stark contrast to a unitary government, in which the central, or national, government has supreme authority. The federal government structure arose as a compromise between these two contrasting forms of government. Supporters of the Constitution used "federalism" to describe a government in which the national and state governments would share power, with federal power being supreme. Federalism is the principle that political authority should be divided across the local, state, and national levels of government. Exactly how that principle works in action has been the subject of debate from America's beginnings to today.

Federalists and Anti-Federalists

High-Yield

As the new nation debated how to structure its government, one of the most contentious issues was whether one nation under a federal government could be maintained without undermining the state governments and individual liberties. Early American leaders held starkly different views on how to structure the new government. The two dominant political viewpoints that emerged were the **Federalists** and **Anti-Federalists**. Their many passionate debates were essential to the development of the foundational documents that helped shape the United States and its form of government. The Federalists wanted a strong central government that could manage the nation's debt, foreign policy, and other political affairs. The Federalists believed that the Constitution would be sufficient to prevent any abuses or excesses of power. Instead, they thought that a strong national government would be better equipped to coordinate and manage the political affairs of the young American nation.

The chief goal of the Anti-Federalists was to restrict the size of the federal government. They strongly supported a separation of powers and a robust system of checks and balances. Even with those protections, however, the Anti-Federalists argued that a large government would be tempted to abuse its power. They claimed that the citizens would not understand such a complex system and be unable to hold it accountable. Because the Anti-Federalists feared a large, national government, they insisted that there be constitutional guarantees to protect the individual liberties of the citizens; this would later become the Bill of Rights.

Anti-Federalist writings, including **Brutus 1,** emphasized the benefits of a small decentralized republic while warning of the dangers to personal liberty from a large, centralized government. One of the Anti-Federalists' main objections was that the new federal government would not be able to effectively govern a territory as large as the United States. The author of *Brutus* 1 wrote, "[I]n a republic of such vast extent as the United-States, the legislature cannot attend to the various concerns and wants of its different parts." The Anti-Federalists believed that government must be close to the people in order to represent the true needs and sentiments of the citizens. This argument stands in contrast with Madison's argument in *Federalist* 10, in which he says that a large republic is key to preventing a small group of people from dominating the government.

Drawing from the participatory model of democracy, the Anti-Federalists also believed that legislators and other government officials should have short terms. When the House of Representatives was proposed, the Anti-Federalists advocated for annual elections in order to keep the legislators more accountable to the voters. Similarly, they believed that House members' districts should be small enough that constituents could keep a close watch on their representatives and be able to vote them out of office if they didn't adequately represent the district.

✔ **AP Expert Note**

Be able to explain the importance of key foundational documents

James Madison, Alexander Hamilton, and John Jay wrote a series of 85 essays called *The Federalist Papers* to argue in favor of a strong national government. The *Anti-Federalist Papers*, most notably *Brutus* 1, were written in opposition to the *The Federalist Papers*. These documents were so seminal in the creation of the Constitution that they are still used today by lawmakers and judges to help interpret the original intentions of the framers of the Constitution.

After nearly four months of debate and compromise, the delegates unanimously accepted and signed the final draft of the Constitution on September 17, 1787. Because the draft required ratification by 9 of the 13 states, the debate moved from the convention in Philadelphia to the 13 state legislatures. Having just fought a war to achieve independence from Great Britain, many Americans strongly distrusted any form of central authority. As such, many citizens and state legislators opposed the proposed Constitution. In particular, opponents criticized the lack of protection for individual freedoms and rights, such as freedom of speech, freedom of religion, and right to a trial by jury. To explain how the new system of government would work and to reassure Americans that their liberties would be protected, Alexander Hamilton, James Madison, and John Jay published *The Federalist Papers* in various newspapers. On December 7, 1787, Delaware became the first state to ratify the Constitution. Throughout 1788, the Constitution's proponents prevailed in most state legislatures, and the new form of government took effect on March 4, 1789.

Despite the official authorization, or **ratification**, of the Constitution, many Anti-Federalists continued to demand that Congress amend the new Constitution to limit federal powers and guarantee individual rights. Soon after, in June 1789, House of Representatives member James Madison introduced a series of proposed amendments to the newly ratified Constitution. The House debated Madison's proposal and passed 17 amendments to be added to the Constitution. Those 17 amendments were then sent to the Senate, where they were consolidated into 12 amendments. After approval by the Senate, the amendments were sent to the states for approval. Two of the amendments were not approved, but the remaining 10 amendments were ratified by three-fourths of the states. The Bill of Rights became part of the Constitution on December 15, 1791.

Current Constitutional Debates

Many of the same debates that were had at the Constitutional Convention continue to be focal points of important political issues. Debate about the role of government power and the protection of civil liberties is especially relevant to the issue of government surveillance today. Surveillance laws provide intelligence and law enforcement agencies with certain legal powers to collect information (e.g., phone records, emails, social media postings) from citizens. Some argue, in the same spirit of *Federalist* 10, that these laws are necessary to gather information that could potentially protect the United States from terrorism and other acts of harm. Critics counter, in the same spirit of *Brutus* 1, that overly broad government surveillance is a power that the government should not possess. Such power, critics say, violates the protected civil liberties of American citizens. The extent

8

of U.S. government surveillance capabilities will undoubtedly continue to be debated. Like the delegates at the Constitutional Convention, today's leaders will have to figure out how upholding the rights and freedoms outlined in the Constitution is to be balanced with the need to provide national security.

Another debate that has proven to be quite controversial concerns the federal government's role in public education. Some believe that because the framers did not comment on education that this is one of the powers left to state government. Over time, however, the federal government's role in education has increased, leading to controversy about the Constitution's intent. This debate reflects tensions inherent in the Tenth Amendment, which reserves to the states and their citizens all powers not mentioned in the Constitution, including authority over public education.

The Fourteenth Amendment, which gives citizenship to all persons born in the United States, provides "equal protection under the law to all people within its jurisdiction." If states fail to provide equal protection to their citizens, then the federal government can issue **mandates**, which are official legal orders, for the states to comply with federal laws or court orders. An example of this is the Supreme Court's decision in *Brown v. Board of Education* (1954), which banned legal segregation in schools. This provided a mandate to the states to desegregate their schools. Since the *Brown* decision, the federal government has passed laws to establish various educational programs and to provide funding for public education. The Department of Education was created in 1979 to help coordinate the federal government's role in education. Some supporters of strong states' rights, often including leaders of the Republican Party, have opposed these efforts, arguing that the federal government should not play such a central role in education. These critics believe that state and local governments are better able to establish and implement education policies and practices.

8.3 LIMITS ON POWER

Key Constitutional Principles

High-Yield

LEARNING OBJECTIVE

- Explain how separation of powers, and checks and balances, limit the U.S. government.

One of the challenges that the framers of the Constitution faced was making sure that increasing the authority of the federal government did not lead to a government with too much power—the memory of British control was still fresh in the minds of most Americans. The framers partially solved this problem through the **separation of powers**, dividing the power of the federal government across the three branches: legislative, executive, and judicial. To make sure citizens' rights are protected and that the government operates effectively, each branch has its own powers and responsibilities, including working with the other branches.

In addition to the separation of powers, each branch has the ability to limit the powers of the others in a system of **checks and balances**. The system of checks and balances means that each branch of government has certain exclusive powers, some shared powers, and the ability to restrain the powers of the other two branches. The principles of separation of powers and checks and balances were set forth and argued for in the *Federalist Papers*, discussed briefly in the previous section.

In *Federalist* 51, James Madison assured his readers that they need not fear that the national government would grow too powerful. He believed that the federal system and the separation of powers would prevent any one part of the government from becoming too powerful. In addition, he said that tyranny would not arise in a government in which "the legislature necessarily predominates."

✔ **AP Expert Note**

Be ready to give varied examples of key constitutional principles in action

Federalism, separation of powers, checks and balances, limited government, and the adaptability of the Constitution are vitally important to understanding the American political system. As you review this material, start to build a list of examples of how these principles have been and continue to be applied; being able to quickly identify or recall examples will help you not only in the multiple-choice section but also on the free-response questions.

The Legislative Branch

Article I of the Constitution gives all legislative powers to a bicameral Congress: a House of Representatives and a Senate (the result of the Great Compromise discussed previously). The system currently provides for a two-year term of office for members of the House of Representatives, elected from the 435 population-based districts. Additionally, voters of each state elect two senators, who serve six-year terms.

The **legislative branch** makes laws, regulates interstate and foreign commerce, controls and implements taxation, creates spending policies, and oversees other parts of the government. The two houses of Congress are fundamentally equal in their legislative functions and roles. However, there are a couple of key differences. Only the Senate confirms presidential nominations and approves treaties, and only the House can initiate and draft revenue legislation. To enact most other laws, both houses must separately agree to the same bill (in exactly the same form) before presenting it to the president for approval.

Legislative action is planned and coordinated by political party leaders in each house. The leaders of each house are chosen by members of their party within their respective houses. Also, in both houses, much of the legislative process is performed within standing committees: groups of members from both parties that typically take the lead in developing legislation. Legislators normally serve on a small number of committees, often for many years, allowing them to become highly knowledgeable in certain policy areas. Committees are chaired by a member of the majority party, and each chair may work closely with the other party's top committee member, called the ranking member. In most committees, the ratio of majority party to minority party members on a committee reflects the overall ratio in each house chamber. Once a law is enacted (i.e., passed by Congress and signed by the president), Congress is responsible for providing oversight of public policy implementation and its effects.

8

The Executive Branch

The **executive branch** carries out and enforces laws. It consists of the president; the vice president; the Cabinet; executive departments; independent agencies; and other boards, commissions, and committees.

Key roles of the executive branch include:

- President—serves as the leader of the federal government, as head of state, and as Commander-in-Chief of the U.S. Armed Forces. The president serves a four-year term and can be elected for a maximum of two terms.

- Vice President—serves to support the president. If the president is unable to serve, the vice president becomes president. The vice president also serves as the president of the Senate.

- The Cabinet—consists of the heads of executive departments. Cabinet members are nominated by the president and must be approved by a simple majority of the Senate (51 out of 100 votes).

The Judicial System

The **judicial branch** consists of the U.S. Supreme Court and the federal judicial system. According to the Constitution, "[t]he judicial Power of the United States, shall be vested in one supreme Court, and in such inferior Courts as the Congress may from time to time ordain and establish."

The number of Supreme Court justices is set by Congress rather than by the Constitution. There have been as few as six justices, but since 1869 there have been nine, including a Chief Justice. All justices are nominated by the president, require confirmation by the Senate, and hold their offices for life. Since justices do not have to run for office, they are assumed to be insulated from political pressure when deciding cases.

The Supreme Court's cases are mostly appellate (i.e., relating to appeals) in nature, and the Court's decisions cannot be appealed to any higher legal or governmental authority, as it is the final judicial authority in the United States. Although the Supreme Court can hear an appeal on any legal issue under its jurisdiction, it typically does not hold trials. Instead, the Court's task is to interpret the law and to rule on how a law should be applied. A case settled by the Supreme Court can have a sweeping impact on the law because its decisions establish precedent that all other courts must follow. Lower courts are required to follow the precedent set by the Supreme Court when issuing rulings on legal issues.

The Supreme Court's power of judicial review was defined by the Supreme Court itself in the case of *Marbury v. Madison* (1803), which is discussed further in the chapter on Interactions Among Branches of Government. Through the process of judicial review, the federal courts can declare legislative and executive acts unconstitutional. This illustrates how the separation of powers and the system of checks and balances work together to guard the citizens against potential government abuse of power.

Consequences of Limiting Power

LEARNING OBJECTIVE

- Detail the effects of separation of powers, and checks and balances, on U.S. politics.

The main objective of the twin principles of separation of powers and checks and balances is to limit the power of the national government and force separate branches to share power. Some of the most important checks and balances include:

- The president, as leader of the executive branch, has the power to check the legislative branch by vetoing laws that Congress passes.

- If the president vetoes a law, Congress may check the veto by overriding the veto through a two-thirds vote in each house of Congress.

- Congress may investigate the executive branch and has the authority to impeach and remove federal officials from office, including the president.

- The president appoints all federal court judges, who must be approved by the Senate.

- Congress must approve presidential appointments that the president makes, and the Senate must approve treaties that the president signs.

- The judicial branch may check both the legislative and executive branches by declaring laws unconstitutional. Also, justices that sit on the Supreme Court serve lifetime appointments, isolating them from any political pressure exerted by the president or Congress.

If the president wants to gain favorable consideration for certain legislative proposals, he or she must make a special effort to cultivate the relationship between members of Congress and make them aware of his or her legislative priorities. If Congress tries to pass legislation that the president does not favor, he or she may threaten to veto the legislation. Through a veto threat, the president can persuade legislators to adjust the content of the bill to be more acceptable to the president. Congress, however, can then override a veto by passing the legislation by a two-thirds vote in both the House and the Senate.

Another important congressional power is the ability to investigate and oversee the executive branch and its agencies, such as the Department of Education and the Department of Agriculture. As part of this responsibility, which is known as oversight, Congress summons senior government officials for questioning and information gathering. Moreover, Congress has also been given some control over executive appointments, which must be filled with the advice and consent of the Senate. Both of these have the effect of checking the power of the president and holding the executive branch members accountable.

In order to insulate judges from political influence, they are given lifetime appointments. However, judges could still be subject to political influence exerted by Congress and other public officials. Although the president has the right to appoint the judges, the Senate must vote to approve the appointments. The judicial branch's main powers over the president are judicial interpretation and judicial review. Judicial interpretation is the power to determine the validity and meaning of executive agency regulations. Judicial review is the judiciary's power to review governmental actions to determine if they violate the Constitution.

One result of the separation of powers and the checks and balances system is that interest groups, influential politicians, and others have multiple access points to the government. For example, an interest group that is concerned with environmental protection may seek support from members of Congress, from public officials in the executive branch, or even from the judicial system. Therefore, citizens, citizens groups, interest groups, etc., have multiple government access points.

Impeachment

As a result of the checks and balances system, one of the most important legislative powers over the executive is that Congress can impeach and remove the president. The Constitution gives the House of Representatives the sole power to impeach a government official, and it makes the Senate the sole court for impeachment trials.

The House of Representatives brings impeachment charges against federal officials as part of its oversight and investigatory duties. Members of the House can introduce impeachment charges and then pass a resolution authorizing an inquiry. The House's judiciary committee has jurisdiction over impeachments and can decide whether to pursue articles of impeachment against the accused official and report the articles to the full House. If the articles are adopted (by a majority vote), the House appoints members to prosecute the subsequent trial, which takes place in the Senate. A conviction on an article of impeachment requires a two-thirds vote of the senators present. If the official is convicted on one or more of the articles, he or she is officially removed from office. The House has initiated impeachment proceedings more than 60 times, but only about a third have led to full impeachments. Only eight, who were all federal judges, were convicted and removed from office by the Senate. Only two presidents, Andrew Johnson in 1868 and Bill Clinton in 1998, have been impeached.

8.4 FEDERALISM

What Is Federalism?

LEARNING OBJECTIVE

- Demonstrate how federalism reflects society's needs.

Federalism, a key part of the Constitution, is the principle that political authority should be divided across the local, state, and national levels of government. The powers of the national and state governments are divided into four basic categories.

The first category is the powers of the national government, which are divided into three subcategories. **Enumerated powers**, or expressed powers, are those that are written in the Constitution. **Implied powers** may be reasonably inferred from the Constitution through the **elastic clause**, a statement in Article I of the Constitution giving Congress considerable leeway to expand the scope of its enumerated powers. The elastic clause is also known as the **necessary and proper clause**. The power to make laws and sovereignty over a territory are **inherent powers**. The Constitution limits these powers in various ways, but it does not specifically grant them because they are assumed to be a natural, or inherent, part of any government.

Reserved powers are those powers that are neither delegated to the federal government nor denied to the states. These powers are not expressly listed but are guaranteed to the states by the Tenth Amendment. Generally, these powers enable state governments to regulate their internal affairs (e.g., fire departments). **Concurrent powers** are those held by both the federal and state governments. The Constitution does not give these exclusively to either the national government or the states. These powers include levying and collecting taxes, making laws, and providing for the health and welfare of citizens. **Prohibited powers**, also known as restricted powers, are denied to the federal government, the state governments, or both. The taxing of exports is an example of a prohibited power.

Part of the Bill of Rights, the **Tenth Amendment** was intended as a further reinforcement of the concept of federalism; it gives the individual state governments any powers that are neither delegated to the federal government nor denied to the states by the Constitution. The **supremacy clause**, found in Article VI of the Constitution, states that the document is "the supreme Law of the Land." All officials of the country must give oaths to support the Constitution. While state constitutions are subordinate to the U.S. Constitution, the exact balance between state and national power has long been the subject of debate.

Federalism's Evolution

High-Yield

LEARNING OBJECTIVE

- Track changes in the balance between federal and state governments over time.

The original interpretation of federalism called for what is known as **dual federalism**. Under this interpretation, the federal government would exercise limited powers, with most power being held by the states. Both of these levels of government were viewed as being able to dominate their own spheres of influence, with the Supreme Court acting as a referee when disputes arose between the two. During the pre-Civil War era (or the Antebellum period) and then the Jim Crow era, dual federalism was criticized for being inadequate for dealing with states that denied freedom (e.g., slavery) and civil rights to their inhabitants as well as for being unable to handle the economic and social changes that were taking place in the United States.

One of the most fundamental and important changes in American government has been the gradual, but significant, evolution of federalism. The territorial expansion of the country in the early nineteenth century, the upheaval of the Civil War, America's development into an industrial and international power, the collapse of world economies in the mid-twentieth century, the struggles of two world wars, and threats of expanding communism have all significantly changed the public's expectations of central powers. More recently, 9/11 and the Great Recession in the early twenty-first century have caused some citizens to favor a larger federal role for certain governmental functions, such as protection against terrorism and financial regulation.

The abolition of the institution of slavery as a result of the Civil War changed the scope of federalism as it applied to the rights of citizenship and was the springboard for applying other federal rights to the states. In particular, the Fourteenth Amendment, ratified in 1868, prohibits the states from denying citizens the rights to which they are entitled by the Constitution, including equal protection and due process.

The Great Depression, which led to increased acceptance of a strong role for the national government in promoting the economic health of the nation, marked the beginning of cooperative federalism. In **cooperative federalism**, federal and state governmental units work together as partners to make policy and to provide goods and services to citizens. Providing various goods and services requires a good deal of collaboration, bargaining, and resource sharing between different levels of government. This interpretation of federalism is distinct from the dual federalism that was prevalent for the first hundred years after the American Revolution.

As the federal government has expanded its responsibilities, **revenue sharing** has become a central feature of its power. When the federal government distributes tax dollars to the states, it attaches rules and regulations to those monies. States are left to decide whether they want to accept the needed funds and adhere to federal rules, or whether they would prefer to attempt to do without the funds and determine their own policies. An example is the federal Race to the Top grants, which have been given only to states that adopt Common Core standards for education. This interpretation of federalism, in which funding is appropriated by the federal government to the states with specific conditions attached, is called **fiscal federalism**.

Today, most federal aid to the states comes in two forms. One type is the **categorical grant**, which is money from the federal government that must be used for a very specific purpose, such as improving public transportation. The other type is the **block grant**, which is financial aid to states that is used within a general policy area. The state maintains discretion over exactly how to spend the money. The federal government has been able to increase its power over state and local governments by controlling how money is allocated to the states. Sometimes this power has stemmed from conditions attached to financial assistance, and sometimes the federal government has even required state and local governments to adhere to policies when funding was not a factor. These obligations are known as unfunded mandates.

Any discussion of federalism must include the courts. Supreme Court rulings concerning federalism have been made since the early 1800s. The Supreme Court has expanded federal power to enable the creation of a national banking system, control of the economy, and construction of vast transportation and communication networks. The balance of power between the national and state governments has changed over time based on U.S. Supreme Court interpretation.

McCulloch v. Maryland *(1819)*

High-Yield

The Supreme Court decision in *McCulloch v. Maryland* **(1819)** held that Congress has implied powers necessary to implement its enumerated powers; this case also established supremacy of the U.S. Constitution and federal laws over state laws. The case came about because, in 1816, Congress chartered the Second Bank of the United States in Maryland. In 1818, the Maryland state legislature passed an act to tax any bank not chartered by the state of Maryland. Since the Second Bank of the United States was not chartered by Maryland, it was taxed. When the Supreme Court heard the case, it had to decide whether Congress has the power to incorporate a bank and whether the state of Maryland could, without violating the Constitution, tax the U.S. Bank. The Court ruled "yes" on the first question and "no" on the second question.

In the Court's majority decision, Chief Justice John Marshall noted that the congressional power established by the Constitution originates from the people, not the states. He wrote that the Constitution, by nature, must be general enough to enable it to be changed as unexpected circumstances arise. There must be some implied powers for Congress, then, hence the language in the necessary and proper clause, or elastic clause, of Article I, Section 8, which established that Congress could use "all means which are appropriate" to uphold the Constitution. Congress does not have the specific power to incorporate a bank, but such a power is implied.

Regarding whether Maryland could tax the federal bank, the Supreme Court decided that the power to tax an entity is also the power to "destroy" it. This is unacceptable, since the states are necessarily lower than the federal government. The bank was deemed an appropriate method for the national government to carry out several of its powers, such as regulating interstate commerce, collecting taxes, and borrowing money.

United States v. Lopez *(1995)*

High-Yield

Another clause of the Constitution that has been interpreted by the Supreme Court is the **commerce clause** (Article I, Section 8), which gives Congress power to regulate trade and commerce. In a significant case, *United States v. Lopez* **(1995)**, the Court ruled that the Gun-Free School Zones Act of 1990 was unconstitutional because Congress had exceeded its authority under the commerce clause. The Court held that Congress may not use the commerce clause to make possession of a gun in a school zone a federal crime, introducing a new phase of federalism that recognized the importance of state sovereignty and local control.

The Court found that the Gun-Free School Zones Act had nothing to do with interstate commerce or economic activity and so struck down the act as an impermissible exercise of congressional power under the commerce clause.

Focus on the important principles of Supreme Court cases

You'll notice key Supreme Court cases discussed throughout this book. It can be easy to get lost in the details, trying to memorize all of the dates and other minutiae of each one. Rest assured that the AP exam is going to focus on larger principles and how those SCOTUS decisions have shaped the way government operates. (A full list of the College Board's 15 required SCOTUS cases can be found in the back of this book.)

Power Distribution

LEARNING OBJECTIVE

- List factors that facilitate and constrain the flow of power within and among U.S. governments.

In the twentieth century, complex problems arose in the United States that could not be solved at one level of government. Supporters of cooperative federalism called for a more pragmatic focus on intergovernmental relations to provide services efficiently. State and local governments have maintained some power as the implementers of programs, but the federal government has played a much stronger role as the initiator of key policies.

To make federalism work, the Constitution imposes certain constraints on both the national and the state governments. States are prohibited from making treaties with foreign countries, coining money, taxing imports or exports, taxing foreign ships, keeping troops or ships in time of peace (except for the National Guard), and engaging in war. In turn, the federal government is obligated by the Constitution to protect states against domestic insurrections. Also, Congress may not force states to enact laws to comply with, or order states to enforce, unfunded mandates. The issue of federal funding to the states has become at times a source of contention between state and national government officials.

🖥 NEXT STEP: PRACTICE

Go to Rapid Review and Practice Chapter 3 or to your online quizzes on kaptest.com for exam-like practice on this topic.

Haven't registered your book yet? Go to kaptest.com/moreonline to begin.

CHAPTER 9

Interactions Among Branches of Government

9.1 THE CONGRESS

Organization

LEARNING OBJECTIVE

- Discriminate among the structures and functions of the two houses of Congress.

The **U.S. Congress** is the legislative branch of the federal government. It is divided into two chambers: the **Senate** and the **House of Representatives**. Article I of the Constitution establishes the structure and powers of each house of Congress. While both chambers participate in the legislative process—any new legislation requires the approval of both the House and the Senate in order to become law—there are some notable differences in their structure and functions.

The design of Congress represents one of the major compromises of the **Constitutional Convention**. While the delegates generally agreed that Congress should be a **bicameral legislature**, there was vigorous debate concerning the allocation of seats. Some delegates wanted to award an equal number of seats to each state. Most of these delegates were from small states and were concerned that their interests would be overwhelmed by those of large states; others who supported giving each state an equal voice wanted to protect the notion of state sovereignty. An opposing faction of delegates wanted to award seats based on population. These delegates, mostly from large states, felt that proportional representation was more fair.

Ultimately, the delegates compromised and agreed to allocate the seats differently in each chamber, a process that exists to this day: in the Senate, each state receives exactly two seats, while in the House of Representatives, each state receives a number of seats in proportion to its population, divided into legislative districts of roughly equal size. Thus, the Senate was intended to protect the interests of the states, while the House of Representatives was designed to represent the interests of the people. This dichotomy is also reflected in the way the framers chose to handle the election of members to each chamber: senators were initially chosen by state legislatures, while members of the House have always been directly elected by the people. Since the passage of the Seventeenth Amendment in 1913, senators have also been directly elected by the people. The overall structure and purpose of each house of Congress, however, has remained largely unchanged.

To further reflect these important differences, the framers chose to establish different term lengths for the members of each house. Because the House of Representatives is meant to be accountable to the people, members serve only two-year terms and must seek reelection frequently. Moreover, all terms expire at the same time, meaning that an entirely new House of Representatives is elected every two years. By contrast, senators serve six-year terms, and their election cycles are staggered so that roughly one-third of the Senate is up for reelection every two years, giving the Senate more long-term stability.

While the number of seats in the Senate (two per state) is prescribed by the Constitution, the number of seats in the House of Representatives is determined by federal law. The number of House seats, currently 435, has changed over time, but typically the House has had more members than the Senate. As a result, debate in the House must proceed much more formally than debate in the Senate. Both chambers follow similar parliamentary procedures, but one key difference is that debate in the House is heavily structured: representatives have limited time to speak, and what they say must be on topic. Senators, on the other hand, are generally allowed more time to speak and are allowed to make off-topic statements in order to delay legislation.

✔ AP Expert Note

Know the history behind the "Upper" and "Lower" Houses of U.S. Congress

Although they were generally opposed to establishing an American monarchy, the framers of the Constitution borrowed heavily from English legal and political traditions in their design for the federal government. The bicameral structure of Congress was strongly influenced by the British Parliament, which consists of an Upper House (the House of Lords) and a Lower House (the House of Commons). By tradition, the House of Lords has represented upper-class landowners and other special interests, while the House of Commons has represented the public at large. In many ways, the Senate is the analogue of the House of Lords: senators were initially appointed rather than elected, and it was assumed that the Senate would protect the interests of landowners and merchants because states would choose members of those classes as their representatives in Congress. Similarly, the House of Representatives is comparable to the House of Commons because its members are chosen by direct election and are intended to represent the interests of the people as a whole. Even today, the Senate is often viewed as more prestigious than the House of Representatives because senators represent larger, state-wide constituencies and because the smaller number of senators overall gives each individual senator greater visibility in the public eye.

Article I, Section 8 sets forth a list of **enumerated powers** that are shared by the Senate and the House, including:

- The power to lay and collect taxes

- The power to coin money

- The power to raise and maintain the armed forces

- The power to declare war

- The power to regulate interstate commerce

In addition, Section 8 contains a **necessary and proper clause** permitting Congress to make any laws that are needed to carry out its enumerated powers, thus authorizing a set of **implied powers** in addition to those explicitly named. Over time, this clause has been used to expand the scope of Congress's legislative authority. For example, in the landmark Supreme Court case *McCulloch v. Maryland* **(1819)**, Chief Justice John Marshall held that the necessary and proper clause authorized Congress to establish a national bank. The necessary and proper clause has been similarly invoked to justify federal legislation concerning a variety of economic, environmental, social, and criminal matters. Due to its inherent flexibility, it is often referred to as the "elastic clause."

Although the House and the Senate share many legislative duties, there are some responsibilities that rest solely with one chamber. For example, the framers, having experienced taxation without representation firsthand during the colonial period, wanted to keep the power of taxation as close to the people as possible; therefore, all tax legislation must originate within the House of Representatives. By contrast, the power to confirm the president's judicial and executive appointments and the power to ratify international treaties rest solely with the Senate, giving states some influence over the domestic and foreign policy of the federal government.

> ✔ **AP Expert Note**
>
> **Be able to explain the reasoning behind the differences in the Houses of Congress**
>
> Many U.S. Government and Politics students can rattle off what the differences are between the Senate and the House of Representatives. The AP exam makers are much more interested in the *why*. You should be prepared to explain the reasons the framers had for creating a bicameral legislature and for allocating certain powers to the House of Representatives or to the Senate, as well as the ways in which those decisions influence politics today.

POLICY MAKING

LEARNING OBJECTIVE

- Cite factors that influence the policy-making process in Congress.

Leadership in the House

The presiding officer of the House of Representatives is the **Speaker of the House**, a position created by Article I, Section 2 of the Constitution but not assigned any specific constitutional duties. Instead, the Speaker's role is defined by the Rules of the House, which are decided every two years at the beginning of each new Congress and which are influenced by common practice. Typically, the Speaker is responsible for a variety of procedural duties, such as presiding over debate, ruling on parliamentary disputes, and making committee assignments. The Speaker also determines when a bill will be considered for a vote by the House. Although the Speaker is elected by the entire House, the voting power of the majority party means that the Speaker will almost always be a member of the House majority. Thus, the Speaker also plays an important role as a partisan leader, using his or her influence to advance the legislative agenda of the majority party.

Other leadership positions in the House are expressly partisan roles. The majority party chooses a **majority leader**, whose primary responsibility is to work with other congressional leaders in the House and Senate—including members of the opposition party—to achieve the majority party's legislative goals. There is also a **majority whip**, who is responsible for enforcing intra-party discipline by encouraging fellow party members in the House to vote in accordance with the majority party's legislative priorities. Similarly, the minority party chooses a **minority leader** and a **minority whip** who perform analogous functions within the minority party.

Leadership in the Senate

The presiding officer of the Senate is the vice president of the United States, who is designated the **President of the Senate** by Article I, Section 3. The Constitution places a clear limit on the vice president's power: unlike the Speaker of the House, the President of the Senate may not cast a vote except in the event of a tie. In practice, the vice president rarely presides over the Senate at all, reserving this duty for high-profile or ceremonial occasions only. In the absence of the vice president, the responsibility to preside over the Senate falls to another constitutional officer, the **president pro tempore**, who is elected by the Senate as a whole. By tradition, the longest-serving senator from the majority party is usually chosen to serve as president pro tempore, and he or she often delegates the responsibility of presiding over the Senate to other members of the majority party. As in the House, each party in the Senate also elects assistant floor leaders known as the majority (or minority) leader and the majority (or minority) whip, who serve functions similar to those positions in the House. However, bipartisan cooperation has traditionally been more common in the Senate than it is in the House.

Congressional Committee System

The committee system was created to manage the volume and complexity of legislative work that would otherwise overwhelm Congress. Each house has about 20 **standing committees** that each specialize in a specific policy area. When a bill is introduced in the House or Senate, it is referred to the appropriate standing committee for review. The standing committee may hold hearings or otherwise gather information relevant to the bill; often, this work is delegated to an even more specialized subcommittee. Once the information-gathering stage has been completed, the bill enters the mark-up phase, where committee members debate the merits of the bill and approve or reject any amendments that have been offered. Ultimately, the committee votes on whether to "report" or "table" the bill. If the bill is reported, the committee recommends it for a vote by the full chamber. If the bill is tabled, no further action is taken, and the bill is stalled indefinitely; most bills introduced in Congress ultimately "die" in committee after being tabled.

Because they determine which bills come to the full chamber for a vote, standing committees wield a considerable amount of power in the legislative process. As a result, assigning members to standing committees is an inherently partisan process. Each committee consists of a mixture of majority and minority members in a ratio that typically approximates that of the chamber as a whole, and each party nominates its own members for service on each committee, subject to approval by the full chamber. The majority party selects a chairperson for each committee to control the committee's agenda, while the ranking member of the minority party on each committee serves as the opposition leader. Given that every chairperson is a member of the majority party, however, it is difficult for legislation that conflicts with the majority party's platform to survive the committee process without being tabled.

Individual members may compete for committee assignments based on the demographics of their constituencies or on other factors, such as the prestige or visibility of the appointment. For example, a senator who represents a state with a large military base might want to serve on the Armed Services Committee, while a House member with lofty political ambitions might seek appointment to a high-profile committee like Rules or Appropriations. Because most members of Congress have some degree of preference regarding their committee assignments, parties often utilize the appointment process as a tool for party discipline by rewarding loyal members with coveted assignments.

Standing committees are permanent committees assigned a particular policy focus, such as Armed Forces, Budget, or Foreign Relations, and their primary task is to review proposed legislation within their legislative jurisdiction. Other committees in the House and Senate serve additional functions.

- **Select committees** (sometimes known as "special" committees) are created for a specific purpose, usually to investigate an allegation of wrongdoing within the executive branch or to consider proposed legislation that does not clearly fall within the jurisdiction of an existing standing committee. Select committees can be dissolved after fulfilling their purpose, but the current select (and special) committees in the House and Senate are treated as permanent committees.

- **Joint committees** are permanent committees that consist of members of both the House and the Senate. Their purpose can be to manage administrative tasks that affect both houses, as does the Joint Committee on Printing, or to investigate and report on important policy matters, as does the Joint Economic Committee.

- **Conference committees** are temporary joint committees created to reconcile the House and Senate versions of the same bill. Once the reconciliation process has been completed, a conference committee is dissolved.

✔ **AP Expert Note**

Know the significance of conference committees in the legislative process

When the House and Senate pass different versions of the same bill, a conference committee made up of members from both houses will work together to reconcile the differences and draft a compromise version of the bill. Due to the changes made by the conference committee, the compromise bill must be voted on by both houses of Congress before it can be presented to the president for his or her signature. In cases where the legislation is especially controversial and the original bill only narrowly passed the House and/or the Senate, the compromise bill may be impossible to pass in one or both houses, thus killing the legislation altogether. In order to avoid this result, members of the House and Senate often work together when drafting the language of a proposed bill, engaging in an informal conferencing process that, if successful, results in the same version of the bill passing both houses during the initial floor vote. This informal process circumvents the need for a formal conference committee and the risk that a compromise bill will not have the support needed to pass one or both houses. It is becoming increasingly common for Congress to use the informal process, with only eight formal conference reports issued during the 114th Congress, which met from 2015 to 2017, compared to more than 60 formal conference reports issued during the 104th Congress, which met from 1995 to 1997, and a fairly stable decline during the intervening years.

Special Procedures in the House

The procedures in the House of Representatives reflect its highly partisan yet also democratic nature: decisions made by the House typically require only a simple majority vote, and many special procedures—even those designed to give a voice to minority interests—reinforce the notion of majority rule.

Rules Committee

After a bill is reported by a standing committee, it is usually then submitted to the **Rules Committee**, which proposes a set of rules for debating that particular bill. Important decisions made by the Rules Committee include whether amendments may be offered, and if so, how many are allowed, and which sections of the bill may be amended. This committee also decides whether floor debate is permitted to take place, and if so, how much debate time will be allocated to each representative.

The constraints put in place by the Rules Committee can significantly affect the likelihood that a bill will pass the House, and the majority party exerts a strong influence over the rule-making process: unlike other House committees, where the ratio of majority to minority members is more balanced, the membership of the Rules Committee tilts heavily in favor of the majority party. While the recommendations of the Rules Committee must be voted on by the full House, the majority party usually has the voting power to ensure that the proposals made by the Rules Committee are adopted easily.

Committee of the Whole

The **Committee of the Whole** is a committee made up of the entire House of Representatives. Typically, the House resolves itself into a Committee of the Whole in order to consider a bill, primarily because the parliamentary procedures for committees are less complex than those of the full House but also because the **quorum** requirement is lower (100 versus 218). The Committee of the Whole is authorized to debate and amend proposed legislation using the rules previously adopted by the House for that bill. Once the debate and amendment process is concluded, the Committee of the Whole dissolves, and the bill is reported back to the full House for a final up-or-down vote.

Discharge Petitions

The majority party exerts a considerable amount of control over the legislative process in the House, but by filing a **discharge petition**, it is possible for individual members to circumvent the majority when a bill is stalled in committee. If successful, this will take the bill from the jurisdiction of the standing committee and bring it to the floor for a vote. Because they require the support of an absolute majority of representatives, discharge petitions rarely succeed, as it is unlikely that enough members of the majority party will agree to support a discharge petition that conflicts with the decisions of their own party's leadership. However, the threat of a discharge petition is sometimes enough to prompt action on a bill that is stuck in committee.

Special Procedures in the Senate

The procedures used in the Senate signal its commitment to bipartisanship and minority party rights by requiring supermajority approval for most legislative business. Senate procedures also reflect its smaller size relative to the House and its resulting ability to proceed less formally.

Cloture

The standing rules in the Senate permit unlimited debate and amendments, and there is no requirement that speeches or amendments be relevant to the subject matter of the original bill. A motion for **cloture** is the only way to end debate and call for a final up-or-down vote, and it requires the approval of three-fifths of the full Senate. Because the majority party rarely holds that many seats, the minority party can often postpone the final vote on a bill through a process known as **filibustering**. During a filibuster, senators use their unlimited speaking time to extend debate indefinitely for a bill they do not support; the only way to end a filibuster is through a successful cloture motion. While actual filibusters are rare today, they are commonly threatened. As a result, controversial legislation effectively requires approval by a three-fifths supermajority.

Unanimous Consent

In order to expedite the legislative process, the majority of Senate business is conducted through a parliamentary procedure known as **unanimous consent**. Under this procedure, the Senate is presumed to act with the mutual consent of all senators unless an objection is raised, allowing the Senate to approve bills and other measures without extended debate or a time-consuming roll call vote. The Senate's standing rules require unanimous consent for any motion to submit a bill for floor consideration, allowing just one senator to block consideration of a bill by placing an anonymous **hold** on the legislation. Usually, a hold is resolved through bipartisan negotiations between party leaders, but if the negotiations fail, the hold can become a filibuster, which can only be ended by a successful cloture motion. Importantly, any method of resolving a hold requires the support of more than just a simple majority.

Ratification and Confirmation Roles

Article II authorizes the president of the United States to make treaties and to nominate judges and other public officials with the "advice and consent" of the Senate. (The House plays no role in either process.) For treaty ratification, a supermajority of two-thirds approval of the Senate is required; for confirmation of judicial and executive branch nominees, only simple majority approval is required.

The Senate utilizes the preexisting committee system for both treaty ratifications and appointment confirmations. As with legislation, these matters sometimes stall in committee. In 2016, for example, the Republican-controlled Senate Judiciary Committee simply refused to consider Democratic President Barack Obama's Supreme Court nominee Merrick Garland, allowing the nomination to expire at the end of President Obama's second term and paving the way for the confirmation of newly elected Republican President Donald Trump's nominee, Neil Gorsuch.

Like legislation, treaty ratifications and appointment confirmations are subject to unlimited floor debate in the full Senate and require a successful cloture motion to end debate and proceed to a vote. Due to recent rule changes, however, judicial and executive branch nominations require only a simple majority to invoke cloture, rather than the three-fifths majority required for legislation.

Budget Process

One of the primary objectives of the legislative branch is to pass an operating budget for the federal government. The expenses in the federal budget can be divided into three primary categories: mandatory spending, discretionary spending, and interest payments on debt. **Mandatory spending** refers to the government's preexisting financial obligations under entitlement programs like Social Security and Medicare. The cost of these programs cannot be reduced without amending their original authorizations, a step that is typically seen as politically unpopular. In 2016, mandatory spending accounted for approximately 64 percent of the federal budget.

Discretionary spending refers to any other expenditures of the federal government (except for debt payments). As its name implies, discretionary spending is optional; the amount of discretionary spending is determined by the annual budget process. In 2016, discretionary spending accounted for approximately 24 percent of the federal budget.

When setting the budget, Congress initially establishes an overall level of discretionary spending. Then, each house refers the matter to its Appropriations Committee, which determines how to allocate discretionary spending among the various federal agencies and programs. As with other legislation, the final budget must be approved by each house of Congress and signed by the president before it can take effect.

✔ AP Expert Note

Be prepared t explain the history of congressional funding practices

The AP exam will expect you to know not just the definition of a process, but also deeper details like how it came to be and how it is viewed today. For example, **earmarking**, the practice of allocating funding to a specific government program, has recently come under fire. It is often criticized as unnecessary spending, especially when it benefits a small number of people—usually voters in the home district of the legislator who proposed the earmark—at the expense of all taxpayers. This type of earmark is referred to as **pork barrel** spending, or pork, and historically it was difficult to avoid because of the back-and-forth bargaining that characterized the budget process, known as **log rolling**. However, within the past decade, several highly publicized examples of pork barrel spending were viewed as evidence of government waste; as a result, earmarking became politically unfavorable, and Congress banned the practice in 2011.

Because mandatory spending comprises such a large portion of the federal budget, it significantly impacts the ability of Congress to pass a balanced budget—that is, a budget in which the government's revenues are equal to its expenditures. As entitlement programs increase in cost, Congress effectively has three options to address the potential imbalance between federal revenues and expenditures:

- Reduce discretionary spending
- Increase tax revenues
- Permit a budget deficit

While both Democrats and Republicans often cite balancing the federal budget as a fiscal goal, in practice it has proven difficult to do so in the modern political era. Budget surpluses, when government revenues exceed expenditures, have occurred, but they have been rare. Instead, the federal budget usually runs at a deficit, and unless discretionary expenses are reduced or taxes are increased, this trend is likely to continue.

9

Effectiveness

Models of Political Representation

In a representative democracy like the United States, voters elect legislators to represent their interests rather than participate directly in the legislative process themselves. Three models of representation are commonly used to describe the different approaches that legislators may take regarding their roles as representatives of the people.

- In the **trustee model** of representation, voters choose a representative who is entrusted with the authority to use his or her own judgment. Under this model, representatives are justified in voting counter to the preferences or interests of their constituencies if they believe that doing so will promote the common good.

- In the **delegate model** of representation, representatives are obligated to vote according to the preferences of their constituencies; they have no authority to substitute their own judgment for that of the voters who elected them.

- The **politico model** of representation is a hybrid theory that incorporates elements of both the trustee and delegate paradigms. The politico model attempts to describe how elected representatives actually behave in practice. In this model, representatives will sometimes act as delegates, usually on issues that are especially important to their constituents, and some-times act as trustees, often when their constituents lack an informed opinion on the matter.

Assessing the effectiveness of an individual representative, or that of an entire legislative body like Congress, often depends on which theory of representation is endorsed by the entity making the assessment. For example, a critic who advocates for the delegate model of representation would likely disapprove of a senator who routinely votes against the express interests of her constituents, but the same senator might be lauded for voting her conscience by a commentator who subscribes to the trustee model of representation.

Political Gridlock

To the extent that the effectiveness of Congress depends on its ability to pass laws and otherwise "get things done," political gridlock represents a failure of Congress to function effectively. The following situations represent common scenarios for political stalemates.

- Each house of Congress is controlled by a different party, and they are routinely unable to compromise; as a result, legislation that passes one house is often unable to pass the other.

- The president is a member of a different party than the majority party of one or both houses of Congress, causing their legislative priorities to conflict. This is especially likely to cause gridlock when the majority party in Congress lacks enough votes to override a presidential veto.

- Even when the House, the Senate, and the presidency are all held by the same party, the minority party in the Senate can filibuster legislation favored by the majority party and prevent it from reaching the president's desk.

One commonly cited explanation for the recent increase in partisanship is **gerrymandering**, the practice of drawing boundary lines for legislative districts so as to favor the party in charge of the redistricting process. Redistricting occurs in every state following the decennial federal census for one of two reasons. If a state gains or loses a House district due to changes in its population, it must redraw its electoral map to accommodate its new number of districts. Even if the number of its districts has not changed, a state must redraw the boundaries of its existing districts using updated census data so that each district is roughly equal in population.

Article I of the Constitution grants each state legislature the power to determine how it will administer federal elections within its borders, including the redistricting process. Thus, the party that controls the legislature controls the redistricting process, and that party often uses its redistricting power to maximize the number of House seats it will control. As a result, fewer House districts are competitive in the general election, magnifying the significance of primary elections. Because the winner of the primary election is typically the one who appeals to the most passionate and ideologically entrenched voters, an increasing number of representatives in the House lack an electoral incentive to compromise, which in turn leads to an increase in the likelihood of political gridlock.

> ✔ **AP Expert Note**
>
> **Know the impact of gerrymandering on electoral outcomes**
>
> The AP exam often tests your understanding of the practical consequences that a key feature or practice has on the political system as a whole. To understand the electoral impact of gerrymandering, it is helpful to know how it might work in practice. There are two primary mechanisms by which a majority party might structure the redistricting process in order to gain a political advantage. The first is "packing," which is the strategy of cramming as many minority party voters as possible into just a handful of districts, known as "majority-minority" districts. The minority party will likely win those seats, but the majority party will have a significant voting advantage in the remaining districts because these districts will contain very few minority party voters. The second is "cracking," which is the strategy of spreading the minority party's voters across as many districts as possible, diluting their strength and potentially preventing the minority party from winning any seats at all. With either strategy, the effect is that the pool of voters within most districts is lopsided in favor of one party or the other.

The Supreme Court has placed some limits on redistricting. In ***Baker v. Carr* (1962)**, the Court first affirmed its authority to review legislative redistricting for constitutional violations. In that case, the Court held that the state of Tennessee's failure to update its redistricting scheme for more than 60 years violated the implicit constitutional principle of "one person, one vote" because, over time, the outdated boundaries had resulted in the overrepresentation of voters in rural districts compared to those in urban districts. Later, in **Shaw v. Reno (1993)**, the Supreme Court prohibited the practice of racial gerrymandering (that is, using race as a factor when drawing the boundary lines for legislative districts).

9.2 THE PRESIDENCY

Powers

LEARNING OBJECTIVE

- Summarize the president's formal and informal powers.

Established by Article II of the Constitution, the **president of the United States (POTUS)** is the head of the executive branch of the federal government. The primary responsibility of the executive branch is to oversee the execution of federal laws, but the president also plays an important role in the legislative process itself: after a bill passes both houses of Congress, it is submitted to the president for approval. In addition, the president serves as the nation's diplomatic head of state and acts as the de facto leader of her political party. As a result, the president uses the express and implied powers of the executive branch to promote a policy agenda.

Formal Powers

The president's formal powers are those that the Constitution has expressly granted to the office of the presidency. Because the framers were concerned about vesting too much authority in a single executive officer, the president's formal powers are limited, and many of them may be exercised only in conjunction with one or both houses of Congress. However, the broad language of the Constitution has allowed custom and practice to define—and in many cases expand—the scope of the president's formal powers.

Veto Power

When a bill has passed both houses of Congress, it must then be presented to the president for signature or **veto**, using a process set forth in the Constitution. Under this process, the president has ten days to consider the bill; if the president signs it, it becomes federal law. Otherwise, the president can exercise veto power by returning the bill to Congress along with a statement of objections. Congress then has the opportunity to override the president's veto by a two-thirds supermajority vote in each house. In practice, due to the supermajority requirement, vetoes are rarely overturned.

If the president fails to sign or veto the bill within the ten-day period, it will become law as if the president had signed it. The only exception occurs when Congress is not in session at the expiration of the ten-day period, at which point the bill effectively dies on the president's desk. This outcome is referred to as a **pocket veto**. Significantly, unlike a formal veto, a pocket veto cannot be overturned because it does not return to Congress for reconsideration and a vote to override the veto. Thus, if the timing is in the president's favor, the president can prevent legislation from taking effect even if the bill had two-thirds support in both houses of Congress.

Military Command

The Constitution designates the president as the **Commander-in-Chief** of the military. Following the precedent established by George Washington, the Commander-in-Chief has no military rank and is considered a civilian leader, ensuring that domestic policy and diplomatic foreign relations are not subordinate to military interests and preventing the military from exerting too much influence over the federal government as a whole. Because no specific duties for this role are prescribed by the Constitution, the scope of the president's role as Commander-in-Chief has fluctuated over time, with some presidents choosing to manage military operations closely and others electing to delegate most of the day-to-day responsibilities to military leaders. Even presidents in the second group, however, have typically opted to exercise their authority over military strategy in high-stakes circumstances.

Foreign Relations

The Constitution grants the president the power to make treaties, with the advice and consent of two-thirds of the Senate, and to appoint ambassadors to represent the United States abroad. In practice, the president, in conjunction with the presidential staff and the State Department, coordinates all official interactions with foreign governments, such as:

- Receiving foreign ambassadors
- Hosting foreign heads of state and other dignitaries visiting the United States
- Negotiating with foreign leaders to promote American interests abroad
- Participating in summit conferences with other heads of state

Informal Powers

The president's informal powers are those that are not expressly granted by the Constitution. Instead, they have developed over time as the circumstances of certain presidencies have resulted in the opportunity or need to expand the scope of the president's authority.

Executive Agreements

The use of **executive agreements** is a prime example of the expansion of the president's authority to conduct foreign relations beyond the express language of the Constitution. Although treaties must be ratified by the Senate, the Supreme Court has held that the president can enter into executive agreements (formal pacts with foreign governments) without the Senate's approval, even though such agreements are not explicitly mentioned in the Constitution. According to the Supreme Court, an executive agreement will have the same legal effect as a treaty so long as the president enters into the agreement under her authority to conduct foreign relations and so long as the agreement does not otherwise violate federal law. Because the process for creating executive agreements is less formal and more expedient than the process for making treaties, executive agreements can be a powerful tool for fostering cooperation with other nations. However, executive agreements only bind the president who signed them and can be rescinded by future presidents who do not wish to adhere to them.

Executive Orders

An **executive order** is a directive issued by the president outside of the legislative process and without express congressional approval. Although the Constitution does not explicitly permit the use of executive orders, the president's authority to issue them derives from the president's express constitutional duty to enforce federal law. The president's ability to make executive orders is somewhat limited: they cannot be used to expand the president's scope of authority beyond those powers delegated to the executive branch by the Constitution or, in some instances, by Congress. However, the president can exert tremendous influence over the operation of the federal government by issuing executive orders that determine how (and to what extent) federal law will be implemented, providing an additional opportunity for the president to shape public policy.

Signing Statements

A **signing statement** is a written statement issued by the president upon signing a bill into law. A signing statement often reveals the president's reasons for signing the bill and opinions on how the language of the bill should be interpreted or implemented by the federal government. Sometimes, the president uses a signing statement to express concern about certain provisions of a bill, indicating that the executive branch will not enforce those provisions or will do so in a limited way. In other instances, the president makes a signing statement for political reasons, such as to encourage public support for the law. Like executive orders, the Constitution does not expressly allow or prohibit signing statements, but the Supreme Court has approved their use. The Supreme Court has yet to determine, however, whether signing statements are part of the legislative record that should be considered when the judicial branch is interpreting the meaning of a law.

Bargaining and Persuasion

The president's ability to promote a policy agenda is directly tied to her aptitude for negotiation: the vast majority of law-making power rests with Congress, and the president is able to exert only indirect influence on the legislative process. For example, the president is unable to introduce legislation in Congress, but he or she can enlist the support of a senator or representative who agrees to introduce legislation consistent with the president's policy vision. Likewise, the president's veto power incentivizes Congress to seek the president's input in the legislative process, since most controversial legislation does not pass Congress with a veto-proof majority.

In addition, many members of Congress are unwilling to engage in a public battle with the president, who occupies a more prominent position in the political landscape and is more likely to "win" a public debate, because a perceived loss could shorten the political career of a representative or senator who challenges the president. For example, a member of the president's party who refuses to advance the president's agenda might lose his next primary election to a challenger who promises to support the president. Similarly, a member of the opposing party in a "swing" district or "swing" state where the president is politically popular may face a strong challenger in the next general election. Because of these electoral pressures, the president is often able to persuade enough members of Congress to support legislation that might otherwise be considered unpopular.

Conflicts with Congress

LEARNING OBJECTIVE

- Identify reasons for tensions between the executive and legislative branches.

A natural tension exists between Congress and the president. By design, each branch of government is meant to serve as a check on the others, leading to conflicts among branches as they navigate the boundaries of their own power and their ability to limit the power of the others.

Judicial Nominations

The power struggle that often occurs during the judicial confirmation process represents a central conflict between the executive and legislative branches. The Constitution directs the president to appoint federal judges with the "advice and consent" of the Senate, so when a vacancy occurs, the president nominates a candidate and the nomination is submitted to the Senate Judiciary Committee for review. Usually, the committee will gather information and eventually hold a confirmation hearing to discuss the candidate's qualifications and judicial philosophy. However, the hearing itself is not explicitly required by the Constitution, and a nomination can stall in committee when it is not supported by the majority party, just as proposed legislation often does. In the past, nominations that made it out of committee could also be filibustered, but due to recent rule changes, judicial nominations are no longer subject to the three-fifths cloture requirement and can be approved by a simple majority of the full Senate.

Arguably, the power to appoint judges is the president's most significant opportunity to build a lasting legacy. Because federal judges are appointed for life, a judicial nominee has the potential to shape federal law and policy well beyond the term of the nominating president. As a result, the Senate tends to regard its role in the process as a significant check on the president's power. Though nominees are typically confirmed when the president and the Senate majority leader belong to the same party, the committee hearing procedure allows members of the minority party to raise concerns about the candidate that can sometimes make it politically inconvenient for the majority party to approve the president's nomination, at which point the president may withdraw the nomination. When the presidency and the Senate are controlled by different parties, the Senate can completely block a president's nomination, though this outcome is rare; in most cases, the president has consulted with Senate majority leaders prior to submitting the nomination in order to choose a nominee that the other party would actually confirm.

9

Executive Branch Nominations

The president is also constitutionally required to seek the advice and consent of the Senate when choosing ambassadors, ministers, consuls, and other public officials. In total, around 1,200 federal executive positions are filled using the nomination and confirmation process, including Cabinet secretaries and agency directors. However, unlike judgeships, these positions are not lifetime appointments; an executive branch nominee, if confirmed, serves at the pleasure of the president and can be removed from office at any time. When a new president is elected, he or she usually dismisses many of these officials and nominates new candidates to fill their posts, especially if the previous president was a member of a different party.

Executive branch nominations are referred to the Senate committee with appropriate jurisdiction—for example, nominations for Secretary of State are submitted to the Foreign Relations Committee—and the committee gathers information about the nominee and holds a confirmation hearing. The confirmation process for executive branch nominations can be contentious, but since these posts are not lifetime appointments, the stakes are lower than for judicial nominees. As with legislation, nominations are sometimes stalled in committee, but historically it has been rare for an executive branch nominee to be rejected in an up-or-down floor vote. Moreover, similar to judicial nominations, executive branch nominations can no longer be filibustered.

> ✔ **AP Expert Note**
>
> **Know the full scope of the president's appointment power**
>
> Not all presidential appointments are subject to the Senate confirmation process. Of the nearly 3,800 appointed positions within the federal government, only about 1,200 require the "advice and consent" of the Senate. The remaining appointments are made solely by the president, allowing the president to handpick appointees that will best implement the president's policy vision, without any congressional input or compromise required.

Recess Appointments

In order to avoid extended vacancies when Congress is not in session, Article II authorizes the president to make recess appointments without the express consent of the Senate. Unless subsequently approved by the Senate, a recess appointment expires at the end of the next legislative session. Historically, recess appointments were fairly common and considered noncontroversial, as Congress was in session for only a few months each year and the president needed to be able to fill vacancies as they arose in order to keep the government operating smoothly.

In modern times, however, Congress is in session for most of the year, significantly reducing the amount of time that a position might stay vacant during a recess. Sometimes, presidents have been accused of purposefully waiting for a brief recess in order to make an appointment because they anticipated a protracted confirmation fight. In order to curb the frequency of recess appointments, the Senate has taken to calling "pro forma" sessions when it would otherwise be in recess. These pro forma sessions are merely procedural devices used to avoid calling a recess; the Senate does not actually conduct any business during a pro forma session. President Barack Obama challenged the use of pro forma sessions to prevent recess appointments, but the Supreme Court upheld the practice in *NLRB v. Noel Canning* (2014).

In theory, Article II allows the president to circumvent a pro forma session and order Congress into recess if the House and the Senate are in disagreement over when to adjourn. This outcome would be especially likely to occur if one house were controlled by the president's political party and the other were not. However, no president has ever exercised this constitutional power.

Policy Disputes

Conflicts between the executive and legislative branches can also arise over policy matters. These disputes are more likely to occur when the White House and at least one house of Congress are controlled by different parties. In such situations, it can be difficult for legislation supported by the president to move through the legislative process because the party controlling the committee system can stall such legislation indefinitely; similarly, legislation that passes Congress without bipartisan support may be vetoed by the president. However, there are incentives for the president and Congress to work together to resolve policy disputes.

Confirmation Process	The president has an incentive to cooperate with the Senate majority leader on policy matters in exchange for more favorable treatment of judicial and executive branch nominees. Conversely, the Senate can leverage its confirmation power to induce a president not to veto important legislation.
Veto Power	When a bill has majority support but not enough support to override a presidential veto, congressional leaders have an incentive to consult with the president and write (or rewrite) legislation that the president is more likely to sign.
Public Opinion	In the event of a legislative stalemate, public support for elected officials often decreases. This concern tends to affect Congress more acutely than the White House, but both branches have an incentive to resolve their differences in order to demonstrate that they can cooperate and accomplish goals despite the partisan divide.
Electoral Considerations	Members of Congress who challenge a politically popular president can undermine their own reelection efforts, as voters will be less willing to support senators or representatives who they see as preventing the president from implementing her policy vision. In particular, members of the president's party risk losing party support during their next campaign, including financial support and endorsements from the president or other party leaders.

Changing Roles

LEARNING OBJECTIVE

- Demonstrate how the president's role has changed throughout history.

The nature of the president's role has changed over time; in particular, the scope of the president's power has gradually expanded despite efforts by Congress and the Supreme Court to limit the president's authority.

Constitutional Origins

For many of the delegates to the Constitutional Convention, one of the more significant defects of the **Articles of Confederation** was its lack of a single executive officeholder, separate from the legislative branch, who could serve as the nation's de facto political and diplomatic leader. At the same time, however, the delegates had to balance their desire to remedy this defect against the concern that consolidating power within a single authority would eventually lead to the establishment of an American monarchy—exactly the type of government they were seeking to avoid. Ultimately, the delegates opted to create the office of the presidency: a single executive authority with a limited role in the legislative process who would serve as the nation's Commander-in-Chief and who, with the consent of the Senate, would appoint judges and other officials to assist with "faithfully executing" federal law.

> ### ✔ AP Expert Note
>
> **Be able to spot connections between current political institutions and historic debates**
>
> The idea of having a U.S. president who serves as a single executive was a contested subject when the American political system was being decided. One of the most notable arguments for the creation of a single executive was made by Alexander Hamilton in *Federalist* 70. Hamilton reasoned that it would be safer to vest the executive power in one person than in a group of people because one person could not easily conceal mistakes by blaming co-executives, leading to greater accountability and an incentive for the executive to work to maintain the public's trust. Hamilton also contended that a single leader would have the "energy" required for the role because this individual would be able to act quickly and decisively without the need to confer with others. As a result, *Federalist* 70 is often cited as a justification for the expansion of presidential authority, especially in times of war or other crises.

In order to protect the presidency from corruption or other undue influences, including those that might cause the presidency to devolve into a monarchy or dictatorship, the framers established the following constitutional restraints on the office:

- Presidential terms are four years, and presidents who wish to serve longer must seek reelection.

- Presidents are not elected by popular vote but are instead chosen by the Electoral College, which is made up of representatives selected by each state and which the framers intended as an additional check on the president's power.

- Presidents must be natural-born citizens and must have actually lived in the United States for at least 14 years prior to seeking office. The intent was to limit the potential for inappropriate foreign influence.

Expansions of Presidential Power

The scope of the president's authority has expanded significantly since the Constitution was initially adopted. The framers did not trust a single, powerful leader and made almost all executive powers contingent on congressional involvement, but over time presidents have found justifications for acting unilaterally, often during a war or other crisis.

For example, during the early days of the Civil War, President Lincoln suspended the writ of habeas corpus, a legal mechanism used by people who have been arrested or imprisoned to petition a court for their release; as a result, federal prisoners could be held indefinitely without trial. The suspension of habeas corpus was challenged by a prisoner of war, and a court of appeals held that Lincoln's actions were unconstitutional on the grounds that only Congress is permitted to suspend habeas corpus. Lincoln ignored the ruling, arguing that it was necessary and constitutionally appropriate for him to have acted in light of the urgency of the situation, especially since Congress could not safely convene due to the war. Ultimately, Congress agreed and passed the Habeas Corpus Suspension Act of 1863, which authorized the president to suspend habeas corpus as he deemed necessary for the duration of the war. Several subsequent presidents—most notably Ulysses S. Grant, Franklin Delano Roosevelt, and George W. Bush—have also suspended habeas corpus with congressional authorization, to varying degrees of legal and political success.

Other prominent examples of the expansion of presidential power include authorizing the military to engage in protracted armed conflicts without a formal declaration of war from Congress, such as during the Vietnam War; issuing greater numbers of executive orders that affect substantive policy making; and creating special commissions that expand the investigative functions of the bureaucracy beyond those authorized by Congress.

> ✔ **AP Expert Note**
>
> **Be prepared to discuss both sides of major issues, such as recent increases in presidential power**
>
> The expansion of presidential authority has prompted some criticism, and the AP exam will expect you to be able to discuss both sides of the debate. Some scholars argue that the framers intended to create a strong executive, while others claim that modern presidents have too much power and believe that presidential authority should be curtailed. See the following table for some evidence for each side; understanding the rationale for both positions will allow you to demonstrate the kind of evenhanded reasoning that will earn you points on the official exam.

9

Benefits of a Strong Executive	Benefits of a Limited Executive
• Can act quickly and decisively when needed (e.g., during a time-sensitive crisis such as a terrorist attack)	• Cannot act without consensus from the legislative branch, preventing a single person from gaining too much control over the policy-making process
• Serves as a much-needed central authority figure in matters of diplomacy and military strategy	• Cannot act on a whim because consensus building is a built-in check that prevents impulsive decision making
• Can adapt to changing circumstances, including technological innovations that impact warfare, more easily than a large group of legislators	• Promotes stability and respect for the rule of law due to the executive's inability to make unilateral decisions
• Unites the country as the only nationally elected public official other than the vice president	

Limits on Presidential Power

The following examples are instances in which Congress or the Supreme Court has used the Constitution to restrict presidential power.

Term Limits

Originally, the Constitution did not place any **term limits** on the office of the presidency. However, George Washington established an unofficial precedent when he declined to run for a third term, and for the next century, most presidents elected to a second term followed this tradition. Ulysses Grant and Theodore Roosevelt were each notable exceptions who sought a third term in office, but Franklin Roosevelt was the first (and only) president to actually achieve the feat, and he kept going: FDR was elected for a third term in 1940 and a fourth term in 1944. (FDR died in office less than a year later.)

In response to Franklin Roosevelt's departure from the two-term tradition, Congress sought to place term limits on the office of the presidency by approving the **Twenty-Second Amendment**, which was officially adopted in 1951. The amendment formalized the two-term tradition by prohibiting the same person from being elected president more than twice; in addition, presidents who serve more than two years of their predecessor's term are only eligible to run for election once. Thus, most presidents are limited to two terms, or eight years, in office, and ten years is the maximum term length for presidents who assume office due to the incapacitation, death, resignation, or impeachment of their predecessors. Significantly, the presidency is the only federal office currently subject to term limits. The passage of the Twenty-Second Amendment reflects the special concerns that arise when a singular executive deviates from tradition, as FDR did when he successfully ran for a third and fourth term.

Line-item Veto

The **line-item veto** refers to the ability of an executive power, such as the president, to veto specific provisions of a bill while signing the other provisions into law. As the Constitution does not expressly authorize the use of the line-item veto, its constitutionality is a matter of considerable debate. It is generally agreed that the line-item veto is not an inherent constitutional power of the president, but experts are split as to whether Congress may authorize the president to use it.

Many presidents have sought the power of the line-item veto, but Bill Clinton is the first (and only) president to have used it, following the passage of the Line Item Veto Act of 1996. The purpose of the law was to reduce pork barrel spending by granting the president the authority to cancel individual appropriations in a budget bill. However, it was politically controversial and was soon challenged in court by several organizations that had been denied their earmarked funding due to President Clinton's use of the line-item veto. Ultimately, the Line Item Veto Act was ruled unconstitutional by the Supreme Court in *Clinton v. City of New York* (1998) on the grounds that it gave the president the power to unilaterally amend or repeal legislation passed by Congress, in violation of the presentment clause of Article I.

The Evolving Bully Pulpit

LEARNING OBJECTIVE

- Cite technological advancements that presidents use to communicate.

The presidential **bully pulpit** refers to the president's unique ability to capture the attention of the public due to his position as the sole executive leader in the United States. The term was coined by Theodore Roosevelt, for whom the word *bully* was a synonym for *excellent*. The bully pulpit is a good example of the president's informal power of bargaining and persuasion: the simple fact that the president is the president means that people will pay attention to what this individual has to say.

Over time, technology has improved the president's ability to communicate with the public as well as with the other branches of government, increasing the significance of the bully pulpit. One notable example of this phenomenon is the president's State of the Union address. During the earliest presidential administrations, the State of the Union was delivered to Congress as a written report. Over time, it became more common for presidents to visit Congress and give a speech instead. In 1947, President Harry Truman delivered the first televised State of the Union address. Today, the State of the Union is an annual event viewed by 40 to 60 million people, giving the president the opportunity to share a vision for the country with a much wider audience than the pre-television era would have allowed.

> ✔ **AP Expert Note**
>
> **Be able to explain how the rise of social media has impacted modern politics**
>
> The AP exam often asks you to explain how current social and cultural trends influence politics. One recent example of this phenomenon is the rise of the Internet and how it has expanded the president's ability to communicate with constituents directly. Through social media platforms, especially Twitter, recent presidents Barack Obama and Donald Trump have been able to make short public statements more frequently, interact with their constituents on a more personal level, and react to events in real time. However, communication via social media may ultimately lead to heightened partisanship. People who rely exclusively on social media for their political news may find themselves in a proverbial echo chamber; as a result, they may be less likely to consider alternative points of view on controversial issues and less likely to support political candidates who promote consensus and compromise.

9.3 THE COURTS

Judicial Review

LEARNING OBJECTIVE

- Summarize the constitutional and legal basis for the development of judicial review.

The federal court system is the judicial branch of the federal government. Article III of the Constitution establishes the **Supreme Court of the United States (SCOTUS)** and authorizes Congress to create "inferior" courts at its discretion. Today, the federal court system consists of 94 trial courts (known as district courts) and 13 appellate courts (known as courts of appeal) in addition to the Supreme Court.

The primary purpose of the federal court system is to adjudicate disputes that arise under federal law. In some cases, these disputes concern the constitutionality of actions taken by the government; for example, a defendant charged with a federal crime might argue that Congress exceeded its constitutional authority when it passed the law that criminalized the defendant's actions. The federal court system's ability to decide these types of cases, known as **judicial review**, is an important feature of the system of checks and balances, but it is not expressly authorized by the Constitution. Instead, the constitutionality of judicial review was defended by *Federalist* 78 and formally established by the Supreme Court in the landmark case of *Marbury v. Madison* (1803).

Federalist *78*

Federalist **78**, authored by Alexander Hamilton, is one of several *Federalist Papers* that discusses the role of the judicial branch. In number 78, Hamilton addresses the concern expressed by some that permitting the courts to declare laws invalid would elevate the judicial branch above the other branches of government. In response, Hamilton confirms that the courts will have the power to void unconstitutional laws and defends the practice, asserting that Congress cannot be expected to police its own authority. Instead, Hamilton argues that judges should have the limited power to invalidate laws that conflict with the Constitution, while also reassuring his contemporaries that the judicial branch is the "weakest" branch of government and that the power to invalidate laws does not carry the same potential for harm as the legislative and executive powers of taxation and criminal prosecution.

Although some have questioned whether the framers of the Constitution intended to authorize the courts to engage in judicial review, Hamilton's defense of the practice in *Federalist* 78 indicates that judicial review was generally understood to have been an implicit power of the judicial branch from the time that the Constitution was first adopted.

Marbury v. Madison

High-Yield

The central dispute in **Marbury v. Madison** (1803) arose from the contentious presidential election of 1800. President John Adams, who had been voted out of office, attempted to nominate as many of his supporters as possible to lifetime appointments within the federal government before his term expired. William Marbury was one of these last-minute appointees, and his nomination was quickly confirmed by the Senate. The outgoing Secretary of State, however, was unable to deliver Marbury's commission to him before Adams's term ended, and the new Secretary of State, James Madison, refused to release it. Marbury then filed a lawsuit against Madison in the Supreme Court, alleging that the Judiciary Act of 1789 had granted the Supreme Court original **jurisdiction** to issue an order, known as a writ of mandamus, to compel Madison to deliver the commission and allow Marbury to take office.

In the Court's written opinion, Chief Justice John Marshall agreed that Marbury had the right to his commission and that the language of the Judiciary Act of 1789 had clearly granted the Supreme Court the authority to issue writs of mandamus. However, Marshall determined that the Court could not issue the writ because the Judiciary Act of 1789 had unconstitutionally expanded the original jurisdiction of the Supreme Court beyond the scope of Article III. Marshall declared it was "iron logic" that the Constitution would prevail when a conflict arose between the Constitution and other federal law; moreover, Marshall asserted the authority of the Supreme Court to adjudicate such a conflict by declaring that it was "emphatically the province and duty of the judicial department to say what the law is." Thus, the doctrine of judicial review was formally established.

Ultimately, the decision in *Marbury v. Madison* was significant in two respects. First, by asserting the constitutional imperative of judicial review, Marshall confirmed an important check on the legislative and executive branches: if either branch exceeds the scope of its constitutional authority, the court system can effectively void the law, regulation, or executive order that violates the Constitution. Second, Marshall strengthened the role of the federal courts in a masterful way. Formalizing the power of judicial review expanded the scope of the court system's constitutional authority, but the fact that Marshall was able to do so while striking down a law that had enlarged the Supreme Court's jurisdiction lent legitimacy to the potentially controversial decision.

Legitimacy

LEARNING OBJECTIVE

- State past and present challenges to SCOTUS legitimacy.

Because federal judges are appointed, rather than elected, and serve lifetime tenures, their philosophical legitimacy is sometimes questioned. Their authority is especially likely to be challenged when they issue rulings that impact a controversial political or ideological dispute. For example, following the Supreme Court's decision in *Bush v. Gore* (2000), many people criticized the majority opinion that halted the recounts in Florida, alleging that the ruling was influenced by partisan bias and that it effectively delivered the presidency to George W. Bush. This concern was reinforced by the observation that the vote to stop the recounts was split along party lines: the five justices appointed by Republican presidents voted to end the recount, while the four justices appointed by Democratic presidents voted to continue it.

Whether valid or not, the criticism of the Supreme Court following *Bush v. Gore* indicated that public support for its authority was waning. In response, current Chief Justice John Roberts has openly prioritized the depoliticization of the Court, promoting consensus among the justices when possible and attempting to avoid making controversial decisions along party lines. However, this objective also meets with criticism; some contend that decisions should be made based on the law itself, not to avoid the appearance of partisan bias. Though the results have been mixed, the efforts themselves demonstrate the Court's awareness of and attempts to preserve its own legitimacy in the eyes of the public.

The Role of Precedent

One legal doctrine that significantly impacts the legitimacy of the court system is the long-standing tradition of **stare decisis**, which holds that **precedent**, once established, should not be reversed except in the most extraordinary circumstances. Adherence to the self-limiting doctrine of *stare decisis* promotes the stability of the court system: decisions made are almost always consistent with precedent, and when changes occur, they are often gradual. In this sense, *stare decisis* can be used to defend the court system's legitimacy, as it demonstrates the judiciary's commitment to consistent, predictable results.

However, critics charge that under *stare decisis*, current and future generations are bound by the rulings of previous jurists, even if they are later judged to be misguided or illogical. For example, the Supreme Court's approval of "separate but equal" racial segregation in *Plessy v. Ferguson* (1896) remained the law of the land for nearly 60 years until it was overturned by *Brown v. Board of Education* (1954); if the Court had not chosen to overlook the principle of *stare decisis*, the decision in *Brown v. Board of Education* would have been to continue to support segregation. Today, many opponents of the decision in *Roe v. Wade* (1973) contend that the unwillingness of the Supreme Court to reverse itself on abortion rights illustrates the problem of *stare decisis*.

Another concern that some critics of *stare decisis* raise is that the doctrine may be applied inconsistently, with justices choosing which precedents to maintain and which to overturn based on their own ideological beliefs. Some detractors even go so far as to argue that the doctrine should be abandoned altogether, as it interferes with a judge's ability to determine objectively what the law is. Its defenders, however, point out that *stare decisis* is a guiding principle, not an absolute mandate, and that many Supreme Court precedents later determined to have been decided wrongly (such as *Plessy v. Ferguson*) have been overturned on sound legal grounds rather than for philosophical or ideological reasons.

> ✔ **AP Expert Note**
>
> **Know the arguments for and against key political principles**
>
> The AP exam makers will often ask you to demonstrate your understanding of the advantages and disadvantages of a particular approach to government, politics, or the law. For a key principle like *stare decisis*, it is important to know not only what it is, but also what reasons are typically given for and against its use by the court system. Throughout this book, there are many examples of other significant ideas that are commonly debated; be sure to focus on the reasoning given by both sides as you review each example.

Another key feature of precedent is that lower courts are bound by the decisions of higher courts. Accordingly, Supreme Court decisions are considered binding precedent, and the judges who preside over other federal courts have to follow them. This aspect of precedent is generally considered noncontroversial, though the staunchest critics of *stare decisis* might argue that it further entrenches wrongly decided precedent into the legal system. Either way, this principle demonstrates the scope of the Supreme Court's authority over the judicial branch.

Judicial Activism versus Judicial Restraint

High-Yield

The ongoing debate between the opposing philosophies of judicial activism and judicial restraint is another factor influencing the legitimacy of the Supreme Court.

Judicial Activism

Judicial activism refers to the belief that a court need not defer to elected officials, nor adhere to established precedent, when engaging in judicial review; instead, a court can use contemporary notions of fairness and equality, as well as changed circumstances, to decide whether or not a law is constitutional.

Judicial activism is generally associated with the political philosophy of liberalism, which holds that the primary purpose of government is to promote justice and equality. Proponents of judicial activism point to the broad, idealistic language of the Constitution as evidence that the framers intended future generations to interpret key constitutional principles such as fairness and equality in light of modern standards and circumstances. Moreover, they believe that the court system is in the best position to safeguard these fundamental constitutional principles from the whims of the majority because judges, who are not subject to the electoral process, are less concerned with political popularity than are members of the legislative and executive branches.

Because of its focus on individual and civil rights such as liberty and equality, the philosophy of judicial activism encourages judges to engage in judicial review and tends to lead to more laws being struck down as unconstitutional. A recent example of judicial activism is the Supreme Court's decision in *Obergefell v. Hodges* (2015), which held that it is unconstitutional for states to deny same-sex couples the right to marry. The Court's decision was based on the Fourteenth Amendment, which was adopted in 1868 and contains no express or implied indication that it was intended to prohibit discrimination based on sexual orientation. Instead, the Court relied on the principles of personal dignity, autonomy, and equality enshrined in the equal protection and due process clauses to justify its conclusion that the Fourteenth Amendment forbids states from prohibiting same-sex marriage.

Judicial Restraint

Judicial restraint is the belief that the courts should generally defer to the judgment of the legislative and executive branches and avoid striking down laws unless they are clearly unconstitutional. Judicial restraint is strongly associated with the political philosophy of conservatism, which advocates for limited government and stresses the need for caution when changing the status quo. Proponents of judicial restraint, who emphasize that the government's authority is derived from the people, contend that the power to define the Constitution should rest primarily with the branches of government that are most directly accountable to the people. According to their reasoning, the legislative and executive branches are better suited for this task than the unelected judges who make up the judiciary.

A commonly cited example of judicial restraint is the Supreme Court's decision in *Gibbons v. Ogden* (1824), in which the Court affirmed that the authority of Congress to regulate interstate commerce includes the power to regulate navigation, deferring to the legislative branch rather than adopting a strict interpretation of the relevant constitutional language. As in this case, the application of judicial restraint often results in an expansion of the authority of the legislative or executive branches of government.

Checks   High-Yield

LEARNING OBJECTIVE

- Explain checks on SCOTUS power.

The executive and legislative branches of government can check the power of the Supreme Court in a variety of formal and informal ways.

Constitutional Amendment

When the Supreme Court issues a decision that interprets the meaning of a constitutional provision, its interpretation of that provision is binding on the other branches of government. Unless the Supreme Court reverses itself in a later case, the only way to overrule its interpretation is through the passage of a constitutional amendment. Since the lengthy amendment process requires at least two levels of supermajority approval, it is rare for the Supreme Court to be overruled in this way, but it has happened in handful of cases. In one notable instance, the Supreme Court's decision in *Dred Scott v. Sandford* (1857), which had held that African Americans should not be considered citizens of the United States, was overruled by the Thirteenth and Fourteenth Amendments, which ended slavery and granted full citizenship rights to all persons born in the United States, respectively.

More commonly, attempts to amend the Constitution following an unfavorable Supreme Court opinion have stalled. For example, after the Supreme Court held in *Texas v. Johnson* (1989) that the free speech protections of the First Amendment extend to flag burning, a Flag Desecration Amendment was introduced in the House of Representatives. If ratified, the amendment would permit Congress to prohibit the practice of flag burning. Although the amendment has widespread public support and has passed the House of Representatives several times, it has failed to garner enough support to pass the Senate. Only after it passed in the Senate would the amendment be able to move on to the state ratification process.

Legislation

Although it cannot overrule the Supreme Court's constitutional interpretations by regular statute, Congress can pass legislation that lessens the impact of an unfavorable Supreme Court decision. When the Supreme Court voids a law for constitutional reasons, Congress will sometimes amend the law to conform to the Supreme Court's ruling. For example, in **Lopez v. United States (1995)**, the Court struck down the Gun-Free School Zones Act of 1990 on the grounds that it exceeded the scope of Congress's authority under the commerce clause; specifically, the Court held that the mere possession of a firearm had not been shown to be sufficiently related to interstate commerce. Congress quickly amended the law to specify that it applies only to firearms that have moved through interstate commerce and, although it has not yet reached the Supreme Court for review, the revised version has been upheld by several courts of appeal. As a result, by making a relatively minor revision, Congress has been able to preserve the substantive policy objective of the law.

Sometimes, Congress is able to use regular legislation to render the Supreme Court's interpretation of a constitutional provision irrelevant. While Congress is not able to expand the scope of its constitutional authority by regular statute, it can pass legislation that limits its power. Thus, even when a law has previously been upheld by the Supreme Court, Congress can not only repeal it but also restrict its own ability to pass such a law again, without resorting to the amendment process.

An example of this type of legislation is the Religious Freedom Restoration Act of 1993 (RFRA), which was passed by Congress in response to the Supreme Court's decision in *Employment Division v. Smith* (1990). The Court held that a "neutral law of general applicability" does not violate the free exercise clause of the First Amendment when it fails to make an exception for religious practices. Public opposition to the decision was remarkably high, prompting Congress to pass RFRA, which requires that laws meet a higher burden for protecting rights under the free exercise clause than the Supreme Court had found constitutionally necessary. While the Supreme Court decided that RFRA requirements could not be enforced against state law in 1997, it upheld the constitutionality of RFRA as it applies to federal law in 2006.

Change of Jurisdiction

Article III outlines the **original jurisdiction** of the Supreme Court and, as the Court itself held in *Marbury v. Madison*, Congress does not have the power to limit or expand the scope of the Supreme Court's original jurisdiction. However, Article III expressly authorizes Congress to regulate the **appellate jurisdiction** of the Supreme Court, and Congress has occasionally exercised this power to insulate its actions from judicial review, a practice known as jurisdiction stripping.

The Supreme Court initially affirmed the constitutionality of jurisdiction stripping in *Ex parte McCardle* (1869). William McCardle, a newspaper publisher who had been arrested for printing "incendiary" articles in violation of the Military Reconstruction Act of 1867, filed a petition for his release in federal district court. When the district court denied his petition, McCardle appealed to the Supreme Court, which had previously been granted appellate jurisdiction to review these types of petitions. However, after McCardle's case was heard by the Supreme Court but before a decision had been issued, Congress passed a law removing the Supreme Court's appellate jurisdiction in such cases. Ultimately, the Supreme Court issued an opinion affirming the constitutionality of the new law and, accordingly, declined to rule on McCardle's claim because it lacked jurisdiction in the case.

Although Congress has the authority to limit the Supreme Court's appellate jurisdiction, it cannot do so retroactively. Once a case has been decided, Congress cannot strip it of its impact by removing the Supreme Court's jurisdiction to have heard the case in the first place. Instead, it can only restrict appellate jurisdiction before a decision has been issued, even if, as in the McCardle case, the Supreme Court has already heard arguments in the case and a decision is imminent.

Confirmation Process

The nomination and confirmation process serves as an advance check on the power of the judicial branch, giving the president and the Senate the ability to vet the qualifications and judicial philosophies of prospective jurists. Because federal judges enjoy lifetime tenure, this process is the only real opportunity to keep unqualified or ideologically unsuitable judges from serving on the federal bench. (While judges are subject to impeachment if they commit "high crimes or misdemeanors," judicial impeachments are rare and cannot be used to remove incompetent or politically unfavorable judges from the bench.)

Although all federal judges are subject to the nomination and confirmation process, Supreme Court nominees tend to receive the most scrutiny from the president, the Senate, and the public. While most nominees are ultimately confirmed, the process is often grueling and can lead to nominees choosing to withdraw their own nominations. For example, Harriet Miers, an attorney who was nominated to the Supreme Court by Republican President George W. Bush, withdrew her nomination after she faced severe criticism from within the Republican Party; the party argued she could not be trusted to consistently represent conservative principles while serving on the Supreme Court because she had no prior judicial experience.

Defiance

Though defiance is not a formal power, the legislative or executive branches could theoretically express their objection to a Supreme Court ruling by refusing to follow or enforce it. Arguably, such an instance of defiance would significantly undermine the system of checks and balances, as that system depends on each branch of government to respect the authority of the others. Notably, in the history of the United States, no executive or legislative officeholder is known to have defied a Supreme Court order, though there have been a few instances when defiance was threatened or when the Supreme Court was at least concerned about the possibility.

For example, the decision in *Marbury v. Madison* may have been influenced by Chief Justice John Marshall's concern that Madison, if ordered to deliver Marbury's commission, might simply have refused. Similarly, following the Supreme Court's decision in *Worcester v. Georgia* (1832), President Andrew Jackson is famously said to have exclaimed, "John Marshall has made his decision; now let him enforce it!" which indicated Jackson's endorsement of defiance as a valid political tool. However, the ruling in that case ordered the state of Georgia, not President Jackson, to release a convicted prisoner, and Georgia ultimately complied with the ruling.

9.4 THE BUREAUCRACY

The Fourth Branch?

LEARNING OBJECTIVE

- Detail the primary characteristics of the federal bureaucracy.

The **bureaucracy** is the administrative arm of the federal government. An extension of the executive branch, the bureaucracy consists of the cabinet departments, agencies, commissions, and government corporations that have been charged with the responsibility to manage the implementation and enforcement of federal law. As the head of the executive branch, the president is also the head of the bureaucracy; however, the bureaucratic system is so complex that most of the day-to-day operations are managed by the employees of each organization.

The federal bureaucracy has a strict hierarchical structure with a clear chain of command: each organization contains multiple levels of management, with each level subordinate to the ones above it. The entire system is massive, containing hundreds of organizations and millions of workers, but its highly organized structure helps to keep it functioning reliably. Bureaucrats often

9

specialize in a particular area of their organization's work, allowing them to complete their portion of a task as efficiently as possible; with so many working parts, however, the bureaucracy is often criticized for moving too slowly.

While the highest ranking officials in each bureaucratic organization are political appointees, the vast majority of bureaucratic employees are **civil servants**, workers who have been hired for their education, experience, and other merit-based qualifications rather than their political affiliations, a practice commonly referred to as **patronage**. The crucial switch from a patronage-based system (commonly referred to as the "spoils system") to a **merit-based system** occurred following the passage of the Pendleton Civil Service Reform Act of 1883, which established a competitive exam-based hiring process for government employees in order to combat the problems associated with political cronyism. Initially, the Pendleton Act applied to only a small percentage of government positions, but over time the scope of its coverage has been expanded to include most of the bureaucracy.

The switch to merit-based hiring has resulted in a bureaucracy that is largely staffed by specialists: workers who are experts in their field. These specialists also experience greater longevity in their careers than their patronage-based predecessors, as federal law protects civil servants from being fired or demoted for political reasons. Thus, bureaucratic employees are able to perform the duties of their jobs without the threat of personal retribution from an unfriendly presidential administration. In return, civil servants can be expected to do their work without regard to their own political beliefs or interests and do not adhere to the policy agenda of the president who appointed them.

Rule-Making Authority

Bureaucratic organizations are tasked with the responsibility of creating **federal regulations**, which are specialized rules that govern the enforcement of federal law. The development of new regulations is governed by the **rule-making process**, a procedure designed to promote fairness, transparency, and oversight in the creation of bureaucratic regulations. The following steps outline the rule-making process:

1. Congress passes a new law that delegates rule-making authority to one of the federal bureaucratic organizations.

2. The designated agency drafts a set of proposed rules and publishes them in the *Federal Register*, an official repository of proposed and final regulations.

3. A public comment period commences, during which interested parties may make comments regarding the proposed rules. In the modern era, these comments can be submitted online through a government website.

4. Once the comment period ends, the agency issues its final rules; however, they do not take effect immediately.

5. Before the final rules are implemented, Congress is given the opportunity to review them and make changes. Any changes made by Congress have to go through the typical legislative process: passage by both houses of Congress and the president's signature (or a veto override).

6. If Congress takes no action, the final rules are published in the *Code of Federal Regulations* and have the same legal effect as federal law.

Once a set of final regulations has been implemented, an agency may issue interpretive rules or policy statements to help the public understand the impact of the new rules. The agency may also publish its own internal guidance documents to assist its employees in the implementation and enforcement of the new rules. Interpretive rules, policy statements, and other guidance documents are binding only to the extent that they accurately reflect the regulation or law on which they are based. Because they have the same legal effect as laws, regulations are also subject to judicial review.

Enforcement

Bureaucratic agencies have significant enforcement powers. When an agency deems that a party is not in compliance with federal regulations, the agency can take a variety of adverse actions against the party to induce compliance, such as withholding a benefit, revoking a license, or issuing a fine. For example, the Environmental Protection Agency (EPA) can fine a business that violates the EPA's clean air regulations.

Bureaucratic organizations also participate in administrative adjudication, the process of resolving disputes that arise under federal regulations. Each agency or other organization has its own quasi-judicial department that specializes in administrative law. Disputes may initially be adjudicated by frontline workers or their supervisors, but if a party appeals, the case is assigned to an administrative law judge (ALJ) who uses the text of relevant laws and regulations as well as applicable precedent to reach a decision. The agency itself may have one or two more levels of review, but ultimately it will issue a final determination in the matter. The final agency determination is subject to review by the federal courts if one of the parties files an appeal.

Authority

LEARNING OBJECTIVE

- Explain ways in which federal bureaus use discretionary and rule-making authority.

The implementation and enforcement powers of the bureaucracy derive from its rule-making authority and its discretionary authority. The bureaucracy's **rule-making authority** refers to its ability to implement federal law by creating regulations pursuant to the rule-making process; the bureaucracy's **discretionary authority** refers to its ability to enforce those regulations by determining whether or not they are being followed, often through the administrative adjudication process.

Because the power to make laws rests with the legislative branch, and because bureaucratic regulations, once finalized, have the same legal effect as federal laws, the bureaucracy's rule-making authority is often cited as an example of **delegation**; that is, Congress has delegated its authority to make laws to the bureaucracy. There are two primary justifications for this delegation of power to the bureaucracy:

- Volume. Requiring Congress to pass laws with the same degree of specificity as federal regulations would overwhelm the legislative branch; regulations are so vast and complex that Congress would not be able to keep up with the work and still perform its other duties.

- Expertise. Many bureaucrats, especially those involved in the rule-making process, are experts in their field; thus, they are better suited for the technical aspects of implementing and enforcing laws than are members of Congress.

In order for proper delegation to occur, Congress must pass **enabling legislation**: a law or part of a law granting implementation and/or enforcement authority to a bureaucratic agency. The enabling legislation must also contain a clear guiding principle for the bureaucracy to follow in order for the delegation to be deemed constitutional.

The following table lists some examples of how bureaucratic entities have exercised their rule-making and discretionary powers.

Bureaucratic Entity	Examples of Authority
Department of Homeland Security	Rule-making: Enact regulations that govern the immigration and naturalization process. Discretionary: Approve or deny visa applications and citizenship petitions.
Department of Transportation	Rule-making: Enact regulations that establish standards for airline safety. Discretionary: Investigate airline accidents and issue fines to non-compliant parties.
Department of Veterans Affairs	Rule-making: Enact regulations that can be used to determine whether a veteran qualifies for disability benefits. Discretionary: Evaluate disability applications and decide whether to approve or deny each claim.
Environmental Protection Agency (EPA)	Rule-making: Enact regulations that establish appropriate methods for disposing of hazardous waste. Discretionary: Investigate alleged violations and issue fines to non-compliant entities.
Federal Elections Commission (FEC)	Rule-making: Enact regulations that specify the required format and content of campaign finance disclosures. Discretionary: Audit disclosures and take enforcement action against non-compliant parties.
Securities and Exchange Commission (SEC)	Rule-making: Enact regulations that clearly define insider trading. Discretionary: Enforce insider trading regulations by pursuing administrative prosecutions.

Congressional Oversight

- Identify methods through which Congress may exercise oversight of the federal bureaucracy.

Congressional oversight of the bureaucracy is an implied power and an important component of the system of checks and balances. Since the authority of the bureaucracy results from a delegation of power by the legislative branch, Congress has the ability to review its decisions, make adjustments to the scope of its power, and influence its actions through the use of budgetary incentives.

In addition to its ability to review and vote down new regulations before they take effect, Congress can use the following tools to exercise its oversight function:

- Committee hearings. Congressional committees can hold hearings to review the work of bureaucratic organizations. Hearings are scheduled for a variety of reasons; for example, routine hearings are held to gather information that will assist Congress in the legislative process, including the formation of the budget. Congress may also hold hearings to review how the bureaucracy handled a specific event, such as the hearings held after Hurricane Katrina to evaluate the government's response to the crisis, or to investigate an allegation of wrongdoing made against a bureaucratic entity.

- The power of the purse. The **power of the purse** refers to the ability of Congress, and especially the House of Representatives, to set the budget for the federal government. Congress can appropriate more money to bureaucratic entities that it favors and less money to those that it disfavors. Thus, if a bureaucratic organization wants more funding, it has an incentive to exercise its rule-making and discretionary authority in ways that appeal to members of the majority party in Congress.

Presidential Supervision

- Define specific ways in which the president can influence, and ways the president is limited by, the federal bureaucracy.

As the formal head of the bureaucracy, the president can use his or her authority to influence the implementation and enforcement of federal law in a variety of ways.

Appointment

The president has the authority to appoint senior bureaucrats who are not part of the civil service, and only about a third of these appointments require confirmation by the Senate. As a result, the president is able to handpick many of the executives who lead bureaucratic organizations, allowing the selection of candidates who are ideologically compatible with the president's own policy agenda. Conversely, because political appointees serve at the pleasure of the president, the president can dismiss them if they fail to act in support of the president's policies.

While the president appoints a few thousand senior bureaucrats, the federal bureaucracy has approximately 2.5 million employees. Thus, the vast majority of bureaucratic workers are civil servants, not political appointees. As a result, the president's ability to direct the day-to-day operation of the bureaucracy is limited, as most bureaucratic workers are not necessarily loyal to the president or her policy agenda, nor can they be fired for their political beliefs or their lack of loyalty to the president. Sometimes, tensions between the president and the bureaucracy can escalate significantly; for example, the ongoing investigation of the 2016 election undertaken by civil servants in the FBI has cast a cloud of speculation over the Trump presidency, leading President Trump and many of his supporters to retaliate by questioning the competency and neutrality of the civil service.

Executive Order

In order to streamline the process of managing the bureaucracy and to have an official record of bureaucratic directives, the president can issue executive orders that instruct a bureaucratic entity to take a specific action. For example, the president could request that the Department of Labor issue new regulations regarding overtime pay. The president can also issue executive orders that direct a bureaucratic organization to refrain from acting, such as by instructing the Justice Department not to pursue prosecutions for low-level possession offenses in states that have legalized marijuana. All executive orders are subject to judicial review; if an executive order exceeds the scope of the president's authority to implement or enforce legislation, it will be found unconstitutional.

Oversight

The Office of Management and Budget (OMB) is the federal agency that supervises the implementation of the president's policy vision within the executive branch. The OMB prepares the president's budget proposal to Congress; though Congress is not bound by the president's proposal, the president can nevertheless reward (or penalize) a bureaucratic entity with a favorable (or unfavorable) prospective funding allocation. The OMB also conducts regular oversight of the bureaucracy, evaluating the effectiveness of and setting priorities for the hundreds of bureaucratic organizations within the executive branch. This review process gives the president valuable information that can be used to dismiss underperforming political appointees, appoint new candidates to fill vacant positions, and issue executive orders to promote the president's policy vision.

 **NEXT STEP: PRACTICE**

Go to Rapid Review and Practice Chapter 4 or to your online quizzes on kaptest.com for exam-like practice on this topic.

Haven't registered your book yet? Go to kaptest.com/moreonline to begin.

CHAPTER 10

Civil Liberties and Civil Rights

10.1 THE BILL OF RIGHTS

Liberties vs. Rights

High-Yield

LEARNING OBJECTIVE

- Distinguish between civil liberties and civil rights in the United States.

The **Bill of Rights** is the formal name for the first 10 amendments to the United States Constitution. These amendments set limits on what the government can legally do to citizens and lay out citizens' rights and liberties; this includes some contested concepts that many are familiar with, such as the right to bear arms and the right to free speech. Often, the terms "civil liberties" and "civil rights" are used interchangeably, but in the United States they are legally distinct categories. The easiest way to tell them apart is to think of the difference between *freedom to do* something (civil liberties) and *freedom from* legal discrimination (civil rights).

Civil liberties include the rights in the Bill of Rights, such as freedom of speech. Typically, a **civil liberty** is freedom to do something, such as speak in a public forum or assemble (First Amendment), though some civil liberties are freedoms *not* to do something, like testify against oneself (Fifth Amendment). The common thread connecting these actions is that they originate from the individual, as choices that an individual can make or not make. Sometimes civil liberties are called negative rights, meaning that they keep the government from acting but do not compel the government to protect citizens. The government cannot prevent its citizens from exercising civil liberties without a "compelling interest," such as protecting public safety.

A **civil right** is typically freedom from legal discrimination aimed at a protected group of citizens, commonly called a protected class. Protected classes include those based on age, sex, disability, religious affiliation, race or national origin, and marital status. Protection from discrimination covers both de facto and de jure discrimination. De facto, or "in fact," discrimination results from policies that are not explicitly discriminatory but have a discriminatory result. De jure, or "in law," discrimination is the explicit expression of discriminatory intent in laws.

Civil rights are sometimes called positive rights because the government has an affirmative duty to protect these rights for people in U.S. jurisdiction, rather than merely refraining from action as in the case of civil liberties.

In legal terms, civil rights are distinct from civil liberties insofar as the government cannot make laws that violate civil rights by discriminating against or between protected classes (at least, not without a very good reason). Such protection is the main achievement of laws like the **Civil Rights Act of 1964**; the **Voting Rights Act of 1965**; and the Education Amendments of 1972, which includes **Title IX**, the portion of federal law that prohibits discrimination based on sex in federally funded education programs. The government has an affirmative duty to intervene in discrimination in the private sphere when such discrimination affects members of the protected classes, while its obligations with regard to civil liberties are more limited.

Some actions, such as marriage, can be protected by civil liberties *and* civil rights. You are free to get married, but doing so is not required; in this way marriage is a civil liberty. However, if the government restricts marriage between groups of citizens in protected classes, marriage becomes a civil rights issue. A famous example is the case of *Loving v. Virginia* (1967), in which the Supreme Court overturned Virginia's ban on interracial marriage on equal protection and due process grounds. American citizens are free from racial discrimination with regard to whom they may marry.

Protected Rights and Liberties

LEARNING OBJECTIVE

- Identify the protections in the Bill of Rights.

The Constitution protects citizens' rights in two key ways. First, it guarantees the rights enumerated (explicitly listed) in the Bill of Rights. Additionally, the Constitution protects rights not enumerated through the Tenth Amendment, and it applies some of the rights contained in the Bill of Rights to the states through the Fourteenth Amendment. The following table summarizes the protections afforded by the amendments in the Bill of Rights. (Full text of the Constitution and its amendments is available in the back of this book.)

First Amendment	Protects the freedoms of speech, the press, religion, assembly, and petition for redress of grievances.
Second Amendment	Protects the right to "keep and bear arms," currently interpreted by the Supreme Court as protecting the ability to have handguns in the home for self-defense.
Third Amendment	Prohibits the quartering of troops in private homes.
Fourth Amendment	Prohibits unreasonable searches and seizures and requires probable cause for warrants. The exclusionary rule stems from this amendment.
Fifth Amendment	Protects against self-incrimination and double jeopardy (being tried for the same crime twice), guarantees due process in federal proceedings, specifies a grand jury indictment process for capital crimes, and prohibits the seizure of private property for public use without just compensation.
Sixth Amendment	Specifies an impartial jury in the district where a crime was committed for criminal trials; guarantees the ability of the accused to face the accuser and call witnesses for the defense; guarantees the right to an attorney, currently interpreted to mean that the government must appoint an attorney for defendants who cannot afford one.
Seventh Amendment	Requires a trial by jury in federal civil cases in which damages exceed $20.
Eighth Amendment	Prohibits excessive bail and fines, as well as cruel and unusual punishments.
Ninth Amendment	Specifies that rights that are not enumerated in the Constitution may nonetheless exist.
Tenth Amendment	Reserves powers not expressly delegated to the federal government for the states or the people.

The First and Second Amendments

LEARNING OBJECTIVE

- Cite specific SCOTUS decisions that have affected how the First and Second Amendments have been interpreted.

First Amendment Jurisprudence

The protections for individual liberty granted by the Bill of Rights are not absolute. Rights can sometimes come into conflict, so judicial interpretation is essential for establishing the scope and limits of particular freedoms. For example, in First Amendment **jurisprudence**, the freedom of speech does not protect deliberate falsehoods, direct incitements to violence, or attempts to cause panic (commonly referred to as "shouting 'fire' in a crowded theater"). Indeed, a number of significant Supreme Court holdings have established limits on each of the protections in the First Amendment, including freedom of religion, speech, press, and assembly.

Religion

There are two clauses in the First Amendment concerning religion: the **establishment clause** and the **free exercise clause**. The difference between these is similar to the distinction between civil rights and civil liberties. One prevents the government from doing something, and the other guarantees citizens a choice to do or not do something. In short, the establishment clause prohibits the government from favoring any one religion and from favoring religion over non-religion. The free exercise clause protects citizens' right to religious belief (though the Court has drawn distinctions between the protections for belief, which are absolute, and the protections for action on that belief, which are not). Often in cases about religion, both of these clauses are applicable.

Cases about religion generally employ balancing tests of some kind, weighing the importance of protecting minority religious belief and practice against majoritarian religious expression and social order. As above, the general rule of thumb is that freedom of religious belief is heavily favored, while religious exercise is not as heavily favored.

The establishment clause reads thus: "Congress shall make no law respecting an establishment of religion." The foundational modern case relating to the establishment clause is ***Engel v. Vitale* (1962)**, in which the Court held that school-sponsored prayer was not permissible under the First Amendment; any prayer composed and promoted by school officials violated the establishment clause; a prayer need not be coercive to be in violation of the establishment clause; and any prayer, no matter how vague, privileges religion over non-religion. Subsequent cases have held other religious exercises unconstitutional, such as student-led prayer at a football game and clergy-led prayer at a graduation ceremony.

Another important establishment clause case is *Lemon v. Kurtzman* (1971), in which the Court found unconstitutional a Pennsylvania statute that allowed reimbursement of private schools with public funds, the majority of which went to Catholic schools. From this case came the Lemon test, a three-pronged test for courts to use in judging establishment questions. In establishment clause cases after *Lemon*, the Court has had to balance the public interest against the prohibition on establishment of religion. Decisions have gone both ways; the Court has upheld the use of vouchers for private schools but has consistently struck down displaying the Ten Commandments on monuments outside and inside government buildings.

The free exercise clause forbids Congress from making any law that prohibits the practice of religion. The foundational modern case relating to this clause is *Sherbert v. Verner* (1963), in which the Court held that South Carolina acted unconstitutionally when it denied unemployment benefits to a woman whose religious beliefs prevented her from working on Saturdays. This case produced the Sherbert test, a three-pronged test for courts to use in judging free exercise questions, which requires a similar balancing of interests as in establishment clause cases.

10

Protections in the free exercise clause were extended to students and their parents in *Wisconsin v. Yoder* (1972), which held that Amish parents were exempt from compulsory education statutes because of their religious belief and practice. The Court found that Wisconsin did not have a compelling interest in requiring students to continue beyond the eighth grade, given the deference to religious belief suggested by the First Amendment and the unique nature of Amish society. *Sherbert* and *Yoder* are the only two major cases in which the Court has relied on free exercise claims to overturn a law; the Court is generally deferential to the government in this area.

Speech

First Amendment jurisprudence on speech follows a pattern similar to court decisions regarding other rights: a slow expansion of individual protections, followed by even more robust protections in the early to mid-twentieth century. Foundational cases include the Espionage Act cases from the First World War, notably *Schenck v. United States* (1919). In those cases, Justice Oliver Wendell Holmes Jr. articulated the "clear and present danger" test, which focused not on the content of the speech but on whether the speech presented an immediate danger to legitimate government or societal interests, regardless of the speaker's intent. As with the Sherbert test, the Court balanced the social good against individual freedom.

The Supreme Court then expanded protections for speech, taking into account the speaker's intent and the likelihood of the speech to create a criminal or negative outcome. The landmark case *Tinker v. Des Moines Independent Community School District* (1969) dealt with symbolic speech by students who were protesting U.S. involvement in the Vietnam War by wearing black armbands. *Tinker* held that students' rights under the First Amendment outweighed the desire of school authorities to avoid controversy, as the armbands in question did not "materially and substantially interfere with the requirements of appropriate discipline in the operation of the school." The protections in *Tinker* are not absolute; speech that is merely obscene is not protected, nor is speech that the Court thinks is overly disruptive, as opposed to the silent protest of the *Tinker* plaintiffs.

As with religious freedom, questions of protected speech are subject to balancing tests that weigh the needs of the government against the rights of individuals. This can lead to different results at different times, as external circumstances change. For instance, in wartime, speech restrictions have been heightened; courts have justified these restrictions as necessary for the war effort. In times of peace as well, courts have considered the needs of society when deciding whether to constrain the rights of the individual.

> ✔ **AP Expert Note**
>
> **Know various applications of free speech protections**
>
> The AP exam will expect you to know and be able to discuss the many ways in which free speech is defined. What counts as speech for First Amendment purposes has expanded as the courts have protected the following types of speech through various rulings: political speech, religious speech, symbolic speech (notably, *Tinker v. Des Moines Independent Community School District*), expressive conduct, anonymous speech, and spending as speech (notably, *Citizens United v. Federal Election Commission*).

Press

Freedom of the press protects more than journalists. The Court has held that the freedom of the press encompasses opinion presented for the public across a variety of platforms and media, including books, magazines, radio, television, blogs, and of course, newspapers. First Amendment jurisprudence concerning the press has traditionally focused on the issue of **prior restraint**, which is the practice of a government telling a publication what it can print or air.

An important case considering prior restraint is *New York Times Co. v. United States* **(1971)**, in which the Nixon administration tried to stop the *New York Times* and the *Washington Post* from publishing the Pentagon Papers, which were classified at the time. The Court found that the Nixon administration did not provide sufficient justification that stopping the publication of the leaked papers was a matter of national security and held that the newspapers' right to publish the leaked documents was protected under the First Amendment. In this decision, the Court essentially outlawed prior restraint.

Another important issue for the press is **libel**, which is the printing of false information that is damaging to the reputation of the person or persons identified. In the 1950s and '60s, Southern officials often used threats and libel suits to suppress public reporting on the violent repression of the civil rights movement. The Court held that anyone alleging libel would have to prove actual malice (knowingly publishing something false or publishing something with reckless disregard for the truth or falsity of the claims), thus establishing a very high burden of proof. Requiring plaintiffs to prove something is false and prove that the publication knew or should have known it was false was a departure from earlier standards, which had placed the burden of proving truth on the defendant. The Court has steadfastly strengthened the protections for the press under the First Amendment.

Assembly

The protections on the freedom of assembly have been applied to the states since the 1930s, but they are limited in similar ways to the protections on speech. The government must be content neutral, meaning it cannot prohibit groups from meeting, even if their ideals or statements are generally considered repugnant, as with the Nazi march in Skokie, Illinois, in the 1970s. A contemporary example involves the Westboro Baptist Church, a group that often protests at military funerals to express views that are offensive to many people. The Court has ruled that the government may impose reasonable restrictions on the time, place, and manner of assemblies; for instance, the government may require groups to have a permit or to make security arrangements for very large gatherings. But the government may not prohibit groups or individuals from assembling based on the content of their message, no matter how objectionable many may find it.

Second Amendment Jurisprudence

The Second Amendment has not been litigated as often as the First, given its comparatively limited scope. The Court had not considered it since the 1930s until a recent pair of linked cases, in which it changed the interpretation of the Second Amendment and incorporated this decision to the states. These cases are important, not least because the Court had considered the Second Amendment so rarely before.

The first modern case, *District of Columbia v. Heller* (2008), is a landmark case that held for the first time that citizens have a right to possess handguns, keep the handguns in their homes, and have access to them for purposes of self-defense. The District of Columbia is under federal jurisdiction, so the Bill of Rights applies, but cases dealing with D.C. are not necessarily applicable to the states.

The second case is **McDonald v. City of Chicago (2010)**, which incorporated the protections the Court mandated in *Heller* to the states. Both decisions noted exceptions to the Second Amendment in terms of the types of weapons permissible and the places they could be carried, and the Court noted that guns could be restricted in sensitive areas such as schools and government buildings (including courtrooms).

> ### ✔ AP Expert Note
>
> **Be able to compare and contrast major principles of SCOTUS cases**
>
> Notice that the discussion of the Supreme Court cases *Heller* and *McDonald* drew specific comparisons between the decisions and pointed out how *McDonald* built upon *Heller*. This is the kind of reasoning that you will be expected to demonstrate on the AP exam, particularly in the SCOTUS Comparison free-response question. To this end, be sure to know the ins and outs of each of the 15 required SCOTUS cases, of which *McDonald* is one. (A full list of these cases can be found in the back of this book, and more details about the specific FRQs can be found in Chapter 13.)

Freedom Versus Security

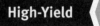

High-Yield

LEARNING OBJECTIVE

- Detail tensions between civil liberties and public safety.

An essential question that courts must consider when dealing with individual liberty claims is the question of public safety. Here again, courts use a balancing test to decide where to draw the line between absolute individual liberty and complete identification with the interests of the state. As a concept, public safety is elastic, and it changes depending on the era in question.

The protections in the First Amendment are relevant to public safety and government interest in a number of ways and are especially sensitive to political concerns, both domestic and international. This political sensitivity can be seen in early limitations on the freedom of speech during wartime, such as in *Schenck*. In times of war or domestic disturbance, the Supreme Court has been quicker to constrain individual speech rights in favor of a government interest. That calculus can change depending on the nature of the conflict, as was evident in *Tinker*.

10

The Second Amendment is more responsive to domestic politics and has obvious implications for public safety and public health. The debate over Second Amendment rights has centered on the types of controls governments can place on individual gun ownership. Some argue that the government should be able to strictly control gun ownership because it is a serious public health issue. Others argue that the government should prioritize individual liberty, having a constitutional duty to ensure access to rights but not to attempt to create positive outcomes. This mirrors the tension between positive and negative conceptions of liberty, in terms of what the government must or must not do to protect individual rights.

The tension between liberty and security is active in discussions about the Fourth Amendment as well. Government surveillance is nothing new, especially at the federal level. The government often spied on domestic opponents of the FBI or other people whom the government saw as a threat, notably in the COINTELPRO program, wherein the FBI worked to surveil and discredit leaders in the civil rights and feminist movements, among others. A contemporary example is the mass surveillance programs run by the National Security Agency (NSA) and disclosed by Edward Snowden in 2013. These programs were notable in that they captured communications by American citizens, in addition to building profiles of metadata: the relevant information about communications without the content itself, such as who sent the communications, to whom they were sent, and what platform was used. Reading communications without a warrant is prohibited by the Fourth Amendment. The government justified the existence of the programs in various ways, claiming they were limited, necessary for national security, and controlled by internal safeguards. Critics have pointed out that the review function of the judiciary cannot be completed when the checks on executive power are controlled by the executive itself.

This type of surveillance is a good example of the tension between civil liberties and public safety. Supporters of government surveillance programs point to the threat of terrorism and argue that the government must do whatever is necessary to protect American citizens. Opponents point to the long American tradition of individual rights, which have been more or less upheld even when the nation has been at war. The Supreme Court has declined to rule on the constitutionality of these programs, and the debate is still ongoing.

Another area of debate is around the treatment of prisoners and what precisely the Constitution means by prohibiting "cruel and unusual punishment" in the Eighth Amendment. The most active area of disagreement has been capital punishment (the death penalty), though there are also substantive disagreements about our system of incarceration and what goals it serves, particularly whether the United States should have a punitive system or a rehabilitative system. Accordingly, some political groups and candidates run "tough on crime" and focus on punishing people who commit crimes, while others focus on the broader conditions that lead to crime.

Capital punishment is inherently irreversible, which raises significant due process questions: if a state mistakenly executes an innocent person, that person cannot be made whole again. The Supreme Court in *Gregg v. Georgia* (1975), the case that restarted capital punishment in the mid-1970s, noted societal approval for capital punishment as a justification. Since *Gregg*, the Court has upheld several restrictions on capital punishment, including banning capital punishment for crimes committed by minors, the mentally handicapped, and for rape and crimes other than murder. The political argument for capital punishment, and for punitive systems of justice generally, weighs the safety of the community greater than the rights of any one individual.

10.2 THE FOURTEENTH AMENDMENT

Selective Incorporation

High-Yield

LEARNING OBJECTIVE

- Summarize the legal basis of selective incorporation.

Incorporation is the application of the Bill of Rights to the states. After explicitly declining to incorporate the protections in the Bill of Rights in nineteenth-century cases, the Court began to apply those protections in the 1920s and onward. The specific legal reason for incorporation is the due process clause of the Fourteenth Amendment.

Many of the common rights in the Bill of Rights were not formally incorporated until the 1950s and 1960s. An example is the right to an attorney in a criminal trial, which was not applied to the states until 1963. The exclusionary rule, the constitutional protection that bars the use of illegally gathered evidence in criminal prosecutions, was not applied to the states until 1961. The Court in the 1950s and 1960s (the Warren Court) was more liberal than previous Courts and generally looked favorably on state action as a mechanism for redress of societal issues, especially racial discrimination. Later Courts have been slower to prescribe government intervention for similar issues. However, incorporation can still happen, as it has most recently in the case of *McDonald v. City of Chicago* (2010), which incorporated the Second Amendment to the states.

Once it was accepted as a concept, justices and legal scholars disagreed in the early to mid-twentieth century about how incorporation should proceed. Some justices argued that if the legal rationale existed to apply one of the amendments to the states, then the same rationale extended to all of the amendments, an approach known as total incorporation. The majority of justices preferred **selective incorporation**, which applied amendments to the states on a case-by-case basis. Selective incorporation is a judicially conservative approach that puts the Court in a reactive position regarding which rights are incorporated. Courts are generally reluctant to issue decisions that might appear to be "legislating from the bench," since legislation is a power reserved to Congress. The issue is functionally moot: most of the enumerated protections in the Bill of Rights have been incorporated to the states, and there is broad agreement among justices, lawyers, and legal scholars that doing so is proper.

Due Process

LEARNING OBJECTIVE

- List and explain specific legal consequences of the due process clause.

The **due process clause** of the Fourteenth Amendment holds that state governments cannot "deprive any person of life, liberty, or property, without due process of law." After many years of legal interpretation and court rulings, due process protections have developed to include prohibition of warrantless searches of premises (such as homes or offices) and private papers (including cell phone data as well as traditional written communications), the exclusionary rule (banning prosecutors from using illegally obtained evidence), the Miranda rule (requiring law enforcement officials to inform accused persons of their rights prior to interrogation), and pretrial rights for accused persons (including legal counsel, a timely and public trial, and decision by a jury of peers), among other protections.

Due process protections are meant to shield people from arbitrary government action. The practical effect of due process is that governments are limited in whether and how they can control the actions of people within their jurisdictions. Due process also affects what the government can do to deprive people of life, liberty, or property, if need be (such as in a criminal case). If a government violates due process, whether through a law or an action, it can be sued by the person violated.

Due process violations can happen during court cases and criminal investigations, and since the stakes are high in those situations, courts take such violations very seriously. Examples of due process violations could include a judge refusing to appoint or allow a defendant to have an attorney, police coercing a confession from a suspect and the prosecutor using that confession at trial, police improperly seizing evidence and the prosecutor using the evidence at trial, or charging someone twice for the same offense (double jeopardy). If a defendant alleged any of these things and could prove that the authorities acted improperly, the defendant could demand a new trial or have the conviction vacated.

Since the protections for fundamental liberties in the Bill of Rights have all been effectively held to apply to the states through the Fourteenth Amendment, states and their agents (police, district attorneys, judges, and other officials) must meet the same standards that federal officials must meet in any area covered by the incorporated rights. This has had the effect of changing trial procedures and police conduct as individual state regulations have been changed by incorporation over time.

Incorporation of Rights

The following table discusses how significant Court cases have incorporated various Bill of Rights protections to the states.

Amendment	Court Case	Significance
First Amendment	*Tinker v. Des Moines Independent Community School District* (1969)	Upheld students' rights to symbolic speech in school while protesting the Vietnam War. It is important that the symbolic speech was not obscene or needlessly disruptive; the Court has upheld some limits on student speech in those categories.
Second Amendment	*McDonald v. City of Chicago* (2010)	Incorporated to the states the individual gun ownership protections the Court mandated in *Heller*. People in the United States have a right to keep handguns in the home for the purpose of self-defense.
Fourth Amendment	*Mapp v. Ohio* (1961)	Applied the exclusionary rule to the states based on the prohibition of unreasonable searches and seizures. Currently, this has implications for privacy rights as mass surveillance and communications metadata are debated.
Fifth Amendment	*Miranda v. Arizona* (1966)	Incorporated the Fifth Amendment protections against self-incrimination; required police to notify suspects of their right to remain silent and their right to legal counsel. There is a public safety exemption to *Miranda*; statements made before a Miranda warning can be admitted at trial as long as they were not coerced.
Sixth Amendment	***Gideon v. Wainwright* (1963)**	Required the state to provide counsel upon request for those who cannot afford a lawyer in criminal cases.
Eighth Amendment	*Gregg v. Georgia* (1976)	Held that the death penalty was not cruel and unusual and did not violate due process so long as the guidelines for juries and judges were standardized and there were no mandatory death sentences.

The Right to Privacy

There are several amendments that seem to suggest a right to privacy, especially the Fourth and the Fifth. For most of the Court's history, the justices did not subscribe to this view and ruled accordingly. In the 1960s and 1970s, however, several cases were decided in accord with the general expansion of civil liberties protections in that era, establishing a right to privacy in certain circumstances. One of the important privacy cases is **Roe v. Wade (1973)**. In *Roe*, the Court held that the right to an abortion was implicit in the privacy right in the Fourth Amendment and limited the ways in which the government could regulate abortion access. The Court issued several decisions based on the idea of a right to privacy but struggled to articulate the precise boundaries of that right. These decisions generally concerned matters of sexual choice and bodily autonomy.

> ✔ **AP Expert Note**
>
> **Be prepared to explain the nuances of the legal analysis of rights**
>
> How courts interpret the Bill of Rights has shifted over time and will continue to shift as legal understandings change. Keep in mind that often, popular conceptions of rights and legal conceptions of rights are different. An example is the way the Supreme Court has interpreted the idea of "privacy" differently in many cases, including *Roe v. Wade*. Other examples include *Griswold v. Connecticut* (1965), which dealt with married couples' access to contraception, and *Lawrence v. Texas* (2003), which dealt with consensual same-sex relationships. It remains to be seen how the modern Court will handle privacy questions as new issues, such as mass surveillance and the bulk collection of metadata, come before the Court.

10.3 SOCIAL MOVEMENTS

The Struggle for Equality

LEARNING OBJECTIVE

- List and explain specific U.S. social movements that opposed discrimination.

Social Movements

Social movements can be broadly defined as collective challenges to authority to achieve collective goals. Authority can be either governmental, political, or social, and it is frequently a combination of all three. Following is a discussion of the composition, tactics, and goals of major American social movements.

The history of social movements in America is different from that of other countries, in large part because of the unusually strong protections for individual rights written in our foundational legal documents, such as the Bill of Rights. Alongside this is the emphasis on equality in our national mythos. In documents like the Declaration of Independence, America is portrayed as a land of opportunity, where all people are created equal, and a place not bound by the rules of hereditary aristocracy, as European countries were. The emphasis on equality of opportunity is a common theme in American rhetoric and notably can be seen in times of national crisis like the Civil War and the Cold War, among others.

It is the tension between that lofty rhetoric and a less-than-equal application of the laws that prompted the growth of social movements in this country, especially after the Civil War. The women's rights movement, along with the civil rights movement and LGBTQ rights movement that followed, started with people who wanted the United States to uphold its promise of legal equality to all citizens.

Composition

Successful movements in America share many traits. They are generally comprehensive, being comprised of individuals and groups that represent diverse perspectives within a given community but united around a shared goal or ideal. Movements often pursue multiple strategies at the same time, depending on the size of the movement. Mass movements, characterized by participation of ordinary citizens, are usually led by community elites who can marshal broad support from the different people and organizations the movement must work with. Leadership can come from within the movement's ranks as well, as members attend training and gain experience in activism. This was how Rosa Parks came to be involved in the civil rights movement before she precipitated the Montgomery Bus Boycott in 1955.

Sometimes movements grow slowly and accrue support over time, and sometimes they seem to grow very quickly in response to a catalyst, either international or domestic. The **Seneca Falls Convention** in 1848 is considered such a catalyst for the women's rights movement in America, especially in promoting suffrage as a movement goal. The gay rights movement is another example, as that movement is commonly said to have begun with the June 1969 **Stonewall Riots**. The LGBTQ rights movement quickly adopted the kind of political tactics used by the women's and civil rights movements, pressuring medical groups to remove homosexuality from a list of mental disorders and working to create legal protections for gays and lesbians on a state-by-state, and community-by-community, basis.

Groups and organizations are an important part of movements, as they contribute organizational structure and can work independently toward movement goals. Important groups for the women's rights movement include the National Women's Party, headed by Alice Paul, who was instrumental in the addition of Title VII to the Civil Rights Act of 1964, which prohibited discrimination based on sex in public accommodations. The **National Association for the Advancement of Colored People (NAACP)** was one of the major groups involved in the civil rights movement and litigated the central civil rights cases, most famously *Brown v. Board of Education* (1954).

In the later stages of the women's movement, the **National Organization for Women (NOW)**, founded by Betty Friedan and other activists, pushed for changes in domestic violence law and supported what would become Title IX. Title IX of the Education Amendments of 1972, signed into law by President Nixon, invalidated discrimination on the basis of sex in federally funded education. It drastically changed the composition of higher education, and eventually the workplace, by removing structural barriers that had prevented women from entering a variety of professional and educational fields.

Tactics

Social movement tactics change from era to era, but all similarly work to exert pressure on policymakers, take the social movement's case to the public, and create a moral frame through which the social movement's demands can be interpreted and understood. For example, the early women's rights movement used petition drives, letter-writing campaigns, and legislative lobbying, working state by state, to change the ability of women to own property and be legally independent.

In 1920, the movement successfully pushed for the passage of the Nineteenth Amendment, which guaranteed women's **suffrage** (the right to vote). Throughout these efforts, leaders like Elizabeth Cady Stanton and Susan B. Anthony challenged the idea that women were naturally subordinate to men and worked to maintain and expand the movement's strategies and partnerships.

Other notable social movement tactics include direct actions such as sit-ins, marches, and other activities that focus less on policy and more on drawing attention to inequities. These tactics are normally aimed at both the public, in order to create an attention-getting situation and educate people about the grievances of the minority, and at business and political leaders, to show the power of the movement to disrupt the status quo and induce those leaders to work with movement leaders on their goals. Often associated with the civil rights movement, these kinds of nonviolent direct actions were championed by leaders like **Rev. Dr. Martin Luther King Jr.**, who saw **civil disobedience** as a crucial way to pressure white leadership to take the civil rights movement seriously, as he explained in "Letter from a Birmingham Jail."

Perception

Domestic and international politics also have effects on movements, as goals shift and tactics and strategies travel between places and times. This can be seen in the women's rights movement, which was happening concurrently in Great Britain and the United States in the 1910s and '20s; American activists adopted more militant tactics from their British counterparts. Similarly, the struggle against British rule in India in the 1930s and '40s and the nonviolent resistance platform of Mahatma Gandhi inspired Dr. King to take up similar tactics here in the 1950s and '60s.

Political concerns can also animate the response to movements. In the mid-twentieth century, charges of Communist infiltration were levied against the civil rights movement, and the FBI surveilled civil rights leaders using the COINTELPRO program, eventually infiltrating the Student Nonviolent Coordinating Committee (one of the more radical arms of the movement) and taking action against the Black Panthers. Charges of Communist sympathies were also used by anti–civil rights leaders to justify their opposition to the movement. But by the same token, concerns over the way that de jure segregation in the United States was perceived overseas led political elites to support the court cases championed by the civil rights movement, such as *Brown*. Concerns over the gap between U.S. rhetoric on democracy in the international sphere and its domestic support of racist policies were very high in the early part of the Cold War.

Goals

Movements generally have an overarching goal or set of goals that they use different tactics to work toward. The women's rights movement worked to change the legal status of women to make them legally independent of men, and it eventually settled on suffrage as an overarching goal. The civil rights movement's goals were to end legal segregation and, ultimately, to create true equality of opportunity in the United States across racial lines. The LGBTQ movement worked for the decriminalization of homosexuality and eventually moved on to marriage as a vehicle for achieving the full legal equality of gay couples and, by extension, gay individuals.

In these movements, there were simultaneous efforts aimed at engaging policymakers through actions such as ballot measures, petition drives, and letter-writing campaigns; engaging the public through education efforts such as leafleting, making speeches, and advertising; and engaging other movements and organizations through coalition building and working on smaller shared goals that advanced the main movement. Successful movements work on multiple fronts at the same time.

Oftentimes movements are working directly in opposition to one another on some issues. An example of this is the pro-life movement, which arose in response to the women's liberation movement and the *Roe* decision. The pro-life movement has pressured state legislatures to restrict abortion access and has kept abortion a live issue through consistent social pressure, utilizing the same type of tactics other movements have used. Social movements are not the prerogative of any one political group.

Government Response

High-Yield

LEARNING OBJECTIVE

• Cite laws and SCOTUS decisions that directly responded to social movements.

Social movements pressure the government to make changes based on movement goals, but the process by which movements successfully change laws or win court cases is complex. Movements must work to create a social and political atmosphere in which laws can be passed and supported by policymakers, even if some of their constituents may not be enthusiastic. Often, movements must work to change older laws or constitutional understandings before moving on to their larger goals.

Examples of this process can be seen in the civil rights movement. The movement pursued a multi-prong strategy, simultaneously working to change social attitudes and educate the public while advancing legal challenges to discriminatory laws and practices and pressuring lawmakers to support new laws that furthered movement goals; cases like *Brown* and laws like the Voting Rights Act of 1965 are examples.

None of this change happens fast, typically. *Plessy v. Ferguson* was decided in 1896. Movement leaders continued to challenge this precedent in the intervening decades, but it wasn't until the 1950s, as the Cold War advanced and political calculations changed, that they had success at the Supreme Court with *Brown* and its companion cases. It wasn't until the 1960s, after successful efforts to educate people about the effects of segregation in the South, that the movement was able to get new laws passed to protect civil rights.

The Civil Rights Act of 1964 and the Voting Rights Act of 1965 were supported by people who overcame internal divisions to push for a common goal. These laws touched on the goals of multiple movements, such as the civil rights movement and the women's rights movement. For example, Title VII of the Civil Rights Act prohibited sex discrimination in public accommodations. The women's rights movement won another victory when it pressured President Nixon to sign the Education Amendments of 1972, which made Title IX law; Title IX prohibits sex discrimination in education.

Usually the government is reactive on civil rights questions, waiting until it is pressured to act. The judicial branch is passive in the sense that cases must be brought by aggrieved parties; the courts cannot identify issues and reach out on their own. Consequentially, social change generally happens before legal change, though the two are related; law shapes society, and society shapes law. Sometimes laws merely codify social agreement, but at other times the law advances rights beyond popular conceptions. This was the case with *Brown*, a decision that was very controversial at the time. In creating an independent judiciary, the founders wanted to give the nation the capability of upholding the rights of minorities despite majority resistance.

Typically, a court makes a decision, or a legislative body passes a law, that reflects the prevailing thinking at the time. People either agree or disagree with the decision or law, and as time passes, public dialogue creates opportunities for movement supporters to organize and persuade others to change their minds on a given issue. After social and political shifts take place and legal understandings change, a court considers the law or decision again, sometimes affirming its previous decision and sometimes reversing itself. In this way, the law both forms and adapts to changing social values.

✔ AP Expert Note

Be able to spot the interconnections among various political events and movements

Success on the AP exam is based not only on what you know, but also on how you can make connections and see the bigger picture. When it comes to the topic of Civil Liberties and Civil Rights, it's helpful to consider entire time periods and the factors that contribute to political and social change.

The 1950s through the '70s, for example, were a volatile time in American society, and this was reflected in constitutional jurisprudence, as well as in social activism and legislative initiatives. Trends in all three areas reinforced each other. Government aid programs, such as Medicare and Medicaid, were made possible when the Supreme Court expanded civil rights protections and championed an expansive view of governmental power; further, such government action to address health care was considered appropriate because of movement activism. Women, African Americans, and LGBTQ people all pressured society at large and the government at every level to expand rights protections, extend fundamental liberties to all people, and address treatment that came to be widely viewed as unequal and unjust.

10

10.4 SCOTUS AND CIVIL RIGHTS

A Mixed Record

LEARNING OBJECTIVE

- Compare the different ways in which SCOTUS has either expanded or restricted civil rights.

Over the history of the Court, protections for minority and individual rights have expanded and contracted in response to broader American social and political realities. The most robust protections for individual liberties were instated between the 1940s and the 1970s. This was largely the era of the Warren Court, which has been the most liberal Court to date. Following is a discussion of the earlier history of the Court, some decisions of the midcentury period, and the narrowing of civil rights protections in the subsequent 50 years.

*The pre-***Brown** *Supreme Court*

In its early years, the Court did not take an expansive view of civil rights, especially for racial minorities. Important cases include *Dred Scott v. Sandford* (1857) and *Plessy v. Ferguson* (1896). Both cases have been overturned as society and the Court have discarded theories of biological determinism and moved away from racial prejudice.

In *Dred Scott v. Sandford* (1857), the Court held that black people, whether free or slave, could not be American citizens and thus did not have standing to sue in federal court. The *Dred Scott* case is widely regarded as one of the most indefensible decisions in the history of the Court. Chief Justice Taney's analysis focused on the historical condition of black people in American society. The two dissents pointed out, among other logical flaws in the majority opinion, that black men could vote in several states and were thus legal citizens. *Dred Scott* was nullified in 1868 by the birthright citizenship clause of the Fourteenth Amendment.

In *Plessy v. Ferguson* (1896), the Court held that public accommodations (public and private facilities that are open to and utilized by the public, such as public transit, restaurants, and hotels) could be segregated by race as long as the facilities for different races were the same, thus establishing the "separate but equal" doctrine. This was the basis for the Jim Crow laws throughout the country in the early and mid-twentieth century. The majority opinion argued that separating the races because of a presumed biological difference did not imply that one was being treated as inferior to another.

When the Court decided *Dred Scott*, the country was on the brink of civil war; riots and other violence erupted frequently, and there was great political unease. Hoping to settle the issue of slavery, the Court ironically pushed the country closer to war with its decision, which radicalized abolitionist groups in the North. In the *Plessy* decision, the Court expressed the widely held conception of the time that people of different races should live separately. The *Plessy* decision led to greater de facto and de jure segregation across the country, including in the northern states as black people left the South in the Great Migration and began changing the racial composition of northern cities. In both cases, the interaction of social attitudes and court rulings is evident.

Historical Expansion

By the 1950s, many ideas had changed; notably, the theories of eugenics and biological racism had fallen from public favor after people learned of the horrors of Nazism in the Second World War. Additionally, black Americans had served with distinction in the armed forces, and veterans, having experienced freedom in other countries, were not satisfied with second-class citizenship in the United States. The civil rights movement gained strength, and several legal challenges to Jim Crow were brought regarding education, leading to the landmark case of *Brown v. Board of Education* (1954).

In *Brown*, the Court held that **"separate but equal"** school facilities were inherently unconstitutional based on the equal protection clause in the Fourteenth Amendment, partially overturning *Plessy*. The case, brought by the NAACP and argued by future Supreme Court justice **Thurgood Marshall**, was actually a consolidation of five cases from different states, all challenging the segregation of public education. The Court explicitly overturned the rationale that racial separation did not imply inferiority of racial minorities, stating that even if conditions in separate schools were equal, the separation was impermissible because it inculcated a sense of inferiority in black children.

There were several other cases striking down de jure segregation in the same era as *Brown*, including cases invalidating racial covenants restricting access to white neighborhoods and cases invalidating the rest of *Plessy* in relation to segregation of public accommodations such as transit. In part, attitudes changed in response to the pressures of the Cold War era, as the Soviet Union successfully used American racial discrimination as a propaganda tool to attack the United States in the international community. As with *Dred Scott*, larger political considerations both domestic and international animated the expansion of civil rights in the midcentury period.

The 1950s through the '70s were a volatile time in American jurisprudence and social and political spheres. Movements pushed for greater government protection of individual rights, and the Court decided cases in favor of expanding those rights, as with *Roe v. Wade* (1973). But since then, those interpretations of the Constitution have gradually been narrowed, again reflecting the general tenor of social attitudes.

Contemporary Narrowing

The Court continued to uphold policies aimed at fostering racial equity, such as race-conscious admissions policies and busing to meet desegregation goals, through the 1970s. But it slowly moved away from results-focused jurisprudence and toward a "color-blind" model, a theory held by some justices that the Constitution forbids any race-conscious action, even one designed to help racial minorities. An intermediate step in that direction is seen in the case of **Shaw v. Reno (1993)**, in which the Court heard a challenge brought by white plaintiffs to redistricting that had resulted in a majority-minority district (a district in which racial minorities were in the majority) in North Carolina. In that case, the Court's majority opinion held that race-conscious districting must meet the standard of strict scrutiny, a high bar for advocates to meet, in addition to being compliant with the Voting Rights Act of 1965. This decision made the creation of majority-minority districts more difficult. The dissenting justices argued that the Court's opinion ran counter to the Voting Rights Act and the Fourteenth Amendment because it hindered efforts to redress the lack of black access to political office in majority-white states.

Color-blind jurisprudence can block affirmative action efforts to address historic disparities. The belief that race is an individual or cultural matter, rather than a sociopolitical issue, can lead judges and lawmakers to be more resistant to race-based strategies to address societal inequality. The claim that talking about race is in itself racist, and the dismissal of the political effects of racism, have grown more prevalent in the Court and in society as the topic of race has become increasingly polarized. Affirmative action in college admissions (when race is explicitly noted in admissions procedures) is an example, as the Court has become more reticent when deciding these cases.

Similarly, justices less sympathetic to government protection of individual rights have gradually replaced more liberal justices. In the 1980s and '90s, this rightward trend resulted in the narrowing of protections for individual rights and liberties and greater deference to government interests. An example is the case of *Employment Division v. Smith* (1990), in which the Court held that hallucinogenic drug use in a religious ceremony was not protected by the First Amendment. The majority argued that as long as laws were generally applicable and applied without discrimination, they did not constitute an impermissible burden on an individual's free exercise rights, no matter the result. This is a departure from the civil rights cases in the 1950s and '60s, such as *Brown*, in which the Court was concerned with the result of laws rather than the application of laws in the abstract.

The Court in recent years has been responding to changes in American society and governance just as earlier Courts did. The end of the Cold War, the cultural conflicts of the 1990s, and the general rightward political turn in the 1980s and '90s have all contributed to the composition of the Court and the way it rules on cases. The Court is less likely to find expansive protections for individual rights in the Constitution and more likely to rule narrowly on the text of the law than to take into account the results of a law. This trend hearkens to an earlier era of jurisprudence that held a more laissez-faire attitude toward civil rights.

NEXT STEP: PRACTICE

Go to Rapid Review and Practice Chapter 5 or to your online quizzes on kaptest.com for exam-like practice on this topic.

Haven't registered your book yet? Go to kaptest.com/moreonline to begin.

CHAPTER 11

American Political Ideologies and Beliefs

11.1 POLITICAL ATTITUDE FORMATION

Core Values

LEARNING OBJECTIVE

- Match particular core values with the specific political attitudes they typically accompany.

Cultural values have a significant influence on the formation of political beliefs. Although the United States has a strong multicultural tradition due to its immigrant origins, certain core values are common within American culture, including individualism, equality of opportunity, free enterprise, rule of law, and limited government. Together, these core values help to shape the **political attitudes** that individuals develop and the **political culture** of the United States.

> **✔ AP Expert Note**
>
> **Keep in mind that the political culture of the United States is not homogeneous**
>
> While American political culture is shaped by common core values, the rich cultural and social diversity of the United States means that individuals may differ in how they interpret or prioritize these values; some individuals may even reject core values entirely. For the AP exam, you should know the general trends that define American political culture, but you should also be prepared to explain how and why individual values, beliefs, and attitudes may differ.

Individualism

Individualism is a social and political philosophy that assigns greater importance to individuals than to society as a whole. Individualistic cultures such as the United States tend to value independence, autonomy, self-reliance, and assertiveness. Individuals are given the freedom to act as they choose, but they are expected to provide for their own needs and take responsibility for the consequences of the choices they make.

As a political philosophy, American individualism promotes personal freedoms and minimal government involvement in daily life. This is reflected in the formation of the Bill of Rights and the ongoing emphasis placed on preserving civil liberties, such as freedom of speech and freedom of religion, that protect the ability of individuals to pursue their own interests and beliefs without unwarranted government intrusion.

A tendency toward individualism also leads to a limited welfare state, as individuals are expected to be self-reliant and not depend on the government for their basic needs. For example, individualism may help to explain why the United States, unlike many other industrialized nations, lacks a government-run universal healthcare system. Similarly, tax policy in the United States is also heavily influenced by individualism: many voters are reluctant to support tax increases if they think the money will be used primarily to benefit others, and politicians who vote to raise taxes are often vilified for doing so.

The alternative to individualism is collectivism, which emphasizes the importance of society as a whole and values selflessness, reliability, sociability, cooperation, and compromise. In collectivist cultures, the needs of the group come before the needs of an individual, and it is considered proper, if not always pleasant, for individuals to make sacrifices for the benefit of society as a whole.

Because individualism and collectivism are on opposite ends of the same spectrum, all cultures—including the United States—exhibit some aspects of both ideologies, and individuals within a culture may hold opinions that are more individualistic or collectivist than the prevailing attitude of their culture as a whole. The United States is notable for its tendency toward individualism, but there are exceptions; for example, social welfare programs like Social Security, Medicare, and Medicaid represent deviations from strict political individualism.

Equality of Opportunity

Equality of opportunity refers to the belief that each person should be given an equal chance to succeed and should not be limited by circumstances outside of that person's control. The American tradition of equal opportunity is rooted in the colonial period, when many younger sons from wealthy English families came to the colonies in order to escape the limitations of primogeniture, a legal custom that granted firstborn sons the right to inherit their parents' entire estates. In the colonies, these younger sons achieved their success through hard work and determination, an early illustration of the now long-standing cultural belief that is commonly known as the "American dream"—that is, the notion that America is a place where people are not limited by the circumstances of their birth and any hardworking person has the opportunity to succeed. Over time, the notion of the American dream has contributed to the country's strong immigrant tradition, as many people have moved to the United States in order to pursue a level of success that might not be available to them in their home country.

Most Americans agree that equality of opportunity is a worthy ideal; however, there is often disagreement over what is required in order to guarantee equal opportunity for all and whether equality of opportunity actually exists in practice. While there are many laws and traditions in place that promote equality of opportunity, there have often been inconsistencies regarding who

11

benefits from them. For example, the framers of the Constitution prevented one type of inequality from growing in the United States by prohibiting federal and state governments from issuing titles of nobility, thus avoiding the inherent inequality associated with a hereditary aristocracy. Yet, the framers did not ban slavery or stipulate that the equality of racial or ethnic minority groups be protected. Over time, the American notion of equality has evolved to include legal and political equality regardless of race or ethnicity.

✔ **AP Expert Note**

Be able to recognize historic and present-day examples of values in action

The AP exam will expect you to know not just what typical core values are in the United States but how these have played out in American politics. For example, over time, the notion of equality of opportunity has become more inclusive. Following the Civil War, the Thirteenth, Fourteenth, and Fifteenth Amendments were added to the Constitution in order to abolish slavery and guarantee equal legal and political rights for all citizens, regardless of race. This is just one example of how American core values have been applied; keep your eye out for more examples in this chapter and throughout your study.

More recently, one area where the application of equal opportunity has been debated has been education. Beginning in the middle of the twentieth century, many colleges and universities began to implement admissions policies that require some degree of affirmative action—that is, these schools consider race when deciding whom to admit as a way of mitigating the negative effects of historical and systemic racial discrimination in the admissions process. The theory behind affirmative action is that the damage caused by discrimination is cumulative; students suffer the negative consequences of discrimination against themselves, but they are also harmed by the past and present discrimination that has disadvantaged their parents. For example, parents who have faced employment discrimination may not be able to afford to live in a community with excellent schools, putting their children at a disadvantage in the college admissions process; an affirmative action policy that considers race as a factor might result in such children being offered admission even if they have lower standardized test scores than other applicants.

It is important to note that equality of opportunity is not synonymous with **equality of outcome**. The American notion of equal opportunity is intertwined with individualism: according to this belief system, everyone should start with an equal chance, but then it is up to the individual to determine what comes next. However, a lack of equal outcomes is sometimes used as evidence of a lack of equal opportunity. For example, a pattern of lower standardized test scores for certain racial or ethnic minorities might be a sign of the cumulative effects of discrimination against previous generations or an indication of bias within the test itself.

Free Enterprise

Free enterprise refers to the ability of people and businesses to make money with minimal interference from the government. The strong cultural tradition of free enterprise in the United States is a natural extension of the values of individualism and equal opportunity, as free enterprise empowers individuals (and the businesses they create) to make the most of their equal opportunity for success. However, American attitudes toward the regulation of capitalism have changed over time.

Due largely to the lasting influence of the free market theory posited by eighteenth-century philosopher Adam Smith, until the early 1900s the federal government took a hands-off approach to managing the economy and regulating business. The period of rapid industrialization that occurred between 1870 and the early 1900s, commonly known as the Gilded Age in American history, created a massive influx of wealth, most of which flowed to industrial magnates like Andrew Carnegie and John D. Rockefeller. At the same time, industrialization caused the number of people working in factories to increase, and businesses trying to maximize profits often required factory employees to work long hours in poor or unsafe conditions. In addition, businesses often failed to maintain consistent quality or safety standards for the goods they produced, sometimes causing harm to consumers.

For many, the negative consequences of industrialization demonstrated that the free market would not always correct unacceptable conditions or outcomes on its own. As a result, many people came to believe that some government intervention was necessary to guarantee fairness and safety for workers and consumers. This shift in thinking helped to initiate the Progressive Era, the period from 1900 to 1920 during which the federal government passed a series of reforms aimed at improving working conditions for factory employees and regulating the safety of consumer products. Initially, many of these reforms were struck down by the Supreme Court, but by the 1930s, political and judicial attitudes had changed, and laws like the Fair Labor Standards Act of 1938, which established a minimum wage and severely restricted child labor, were upheld under Congress's power to regulate interstate commerce.

Today, the notion of free enterprise is still evolving. Some Americans would prefer a more laissez-faire approach to government regulation, believing that market pressures will usually prevent businesses from putting their employees or customers at risk. Conversely, others believe that some regulation is necessary in order to prevent businesses from prioritizing profits over other concerns, such as worker safety or the health of the environment. As with the other core values, opinions about free enterprise exist on a spectrum: most people agree that at least some regulation is beneficial, but there is considerable disagreement about where to draw the line.

Rule of Law

The **rule of law** is the principle that everyone—including corporations, organizations, and government leaders—should be held accountable to the same legal standards; in other words, no one is "above the law." The appreciation of early Americans for this concept in part explains why the United States is a democracy, with leaders who are elected and therefore accountable to the people, rather than a monarchy or some other form of government in which the people in power are granted a special status that places them above the reach of the law. As a result, the concept of the rule of law reinforces the notion of equality.

In the United States, the Constitution is the ultimate source of the rule of law, and the system of checks and balances helps to ensure that the rule of law is followed. For many, the most important institutional check is the independent judiciary, since federal judges and many state judges are appointed rather than elected and need not consider popular opinion when striking down laws, unlike Congress, which must consider popular opinion when making laws.

Limited Government

The political value of **limited government** is closely related to the notion of the rule of law, as a limited government is one that derives its power from the law itself; without a law granting it the authority to act, a limited government has no power. The framers of the Constitution created a limited government in part because of their experience living under English rule; though limited by the Magna Carta, the British monarchy's power was more expansive than what the framers envisioned for the U.S. federal government.

The notion of limited government continues to influence American political culture today. For some, limited government is a core political value, and reducing the size of the federal government is an important goal. For others, however, having a limited government is often a lower priority, and the government is often considered an essential part of the solution to social and economic problems.

Cultural Influences

LEARNING OBJECTIVE

- List means by which people's political attitudes are formed.

Political socialization refers to the process by which people form their political attitudes and beliefs. The process begins early in life through the combined influences of family, school, peers, and the media.

Early Influences on Political Socialization	
Family	Most people share the same political affiliation as their parents or other close family members. Sometimes, this is because their parents made a deliberate effort to share their political beliefs and values with them as children, but people can also learn about their parents' political opinions in less overt ways. Sometimes, people develop political beliefs that are opposite to those of their parents as a form of rebellion, but it is more common for children to share the same political beliefs as their parents than it is to reject them.
School	Most primary and secondary schools in the United States offer some form of civics instruction that teaches students about American political values. The curriculum itself, and the way it is presented by the teacher, can influence students' understanding of and appreciation for those values.
Peers	While younger children aren't likely to discuss politics in a meaningful way, by the time they reach high school, most teenagers will probably have at least some friends who hold vocal political beliefs. As with the other decisions they make, teenagers can be influenced by their friends' political opinions for good reasons, such as experiencing sympathy for a friend who was racially profiled by the police, and bad reasons, such as peer pressure.
Media	The influence of media can be direct, such as when someone watches a television news program or reads a newspaper, or indirect, such as when someone views a television show or movie with political themes, however subtle, primarily for entertainment value.

Another important factor that influences political identity is membership in different **social groups**, which are formal or informal groups of people who share similar characteristics and feel a sense of unity with one another. Social groups are typically defined by demographic characteristics, such as race, gender, age, or income level. Because of their shared experiences, members of a social group often share similar political values and beliefs.

Political socialization is a lifelong process; as time passes, individuals are exposed to new people and ideas, significant cultural or historical events, and personal experiences that may cause them to reevaluate their political beliefs.

- **Generational effects** are the results of significant historical or cultural events that can have long-term effects on the political attitudes of an entire generation of people. For example, people who lived through the Great Depression and experienced the economic recovery ushered in by the New Deal may be more likely to support policies that allow the government to spend its way out of an economic recession. Similarly, people who lived through the Watergate scandal and the resignation of President Nixon may be less trusting of elected officials and more supportive of the freedom of the press.

- **Life-cycle effects** refer to fluctuations in political beliefs that can occur due to changes in personal circumstances during the course of a person's life. For example, a young adult starting out in her career may not have a strong opinion about taxes or may favor a

11

progressive tax policy (one in which people who earn more pay a higher tax rate). But she may modify that view when she is older, more established in her career, and, perhaps most importantly, earning more money.

11.2 POLLING

Methods

LEARNING OBJECTIVE

- Identify the salient characteristics of polling.

Polling, or the monitoring of public opinion, has been a key part of the political process for most of the last century. Public opinion polls are used to determine how people feel about policy issues and the effectiveness of their political leaders. In the United States, it is common for politicians and political candidates to use public opinion polls to determine which programs and policies they should publicly support, but it is also not unusual for a politician to deviate from public opinion and support an unpopular program or policy.

There are several categories of public opinion polls. A **benchmark poll** is taken at the beginning of a particular election cycle to give a candidate an idea of where she initially stands with the voting public and where to focus her campaign resources to effectively persuade the electorate to vote for her. **Tracking polls** are taken repeatedly over several consecutive time periods (for instance, every day, or every week) to get an idea of how opinions are changing over time. Data is often averaged over the last several time periods, and as new time periods are added, data from the older time periods drops out.

Exit polls are taken on election day at polling sites to find out how people voted. The results of exit polls are often widely publicized; since they ostensibly reflect which candidates people actually voted for, they tend to be seen as more reliable than other types of polls. However, there are some criticisms of the reliability of exit polls. For example, some voters may be reluctant to reveal whom they voted for, especially if they feel the vote they cast may not be socially acceptable. Exit polls may also have an unwanted electoral impact. If it is widely reported that one candidate is projected to be the winner, potential voters may decide to stay home; either they are complacent because they think their candidate has already won, or they may think there's no point in voting for their candidate since the other candidate has already "won" the election. Some credit the contentious recount in Florida during the 2000 presidential election to this phenomenon, citing the media's decision to call the state for Democratic candidate Al Gore before the polls had closed in the western part of the state, where voters tended to be more politically conservative, as a potential factor in suppressing Republican turnout.

11

✔ **AP Expert Note**

Know how public opinion polls might influence an election

Public opinion polling is a significant feature of most election cycles. Often, polls are explicitly aimed at asking respondents whom they will vote for, but polling questions can also be designed to determine the respondents' opinions on various political issues. The AP exam might give you a set of polling data and ask you what impact it is likely to have on an election. To prepare for this type of question, consider the ways in which a political candidate might respond to different polling results (such as using public opinion data to reshape campaign strategy) and the ways that polling data might impact a campaign's fundraising efforts (such as donors deciding not to spend money on a candidate who seems to have little chance of winning).

Credibility

High-Yield

LEARNING OBJECTIVE

- Cite factors affecting the credibility of polls.

In order to be useful, opinion polls must be reliable. Credible **scientific polling** requires a randomly chosen, relevant **sample**; a large enough sample size; and clear, unbiased questions.

Random Sampling

One key feature of scientific polling is random sampling. In order to be reliable, the people who are surveyed have to be chosen at random. Otherwise, the group of people chosen may not be representative of the entire population; in other words, a non-random sample, as a group, may be more or less likely to hold certain beliefs or opinions when compared to the population as a whole.

A common example of this type of sampling error occurs when taking a **straw poll**, which is an unofficial survey taken from a group of people who have already assembled for a different purpose. For example, a candidate hosting a rally might take a straw poll of the constituents in attendance to gauge their opinion on an important policy matter. However, the candidate would be unwise to use the results of the straw poll to determine his official position on the policy, since the people who chose to come to his rally are, as a group, likely to hold similar political beliefs, and their beliefs may differ significantly from those of the candidate's constituency as a whole.

Sample Size

In order to be reliable, polls must survey enough people. It would be incredibly inefficient to poll the entire population, so the size of the sample, or those who will actually be surveyed, must be determined. A larger sample may lead to more accurate results, but the larger the sample, the more expensive and time-consuming it is to collect and analyze. **Pollsters** consider a number of factors when determining sample size, including the size of the total population being sampled.

Generally speaking, the larger the sample size, the more reliable the results of the poll. In order to assess the reliability of a given poll based on its sample size, polling data is often reported with its **margin of error**, which is the maximum expected difference between the results of the poll and the opinions held by the population as a whole. For example, if a poll reports that 48% of people support Candidate A with a 3% margin of error, then the percentage of people who support Candidate A within the population as a whole should be between 45% and 51%.

> ✔ **AP Expert Note**
>
> **Be able to explain why a particular polling result is or is not credible**
>
> The AP exam commonly asks you to evaluate the credibility of a particular poll or polling result. Make sure you know the requirements for a credible scientific poll and that you can recognize when those requirements have (or have not) been met.

Clear, Unbiased Questions

A reliable scientific polling also requires clear, unbiased questions. If the wording of a question is unclear, then the intent of the question may not be understood by many of the respondents, thus compromising the reliability of the poll's results.

Similarly, biased questions may lead respondents to give responses that don't accurately reflect their opinion about an issue. For example, a poll that asks people how they feel about the government imposing a "death" tax is probably going to have different results than a poll that asks for opinions about the estate tax.

11.3 IDEOLOGY AND POLICY

Political Platforms

LEARNING OBJECTIVE

- Distinguish between traditional Democratic and Republican platforms.

Since the 1860s, the dominant political parties in the United States have been the Democratic Party and the Republican Party; their current platforms emerged in the mid-twentieth century.

✔ AP Expert Note

Be able to discuss the "how" and "why" of the two-party system

The longevity of the American two-party system is typically attributed to the "winner-take-all" method of federal elections, also known as plurality voting, which limits the ability of third parties to gain traction because voters elect only one representative for each seat and only the candidate with the most votes wins; a third party whose candidate fails to get the greatest share of the votes gains nothing in a plurality voting system. By contrast, multi-party systems are common in countries that utilize a proportional method for voting, in which the same group of voters elects multiple representatives, and seats are apportioned to each party based on the number of votes it receives. This system allows third parties that receive only a small portion of the vote to potentially win seats in an election.

Other factors may also limit the ability of third parties to improve their electoral success. In most states, the candidates of the two major parties are typically granted an automatic spot on the ballot, but third-party candidates may have to petition to be included. In addition, the immense spending power of the two major parties puts third-party candidates at a significant electoral disadvantage. And even when third-party candidates win seats, they often have to caucus with one of the two dominant parties in order to hold any influence over the legislative process. Moreover, the party that they caucus with may significantly restrict their access to positions of power.

Democratic Party Platform

The **Democratic Party** believes that the federal government should play a key role in providing for the overall welfare of the American people. As a result, the Democratic Party advocates policies that promote quality and affordable human services such as healthcare, education, and housing. More broadly, the Democratic Party believes that the federal government can improve the welfare of the American people by funding scientific advancement and the arts, as well as by protecting the environment. In addition, the Democratic Party advocates government regulation of the economy as a means of promoting economic prosperity for all levels of income earners, especially low- and middle-class workers.

The Democratic Party is considered the more liberal of the two major parties; thus, it is strongly associated with the political philosophy of **liberalism**, which holds that an important purpose of government is to actively promote equality and justice. Consequently, the Democratic Party promotes legal and political equality for traditionally disadvantaged groups, including women and people of color, and advocates for reforms that will make the justice system more fair for all parties. Similarly, the Democratic Party supports tax policies that are based on ability to pay, requiring wealthy taxpayers to shoulder what the Democratic Party believes is their fair share of the tax burden. The Democratic Party is also known for its progressivism, meaning that it tends to support policies that reform or improve the status quo. In recent years, examples of the Democratic Party's progressivism include its support of gay marriage and other LGBTQ rights and its advocacy of universal healthcare.

Republican Party Platform

The **Republican Party** believes that individual liberty is paramount and the role of the federal government should be limited in order to preserve as much personal freedom as possible. As a result, the Republican Party tends to support policies that protect individual rights, such as freedom of speech or gun ownership, from intrusion by the government. More broadly, the Republican Party advocates for robust military spending in order to protect personal liberties from threats made by foreign governments and other external groups, such as non-governmental terrorist organizations.

The Republican Party is considered the more conservative of the two major parties. As a political philosophy, **conservatism** encourages a smaller, decentralized government structure and promotes free enterprise and private property rights. Accordingly, the Republican Party generally opposes economic regulations that inhibit people from making their own choices regarding employment, investment, or consumer spending. Similarly, the Republican Party favors tax policies that keep the rate of taxation low, especially for corporations and the wealthy, with the intent of encouraging investment and rewarding successful behaviors.

Conservatism is also strongly associated with adherence to traditional social values. For example, the Republican Party tends to favor policies that promote traditional family structures. Republicans are also more likely to favor capital punishment and other measures related to preserving law and order.

Another ideological doctrine that significantly influences the Republican Party is the notion of **American exceptionalism**, which holds that the United States occupies a unique place in world history as a long-standing democratic republic committed to personal liberty. As a result, Republicans tend to hold great reverence for the Constitution, especially the Bill of Rights and the doctrines of federalism and separation of powers. Republicans are not likely to support laws that they perceive as deviating from these principles.

Historical Change

LEARNING OBJECTIVE

- Track changes in U.S. political debates and public policies over time.

One potential explanation for the longevity of the Democratic and Republican parties is their ability to adapt to changing political trends. For example, when the Republican Party was initially founded, it advocated for a strong central government. However, due to the rise of industrialization during the latter part of the nineteenth century, Republicans came to support a laissez-faire approach to economic regulation and a more limited federal government in order to promote business interests and gain the support of a new class of wealthy American voters.

The Democratic Party has also experienced shifts in its ideology over time. Founded by supporters of then-presidential candidate Andrew Jackson, the Democratic Party initially advocated for a limited federal government and emphasized individual freedom and states' rights. In the early twentieth century, the Democratic Party began to experience a split between progressive Democrats in the North and conservative Democrats in the South. Initially, the party was able to build a successful coalition from these two groups, but eventually the more conservative southern Democrats, often referred to as "Dixiecrats," started to break away from the party. Dixiecrats ran their own candidate for president, Strom Thurmond, in 1948, and within a few decades, many of the people who had aligned with the Dixiecrats had migrated to the Republican Party. This shift positioned the Republican Party as favoring states' rights, leaving primarily progressives in the Democratic Party.

Market Regulation

LEARNING OBJECTIVE

- Distinguish among conservative, liberal, and libertarian positions on market regulation.

The libertarian, conservative, and liberal views on market regulation exist on a continuum. As a political philosophy that embraces liberty as its core value, **libertarianism** advocates for minimal government regulation. The libertarian approach is often associated with laissez-faire economics because both ideologies endorse the free-market system and its ability to self-regulate. For libertarians, a laissez-faire economic system promotes individual freedom by allowing people to have maximum control over their own economic choices and enjoy all the rewards of their efforts. Libertarians believe that government has a key role to play in protecting private property and settling trade disputes between private parties, but they otherwise oppose government regulation of the economy.

Like libertarians, conservatives tend to oppose government intervention in the private economy. While they are not completely opposed to economic regulation, they strongly prefer regulations that protect business interests and encourage economic growth; regulations that restrict what businesses can do or impose additional costs on businesses, such as environmental and labor regulations, are generally disfavored. Conservatives also tend to endorse **fiscal conservatism** as a means of indirectly stimulating economic growth. Proponents of fiscal conservatism believe that government should be as small and inexpensive as possible. They prefer a balanced budget, in which the amount of money spent by the government is roughly equal to the amount of revenue it collects. In order to achieve these goals, fiscal conservatives advocate both lower tax rates and reduced government spending.

By contrast, political liberals tend to support government regulation of the economy, especially when the goal is to promote economic equality. For example, liberals are more likely to support minimum wage laws and other regulations that lead to increased wages, especially for the poorest segments of the population. Similarly, liberals tend to favor graduated tax policies that subject wealthier individuals to a higher tax rate.

11

Be familiar with types of market regulation

Market regulation is generally divided into two categories: **monetary policy**, which refers to actions taken by central banks to control the money supply and raise or lower interest rates, and **fiscal policy**, which refers to the government using its powers of spending and taxation to influence the economy. Monetary policy is managed by the Federal Reserve Board, an independent executive agency that serves as the head of the central bank of the United States. The Federal Reserve lends money to private banks, and it controls the money supply by changing the interest rate it charges banks to borrow money. In simple terms, when interest rates go up, banks borrow less, and the money supply decreases, slowing inflation; conversely, when interest rates go down, banks borrow more, increasing the money supply but also increasing inflation. Fiscal policy, on the other hand, is managed by Congress via the normal legislative process.

Economic Models

LEARNING OBJECTIVE

- Distinguish between Keynesian and supply-side perspectives on fiscal and monetary policy.

In order to understand the competing theories of Keynesian economics and supply-side economics, some familiarity with the classical economic model of supply and demand is required. In economics, "supply" refers to the amount of a good or service available to be sold, while "demand" refers to the amount of the same good or service that consumers want to buy. The classical model of supply and demand holds that the price of a good or service is determined by the price at which the supply and demand are equal; this is often referred to as the "equilibrium price" of the good or service. Under the theory of supply and demand, every good or service will eventually reach its equilibrium price.

Classical economic theory also incorporates a principle known as the law of markets, which holds that aggregate supply and aggregate demand will always equalize; in other words, the overall supply of all goods and services produced by an economy will match the overall demand of all consumers within that economy. A key tenet of the law of markets is that potential demand will always outpace actual supply, meaning that it is not possible to have an excess supply (also known as an overproduction). Because of this principle, classical economics promotes a laissez-faire approach to market regulation; the government need not intervene in the economy because the law of markets will result in an overall equilibrium, full employment, and general prosperity.

Keynesian Economics

Keynesian economics refers to a set of economic theories that were developed by British economist John Maynard Keynes, primarily in response to the worldwide Great Depression that began in 1929. Keynes challenged some of the principles of classical economics, including the law of markets, by arguing that overproduction was possible and in fact had led to the severely high rates of unemployment experienced by the United States and other countries during the Great Depression.

Keynes asserted that aggregate demand is not stable and not potentially infinite, as classical economists had contended, but volatile and limited. When demand is low, an economic recession (or depression) can occur as production slows down in response to reduced demand. Alternatively, when demand is high, inflation can occur.

To avoid these problems, Keynes advocated for market regulation when needed to stabilize aggregate demand. In response to the Great Depression, Keynes recommended that governments increase spending and reduce taxes, even if those tactics required the government to operate with a budget deficit; Keynes theorized that spending more money on government projects would directly increase demand for the goods and services that those projects required, while cutting taxes would indirectly increase demand by giving individual consumers and businesses more discretionary income to spend. By increasing demand, the supply of goods and services would increase as well, allowing more people to find jobs and thereby reducing the unemployment rate. Many governments, including the United States, adopted Keynesian-style economic policies, which are often credited with having ended the Great Depression.

> ✔ **AP Expert Note**
>
> **Be able to explain what economics look like in practice**
>
> The AP exam is all about the application of principles, so be sure that you can discuss examples, especially for more complex topics. For instance, President Franklin D. Roosevelt, who initially advocated classical economic theory, eventually came to embrace Keynesian economics as he sought a way to end the Great Depression. The New Deal, which established numerous public works projects, is a textbook example of using government spending to increase aggregate demand during an economic depression. In addition, while he had promised to balance the federal budget during his first presidential campaign, FDR ultimately reversed his position and recommended deficit spending in order to hasten the country's economic recovery.
>
> On a smaller scale, the stimulus packages endorsed by presidents George W. Bush and Barack Obama during the brief economic recessions of the early twenty-first century also exemplify Keynesian principles. The stimulus packages contained a combination of government spending and tax cuts designed to increase demand, or "stimulate" the economy. As these recessions were short-lived, many believe that the stimulus packages were responsible for preventing the recessions from becoming severe, long-term economic downturns.

Supply-Side Economics

Following its apparent success in halting the Great Depression, Keynesian economics came to replace classical economics as the dominant economic theory of the mid-twentieth century. Indeed, the United States and other countries that adopted monetary and fiscal policies consistent with Keynesian economics experienced an economic boom during the 1950s and 1960s. However, by the end of the 1970s, the American economy was experiencing stagflation, a combination of high inflation and high unemployment, despite a lack of change in aggregate demand. Some economists theorized that Keynesian economic principles, which focused on managing demand, had failed. These economists suggested that the government instead use monetary and fiscal policies to manage supply, developing a set of theories known as **supply-side economics**.

Supply-side economists believe that an economy is prosperous when conditions are ideal for the suppliers of goods and services. Thus, they favor lower taxation, especially for corporations and the wealthy, who are the economy's primary suppliers. If suppliers paid less in taxes, supply-side economists posit, they would have more money to invest in their businesses, stimulating production and keeping employment levels high. In addition, workers would get to keep a larger portion of their paychecks, giving them greater incentive to work and more discretionary income to spend, further increasing production and encouraging economic growth. Supply-side economists predict that lowering tax rates would actually cause tax revenues to increase, since more wealth would be created overall.

President Ronald Reagan was a vocal proponent of supply-side economics and advocated for tax cuts in order to stimulate the stagnant economy he inherited when he took office in 1981. In addition, Reagan promoted deregulation of the economy as a means of giving businesses greater freedom to make investments that would stimulate production. There is some indication that Reagan's fiscal and monetary policies were successful; for example, the unemployment rate declined steadily after the first year of Reagan's presidency. However, economists are divided over the merits of supply-side economics; critics allege that the theory harms society as a whole by favoring the wealthy at the expense of the less affluent, and they dispute the claim that lowering taxes is likely to increase government revenues. Despite these criticisms, supply-side economics remains a popular theory among fiscally conservative Republicans, who favor lower taxes and limited market regulation.

Government Intervention

LEARNING OBJECTIVE

- Distinguish among conservative, liberal, and libertarian views on government intervention.

As with market regulation, the conservative, liberal, and libertarian perspectives on government intervention exist on a continuum. Libertarians tend to oppose any government involvement in the social or economic affairs of private citizens, except as needed to protect property rights or personal liberty. For libertarians, government intervention is not appropriate if its only purpose is to protect individuals from the negative consequences of their own decisions; instead, government intervention is justified only when it is done to protect third parties from the decisions of others, as in the case of laws against theft or murder. Thus, libertarians oppose economic regulations, such as laws that establish a minimum wage or seek to improve working conditions, and laws that criminalize or otherwise restrict personal choices such as smoking marijuana.

Conservatism is also associated with the principle of limited government intervention, but conservatives are more willing than libertarians to permit some government intrusion into private life, especially when the intrusion would promote national security or traditional moral values. However, conservative Republicans are likely to oppose laws that interfere with economic, educational, or religious choices.

Liberalism typically advocates greater government intervention within the economic sphere than do conservative or libertarian ideologies; for example, liberals tend to support minimum wage and overtime laws, laws that promote workplace health and safety, laws that prevent environmental degradation, and consumer protection laws. On social issues, however, liberals are more likely than conservatives to oppose government intrusion.

Social Issues

LEARNING OBJECTIVE

- Distinguish between conservative and liberal perspectives on social issues.

Social policy refers to the government's role in promoting the welfare of its citizens. Social programs may promote equal access to important quality of life factors like affordable healthcare, education, or housing, or they may offer assistance (financial or otherwise) to individuals who are economically disadvantaged.

In the United States, a handful of social programs, especially Social Security and Medicare, have fairly widespread support, but in general conservatives are less likely to favor social programs than are their liberal counterparts. In part, this is because conservatives are more likely to value individualism and self-reliance. For conservatives, social programs that shift economic risk from the individual to the government seem to contradict this core political value. In fact, conservative support for Social Security and Medicare may be more practical than ideological; eliminating or significantly reforming either program is certainly politically unpopular and possibly economically infeasible, given the vast number of senior citizens who depend on their Social Security income. Either way, conservatives are not likely to support the addition of new social programs like universal healthcare and often advocate reducing or eliminating those that already exist. They may also support placing limits on who can receive assistance from a social program, or for how long. For example, conservatives may support a work requirement for individuals receiving food stamps as a means of encouraging them to work toward self-sufficiency.

Conversely, liberals tend to be more supportive of social programs, especially those that promote equality or help traditionally disadvantaged groups. In part, this is because liberals are more likely to value equality over individualism. Thus, liberals are more likely to support government efforts to fund equal access education and healthcare, as well as programs like food stamps and public housing that are intended to offer financial and other forms of support to individuals who are economically disadvantaged.

NEXT STEP: PRACTICE

Go to Rapid Review and Practice Chapter 6 or to your online quizzes on kaptest.com for exam-like practice on this topic.

Haven't registered your book yet? Go to kaptest.com/moreonline to begin.

CHAPTER 12

Political Participation

12.1 VOTING

Rights

LEARNING OBJECTIVE

- Detail significant U.S. voting rights protections.

When the U.S. Constitution was ratified in 1788, it contained no stipulations concerning suffrage (the right to vote). Instead, the Constitution left voting rights up to the individual states. Prior to the 1820s, most states permitted only a limited number of white men to vote. Some states employed a variety of restrictions, including property ownership and religious affiliation requirements. States gradually abandoned many of their voting restrictions, and by the 1860s, white men had achieved near-**universal suffrage** in the United States. While voting rights were expanding for white men, however, states actively barred women, African Americans, Native Americans, and many immigrants from voting.

African Americans

In the aftermath of the American Civil War, which ended in 1865, a movement was launched to obtain voting rights for African American men. After the United States officially ended slavery with the **Thirteenth Amendment**, it adopted the **Fourteenth Amendment** to define African Americans as full U.S. citizens. The Fourteenth Amendment, however, did not directly guarantee African American men the right to vote. This prompted Congress to propose the **Fifteenth Amendment**, which was ratified in 1870. This amendment states, "The right of citizens of the United States to vote shall not be denied or abridged by the United States or by any State on account of race, color, or previous condition of servitude." African American men were finally legally guaranteed the right to vote.

This newly gained right to vote continued to be suppressed, however, through intimidation tactics and a variety of restrictive measures such as poll taxes and literacy tests. Many African Americans could not afford to pay the poll taxes, especially given the poor economic conditions in the South. Poor whites who could not afford to pay the poll taxes were assisted by white supremacy groups, such as the Klu Klux Klan (KKK), which would pay the poll taxes for whites in order to continue the system that disenfranchised black voters. The literacy tests often required perfect scores and were frequently designed to be confusing. Again, white voters received preferential treatment. They were able to bypass this requirement through a "grandfather clause" unavailable to black voters: those who had been allowed to vote in that state prior to the Civil War, and their descendants, did not have to complete literacy tests.

Laws like these that discriminated against African Americans, from Reconstruction through the mid-1960s, are known collectively as **Jim Crow laws**. Therefore, despite the constitutional protections provided by the Civil War Amendments, African Americans in the South were largely disenfranchised until 1965. For example, in 1960, less than 10 percent of blacks in Mississippi were registered to vote.

The civil rights movement renewed efforts to enforce voting rights for African Americans. In 1964, the **Twenty-Fourth Amendment** was adopted to prohibit poll taxes in federal elections, removing a significant barrier for registered voters. To further remedy issues with voting rights restrictions, Congress passed civil rights bills in 1957, 1960, and 1964, all of which contained voting-related provisions. However, it was not until the passage of the Voting Rights Act of 1965 that significant voting protections were extended to all black people. The Voting Rights Act outlawed literacy tests and other tactics that limited **voter registration** (the process of officially signing up to vote) and the actual process of voting. Under this act, federal officials were sent to the South to ensure that African Americans were allowed to vote free from fear and intimidation. Additionally, this act required local governments to submit changes in their voting and electoral practices to the U.S. Department of Justice in order to ensure they were not discriminatory.

✔ **AP Expert Note**

Be able to trace the historical progression of voting rights

The AP exam will expect you to be able to draw sophisticated connections, including how historical events have built on one another. For example, to say that the Fifteenth Amendment granted African Americans the right to vote is not enough; you should be able to recognize how the civil rights movement and the Voting Rights Act of 1965 further cemented this right for all African Americans.

Women

When the Fifteenth Amendment was adopted in 1870, it applied only to black men. Like white women, black women would remain legally disenfranchised for 50 more years. Led by notable activists such as Elizabeth Cady Stanton, Lucretia Mott, Lucy Stone, and Susan B. Anthony, the women's suffrage movement emerged during the second half of the nineteenth century. The movement advocated greater educational and job opportunities for women. By empowering women, the suffragists were able to gradually overcome their opposition. In 1890, Wyoming became the first U.S. state in which women were able to vote, and by 1918, women had acquired the right to vote in 15 states. Finally, in 1920, the United States adopted the **Nineteenth Amendment**, guaranteeing all women the right to vote.

Other Expansions

Following the expansion of suffrage for African Americans and women, the next major wave of voting rights came in 1971 when the voting age was lowered from 21 to 18. The movement that advocated for this change was born during the Vietnam War era. Youth-led antiwar activists argued that those who risked their lives in war ought to have a voice in governing the country they were defending. Politicians who supported the Vietnam War also supported lowering the voting age to 18 so that soldiers under 21 years old could vote. In 1971, a proposal to lower the voting age from 21 to 18 was adopted by both houses of Congress and sent to the states for ratification. Three months later, the states ratified the **Twenty-Sixth Amendment**, making it the fastest amendment ever to be ratified. **Voter eligibility** is currently open to any U.S. citizen who is at least 18 years old on election day and not disqualified due to a felony conviction; some states add additional criteria that trigger disqualification, such as being declared mentally incompetent by a court.

Another major change in U.S. voting processes occurred in the early twentieth century; prior to 1913, U.S. senators were not directly elected by American citizens. Instead, Article I, Section 3 of the Constitution required that each state legislature choose the state's two senators. By the early twentieth century, most Americans had concluded that this method of selection was undemocratic and corrupt. In 1912, an amendment was proposed in Congress to end this practice and to require that senators be directly elected by the citizens of each state. After passing Congress, the amendment was then ratified by two-thirds of the states in 1913, becoming the **Seventeenth Amendment** to the Constitution.

Behavioral Models

LEARNING OBJECTIVE

- Distinguish among rational-choice, retrospective, prospective, and party-line voting models.

The expansion of voting rights has theoretically made the United States more democratic, but in practice, there is a difference between who *can* vote and who *does* vote. Traditionally, young adults have voted in far smaller numbers than have older adults. Likewise, minority groups tend to vote in smaller numbers than whites. The motivations for voting are complex. A person is far more likely to vote, for example, if that person is interested in a particular campaign, has strong feelings of civic responsibility, and believes voting can lead to a positive outcome. To help describe how people weigh various factors when making voting decisions, political scientists have created a number of voting behavior models.

Retrospective voting is a theory that voters may make voting decisions based on the past performance of a candidate or party. If those in office have kept their promises, voters may be more inclined to vote for them again. Often, in periods of strong economic growth, voters who have benefited financially will vote for the current party in power. In 1980 Ronald Reagan asked the famous question: "Are you better off today than you were four years ago?" The question challenged voters to think about their economic well-being. Because the economy was quite weak in 1980, many realized they wanted change and elected Reagan as president. In contrast, **prospective voting** is a theory that voters decide based on predictions of how a candidate or party will likely act once elected. Voters compare the political values, campaign promises, and party platforms of the various candidates and then vote for the candidate whom they are most likely to benefit from after the election.

In economics, to explain consumers' purchasing decisions, analysts sometimes use a rational-choice model. If a consumer has a dollar to spend, he or she tries to get the best possible return for that dollar. Similarly, political scientists use the **rational-choice voting** model to describe voting behavior. With only one vote to cast in any given election race, a citizen tries to get the best return for that vote. In the rational-choice voting model, a voter considers the various candidates and their positions and then votes for the candidate whose platform will likely give the voter the most favorable outcome.

For many citizens, the election environment is complicated due to the number of races, candidates, and issues; researching the candidates and the issues takes considerable time. Nevertheless, most citizens want to cast meaningful votes. To achieve this goal, voters sometimes take shortcuts; the most common shortcut is to vote based on party affiliation. Strictly using political party identification to make voting decisions is called **party-line voting**, also known as straight-ticket voting. For example, if a person casts a ballot for only Republicans or for only Democrats, the person is using straight-ticket voting. Since the 1960s, more voters have adopted split-ticket voting, the practice of voting for candidates from different political parties during an election in which multiple offices are being decided. For example, a split-ticket voter may vote for a Republican candidate for the House of Representatives and also vote for a Democrat for the Senate.

Turnout

LEARNING OBJECTIVE

- List major factors affecting election turnout.

Voter turnout is the percentage of eligible voters who cast a ballot in an election. A long history of political science research has shown that the following demographic factors substantially impact voter turnout: education, age, race, religious affiliation, income level, and gender. Voter turnout also varies by election type and from state to state, since each state produces its own ballot and determines rules for voter eligibility.

Demographic Factors

High-Yield

Education has a strong positive correlation with turnout: the higher a person's level of education, the more likely the person is to vote. Those with stronger educational backgrounds are generally better able to understand the issues, read about or watch the news, and distinguish among the candidates' positions. Research indicates that younger adults, particularly those under 30, vote less often than middle-aged voters. Those between the ages of 55 and 65 usually have the highest turnout. Then, there is a decline in participation for those over 65.

For all education levels and ages, citizens are more likely to vote if they believe their votes can bring about real political outcomes and positive change. This belief is part of a larger concept called **political efficacy**, which is the citizens' faith and trust in government and their belief that they can understand and influence political affairs. A large proportion of U.S. citizens choose to not vote. The following table shows the percentage of American adults who voted in presidential elections from 2000 to 2016. Less than two-thirds of citizens actually vote in presidential election years.

Presidential Election Year	U.S. Citizens Who Reported Voting
2000	59.5%
2004	63.8%
2008	63.6%
2012	61.8%
2016	61.4%

As groups, both African Americans and Hispanics are less likely to vote than whites. However, the differences are primarily based on socioeconomic status. After the data has been adjusted for income and education, it shows that African Americans are as likely or more likely than whites to vote in many elections. The following table shows the turnout rates by race for the presidential elections from 2000 to 2016. With the exceptions of 2008 and 2012, when African Americans had the highest turnout, whites have generally had the highest turnout. Hispanics have consistently trailed behind both African Americans and whites in turnout.

	2000	2004	2008	2012	2016
Whites	58%	64%	65%	62%	65%
African Americans	53%	61%	69%	67%	60%
Hispanics	39%	43%	47%	43%	45%

In every presidential election since 1980, voter turnout for women has exceeded voter turnout for men; in fact, women have cast between four and seven million more votes than men have. Women are also registered to vote at higher rates than men. In 2012, nearly 82 million women were registered, compared to 71 million men. In addition, since 1980, larger proportions of women than men self-identify as Democrats. In the 2012 presidential election, women were 10 percentage points more likely than men to vote for the Democratic candidate Barack Obama (55 percent of women versus 45 percent of men).

Election Types

Voter turnout is normally much higher in general elections than in primary elections. A **primary election** is a nominating election in which party members choose which of their party's candidates will run in the general election. There are a number of reasons why turnout is lower for primaries. First, in some state primaries, a citizen is only allowed to vote for candidates who belong to his or her political party; this also means that independents (voters not belonging to a party) are far less likely to participate in primaries. Second, because several candidates often compete for the party's nomination, voters are less able to use party identification to make voting decisions. For example, in the 2016 Republican primary, Republican voters had to sort through 17 major candidates who entered the race. Since researching the candidates takes time and effort, voters may choose to not participate in the primary vote. Lastly, most primary races receive significantly less media coverage than general election races.

Turnout can also be affected by the type of primary the state has. Some states have **open primaries** in which voters are allowed to vote for candidates from any party. For example, a Democrat can vote for a Republican candidate or a Green Party voter can vote for a Democratic candidate. During **closed primaries**, participants must be registered with a political party to vote for one of its candidates. For example, a Democrat can only vote for a Democratic candidate. Most state political parties favor closed primaries because they believe it ensures that the winning nominee is truly backed by the party. However, in closed primaries, independents are not allowed to vote, and those who prefer a candidate from another party may choose to not vote. Both of these factors, therefore, diminish the turnout.

General elections, which occur every November, are held to choose among the candidates nominated by the various political parties or running as independents. National candidates for the presidency and Congress as well as state and local candidates must participate in the general election to be elected. Given the importance of the general election, voters turn out in much larger numbers than they do for primary elections.

Turnout also tends to be higher in years in which the president is elected than in midterm election years. **Midterm elections**, which occur in even-numbered years between presidential election years, mainly consist of congressional races. Media coverage for presidential elections is much more intense and widespread, producing more information about the experience, character, issue positions, and leadership potential of the candidates. People are less likely to vote if they are not familiar with the issues and candidates, and voters are less likely to know about congressional candidates than presidential candidates. Given the greater perceived importance of the presidential election, it is not surprising that voter turnout is higher than that of midterm elections. The graph illustrates the significant increase in turnout in presidential elections compared to congressional elections.

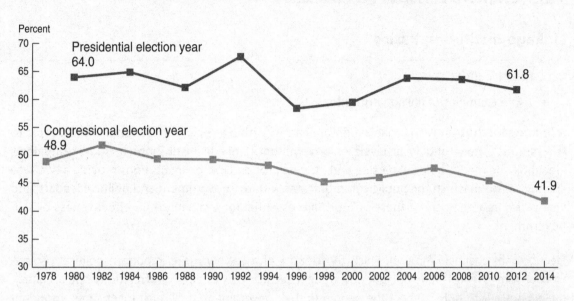

Voting Rates in Congressional and Presidential Elections: 1978 to 2014

Voting Laws

While demographics and political efficacy are influential factors for turnout, voting laws and regulations on the state level are also very important. Registration laws, voter identification laws, and polling place accessibility affect turnout. In general, states see an increase in turnout when they make registering to vote easier, forgo strict photo identification requirements, and have more polling locations.

Currently, one of the most controversial issues concerns **voter identification laws**, which require voters to present proof of their identities before casting ballots. More than 30 states have laws that either request or require voters to show a form of identification at the polls. Proponents of these laws argue that requiring identification prevents in-person voter fraud and increases public confidence in the election process. Opponents, however, argue that there is very little voter fraud and that requiring identification adds an unfair barrier to voting for some citizens because those with lower levels of income and education often lack the resources to get a government-issued ID.

On the federal level, the National Voter Registration Act of 1993, popularly known as the **motor-voter law**, was enacted to make registering to vote easier. It enables people to register to vote when they apply for driver's licenses and permits registration through the mail as well as at some state offices. The law also prohibits states from canceling a voter's registration due to a failure to vote.

✔ **AP Expert Note**

Be prepared to discuss controversial current events

Hot-button topics, such as voter ID laws, are an integral part of AP U.S. Government and Politics, and you can expect to see some on the official exam. It's important to keep your focus on treating each side of a given issue in an evenhanded manner and on recognizing larger themes and connections to other topics.

12.2 LINKAGE INSTITUTIONS

Linkage Institution Basics

LEARNING OBJECTIVE

- Cite examples of linkage institutions.

A **linkage institution** is an organization or channel within a society that connects the people to the national, state, and local levels of government. Linkage institutions include campaigns, elections, the media, political parties, and interest groups. Linkage institutions provide a two-way channel through which the public communicates with the government and political leaders, and vice versa. In a democracy, these linkages are essential for evaluating the effectiveness of self-government.

Elections are channels through which the citizens of a society make important political choices. Elections are essential for democratic government because they establish and reaffirm popular control. If elections are to truly connect the people to their government, they must meet some important criteria. The first is universal suffrage, meaning that all citizens who can be responsible for their own actions are permitted to vote in order to protect and promote their own interests. Second, elections should offer the citizens a meaningful choice, or the ability to select among credible candidates. Lastly, democratic elections require political equality, meaning that all votes are equal.

Another important linkage institution is the **media**, in particular the news media and social media. Media organizations affect politics in a variety of ways:

- focusing attention on important issues, often influencing what issues citizens believe are important
- creating platforms in which issues are addressed by political leaders, public officials, citizens, etc.
- influencing the content, tone, and time frame of political debate and conveying and evaluating the decisions of public officials

As such, media organizations play two vital roles for democracy: channeling or transmitting information to the citizens, and influencing the way that voters perceive and interpret this information. Both the media and elections will be discussed in more specific detail later in this chapter.

Political Parties

LEARNING OBJECTIVE

- Identify processes that political parties use to influence U.S. political life.

In all societies, people need to work together to solve problems and manage their limited resources. In modern U.S. politics, such collective action is taken up by two important types of organizations: political parties and interest groups. **Political parties** are organized groups of people with shared political values who seek to gain governmental control through winning elections. National political parties hold **party conventions** (meetings to select candidates and set priorities) every four years to create a party platform. The platform is a compilation of the party's official positions and priorities on issues and governance. The platform guides members of Congress in drafting legislation. A party tries to guide proposed laws through Congress and informs party members of how they should vote on important issues. A political party also nominates candidates to run for state government, Congress, and the presidency. Finally, it coordinates political campaigns and mobilizes voters.

While the nomination and promotion of political candidates is probably the parties' most visible function, parties play several other important roles in a democratic society:

- organizing and articulating public policy priorities as identified by party members and supporters
- educating voters and citizens about the workings of the political and electoral system
- promoting and articulating general political values to generations of citizens
- channeling public opinion from citizens to government
- recruiting and training candidates for public office

Adapting Political Parties

LEARNING OBJECTIVE

- List factors that influence political parties to change over time.

Political factions—from which organized parties evolved—began to appear almost immediately after the establishment of the federal government. Those who supported President Washington and his administration would form the Federalist Party, while those in opposition joined the emerging (Jeffersonian) Democratic-Republican Party. By the 1820s, the Federalists had lost popular support, and the Democratic-Republicans had split into factions, eventually forming the Democrats and the Whigs. Though the Whig Party lasted only a short time, it has had a lasting impact on American democracy. When the Whig Party collapsed, many of its members formed the modern Republican (GOP) Party and elected Abraham Lincoln as the first Republican president. During the Great Depression in the 1930s, the electorate divided along economic lines; wealthy voters were more likely to vote Republican, and less-wealthy voters, including a large number of southerners, were more likely to vote Democratic. A significant shift in party allegiance by a large number of citizens is known as a **realignment**. An election that signals a party realignment is called a **critical election**. The 1932 election of Franklin Roosevelt is an apt example of a critical election, in that it ended a long period of dominance by the Republican Party.

12

During the 1960s, another realignment occurred. White southerners became increasingly disillusioned with the Democratic Party because of the party's support for civil rights, school desegregation, and other social programs. Therefore, white southerners started leaving the Democratic Party and joining the Republican Party. After the 1960s realignment, the Democrats continued to benefit from the support of minority groups, notably African Americans and Hispanics. The Democrats have also benefited from an increase in support from women and young voters over the past three decades. In contrast, Republicans have overall become more white, more male, and more suburban and rural. The Republican Party has gained more support from Protestants, in particular those who identify as Christian evangelicals. Although it has gained support in the South and Southwest, the Republican Party has lost support in the Northeast.

Another adaptation that has occurred over the past 40 years is the shift from a party-centered campaign to a candidate-centered campaign. In the nineteenth century, political "machines" and party "bosses" often took advantage of immigrants by trading jobs in exchange for voter loyalty. These machines built large party coalitions that endured for decades. A **party coalition** occurs when different political parties cooperate on a common political agenda. Today, this type of corruption has been reduced, and party bosses have been eliminated. Some people believe that the major parties are now in decline. Party loyalty is no longer critical for economic advancement, and easy movement across the country has fragmented loyalties to state and local political parties. An increasing number of independents, lower levels of voter turnout, and voter distrust of political parties have likewise weakened the political influence of the parties.

In the years before television and social media, voters typically received information about a candidate directly from the candidate or someone working on behalf of the candidate. The parties were extremely important organizers of this *grassroots*, or "boots on the ground," type of campaigning in which ordinary citizens advocate for a candidate or issue. Today, campaigns are mostly conducted through mass-media channels and consequently have become less dependent on the work done by the political parties. Candidates themselves form their own political organizations: professional campaigns that work for the candidate rather than for the party. Both presidents Barack Obama and Donald Trump have shown that parties have become increasingly dependent on candidates who can generate their own enthusiasm and fundraising.

Third-Party Candidates

LEARNING OBJECTIVE

- Detail U.S. political structures that impede third-party candidate success.

Today, the United States is a multi-party system. The Democratic Party and the Republican Party are the most powerful. **Third parties**, such as the Reform, Libertarian, Socialist, Constitution, and Green parties, can run candidates in presidential and congressional elections. While third-party candidates sometimes win local or state office, they almost never win national elections. One of the more significant challenges that third-party candidates face is the **winner-take-all** system, in which the candidate who receives the greatest number of votes in a state wins, with few exceptions, all the electoral votes of that state.

12

Third parties also are generally unable to get federal campaign funding from the government. Campaign finance rules say that a political party can only get government funding if it received a certain percentage of votes in the previous election. Therefore, typically only the Democratic and Republican parties garner enough votes to secure government funding for their campaigns.

The Libertarian and Green parties had some success in 2016, tripling their vote share from 2012. Both parties ran more television ads than they had in previous elections and received more media attention from the cable news channels (e.g., CNN). Still, they faced challenges that went beyond those noted above; they lacked campaign funding and had trouble getting their candidates on the election ballots in some states. Given the enormous advantage that the two major parties have, winning as a third-party candidate is a seemingly impossible task.

Despite their inability to win national elections, third-party candidates can be very influential. In 2000, Green Party candidate Ralph Nader, who is known as an activist for consumer protections, environmental rights, and social justice, earned a substantial amount of votes in a few states, most notably Florida. Many assume that Nader's voters would have preferred Al Gore over George W. Bush if Nader had not been on the ballot. Had those votes indeed gone to Gore, then Gore would have likely won the election.

Even when third-party candidates do not impact the election outcome, the policies and issues that they promote may get incorporated into the political platforms of the Democrats and/or Republicans. For example, many of the policy positions advocated by Reform Party candidate Ross Perot in the 1992 election were adopted by the Republican Party. Thus, in this important way, third-party candidates do leave their mark on American politics.

Interest Groups

High-Yield

LEARNING OBJECTIVES

- Identify positive and potentially negative effects of interest-group politics.

An **interest group**, also referred to as a special-interest group, is any association of individuals or organizations that is organized on the basis of one or more shared concerns or issues and that attempts to influence public policy in its favor. There are a variety of interest groups, all with political priorities and opinions about what the government should do. Because they are usually not officially affiliated with any political party, they generally have no trouble working with either of the two major parties. In some cases, though, interest groups do have ideological or political priorities that cause them to heavily favor one party or the other. Interest groups use four major strategies to do their work: lobbying, electioneering, litigating, and influencing public opinion. To make any of these strategies work, interest groups first need to raise a sufficient amount of money. They do this in part by convincing people to become members of their group and contribute to the cause.

The most powerful way that a well-funded interest group can affect public policy and the government is through **lobbying**. Lobbyists meet with members of Congress and their staff members, provide evidence at hearings, petition for issues, participate in campaign fundraising, and even draft memos and potential legislation. Interest groups are known for hiring recently retired members of Congress and the executive branch as well as other political insiders as lobbyists. These lobbyists can use their inside experience to outmaneuver other groups. Suggestions of impropriety caused Congress to mandate a waiting period before former members can conduct private consulting. Because some major lobbies have vast resources, their influence over campaigns and parties remains controversial. Current examples include Republican connections to energy company interest groups and Democratic connections to labor union interest groups.

Interest groups also engage in **electioneering** because they have a vested interest in getting the right people into office and making sure they remain there. Thus, interest groups are very active in political campaigns. If an interest group is unable to get a desired result from Congress or a federal agency, it may resort to litigating or turning to the judicial system to reach its goal. Interest groups often issue ratings and analyses of judicial nominees, file legal briefs, and undertake lawsuits. Perhaps the most famous example of this occurred when the NAACP was able to get the Supreme Court to rule that segregation of America's public schools was unconstitutional. Lastly, interest groups attempt to shape public opinion in a variety of ways, such as by publishing research study findings, using the media, and putting on public events like marches.

Some interest groups have more broadly defined goals than others. For example, AARP (formerly the American Association of Retired Persons) has nearly 40 million members and advocates on behalf of individuals age 50 and over on a wide range of issues including insurance access, health care, employment, and consumer and financial protection. AARP represents people across the political spectrum. Other interest groups are called single-issue groups. A **single-issue group**, as the name suggests, is an interest group that focuses on a single issue, such as the environment, gun rights, or foreign policy. Many of these groups, such as the National Rifle Association (NRA), are very well-known and capable of launching high-profile media campaigns to mobilize their members.

The close relationship that interest groups develop with Congress and the executive branch is referred to as the **iron triangle**. Agencies and departments within the executive branch (i.e., the federal bureaucracy) keep close contact with interest group lobbyists who want to influence the government. Interest groups may provide research and statistics to the executive departments. Both lobbyists and bureaucrats value contact with congressional committees and subcommittees that shape the laws regarding their interests. Members of Congress want interest group money and do not want to alienate such powerful interest group support. Bureaucrats may want jobs as lobbyists or funding for various projects. Working together, these three groups have a significant impact on many government policies.

Iron Triangle

Congress

electoral support

funding & political support

friendly legislation & oversight

policy choices & execution

congressional support, via lobby

Interest Group

low regulation, special favors

Bureaucracy

Interest groups give some citizens the opportunity to become more civically engaged. However, not all citizens have the financial resources or ability to participate equally. Socioeconomic status is the top predictor of who will likely join groups. Many people are concerned that the prominence and influence of the interest group system gives disproportionate political weight to the views and interests of the wealthiest citizens.

✔ **AP Expert Note**

Be prepared to apply principles from the foundational documents

In *Federalist* 10, James Madison famously warned of the dangers of factions, by which he meant "a number of citizens, whether amounting to a majority or minority of the whole, who are united and actuated by some common impulse of passion, or of interest, adverse to the rights of other citizens, or to the permanent and aggregate interest of the community." In other words, Madison was wary of the conflicts caused when powerful groups advocate for certain issues that do not apply to the broader public. In a similar manner, critics today claim that interest groups do not work for the public good. Others point out that the group leaders and lobbyists are not elected officials, yet they have tremendous access to government officials and influence on policy.

Being able to spot connections like this between government and politics topics and one or more foundational documents will be crucial to your exam success, especially on the free-response section. (A full list of the College Board's nine foundational documents and key information about them can be found in the back of this book.)

Proponents of interest groups say that the proliferation of interest group activity reflects a positive aspect of the American system of government. American citizens have the lawful right to assemble and to directly petition the government. Such participation is an important aspect of a thriving democratic society. Others reject this positive view of interest groups.

People don't necessarily have to join interest groups in order to benefit from the work interest groups do. Thus, a common problem that some interest groups face is called the **free-rider problem**, which refers to the difficulty an interest group has in acquiring members even though the community at large freely reaps the benefits obtained by that interest group. For example, an interest group dedicated to improving environmental quality standards will, if successful, improve the environment for everyone, even those who are not members of the interest group. Some people, therefore, feel as if they lack an incentive to join an interest group and pay dues because they will receive the benefits anyway. Consequently, some groups decide to close membership and to provide private benefits only to group members. These groups tend to attract wealthier citizens, giving them a financial advantage and thus more political power.

Policy Outcomes

LEARNING OBJECTIVE

- Detail major influences on public policy outcomes.

Membership size, financial resources, ability to generate coverage for their cause, connections with policymakers, favorable relationships with political parties, and the ability to provide information are all important factors that affect interest group influence. Interest groups are important linkage institutions that can greatly affect public policy outcomes, but they are not the only players. Other stakeholders, such as political parties, government officials, and businesses, also work to influence policy direction, often through lobbying, mobilizing strategic partnerships, and using their platforms to advocate for their positions. Therefore, rarely ever are policies developed purely through the political process; instead, they are influenced through various interactions and compromises.

Public policies are also influenced by a variety of additional factors. These factors include economic conditions, public opinion, media coverage, and scientific and technological change. As a result of the wide variety of linkage institutions and other factors, which can push and pull policy in different directions, public policy change often happens slowly.

12.3 ELECTIONS

Election Basics

LEARNING OBJECTIVE

- Identify the impact of presidential elections' discrete components.

Regular, free, and competitive elections work to preserve American democracy by affirming popular control of the government. In addition to selecting public officials, elections encourage and frame policy debates as well as influence the decisions made by public officials. As such, elections provide citizens a mechanism for making important political decisions.

Although the Constitution explains how candidates for the presidency are elected, it does not specify how candidates are to be nominated, nor does it mention the role that political parties are to play in elections. Primary elections and caucuses are managed at the state level by the individual political parties. In other words, the Democrats manage their own primaries, and the Republicans do likewise. Currently, 30 states hold primaries; other states use a caucus to select nominees. A **caucus** is a private meeting run by a political party in which members of the party vote for candidates. In most caucuses, voters physically divide into groups according to the candidate they support, and undecided voters cluster in a group of their own. Each group delivers campaign-style speeches supporting its candidate and tries to convince others to join its group. At the end of the caucus, party organizers count the participants in each candidate's group and tally how many delegates each candidate has won. The delegates will later attend a convention to formally vote in the nomination process.

States' political parties decide whether they want to hold a primary or a caucus. A few states have both caucuses and primaries. In Alaska and Nebraska, for example, Republicans hold primaries while Democrats hold caucuses. In Kentucky, Democrats use a primary while Republicans convene a caucus.

For many years, Iowa has held the first presidential election caucus, generally in January or early February of the election year, and New Hampshire has held the first primary a short time later. Because these and other early contests often decide which candidates have enough support to seriously compete for the presidency, candidates campaign vigorously in these early states. To get the attention of candidates and the media, more and more states have scheduled their primaries and caucuses early in the election year. This trend is often referred to as frontloading, a major consequence of which is that the nominees of the major parties are often known well before the national party conventions, which are held in late summer.

At the nominating conventions, party members discuss and vote on the party's platform, which outlines the party's basic ideological principles, stances on various issues, and campaign objectives. Over the course of four or five days, candidates, notable politicians, public officials, and even celebrities deliver speeches. While some speakers focus on governmental issues, policy matters, and election rules, others deliver highly emotional, pep rally–like addresses designed to energize the party. Perhaps most importantly, it is during the convention that the party officially nominates its candidates for president and vice president.

If no candidate has a majority of the party's delegates going into its convention, then the delegates pick a presidential candidate in what is called a brokered or contested convention. In the first round of voting, delegates vote for the candidate who won their respective states, and if no one gets a majority, delegates may select any candidate in subsequent rounds of voting. Balloting continues until one nominee receives a majority of votes. The last time there was a contested convention was in 1976, when President Gerald Ford and challenger Ronald Reagan both came close but failed to win enough delegates to secure the nomination outright. Ford went on to win the nomination.

12

The Presidential Election Cycle	
Spring of the year before an election	Candidates announce their intentions to run
Summer of the year before an election through spring of the election year	Primary and caucus debates take place
January to June of the election year	States and parties hold primaries and caucuses
July to early September	Parties hold nominating conventions to choose their candidates
September and October	Candidates participate in presidential debates
Early November	Election Day
December	Electors cast their votes in the Electoral College
Early January of the next calendar year	Congress counts the electoral votes
January 20	Inauguration Day

The Electoral College

High-Yield

LEARNING OBJECTIVE

- Provide prominent arguments for and against the Electoral College.

Once the presidential election is held in November, the process of electing a president continues. Unlike candidates in other U.S. elections, the president and vice president are not elected directly by the citizens. Rather, they are voted for by electors through a process called the **Electoral College**. These votes are referred to as electoral votes. Including the 3 in Washington, D.C., there are a total of 538 electoral votes. The number of electoral votes in each state is equal to the number of its U.S. representatives and senators. In mid-December, the electors of the Electoral College go to their respective state capitals to formally vote for president. A majority of 270 electoral votes is needed to elect the president.

Then, the electoral votes are counted in a joint session of Congress. The President of the Senate (who is also the vice president) presides over the official vote count and announces the results. The president-elect takes the oath of office and is sworn in as president on January 20 in the year following the election.

In the unusual event that no candidate gets a majority of electoral votes, the House of Representatives elects the president from the three candidates who received the most electoral votes. Each state's House delegation has one vote. The only time this has happened was during the 1824 election; the House elected John Quincy Adams as president. The House votes only for the president, not the vice president. In the event that the House elects the president, the Senate has the responsibility of choosing the vice president from the two vice presidential candidates with the most electoral votes.

Impact on Democracy

In the 2000 U.S. presidential election, Al Gore lost to George W. Bush even though Gore had received more popular votes (i.e., votes from individual citizens) nationally. In fact, Gore received over 500,000 more votes than Bush. Bush, however, received more electoral votes and thus won the election. In 48 of the 50 U.S. states (except Nebraska and Maine), if a presidential candidate wins the state's popular vote, then the candidate gets all of that state's electoral votes. In this winner-take-all system, even if a candidate wins as little as 51 percent of the popular vote in a state, the candidate gets all of the state's electoral votes. Thus, winning a state by a large margin in the popular vote gets the candidate the same number of electoral votes as winning the state by only a single popular vote.

One of the more controversial debates in American politics is whether the Electoral College is beneficial or harmful to the democratic process. Proponents of the Electoral College argue that the system protects smaller states. If elections were based strictly on the popular vote, then candidates would mostly campaign in major population centers such as New York and Texas. Farmers in Wisconsin and Nebraska, factory workers in Michigan and Illinois, and people living in rural areas might be left out of the process. With the Electoral College, a presidential candidate needs to earn electoral votes from multiple regions of the country. Therefore, a candidate must build a campaign with a trans-regional focus. Those who favor the Electoral College argue that this is an essential safeguard of the democratic process. Supporters of the Electoral College also argue that the system does reflect the popular vote outcome, but on the state level. Further, supporters view the Electoral College as a safeguard against the public electing someone who is widely popular but not qualified to become president.

One of the chief arguments against the Electoral College is that it is possible for a candidate to win the national popular vote but still lose the electoral vote contest and therefore the election. This has happened five times: John Quincy Adams, Rutherford B. Hayes, Benjamin Harrison, George W. Bush, and Donald Trump each became president without winning the popular vote. Critics say that such outcomes diminish the voting power of the people.

Other critics of the Electoral College say that candidates tend to campaign mainly in **swing states**. These are states in which the race is close enough that either of the two major party candidates has a chance to win. Common swing states in recent presidential elections have included Ohio, Florida, Nevada, and New Hampshire. In many other states, the presidential race is rarely close. For example, over the past 30 years, the Republican candidate has always won Texas, and the Democratic candidate has won California. Thus, candidates often do not campaign as much in these states as they do in the swing states.

Congressional Elections

LEARNING OBJECTIVE

- Identify the impact of congressional elections' discrete components.

Running for Congress is in many ways similar to running for president. Candidates for Congress often raise enormous sums of money, undertake an extensive mass media campaign, and rely on professional political managers, strategists, and consultants. Congressional campaigns have some important distinctions, however.

12

A candidate for the presidency has to be a natural-born citizen who is at least 35 years old and has resided in the United States for at least 14 years. There are parallel, but somewhat less stringent, requirements for prospective members of Congress. A candidate for the U.S. House of Representatives must be at least 25 years old, a U.S. citizen for at least seven years, and a legal resident of the state she wishes to represent. The framers intended members of the House of Representatives to be close to the constituents they represented. To make sure representatives heeded public sentiment, the framers mandated that all 435 House members face elections every two years. Each state is entitled to one seat in the House, with additional seats allocated according to population. South Dakota, for example, has a very small population and therefore has only one representative. By contrast, California, the most populous state, has 53 representatives.

A candidate for the U.S. Senate must be at least 30 years old, a U.S. citizen for nine years, and a legal resident of the state he seeks to represent. U.S. senators serve six-year terms that are staggered so that approximately one-third of the 100 Senate seats come up for election every two years. The Senate was designed for its members to represent an entire state and to provide equal representation for each state, regardless of population. Thus, small states possess as much influence as large states in the Senate.

Unlike the president, who can only serve two four-year terms, there are no term limits for representatives or senators. Also, members of Congress are elected based on the popular vote rather than the Electoral College. The candidate with the most votes wins the House or Senate race.

Campaigning

LEARNING OBJECTIVE

- List the pros and cons of the manner in which political campaigns are currently conducted.

Campaigning is a huge part of the election process. After the nominating convention, the presidential candidates hit the campaign trail for the general election. Candidates travel the country, explaining their stances on the issues of the day and their plans to govern. A similar process occurs on the state level with congressional candidates. While they do not have to be nominated by a convention, congressional candidates campaign vigorously in the run-up to the November general election. Debates, rallies, and advertising are major components of general-election campaigning. Candidates typically build massive campaign operations that employ professional campaign managers, strategists, and consultants. Modern campaigns also heavily rely on media and communications experts to craft their political brands, slogans, advertisements, and media messaging.

Voter turnout in primaries is relatively low; only the most motivated voters tend to participate, and these voters tend to be passionate about policies and positions that are important to their party. During the primaries, therefore, presidential and congressional candidates tend to focus on these issues, and they may take extreme positions to appeal to the people most likely to vote. As a result, Democratic Party primaries may become contests among different left-leaning positions. Likewise, Republican primaries can be contests among various conservative ideologies. Once nominated for

12

the general election, candidates often soften their position on issues, especially those that are controversial. Candidates occupy this middle ground in order to attract more mainstream party members, independents, and any voters who would not support highly partisan candidates.

Congressional elections rarely get as much attention as presidential elections, but they are none-theless high-stakes elections. One major factor influencing the outcome of congressional and presidential elections is **incumbency advantage**, which is the edge, or advantage, that current officeholders (i.e., incumbents) possess as they run for reelection. Incumbents are typically much better funded and are better recognized by voters. An office is considered a competitive seat if it is currently held by an incumbent. Incumbents who run for reelection have a distinct advantage over their challengers. First, incumbents are usually well-known by the voters since they have already been serving in office. Second, incumbents often have better campaign operations and fundraising mechanisms. If the incumbent decides not to run for reelection, the office is called an open seat.

Campaign Finance

High-Yield

LEARNING OBJECTIVE

- Detail U.S. legal constraints on campaign finance.

One of the most important requirements for running a campaign, especially for president, is money, and a lot of it. In the 2012 presidential campaign, candidates Barack Obama and Mitt Romney each spent more than $1 billion. This was the largest amount of money ever spent by two candidates, or at least it was until the 2016 election cycle, when Hillary Clinton and Donald Trump collectively spent more than $2.5 billion. In addition to the money raised by the campaigns themselves, cor-porations, unions, and the previously discussed interest groups raise massive sums of money in support of candidates and political initiatives.

Interest groups set up **political action committees (PACs)** to raise campaign contributions from their members to support or oppose candidates, legislative proposals, ballot initiatives, and other policy matters. Often established to support a specific candidate or issue, PACs represent one way interest groups can contribute to a campaign without violating restrictions on political spending. After the Supreme Court's decision in *Citizens United v. Federal Election Commission*, a new type of PAC emerged: the super PAC. Unlike regular PACs, **super PACs** do not have a specific, identifiable political cause. Instead, super PACs are created to support individual candidates for office without having any direct link to that candidate's campaign. They cannot give directly to the candidates or their campaigns, but they are allowed to raise unlimited amounts of money from corporations, unions, associations, and individuals. Then, they spend the raised money to advocate for or against political candidates and issues.

12

Federal Election Laws & Supreme Court Cases

The Tenth Amendment of the Constitution preserves for the states all powers not explicitly delegated to the federal government. This amendment provides the basis for states to control the administration of elections, including campaign finance regulation. Congress, however, also plays a major role in election administration.

In 1907, Congress passed the Tillman Act to prohibit corporations from donating money to candidates running in national elections. Congress would enact various other laws to limit how much money people could give to candidates, how candidates could spend donations, and what spending information candidates must disclose to the public. Despite these efforts to control election spending, the government lacked the ability to enforce spending rules until Congress passed the **Federal Election Campaign Act (FECA)** in 1971. FECA provided a set of rules to regulate the reporting of campaign contributions and expenditures. FECA also outlined contribution rules for corporations and organizations to follow. FECA was amended in 1974 to place legal limits on campaign contributions and expenditures and to establish the **Federal Election Commission (FEC)**. The FEC is an independent regulatory agency that administers and enforces election laws and federal campaign finance rules. The FEC has jurisdiction over the financing of campaigns for both Congress and the presidency.

Buckley v. Valeo (1976)

In *Buckley v. Valeo*, the Supreme Court had to decide this question: Did the limits placed on election expenditures by the Federal Election Campaign Act violate the First Amendment's freedom of speech and association clauses? In this complex case, the Court came to two important conclusions. First, it upheld the constitutionality of limits on individual contributions to candidates. The Court concluded that FECA could restrict individual contributions in order to safeguard America's system of representative democracy. Second, the Court held that governmental restriction of independent expenditures in campaigns, the limitation on expenditures by candidates from their own personal funds, and the limitation on total campaign expenditures *did* violate the First Amendment. *Buckley v. Valeo*, therefore, established the principle that political campaign money is considered speech.

Bipartisan Campaign Reform Act of 2002

The **Bipartisan Campaign Reform Act of 2002**, more commonly known as the McCain-Feingold Act, tried to end the influence of soft money. **Soft money** is not regulated by federal campaign laws. It can be raised in unlimited amounts by political parties for party-building purposes such as voter registration and get-out-the-vote efforts. **Hard money**, on the other hand, is money that is limited and regulated by law. Hard money can be given to a party or candidate. This reform banned all soft money contributions to political parties, increased the limits on hard money contributions, and restricted the ability of corporations, nonprofit organizations, and labor unions to broadcast political advertisements that included a candidate's name or picture.

12

Citizens United v. Federal Election Commission (2010)

In a previous Supreme Court case, *McConnell v. Federal Election Commission* (2003), the Court largely upheld the Bipartisan Campaign Reform Act. The majority opinion stated that the government's restriction on free speech was minimal and justified by an interest in preventing potential corruption threatened by large financial contributions. The results of this opinion were retried just seven years later by the Supreme Court in *Citizens United v. FEC*.

In ***Citizens United v. Federal Election Commission* (2010)**, the Supreme Court overruled parts of *McConnell v. FEC* by a 5-to-4 vote. The Court concluded that corporations, nonprofits, and labor unions have the same political speech rights as individuals under the First Amendment. This case struck down the Bipartisan Campaign Reform Act's ban on soft money, thereby allowing corporations and associations to spend unlimited amounts of money on political ads that call for the election or defeat of individual candidates.

✔ AP Expert Note

Be able to explain the impact of major court cases

Citizens United is one of the College Board's 15 required Supreme Court cases, and with good reason, as it represents a major shift in campaign finance law. On top of this, given the Supreme Court's broad interpretation of First Amendment protections, *Citizens United* demonstrates the various ways that the Constitution can be interpreted. Note that it is not just the ruling itself, but also the factors, causes, and effects tied to that ruling, that will be important on the official exam.

12.4 THE MEDIA

Mass Media's Political Role

LEARNING OBJECTIVE

- List specific influences of mass media on politics.

Closely related to the discussion of voting, political parties, and elections is the role of the news media. It is through the news media that nearly all Americans receive information about politics and current events. The media is a powerful and diverse linkage institution that influences politics and public opinion. The term *media* encompasses a wide range of communication formats such as newspapers, magazines, television, radio, Internet news and political sites, and social media. Together, these news sources inform a large, widely dispersed public and are therefore known as the **mass media**. The term **traditional media** describes media sources that predate the Internet, such as newspapers, radio, and television. The term **news broadcasting** refers to the communication of various news events and other information via television, radio, or Internet.

The media's role in presenting political information is as old as U.S. politics. However, the idea that the news media should not be **biased** (favoring one political view) did not fully develop until the early twentieth century. Essays, leaflets, and books in colonial times were often printed in order to sway public opinion. The advent of daily papers aided in the distribution of political news, but early newspapers would be considered quite biased by today's standards. The development of radio and television and, later on, the Internet allowed citizens to actually see or hear a political speech as it happened, thus enabling people to process political information that had not been filtered by the media.

The Development of Media in the United States	
Late 1700s to the mid-1800s	Very few daily newspapers existed. Instead, news was often distributed via pamphlets and essays (e.g., *Common Sense* by Thomas Paine). Organized reporting was done for political reasons and was directly controlled by supporters of different parties. The media was intended to be partisan and to convey political attacks, which were often personal and vicious.
Late 1800s	Newspapers became national businesses (e.g., William Randolph Hearst's *New York Journal* and Joseph Pulitzer's *New York World*), and selling popular stories that would attract readers and earn profits was the key. News organizations sought to shape public opinion and government policy. Newspapers were also central in helping to enact progressive reforms. Stories about the powers of trusts such as Standard Oil were good for the newspaper business and created pressure for political changes. In this way, the press began helping to set the political agenda.
Early 1900s	Theodore Roosevelt established the presidential "bully pulpit" by speaking directly to the press as a way to advance his agenda. Roosevelt saw the media as a channel through which political leaders could speak directly to the people. His administration took the first steps in creating media events and press conferences. The press came to rely on the president and was often openly supportive of him to continue getting information. A reporter who was overly critical would be shut out from conferences and inside information. The development of radio opened a new form of communication between leaders and the public. Franklin Delano Roosevelt used "fireside chats" as a form of agenda setting. The president's staff knew they could reach millions with personal messages.
Mid-1900s	The development of network television and the expansion of radio, as well as the increasing number of families who gained access to these forms of media, characterize the mid-twentieth century. Events such as the Cuban missile crisis and the Kennedy assassination were broadcast to the entire nation and became media events. During the Vietnam War and Watergate, the media took on the role of investigator, or "watchdog." Growing public mistrust of government led to media focus on government flaws and mistakes.
Late 1900s to early twenty-first century	The development of cable news networks (e.g., CNN, Fox News, and MSNBC) has led to a 24-hour news cycle. The creation of the Internet and the explosion of talk radio has led to the prevalence of "attack journalism" and partisan political coverage. Conservative and liberal groups try to outdo each other in media attacks in order to drive higher ratings.

12

A Changing Media Landscape

LEARNING OBJECTIVE

- Track recent trends altering the media's effect on U.S. political life.

Over the last decade or so, the Internet has become a major source of news and information about politics. Newspapers and print media have had to adapt the way they disseminate information by offering access to most or all of their daily news via online sites. Likewise, many traditional radio programs can now be listened to online. Government officials, political analysts, and others now heavily rely on online blogs, news sites, and social media channels. Various political groups and candidates use Twitter, Facebook, YouTube, and other social networking sites to recruit and organize supporters as well as raise money for their causes. Lastly, the Internet provides average citizens the means to research their government. For example, a person interested in the Supreme Court and its work could visit the SCOTUS blog, which provides information on court cases and decisions, judicial nominations, and other legal questions. Government records and statistics that were once available only inside major libraries are now readily accessible to the public.

✔ AP Expert Note

Know the various ways that the media affects modern-day politics

Given how vital the media is in terms of maintaining democracy and keeping the government accountable, some have nicknamed the media "the fourth estate." In other words, members of the media are considered almost like a fourth branch of government. Describing journalists and media outlets in this way is an acknowledgment of the influence they have on the American people. This chapter outlines the details and methods behind this influence, a topic that has only become more prominent in the age of the Internet and social media.

Most citizens lack the time and interest to be thoroughly informed about politics and current events. Therefore, journalists and others who create content for the media monitor what the government and politicians are doing and alert the public when it needs to pay attention. As the media responds to and participates in the political process, it helps to influence public opinion. In this role, the media engages in **agenda setting**, which is its ability to influence the importance placed on the topics in the public agenda.

The study of **media effects** analyzes how much people's political attitudes and opinions are affected by exposure to media coverage. The media, despite any claims to the contrary, is not a simple mirror that reflects news events. There is a great deal of evidence to suggest that the media impacts its audience by what is reported, what is not reported, and how certain information is presented. There are four basic media effects that influence people on a subconscious level.

1. Framing: The influence on public opinion due to how a story is covered.

2. Slant: The bias in a report that covers one policy or politician positively without providing similar coverage of the other side.

3. Filtering: The effect on public opinion of media officials' decisions about which news events to report.

4. Priming: The impact on the public's view of a topic or person due to positive or negative coverage of it.

Until the 1990s, the three major television news networks (ABC, CBS, and NBC) together claimed more than 80 percent of all news consumers. Over the past 30 years, the networks have faced a growing list of competitors, especially from cable television. **Cable news** channels are dedicated to broadcasting the news; the name comes from the boom of cable television in the 1980s. To capture more viewers, cable news providers must select coverage and programming that is interesting, visually appealing, and often even entertaining.

Because there are so many coverage sources, news providers often target highly segmented listening and viewing audiences. For example, certain talk-radio programs target conservatives, while others target liberals. The same is true for some cable news channels; for instance, MSNBC has a more liberal audience, while Fox News has a more conservative audience. Another result of the increase in media competition has been **horse-race journalism**, a practice in which journalists and media providers focus almost exclusively on which candidate is winning or losing in the polls and on candidate personalities and differences. Some critics argue that this type of journalism prevents important news and issues from being covered in the media, leading to a less-informed public.

The **equal-time rule** dictates that television and radio broadcast stations provide equal airtime to all political candidates who request it. This means, for example, that if a station gives a certain amount of time to a presidential candidate, it must do the same for another candidate who requests it, at the same price if applicable. The equal-time rule was created because the Federal Communications Commission wanted to ensure that broadcast stations could not easily manipulate the outcome of an election by presenting one candidate while excluding others. The equal-time rule should not be confused with the now-defunct Fairness Doctrine, which dealt with presenting balanced points of view on matters of public importance.

Online and social media present even more diversity in terms of coverage quality and depth. The Internet is a free market of political news in the sense that no one can regulate, control, or ban information. Consumers themselves must decide what is fact, what is opinion, and what is falsehood. The proliferation of competing online information may weaken the power of the news media relative to the days when news media monopolized our attention.

Social Media

Social media has also changed the way campaigns are conducted by giving candidates a new platform and a new way to target voters. Most consider Barack Obama the first presidential candidate to effectively utilize social media. In the 2008 presidential election, John McCain, Obama's opponent, focused on traditional media in his campaign. In contrast, Obama developed a powerful online presence using platforms such as Facebook, MySpace, YouTube, and podcasts. These efforts made it possible for information to be easily shared between people. It also helped Obama

12

connect with a younger generation, gaining many first-time voters. By election day, Obama had over two million Facebook supporters, while McCain only had 600,000. Obama had more than 100,000 Twitter followers, and McCain had fewer than 5,000.

In the 2016 election, the Donald Trump and Hillary Clinton campaigns moved online and created websites to distribute information. They used search engine results to target voters with ads. They used the Internet to reach out to potential donors, raising millions of dollars online. Trump and Clinton used social networks such as Facebook, Twitter, and YouTube to interact with supporters and get the attention of potential voters.

Mass media has been changing rapidly, as the Internet supports a growing number of news information providers and fewer people rely on print media, television, and radio for news. While it is an influential force, the media itself is influenced by the need to attract consumers. Given the great variety of media sources, it is challenging to argue that the media as a whole has a particular ideological bias. There is general agreement, however, that a free and open press is a vital part of American democracy.

Key Media Roles
Educating voters on how to exercise their democratic rights
Reporting on the development of an election campaign
Providing a platform for political parties and candidates to communicate their message to the electorate
Providing a platform for the public to communicate their concerns and opinions to political office holders, candidates, and government officials
Organizing and hosting debates so that the parties and candidates can interact with each other
Reporting results and monitoring vote counting
Monitoring the election process itself in order to evaluate the fairness and legitimacy of the process

 **NEXT STEP: PRACTICE**

Go to Rapid Review and Practice Chapter 7 or to your online quizzes on kaptest.com for exam-like practice on this topic.

Haven't registered your book yet? Go to kaptest.com/moreonline to begin.

CHAPTER 13

The Free-Response Section

FREE-RESPONSE STRATEGY

Section II Overview

The 1 hour and 40 minute free-response section is worth half of your total exam score and consists of 4 questions, all of which are required. You should devote about 20 minutes to each of the first 3 questions, which will ask you to write short responses to questions relating to a stimulus. You should plan to spend about 40 minutes on the final prompt, which will lay out specific criteria you must meet when constructing a longer essay with a thesis.

> ✔ **AP Expert Note**
>
> **Treat the free-response section as a marathon (and train accordingly)**
>
> 100 minutes can feel like no time at all when you have to write 4 free-response questions, but it is actually a long time for your brain to maintain sharp focus—especially after you have already spent 80 minutes on the multiple-choice part of the exam (Section I). However, if you practice writing free-response questions, including sticking to the timing and pacing required for Section II, you will build up the necessary stamina and feel much more prepared and confident on the official exam.

Question Types

Every AP U.S. Government and Politics exam will contain the same four free-response question (FRQ) types, always in the following order:

1. **Concept Application:** Apply government and politics concepts to a scenario described in a paragraph.

2. **Quantitative Analysis:** Interpret data from an information graphic, and apply the data to government and politics concepts.

3. **SCOTUS Comparison:** Compare a provided description of a non-required Supreme Court case to a required Supreme Court case.

4. **Argument Essay:** Construct an essay with a thesis, support it with evidence, and respond to a view that opposes the thesis.

Most free-response prompts will contain three or four tasks (labeled A, B, C, D). Although each type of question is distinct, they share some common characteristics. Often, a question draws from two or more areas in the course; for instance, the prompt may ask you to relate the topic of government bureaucracy to the topics of public policy and voting patterns. The free-response questions are also often structured to ask progressively more challenging tasks that will help you think through the prompt and build your answer. For example, Part A of the question may ask you to simply identify a trend based on data provided, Part B to describe the historic precedents for this trend, and Part C to explain how this information would apply to a present-day scenario.

Scoring

Readers will score each individual prompt according to a rubric. The rubrics for the Concept Application, Quantitative Analysis, and SCOTUS Comparison questions are straightforward: if a prompt requires you to complete five tasks, you can earn one point for successfully completing each task, for a total of five points for that prompt. The rubric for the Argument Essay is a bit more complex and relates to demonstrating certain skills, such as thesis construction and use of evidence. (Scoring information and sample rubrics will be provided in the following sections about each specific question type.)

> ✔ **AP Expert Note**
>
> **Keep in mind that each free-response question is weighted equally**
>
> Although the first three prompts might include varying numbers of tasks, and the Argument Essay will take you more time to write, each free-response question is worth the same amount: one quarter of your Section II score. Section II, as a whole, counts for half of your overall exam score. This means that each free-response question is worth 12.5% of your total exam score! Therefore, it is important to take every question seriously and respond to each one fully.

The Kaplan Method for Free-Response Questions

While there are four different kinds of free-response questions on the AP U.S. Government and Politics exam, you can and should approach every prompt using the same Kaplan Method. Employing a methodical, strategic approach will help ensure that you effectively address every part of every question. Just follow these four steps (which spell out AP-AP)!

1. **Analyze the prompt.**

2. **Plan your response.**

3. **Action! Write your response.**

4. **Proofread.**

Let's look at the Kaplan Method steps in more detail.

Step 1: Analyze the Prompt

Take the time to understand each and every part of the prompt. If you don't answer each of the prompt's required tasks, it will be impossible to earn a high score for that question! Analyzing the prompt means thinking carefully about the following components.

- **The stimulus.** The first three prompts will all include a stimulus, paragraph(s) or an information graphic that serves as the base of the questions that follow. Whether text or visual, analyze the stimulus just as carefully as you do the questions themselves. Take notes, underline key facts, and mark data trends. Most of the questions will be based directly on information from the stimulus, so it is essential to fully understand the stimulus.

- **The content of the questions**. Consider exactly what topics the questions address. Underline key terms and requirements. Some prompt parts might ask for more than one item—perhaps a "similarity" and a "conclusion based on the similarity"—so make sure you address them all. Read all the questions before starting work on your responses; often, the questions ask for related information or build upon each other, so understanding the set as a whole will help you plan out your response.

- **The action words.** Next, make sure you know exactly what you have to do with the content: *identify, explain,* etc. Consider circling the action words so you make sure you do the correct required action, noting especially when prompts ask you to do more than one. While we often use these action words somewhat interchangeably when speaking, consider carefully how each action word calls for a slightly different treatment of the content. Some examples, from simple to complicated, include:

  - *identify*: point out a trend or piece of information

  - *describe*: fully lay out the details of something

  - *explain*: describe something, including *why* or *how* factors (e.g., what causes it, why it's important)

  - *analyze*: explain something, considering multiple perspectives, and assert a claim based on evidence and logic

So before doing anything else, take a few minutes to analyze the prompt's stimulus, question content, and action words. You must have this foundation to successfully answer any free-response prompt.

13

Know commonly tested free-response question topics

At least one of the four free-response questions on every AP U.S. Government and Politics exam will include the topic of public policy. While prepping for the exam, consider brainstorming ways that the branches of government, the public, and linkage institutions can each influence the creation of public policy. (For example, the president could issue an executive order regarding policy; interest groups could lobby Congress to make a law about a policy.) Other highly tested free-response question topics include: federalism, separation of powers, checks and balances, and political behaviors.

Step 2: Plan Your Response

This is the *most important* factor in writing a quality response. Planning is never a waste of time; rather, it is a crucial step to creating an effective response that addresses every part of every prompt. The test makers expect you to take time to plan your responses and have built this into the exam timing, so take advantage of it. Ultimately, planning saves you time by helping you write a focused response. You only have time to write each response once, so make it count!

Here are some tips to help you make your plan:

- Think about what you will write for each part of each prompt. Jot down brief notes—phrases and/or examples—for each part.

- When asked to *describe*, *discuss*, or *explain*, see if you can come up with an example to help support your response.

- Double check your notes against the prompt to make sure you didn't skip any required tasks.

- Devote an appropriate amount of time to each part, depending on the complexity of the required task. (Parts that only ask you to *identify* something will require less time than parts that ask you to *explain* or *describe*.)

Step 3: Action! Write Your Response

After thoroughly completing the pre-writing steps, actually writing the response should be relatively easy: just use the notes you jotted down in Step 2 to write your paragraphs. You may choose to label your paragraphs according to the part of the prompt they address (A, B, C) in order to stay organized, but you don't have to. The most important thing is to make sure to write full paragraphs; lists or outline-style notes will not earn you points on the exam.

General writing strategies were laid out in Chapter 2, but overall, keep in mind that your responses should clearly focus on the required tasks, provide full explanations, and firmly assert your points.

13

✔ AP Expert Note

Be strategic with the information you provide

Don't just write as much as you know about the topic of a prompt; rather, respond with information that satisfies each specific requirement. For example, if a free-response prompt asks you to "identify the principle established in *Marbury v. Madison*," don't waste time explaining all the facts of this complicated case. Just write enough to identify that the case established judicial review, and move on!

Step 4: Proofread

Try to leave a minute or two to briskly proofread. Your responses need not be perfect, but you should quickly correct any glaring errors that might distract your readers from your content. If you catch a mistake, just neatly cross it out and write the correction above. Try to avoid erasures or other potentially messy alterations. There's no time for a complete overhaul of the response, but if you made a plan, there won't be any need for one!

A Note on Timing and Pacing

Now that we've established the Kaplan Method (AP-AP) to apply to every free-response question, let's review timing considerations. You should respond to each prompt for an amount of time that is proportional to the work involved. Prompts 1–3 should each take approximately 20 minutes to analyze, plan, write, and proofread, while Prompt 4 is a longer essay that should take 40 minutes for all of those same steps.

You are working over a long total time span, 1 hour and 40 minutes, so pacing yourself among four prompts will require some effort and practice. Consider wearing a standard wristwatch to help pace yourself in case there is no clock available in the testing room. And just as importantly, practice the free-response sections on the practice tests under timed conditions. It's easy to overestimate how long 1 hour and 40 minutes will feel on the day of the exam, so practicing an entire free-response section with a watch will greatly increase your familiarity with the required pacing.

One final reminder about pacing: although your time should be appropriately allotted among the four prompts, you do not necessarily have to respond to the prompts in order. As long as you write within the correct area of your lined booklet, feel free to start with whichever prompt is easiest for you to help build your confidence to complete the whole section.

13

Remember to "AP-AP"

Recall that the steps of the Kaplan Method for Free-Response Questions spell out AP-AP. Follow all of the steps of this easy-to-remember acronym every time you encounter a free-response prompt, both in practice and on Test Day. By making the Kaplan Method second nature, you won't have to think about what you're doing, and can instead focus on the quality content you're writing.

CONCEPT APPLICATION

Overview

Question 1 of the free-response section will always be the Concept Application prompt. This prompt will begin with a stimulus that is a short paragraph or two describing a political scenario. The paragraph(s) could be an excerpt from news media, a description of a political situation, a summary of information, or something else.

The questions that follow the stimulus require you to apply course concepts to the given scenario. For instance, you could be asked how different branches of government might respond to the scenario, or how a conservative or liberal viewpoint might impact someone's support of or opposition to the scenario. Whatever you're asked, you'll need both a careful understanding of the prompt and your knowledge of government and politics concepts to tackle the Concept Application question.

Strategy

As you will for every free-response question, follow the 4-Step Kaplan Method. Before walking through a sample prompt step-by-step, let's look at some special considerations for the Concept Application question.

- When analyzing the stimulus, carefully note relevant details. Paraphrase the political scenario in your own words before looking at the questions.

- Concept Application questions often build on each other, asking you to use your response for one part to answer another part. Therefore, carefully plan your response before you start writing in order to make sure you choose answers that you can apply to later parts of the prompt if needed.

The following is a step-by-step walk-through of a sample Concept Application question.

Sample Question

A new political party, the Health & Wealth Party, forms to focus on those policies which members believe will address the most significant threats to the health and prosperity of the general population. Their key platform favors requiring manufacturers of high-sugar snack foods to produce an equal ratio of low-sugar snack alternatives offered at the same price to consumers. In addition, they advocate using tax money to subsidize low-income families with funds to buy the low-sugar snacks. To increase "wealth," the party supports significantly lowering taxes on corporations, with the intent of attracting new businesses to the United States. Finally, they also propose drastically reducing income taxes for all Americans, making up the difference in the budget by slashing military spending for foreign affairs.

After reading the scenario, respond to Parts A, B, and C.

(A) The Health & Wealth Party's platform contains elements that reflect conservative, liberal, and libertarian viewpoints. For each of the three viewpoints, identify one element of the Health & Wealth Party platform that reflects that viewpoint's typical ideology.

(B) Describe a way in which the Health & Wealth Party's nominee, if elected to the presidency, could attempt to implement the policy regulating snack manufacturers.

(C) Explain one reason why it is difficult for third-party candidates, like the Health & Wealth Party nominee, to win presidential elections.

Step 1: Analyze the Prompt

Closely read the political scenario (the stimulus), marking important details. When finished, briefly paraphrase the paragraph in your own words, either in your head or in the margins, to solidify your understanding of the scenario before reading the questions. A sample paraphrase for this prompt could be: *Party for regulating snack companies, but otherwise supporting businesses, and lowering taxes & foreign military spending.* Note that on a detail-heavy scenario such as this, it is especially important to paraphrase the paragraph.

As you did with the stimulus, read all the questions carefully, underlining exactly what each asks for. Box, underline, or otherwise mark the action words in each question (which, for this sample prompt, are *identify, describe,* and *explain*). Make sure to respond in a way that fulfills what each action word requires.

13

Step 2: Plan Your Response

The following showcases a high-scoring writer's thought process and written notes for planning a response to this prompt.

Part A: Need to ID a detail for each of the three views.

- Conserv.: traditional values + pro-market policies --> lower taxes on business
- Liberal: more gov't involvement for equality --> regulate manuf. & subsidies for poor
- Libert.: ind. liberty + low gov't involvement --> lower income taxes & military spending

Part B: Need to think of how a pres. could impact a policy about reg. snack manufacturers, including details to describe my answer.

- Commerce clause is relevant
- Pres. could meet w/ Congress, persuade to make committee & draft bill
- Pres. could endorse candidates who agree on issue

Part C: Need to think about difficulties faced by third-party candidates during elections (not while in office). Need to fully describe the issue, including the why/how, to count as explaining.

- Hard to win votes in electoral college due to winner-take-all system and entrenchment of major parties
- But an election based only on popular vote would likely not create a clear majority winner

Step 3: Action! Write Your Response

Now you'll just write out the information you planned! As you write, remember to keep your paragraphs organized and your writing legible. Refer back to the question's action words to make sure you're doing the correct tasks. See the sample high-scoring response and the explanation of what features make it high-scoring at the end of this section. One of the best ways to improve your own free-response answers is to read sample responses, thinking carefully about what makes the responses effective and what features you can copy.

Step 4: Proofread

Leave a minute or so for a quick proofread, neatly correcting any errors you catch.

Sample High-Scoring Response

Parts of the Health & Wealth Party's platform reflect different political ideologies. Their stance on lowering taxes for businesses is a conservative view, as it reflects less government involvement in the economy. The plank about increased regulation of snack manufacturers, however, is a more liberal view about regulating the economy. The goal of lowering overall taxes and foreign military spending reflects a libertarian preference for less government.

The party's goal of regulating snack manufacturers could be addressed by a president. Since regulating a food company would likely fall under Congress's authority due to the commerce clause, the president could try to influence Congress. For instance, the president could formally and informally meet with Congress members to persuade them to draft a relevant bill, encourage (or pressure) them to call a special committee to research the issue, and try to influence the committees that handle health and nutrition. In addition, the president could endorse candidates who agree with the regulations during the midterm elections to get agreeable Congress members working on the policy.

However, a third-party candidate winning the Electoral College would be very difficult in our current two-party system. Since most states have a purely winner-take-all system for electoral votes, a third-party candidate would have to beat out both major party candidates in order to earn any electoral votes in a state. And even if a candidate did win a few states' electoral votes, he or she would still be far from winning the required 270 electoral votes to become president. Still, using a majority of popular votes to win the presidency would also be problematic: with 3 or more candidates running, it would be unlikely that any candidate would win the majority of votes. So, the winner-take-all system might be practical, even if it creates a challenge for third-party candidates.

Sample Response Explanation

The writer of this high-scoring response includes many effective elements:

- **Organization:** The response addresses one part in each paragraph. Although this is not required, it makes it much easier for the reader to follow and score your response.

- **Sentences:** Although Part A requires only identification, the writer still uses a paragraph for the response, adding just a little explanation to justify his or her classifications of the party planks. Use paragraphs and complete sentences for all parts of your responses; never use just phrases or lists.

- **Addressing each action word:** Note that the responses for Parts B and C are longer than the response for Part A. Part A only required *identification*, while B required *description* and C required *explanation*. The response for Part B provides a full description of a presidential action. The response for Part C effectively *explains* by discussing multiple reasons why the Electoral College is the way it is, including both how the system puts third-party candidates at a disadvantage and why the system is still practical.

13

Scoring for Question 1: 3 points (1 + 1 + 1)

The following is a general rubric an AP reader might use to grade this free-response question. When you practice FRQs, use both the sample responses and this scoring information to assess your own writing.

Part A (1 point)

One point for identifying a component of the platform for each view: conservative, liberal, and libertarian. Note: Some components could fall under more than one label.

- Example conservative components: lowering taxes on businesses, lowering income taxes, seeking more balanced budget

- Example liberal components: regulating snack manufacturers, providing subsidies for lower-income families, lowering military spending

- Example libertarian components: lowering taxes on businesses, lowering income taxes, lowering foreign military spending, seeking more balanced budget

Part B (1 point)

One point for describing a way the president could impact policy.

- Example ways include: calling a special committee/commission to research and influence the issue, persuading Congress members to create legislation that addresses the policy, appointing positions to the Food and Drug Administration that support the policy, issuing an executive order to the FDA, endorsing candidates who support the policy, using the "bully pulpit" to rally public support and put pressure on Congress, highlighting the issue in the State of the Union address, proposing a budget that includes provisions for the policy, threatening to veto a bill unless Congress makes provisions for the policy

Part C (1 point)

One point for explaining a difficulty faced by third-party candidates.

- Example difficulties include: less financing, difficulty of getting onto ballots, heavy political entrenchment of the two-party system, winner-take-all nature of Electoral College makes it difficult to score electoral votes, voter discouragement (wanting to make sure their vote "counts"), major parties' tendency to adopt platform planks that try to appeal to potential third-party voters

QUANTITATIVE ANALYSIS

Overview

Question 2 is the Quantitative Analysis prompt. This FRQ begins with an information graphic, such as a table, chart, graph, or map. The information graphic will depict some kind of politically relevant data—presidential election results, political affiliations of federal judges, or voter turnout by state, for instance.

The prompts that follow will require you to both analyze the information graphic and relate its data to government and politics concepts; later parts will likely require increasingly complex tasks.

- Part A usually asks you to *identify* a piece of data or a trend from the information graphic.

- Part B will likely ask you to *analyze* the information graphic, perhaps by explaining a possible reason for the graphic's data trends or by using the data to draw a conclusion.

- Part C will then involve *applying* the information graphic to a course concept; for example, the question could ask how a table's depiction of popular vote results in a presidential election reflects the structure of the Electoral College system.

Strategy

As always, follow the 4-Step Kaplan Method. Also, consider the following special strategies for the Quantitative Comparison question:

- Take time to analyze the information graphic. The information graphic is just as important to answering the questions as the text stimulus on other prompts, and it requires some special analysis. Components such as titles, labels, and keys are vital for correct interpretation of the graphic. Ask yourself exactly what data the information graphic is depicting (and what data it is *not* depicting) and note relevant trends before you look at the questions.

- At least one question will require you to identify a specific trend or data point from the information graphic. On such questions, focus only on the relevant part of the graphic and pinpoint the data you need.

- When appropriate, refer to data from the information graphic in your response, and be specific (e.g., "only four amendments were passed in the nineteenth century" rather than "few amendments were passed in the nineteenth century").

Sample Question

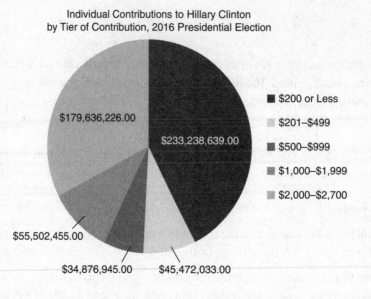

Individual Contributions to Hillary Clinton
by Tier of Contribution, 2016 Presidential Election

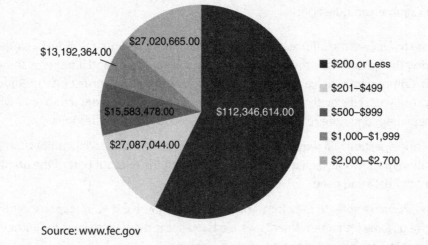

Individual Contributions to Donald Trump
by Tier of Contribution, 2016 Presidential Election

Source: www.fec.gov

Use the information graphic to respond to Parts A, B, and C.

(A) Identify the tier of individual contributions to Hillary Clinton's campaign that accounts for the third largest proportion of her total.

(B) Describe a similarity or difference between the data for individual contributions for each candidate and draw a possible conclusion based on this similarity or difference.

(C) Explain a reason that individual contributions are capped at $2,700, and explain a possible impact of this cap on elections.

13

Step 1: Analyze the Prompt

Carefully analyze the components of the information graphic: titles, labels, and general trends. Notice that the information graphic contains two pie charts. Both depict individual contributions at different tiers to presidential candidates in 2016; one shows contributions for Clinton, one for Trump. The contribution tiers are the same for both candidates. Contributions of $200 and less represent the lowest tier; this tier makes up the biggest proportion of both candidates' contributions from individuals. Note that there must be a limit at $2,700 since the tiers don't go any higher. Clinton also had a large proportion of contributions at the highest tier, while Trump's were a bit more evenly distributed among the middle-high tiers. The dollar totals show that Clinton had a much higher total amount of contributions.

Next, carefully read and mark the important parts of each question, paying special attention to questions that ask for multiple things; note that Part B asks you to both *describe* and *draw a conclusion* and Part C includes two things you must *explain*. Keep in mind that Quantitative Analysis questions generally ask you to first read data from the information graphic, then make some analysis of the data, and finally apply the data to a course concept.

Step 2: Plan Your Response

Brainstorm how you will address each response part based on your analysis in Step 1. See the following thoughts and notes that a high-scoring writer might make.

Part A: Need to find the 3rd largest tier on Clinton's pie chart.

- $1,000–$1,999

Part B: Need one similarity or difference, and a conclusion based on this info.

- similarity: <$200 largest proportion
  concl.: many want to support candidates; even small contributions add up

Part C: Need to fully explain two things.

- caps on ind. contribs b/c concerns about buying elections, campaign finance laws
- cap probably helps limit the total amount at the highest tier; caps help equalize contribs among candidates & limit scope of campaigning (ex. of candidate highly supported by wealthy)

Step 3: Action! Write Your Response & Step 4: Proofread

Then, use your plan to write out your response, leaving a minute at the end to complete a brisk proofread. Remember that it is suggested you spend about 20 minutes each on Questions 1, 2, and 3. See the following for a sample high-scoring response and an explanation of its high-scoring features.

13

Sample High-Scoring Response

The third largest proportion of Clinton's individual contributions total was the tier of $1,000–$1,999.

A similarity in the data about individual contributions is that both candidates' most common donation is the lowest-tier amount, $200 or less. This suggests that both candidates have widespread support among less-wealthy voters. To constitute such a high percentage of the total contributions even though it is the lowest tier, this indicates that many individuals must have contributed to the campaigns.

Individual contributions to candidates were capped due to concerns about money having too large of an influence on elections, threatening what is supposed to be a democratic process in which every voter has an equal voice. In an unregulated system, a wealthier candidate with wealthier supporters could overrun the media with political messages, perhaps having such an overwhelming impact on public opinion that the election was essentially purchased by the side with more money at its disposal. To prevent this, Congress passed campaign finance laws; limiting individual contributions perhaps prevents a disproportionate influence by wealthy supporters. These laws thus help equalize contributions among candidates, making elections more fair. Limits help minimize the potential for out-of-control campaigning with essentially limitless money for candidates to spend.

Explanation of Sample Response

Note the following successful elements of this high-scoring response:

- **Organization:** The writer uses one paragraph for each part of the response and follows the plan from Step 2, helping to ensure that the response addresses every required task.

- **Complete sentences:** The writer uses full sentences for every part of the response—even the brief identification task in Part A.

- **Specific data from the information graphic:** The writer uses specific data for the response to Part B.

- **Addressing each action word:** The writer addresses each action word appropriately. For instance, in Part A, the writer uses a brief sentence to address the requirement of *identification*. In contrast, Part C requires two *explanations*, so the writer fully explains both a reason for and an impact of contribution caps, effectively incorporating an example of a candidate with many wealthy supporters to help support the explanations.

Scoring for Question 2: 5 points (1 + 2 + 2)

Part A (1 point)

One point for identifying $1,000–$1,999 as the third largest proportion for Clinton's campaign.

Part B (2 points)

One point for describing a similarity or difference.

- Example similarities: both candidates had lowest tier (<$200) make up the largest percentage of contributions; middle tiers were similar for both candidates

- Example differences: Clinton's second-highest percentage tier was the highest contribution level ($2,000+) and made up about a third of her total contribution amounts, while Trump had a near-tie for the second-highest percentage tier ($200-$500 and $2,000+); Clinton had much higher total contribution dollars than Trump both at each tier and overall

One point for drawing a logical possible conclusion based on the similarity or difference.

- Example conclusions: based on high percentage of lowest-tier contributions, both candidates may have had large numbers of supporters who could not afford contributions at higher tiers; based on Clinton's larger percentage of highest-tier contributions, she may have had a greater number of wealthy supporters than Trump; Clinton lost the election although she had more individual contribution dollars than Trump, suggesting that the candidate with the highest contributions from individuals does not necessarily win the election

Part C (2 points)

One point for explaining a reason for the cap on individual contributions.

- Example reasons for the cap: concerns about wealthy individuals and corporations "buying" elections have led to campaign finance laws and contribution caps; cap reflects attempts to limit spending on pervasive advertising, especially "attack ads"; cap reflects restrictions such as Bipartisan Campaign Reform Act of 2002's regulations on "soft money" contributions by individuals

One point for explaining a possible impact of the cap on elections.

- Example impacts on elections: limits potential for elections to be dominated by wealthy contributors; potentially limits unfair advantage of candidates who have more wealthy supporters; forces individuals who wish to contribute more than the cap to use other avenues of financial support, such as political party committees and PACs, which increases such institutions' influence on elections

SCOTUS COMPARISON

Overview

Question 3 is the SCOTUS Comparison FRQ. It begins with a two-paragraph stimulus that describes the background and holding for a non-required Supreme Court case. Don't worry: you are not expected to have any outside knowledge of the non-required case. All the information about the case needed to answer the question will be provided. (Note: Lists of College Board's 9 foundational documents and 15 required SCOTUS cases, and some key information about each, are available in the back of this book.)

The prompts that follow the stimulus will ask you to relate the non-required case to one of the required SCOTUS cases. Specifically:

- Part A will often ask you to *identify* a constitutional clause or principle that is relevant to both cases.

- Part B will often require you to compare or contrast the two cases, perhaps asking you to *explain* why the facts of the cases resulted in different holdings.

- Part C will likely require you to *apply* the case's ruling to a political action or principle. For instance, you could be asked how citizens could react to a ruling with which they disagree.

Strategy

Because it compares the reasoning of two court cases, the SCOTUS Comparison question may be the most abstract and complex prompt you encounter on the free-response section. It is therefore extra important to use the Kaplan Method in order to organize your ideas and logically think through your response. Also, consider these factors that are specific to the SCOTUS Comparison FRQ:

- The stimulus will explain a new case to you. (Remember, you are not expected to have any outside knowledge of the new case.) Since court case backgrounds and holdings are nuanced, pay very close attention to the details and reasoning of the new case. Consider writing a brief paraphrase of the case holding in your own words.

- The questions will always refer to one of the required SCOTUS cases. It may be helpful to spend a few moments reviewing what you know about the required case; jot down the main idea of the required case's holding before getting too far into the questions.

  - If asked why the cases resulted in similar or different holdings, carefully consider the background of both cases: what essential difference or similarity between the two led the Court to the individual holdings?

Sample Question

In Utah in 1874, George Reynolds was indicted by a grand jury and later found guilty of bigamy (marriage to more than one person) under the federal Morrill Anti-Bigamy Act, passed by Congress in 1862, which prohibited residents of territories to marry someone while still married to someone else. Reynolds, a member of the Church of Jesus Christ of Latter-Day Saints (LDS Church), presented himself as a test case to challenge the Morrill Act, arguing that the law violated LDS Church members' First Amendment freedom of religion rights. Reynolds argued that it was his religious duty to marry multiple wives, and thus the practice should be protected under the First Amendment.

The case was appealed to the Supreme Court, and in *Reynolds v. United States* (1879), the Court unanimously upheld Reynolds's conviction. In its holding that the Morrill Act did not violate the First Amendment's protections of religious freedom, the court distinguished between religious belief and religious action. While Congress cannot legislate against the former, it can regulate religious action; in this case, the holding justified the prohibition of the action of bigamy based on the tradition of English law. In addition, the Court concluded that "to permit this would be to make the professed doctrines of religious belief superior to the law of the land, and in effect to permit every citizen to become a law unto himself," perhaps leading to claiming practices like human sacrifice as protected religious actions.

Based on the information given, respond to Parts A, B, and C.

(A) Identify the constitutional clause that is common to both *Reynolds v. United States* (1879) and *Wisconsin v. Yoder* (1972).

(B) Based on the constitutional clause identified in Part A, explain why the facts of *Wisconsin v. Yoder* led to a different holding than the holding in *Reynolds v. United States*.

(C) Describe a political action that members of the public who disagree with the holding in *Reynolds v. United States* could take to attempt to impact the legality of bigamy.

Step 1: Analyze the Prompt

Since court cases involve abstract reasoning and many details, learning about new cases is a complex task. To help keep the information from the stimulus straight, underline or jot down the key facts and write a paraphrase of the ruling. The following is an example of brief notes a high-scoring writer might make.

Key details:

- R found guilty of violating federal law against bigamy
- R claimed law violated 1st Am. right, since bigamy part of LDS Church belief

Holding:

- conviction upheld, law did not violate 1st Am.., religious beliefs v. actions, actions may be limited or otherwise anything could be claimed to be a justified religious action

After analyzing the questions for the content and action words (in this case, *identify, explain, describe*), review the required SCOTUS case (introduced in the question stem). Consider writing a few quick notes to refresh your memory about the required case so that you can keep the cases straight and make a solid plan for answering the various parts of the prompt.

13

Wisconsin v. Yoder:

- Amish children stopped attending school after 8th grade, breaking WI law
- Amish believed more edu. bad
- Court ruled with Amish parents: requiring more edu. violated free exercise clause (by 14th Am.) b/c action based on sincere belief and not harmful to students/society

Step 2: Plan Your Response

The following is an example of how a high-scoring writer might plan an answer to this question, including the writer's thought process and notes.

Part A: Free exercise clause.

Part B: Need to note the difference in the reasoning of the rulings, and what led to different holdings.

- R v. US: law against bigamy const. b/c not all religious actions are protected by free ex. clause, only beliefs; bigamy can be prohibited based on tradition - action not protected
- Y v. WI: law requiring more edu. unconst. b/c stopping edu. based on sincere belief & not harmful - action protected

Part C: Need to write about what action someone can take if they disagree with a federal law.

- petition Congress members to change law
- elect new reps. who will change law

Part 3: Action! Write Your Response & Step 4: Proofread

Use your plan to write each part of the response, and briskly skim for errors when finished.

See the following high-scoring response, and be sure to read the points in the explanation about what makes this response effective. Think about what features you can incorporate into your own free-response answers.

Sample High-Scoring Response

Both cases concern the free exercise clause of the 1st Amendment, since both have to do with laws that prohibit acting in accordance with religious beliefs. However, the rulings in the cases differed due to the Court's interpretation of the religious actions involved. In general, the government cannot pass a law that prohibits someone from exercising their religion. In Reynolds v. US, Reynolds argued that the federal law against bigamy violated his right to practice his religion, believing the practice to be a duty as a member of the LDS

Church. In *Wisconsin v. Yoder*, some Amish parents had stopped sending their children to public school after 8th grade, believing that further education was unnecessary and even harmful to their faith. The Court sided against Reynolds, but with the Amish parents. In Reynolds, the Court determined that not all religious actions are protected by the 1st Amendment; otherwise, people could claim that any action, no matter how controversial, was necessary for practicing their religion. Although the government cannot legislate against belief, it could, in this case based on tradition, legislate against the action of bigamy. However, in Wisconsin, the Court held that the state could not force the students to continue in public education because the action was based on a sincere, non-harmful, religious belief. Thus, the Amish action, unlike bigamy, was a protected religious action under the 1st Amendment.

As with any Court ruling about a federal law, citizens can take political action to protest it, such as trying to influence Congress. Citizens could attempt to get Congress to change the law by writing and trying to persuade their representatives. Also, citizens could draw attention to the issue during future elections and attempt to elect candidates who would support changing the law prohibiting bigamy.

Sample Response Explanation

Note a couple of the successful features of the high-scoring sample response:

- **Organization:** The writer combines the responses for Parts A and B into the same paragraph, which is effective since the response for Part A is very brief. Although the first paragraph of the response is lengthy, it reflects the complexity of the explanation required for Part B.

- **Addressing each action word:** Part B's *explanation* requires both a summary of the required case, *Wisconsin v. Yoder*, and a comparison explaining the difference between the two cases. When you see the action words like *describe* or *explain*, be sure to include a full, detailed discussion that covers all relevant points/sides. Although the question may seem to be asking for only one item, the rubric may score the question out of two points due to its complexity.

Scoring for Question 3: 4 points (1 + 2 + 1)

Part A (1 point)

One point for identifying the free exercise clause (of the First Amendment) as relevant in both cases.

Part B (2 points)

One point for identifying relevant facts about *Wisconsin v. Yoder*.

- Example facts: ruling held that requiring students to attend public school past 8th grade violated Amish parents' right to free exercise of their religion

One point for explaining why the facts in both cases led to different holdings.

- Example explanations: both cases concern free exercise of religious actions based on beliefs; in *Reynolds*, the Court determined that not every action that is claimed to be religious is protected; in *Reynolds*, the action was determined to violate traditional law, while in *Wisconsin*, the Court found no justification to prohibit the action, which they deemed was based on legitimate religious beliefs and did not result in the students burdening society; the scenario in *Wisconsin* did not fit the extreme examples of constitutionally limited religious actions as outlined in *Reynolds*

Part C (1 point)

One point for describing a valid political action of dissenters.

- Example actions: petitioning their representatives to change the law prohibiting bigamy, campaigning for/voting for candidates to Congress who would support legislation to permit bigamy, forming an interest group focused on the issue, organizing protests to draw attention to the Supreme Court ruling

ARGUMENT ESSAY

Overview

Question 4 will always be the Argument Essay. These questions begin with a brief paragraph about a given topic, such as the balance between federal and state powers. The prompt will then give specific instructions about how you must format your essay, including a list of several required foundational documents that are relevant to the topic at hand. You will need to discuss one of the listed documents as well as another piece of specific evidence from your own knowledge. (Note: A full list of College Board's 9 foundational docs and 15 required SCOTUS cases is in the Resources section at the back of this book.)

Strategy

The Argument Essay differs substantially from the other free-response questions on the AP U.S. Government and Politics exam, but you can and should still follow the Kaplan Method (AP-AP). It is recommended that you take 40 minutes to plan and write your Argument Essay (as opposed to 20 minutes each for the other free-response questions), so just double the time it typically takes you to complete each step of the Method.

While the scoring for the first three free-response questions is more straightforward—you earn points (or not) based on fully addressing each part of the prompt—the scoring for the Argument Essay is a little more complex. The following rubric outlines what the AP readers are generally looking for when they grade your Argument Essay; note the various categories and the ways you can earn points. (You will also see a prompt-specific sample rubric later in this section.)

General Rubric (6 points)

Category	Scoring Criteria	Notes
Thesis	**1 pt** for stating a claim that can be defended, is responsive to the issue posed, and sets up a line of reasoning.	The idea of "because" or "why" should be clear. You cannot earn a point if all you do is state the topic or prompt in different words.
Support	**1 pt** for presenting a piece of evidence relevant to the topic. **OR 2 pts** for using a single piece of evidence appropriately supporting your thesis. **OR 3 pts** for using two pieces of evidence appropriately supporting your thesis.	Your evidence should directly relate to the claim(s) made by your thesis. You cannot earn more than 1 point if you haven't stated a thesis.
Reasoning	**1 pt** for explaining why or how the evidence you are presenting supports your thesis.	Again, a thesis must have been stated. Also, be sure to specifically address at least one piece of evidence here.
Reply to Alternative Viewpoint	**1 pt** for offering a point of view different from or opposing yours, and going on to rebut it, refute it, or concede it.	You need to explicitly state an alternative viewpoint, and either argue against it (rebut), attempt to prove it false (refute), or grant that it has some validity (concede).

Sample Question

Construct an argument that explains which of the three models of representation—trustee, delegate, or politico—best reflects the founders' intentions with regard to the relationship between legislators and their constituents.

In your essay, you must:

- Formulate a defensible thesis that establishes a chain of reasoning.

- Provide evidence for your thesis with at least two pieces of relevant, accurate information.

  ○ Take at least ONE of your pieces of evidence from the following list of foundational documents.

    ▪ *Federalist* 10

    ▪ *Brutus* 1

    ▪ U.S. Constitution

  ○ Take your other piece of evidence from a different foundational document from the list above OR from your own study.

- Logically explain why your evidence supports your thesis.

- Present and reply to an alternative viewpoint using refutation, concession, or rebuttal.

13

Step 1: Analyze the Prompt

The Argument Essay question format is relatively straightforward, and the language will largely be the same for all Argument Essay prompts except for two parts: the topic and the short list of relevant foundational documents. With this in mind, analyzing the prompt for this question type is easy! Just make sure you have a solid grasp of the topic, and then continue to the planning stage.

Step 2: Plan Your Response

You'll want to create a brief outline before you start writing, just like you would for any other full-length essay. As you saw from the rubric, AP readers are interested in your thesis development, your use of evidence, and your treatment of an alternative view. Everything you write should be toward one or more of those ends.

You will need to state a thesis that specifically addresses the prompt and makes a claim. Avoid rewording the prompt or being too general. A good question to ask yourself is, "Am I actually taking a position on this issue that someone else might argue against?" Also, while the Argument Essay necessitates a longer, more detailed response than the other free-response question types, it does not require a formal introduction; in fact, writing a lengthy introduction can take up valuable time and frustrate the AP reader who is scoring your essay. Assert your thesis as soon as possible, and then move into the rest of your response.

It is important to note that the Argument Essay's topic and prompt wording will always intentionally allow for multiple positions. Therefore, you should be strategic and choose the position that you can best back up with evidence. You may even advocate for a different position than the one you personally agree with! To that end, no matter how strongly you feel about a topic, always present your evidence and claims in a balanced manner. Throughout your essay, even and especially when responding to an alternative viewpoint, avoid wording that makes it seem like your argument is simply your personal opinion (e.g., "I think" or "I believe," or any language that is overly emotional). With all of this in mind, a high-scoring writer might write the following outline:

Thesis: Trustee is the best model (ideals of Constitution)

Evidence:

- From list: Federalist 10
    - Madison's fear: large country + big gov't = factions (many groups disagree)
    - Trustee can mediate, come to concl, act in best interests
- From my own study: social mov'ts
    - Needed trustee model to make change
    - Civil rights and women's rights movements
    - The Civil Rights Act of 1964 and Voting Rights Act of 1965

Response to alternative view: Anti-Feds would fear large repub (Brutus), but pol system in place would keep trustee honest

Part 3: Action! Write Response & Step 4: Proofread

Use your plan to write each part of the response, and briskly skim for errors when finished. See the following high-scoring response, and pay extra attention to the rubric and scoring notes so you see how to apply this model to your own writing.

Sample High-Scoring Response

The trustee model of legislative representation is the best reflection of the founders' intentions in setting up American democracy because it offers the best hope for what the Preamble to the Constitution calls "a more perfect union," one that will bring together warring factions and increase harmony.

As James Madison pointed out in Federalist 10, it is inevitable that a republic will contain many groups which vehemently disagree. The bigger a country grows, the more frequent and violent factional clashes are likely to become. Madison was looking ahead to a U.S. that would burst the bounds of the original colonies and create more factionalism. This vision of an expanding, clashing nation makes the trustee model very appealing. A trustee Congressperson is one who will listen to all sides, make an independent judgment, but then go on to explain it so that opponents may be persuaded to change their minds, thus bringing resolution to conflicts.

A trustee is a representative willing to do the principled thing even if the public thinks otherwise. Many issues in our history have seemed so polarized that they were beyond resolution and could not wait for popular consensus. This was the case with civil rights issues and legislation in the 1960s. Technically, African Americans had the right to vote since the passage of the Fifteenth Amendment in 1870. However, this right was violently suppressed through intimidation tactics and a variety of restrictive measures such as poll taxes and literacy tests. It was not until the passage of the Voting Rights Act of 1965 that substantial voting protections were extended to all black people. The Voting Rights Act outlawed literacy tests and other tactics; under this act, federal officials were sent to the South to ensure that African Americans were allowed to vote free from fear and intimidation, and the election practices of local governments were held under greater scrutiny. Civil rights movement leaders had challenged discriminatory practices for decades, but due to intense polarization in society, there was not public consensus on how to address racism in voting practices, or even agreement as to whether to address it at all. Legislators had to go against the opinions of the majority in order to act in a way that advanced American ideals for all citizens, and the public eventually caught up.

Similarly, legislators pushed through the Civil Rights Act of 1964 which was supported by people within social movements but not by the general populace. Additionally, the Civil Rights Act of 1964 touched on the goals of not just the civil rights movement but also the women's rights movement; for example, Title VII of the Civil Rights Act prohibited sex discrimination in public accommodations. Members of these movements had been working for years to get society at large to expand rights and protections to all people. However, if legislators had waited to act until a majority of their constituency approved of these civil rights bills, the bills may never have passed. In this way, the trustee model can be used to uphold the rights of the minority despite majority resistance.

The trustee idea would have been opposed by Brutus and other Anti-Federalists. Brutus 1 warns that a large republic would necessarily be disconnected from its people. Following this logic, a concern with the trustee model would be that the representative would deviate too far from the will of the people and become despotic. But it is important to note that the people have the ultimate voice if they disagree with the trustee's judgments: the power of the ballot. The legislator's desire to stay in power is a strong check on him or her, acting as an incentive to listen to constituents.

All in all, the trustee is in the best position to reduce the intense factionalism Madison feared. Even before the advance of mass media, the trustee had many means to learn of the people's different views and to explain why the legislator was voting a certain way, or advancing this or that philosophy. This give and take of ideas surely helped to get the republic through its rocky early decades, and also helped the country to recover from the volatile growing pains and changes in the mid-twentieth century by finding ways to bring people together and advance equal rights for all.

Sample Response Explanation and Scoring

Note the following successful features of the high-scoring sample response:

- **Thesis (0–1 pt):** The writer sets up a clear *X because Y* sentence to introduce the thesis, which could be paraphrased as, *The trustee model brings about harmony*. Everything that follows is connected to the founders' ideal of harmony. The writer would therefore earn 1 point for Thesis.

- **Support (0–3 pts):** There is more than enough evidence to gain the full 3 points for Support, as the writer explains Madison's argument in *Federalist* 10 and elaborates upon relevant historical examples of disharmony that those acting as trustees helped to fix through assertive actions. In addition, the references to the Constitution and *Brutus* 1 (while unnecessary for earning full credit in Support) show a strong command of course material.

- **Reasoning (0–1 pt):** The writer earns the 1 point for Reasoning by clearly explaining how a trustee offers the best hope for Madison's vision. Specifically, the writer asserts in paragraphs 3 and 4 how trustees could not wait for public opinion in order to act.

- **Reply to Alternative Viewpoint (0–1 pt):** There is a whole paragraph at the end dedicated to rebutting the Anti-Federalists' objections. In this way, the writer makes it clear that this requirement has been met and earns the final 1 point.

Question-Specific Rubric: 6 points (1 + 3 + 1 + 1)

Category	Types of Appropriate Responses	Notes
A: Thesis (1 pt for stating a claim that can be defended, is responsive to the issue posed, and sets up a line of reasoning)	"The trustee/delegate/politico model of representation most closely reflects the founders' intent in that _____."	You cannot earn a point if all you do is list the three models and echo the idea that all deal with the legislator/constituent relationship. The blank indicates that you should provide an answer to the question, "Why?" Why is this model the closest reflector?
B: Support (1 pt for presenting a piece of evidence relevant to the topic)	A correct statement about, or definition of, one of the three models, including relating it to the given context.	The response must define one of the three models and discuss the founders' original intent.
OR B: Support (2 pts for using a single piece of evidence appropriately supporting your thesis)	*Federalist* 10—The dangers inherent in factions, and government's ability to control factions' effects. U.S. Constitution—Passage of the Seventeenth Amendment, providing for direct election of senators. *Brutus* 1—Warning that a large republic must create a disconnect between representatives and the people.	Including a relevant reference from one of the listed founding documents is important.
OR B: Support (3 pts for using two pieces of evidence appropriately supporting your thesis)	"The Internet makes it easy for voters to let their representatives know what's on their minds." "Mass media, unimagined in the founders' day, offers unprecedented access for elected officials to both present their views and hear those of their constituents." "The U.S. population is almost 11,000 percent larger than when the Constitution was drafted, which means a diversity of viewpoints virtually impossible for any sitting Congressperson to reconcile."	Your second piece of evidence can come from your reading or general knowledge. Be sure it is relevant to the matter at hand.

(*Continued*)

(*Continued*)

Category	Types of Appropriate Responses	Notes
C: Reasoning (1 pt for explaining why or how your evidence supports your thesis)	"The inevitability of quarreling factors, correctly identified in *Federalist* 10, means that any position a representative takes is sure to alienate some large group of constituents. So he or she might as well opt for the wise position rather than the popular one, and then try to persuade the electors of that wisdom."	Note that each example falls into the broad form of "[Evidence], and thus [Conclusion]." Don't just assume that readers will know how your evidence supports your thesis. Tell them how it does.
	"The speedy passage of the Seventeenth Amendment, which allows for the direct election of senators, indicates that the founders who argued for the delegate model anticipated the view that the representative is the people's servant, not their tutor."	
	"*Brutus* 1 indicated that the larger the republic, the more disconnected the government would become from its citizens. However, the delegate model combats that disconnection because it hitches legislators' votes to the majority opinion."	
D: Reply to Alternative Viewpoint (1 pt for offering a point of view different from yours and going on to rebut, refute, or concede it)	Present a weakness of the model you've chosen as the best reflection of founders' views, or present a defense of one of the other two models as a better reflection. Then reply to this alternative with a rebuttal, refutation, or concession.	You can't just bring up the alternative perspective and expect to get the point. You need to reply to it in some way, either by arguing against it or granting that it has some truth.

In this chapter, you've learned about the structure of the FRQ section and the steps to crafting successful responses. To maximize your scoring potential, however, you'll need to apply what you learned. Practice by responding to the free-response questions from the practice exams. You can do this as part of taking a full-length exam, or you can take the FRQ section on its own. You can even practice answering one FRQ at a time. Whatever your approach, be sure to write under timed conditions. (As a reminder, you will have 100 minutes total on the official exam; the recommended timing breakdown is 20 minutes for each of the first 3 FRQs, and 40 minutes for the final FRQ, the Argument Essay.)

Make sure to compare your answers against the samples and scoring information provided and to carefully consider whether you met each requirement. If possible, ask someone else to help you fairly assess your responses. Then, reflect on which successful qualities you displayed in your responses, as well as which qualities you should try to adopt on your next practice set. Remember, the free-response section makes up half of your total exam score, so it's worth it to prepare thoroughly!

PART 4

Practice Exams

How to Take the Practice Exams

Taking a practice exam gives you an idea of what it's like to answer AP questions under conditions that approximate those of the official exam. You'll find out which areas you're strong in and where additional review may be required. Any mistakes you make now are ones you won't make on the actual exam, as long as you take the time to learn where you went wrong.

For the most accurate results, you should approximate real test conditions as much as possible. Before taking a practice exam, find a quiet place where you can work uninterrupted. Time yourself according to the official exam parameters for each section (1 hour 20 minutes for Section I and 1 hour 40 minutes for Section II). Make sure you have all of the supplies you need, including pencils and answer grid for the multiple-choice section, and pens and lined paper for the free-response section. (The proctor will provide the official answer grid and booklet of lined paper when you take the official exam.)

As you take the practice exams, remember to pace yourself. Train yourself to be aware of the time you are spending on each question. Try to stay alert to certain strategies or approaches that can help you to handle the various questions more effectively.

After taking each practice exam, complete the following steps.

1. Self-score your multiple-choice section using the answer key immediately following each exam.
2. Read the answers and explanations for the relevant exam, located in the back of your book. These detailed explanations will help you identify areas that could use additional study. Even when you have answered a question correctly, you can learn additional information by looking at the explanation.
3. Self-score your free-response questions using the rubric and sample essays in the answers and explanations. Comparing your writing to these exam-like samples will help you assess how the AP readers would likely score your essay.
4. Navigate to the scoring section of your online resources (kaptest.com/moreonline) to input all of these raw scores and see what your overall score would be with a similar performance on Test Day.

Finally, it's important to approach the exam with the right attitude. You're going to get a great score because you've reviewed the material and learned the strategies in this book.

Good luck!

Practice Exam 1

Practice Exam 1 Answer Grid

1. A B C D	15. A B C D	29. A B C D	43. A B C D
2. A B C D	16. A B C D	30. A B C D	44. A B C D
3. A B C D	17. A B C D	31. A B C D	45. A B C D
4. A B C D	18. A B C D	32. A B C D	46. A B C D
5. A B C D	19. A B C D	33. A B C D	47. A B C D
6. A B C D	20. A B C D	34. A B C D	48. A B C D
7. A B C D	21. A B C D	35. A B C D	49. A B C D
8. A B C D	22. A B C D	36. A B C D	50. A B C D
9. A B C D	23. A B C D	37. A B C D	51. A B C D
10. A B C D	24. A B C D	38. A B C D	52. A B C D
11. A B C D	25. A B C D	39. A B C D	53. A B C D
12. A B C D	26. A B C D	40. A B C D	54. A B C D
13. A B C D	27. A B C D	41. A B C D	55. A B C D
14. A B C D	28. A B C D	42. A B C D	

SECTION I

80 Minutes

55 Questions

Each of the following 55 multiple-choice questions or incomplete statements is accompanied by four possible answers or completions. Select the answer choice that best answers the question or completes the statement.

Questions 1 and 2 refer to the graph below.

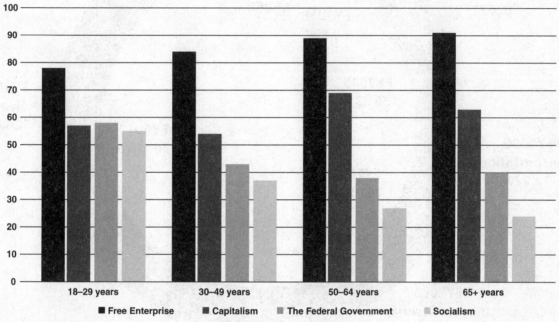

View of Political Concepts (% positive by age)

Source: Gallup, 2016

1. Which of the following statements is most accurately supported by the data in the graph?

   (A) Views of the federal government tend to become increasingly negative in older demographic groups.

   (B) Socialism has a more positive reaction only among the 18–29 year old demographic.

   (C) Across all demographics, free enterprise has a less positive image than capitalism.

   (D) Those in the 65+ demographic hold more positive views in every category polled than those in the 30–49 year old demographic.

2. A conservative response to the trends depicted in the graph most likely would include

   (A) creating a tax credit for people who start their own small businesses

   (B) encouraging state and local governments to lower taxes on businesses while increasing welfare spending

   (C) increasing regulation of Wall Street banks in order to appeal to 18–29-year-old voters

   (D) slashing federal spending on Medicare to make funding available for free college

GO ON TO THE NEXT PAGE

Questions 3 and 4 refer to the graph below.

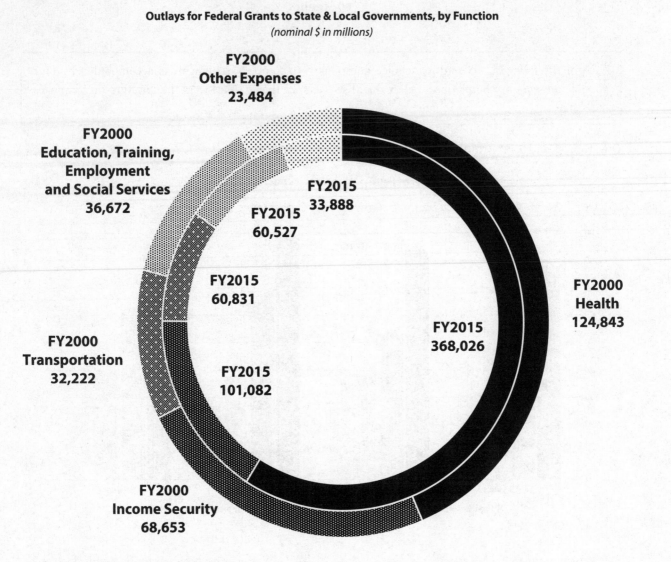

Outlays for Federal Grants to State & Local Governments, by Function
(nominal $ in millions)

FY2000
Other Expenses
23,484

FY2000
Education, Training,
Employment
and Social Services
36,672

FY2015
33,888

FY2015
60,527

FY2015
60,831

FY2000
Health
124,843

FY2015
368,026

FY2000
Transportation
32,222

FY2015
101,082

FY2000
Income Security
68,653

Source: Congressional Research Service, 2018

GO ON TO THE NEXT PAGE

3. Which of the following statements accurately describes the information presented in the graph?

(A) Income security grants shrank in terms of overall dollars spent between 2000 and 2015.

(B) Transportation grants nearly doubled in terms of dollars spent between 2000 and 2015.

(C) Healthcare grants tripled between 2000 and 2015 but also shrank in the same span as a percentage of all grants.

(D) More money was spent overall on federal grants in fiscal year 2000 than in fiscal year 2015.

4. Based on the trends depicted in the graph, which of the following is likely?

(A) The federal government will defer to state and local governments when it comes to the allocation of grant funds.

(B) State and local governments will become increasingly powerful due to lessening dependence on federal funding.

(C) The federal government will increase its power over state and local governments through their dependence on larger grants.

(D) State and local governments will increasingly make their own decisions when it comes to things like healthcare spending.

GO ON TO THE NEXT PAGE

Questions 5 and 6 refer to the graph below.

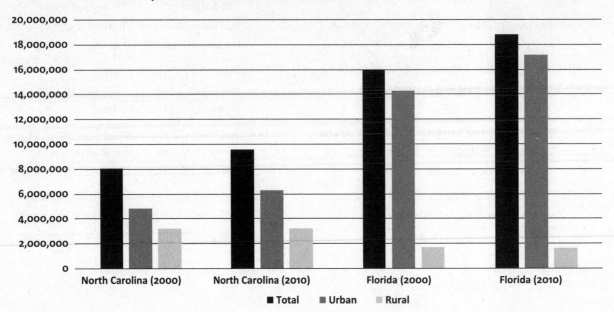

Total Population, Urban and Rural, in North Carolina and Florida (2000–2010)

Source: census.gov

5. Which of the following statements is reflected in the data in the bar graph?

   (A) Urban population growth outstripped rural population growth in Florida but not in North Carolina.

   (B) North Carolina's total population grew more than Florida's total population did.

   (C) Florida's rural population decreased by a far greater amount than North Carolina's rural population did.

   (D) Florida's urban population increased by a greater amount than North Carolina's total population did.

6. Which of the following is a likely consequence of the trends depicted in the bar graph?

   (A) The Democratic Party will have a greater chance of winning the electoral votes of both states.

   (B) Rural voters will maintain their current political power in North Carolina even as its total population grows.

   (C) The Republican Party will retain its hold on North Carolina but likely lose Florida to Democratic control.

   (D) The Republican Party will have a greater chance of winning the electoral votes of both states.

GO ON TO THE NEXT PAGE

Questions 7 and 8 refer to the graph below.

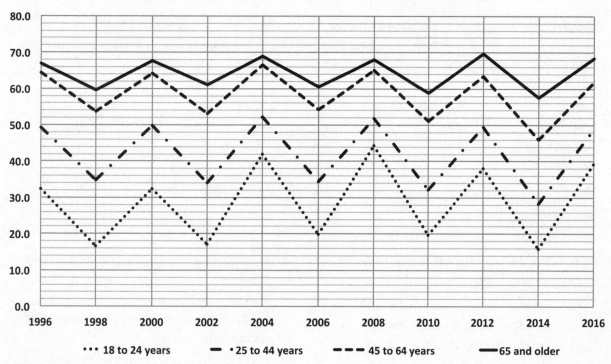

Voting-Eligible Population Turnout Percentages by Age Group (1996 - 2016)

• • • 18 to 24 years   — • 25 to 44 years   — — 45 to 64 years   —— 65 and older

Source: census.gov

7. Which of the following is an accurate statement about the information in the line graph?

(A) Turnout in midterm elections by those 65 and older has been steadily rising.

(B) Turnout by 25–44-year-olds has never risen above 50 percent of the voting-eligible population.

(C) Turnout in presidential elections by 18–24-year-olds has consistently beaten midterm turnout by 25–44-year-olds.

(D) Turnout by 25–44-year-olds in presidential elections is comparable to the turnout by 45–64-year-olds in midterms.

8. Based on the information in the graph, which of the following is the most likely implication for public policy?

(A) Major events like 9/11 will drive an increase in turnout as voters involve themselves in major new political issues.

(B) The senior vote reliably turns out at high levels in all elections, giving the Democratic Party a reliable base.

(C) Youth turnout in the midterms is low, so issues important to them will only receive attention in presidential elections.

(D) An overall general decline in voter turnout will lead to political extremism as parties focus on their partisans.

GO ON TO THE NEXT PAGE

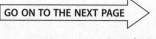

Questions 9 and 10 refer to the table below.

Social Media Posts by Candidates, Presidential Election 2016

Month	@realDonaldTrump		@HillaryClinton	
	Number of Posts	Average Posts per Day	Number of Posts	Average Posts per Day
June	304	10	385	13
July	378	12	815	26
August	327	11	523	17
September	290	10	779	26
October	529	17	957	31
November 1–7	89	12	282	40
Overall	1917	12	3741	26

Source: Twitter, 2018

9. Which of the following statements is reflected in the data in the table?

   (A) For both candidates, the average posts per day increased each month leading up to the November election.

   (B) Considering only full months, both candidates had their fewest number of monthly posts in September.

   (C) For each full month on the table, Clinton averaged more posts per day than Trump.

   (D) Trump made 89 posts per day during the week leading up to the November 8 election.

10. Given that Clinton won the popular vote while Trump won the electoral college vote, which of the following is an accurate conclusion based on the data in the table and your knowledge of influences on voters?

    (A) Social media posts are a tool used by modern political candidates, but they are not the only influence on voter behavior.

    (B) There is a cause-and-effect relationship between number of votes received and number of social media posts made by a candidate.

    (C) Voters were disenchanted by the quantity of Clinton's social media posts.

    (D) The number of social media posts made by presidential candidates will continue to increase in future elections.

GO ON TO THE NEXT PAGE

Questions 11–13 refer to the passage below.

The judicial Power of the United States, shall be vested in one supreme Court, and in such inferior Courts as the Congress may from time to time ordain and establish. The Judges, both of the supreme and inferior Courts, shall hold their Offices during good Behaviour, and shall, at stated Times, receive for their Services, a Compensation, which shall not be diminished during their Continuance in Office.

The judicial Power shall extend to all Cases, in Law and Equity, arising under this Constitution, the Laws of the United States, and Treaties made, or which shall be made, under their Authority. . . . to Controversies between two or more States;— between a State and Citizens of another State,—between Citizens of different States,—between Citizens of the same State claiming Lands under Grants of different States, and between a State, or the Citizens thereof, and foreign States, Citizens or Subjects.

In all cases affecting ambassadors, other public ministers and consuls, and those in which a state shall be party, the Supreme Court shall have original jurisdiction. In all the other cases before mentioned, the Supreme Court shall have appellate jurisdiction. . . .

The trial of all crimes, except in cases of impeachment, shall be by jury; and such trial shall be held in the state where the said crimes shall have been committed; but when not committed within any state, the trial shall be at such place or places as the Congress may by law have directed.

—*Article III of the Constitution*

11. Which of the following is an accurate statement based on the information in the passage?

    (A) The Supreme Court holds original and appellate jurisdiction, and nearly all criminal cases must be tried by a jury.

    (B) Congress holds the power to regulate the Supreme Court and must decide where trials should take place.

    (C) The Supreme Court holds only appellate jurisdiction, and courts created by Congress hold original jurisdiction.

    (D) The judicial power was created to try all cases equally, and all criminal cases must be tried by a jury.

12. Which of the following actions would likely be considered constitutional based on the excerpt?

    (A) Congress creating a court to hear the case of a lawsuit against North Carolina for the first time

    (B) The Supreme Court deciding that a case committed online across multiple states will be tried in Boston

    (C) A court trying a president's impeachment case in front of a jury

    (D) A court trying a crime in Orlando that was committed in Tampa

GO ON TO THE NEXT PAGE

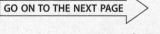

13. The Constitution's use of the phrase "shall hold their Offices during good Behaviour" is most likely referring to which of the following aspects of the judiciary?

    (A) Supreme Court justices are nominated by the president.

    (B) The Supreme Court is the highest-ranking court in the country.

    (C) Supreme Court nominees must be approved by the Senate.

    (D) The Supreme Court features lifetime tenure for its members.

GO ON TO THE NEXT PAGE

Questions 14–17 refer to the passage below.

Yet, I confess, I see great difficulty of drawing forth a good representation. What, for example, will be the inducements for gentlemen of fortune and abilities to leave their houses and business to attend annually and long? It cannot be the wages; for these, I presume, must be small. Will not the power, therefore, be thrown into the hands of the demagogue or middling politician, who, for the sake of a small stipend and the hopes of advancement, will offer himself as a candidate, and the real men of weight and influence, by remaining at home, add strength to the state governments? I am at a loss to know what must be done; I despair that a republican form of government can remove the difficulties. Whatever may be my opinion, I would hold it however unwise to change that form of government. I believe the British government forms the best model the world ever produced, and such has been its progress in the minds of the many, that this truth gradually gains ground. This government has for its object *public strength* and *individual security*. It is said with us to be unattainable. If it was once formed it would maintain itself. All communities divide themselves into the few and the many. The first are the rich and well born, the other the mass of the people. The voice of the people has been said to be the voice of God; and however generally this maxim has been quoted and believed, it is not true in fact. The people are turbulent and changing; they seldom judge or determine right. Give therefore to the first class a distinct, permanent share in the government. They will check the unsteadiness of the second, and as they cannot receive any advantage by a change, they therefore will ever maintain good government. Can a democratic assembly, who annually revolve in the mass of the people, be supposed steadily to pursue the public good? Nothing but a permanent body can check the imprudence of democracy. Their turbulent and uncontrouling disposition requires checks.

—Alexander Hamilton, as quoted in *The Records of the Federal Convention of 1787, vol. 1* (1911)

14. Based on the text, which of the following statements best summarizes Hamilton's argument?

    (A) Wealth is not just a sign of wisdom, but of godliness.

    (B) The judicial branch should have lifetime appointments.

    (C) The masses cannot be trusted to rule themselves.

    (D) Good government is built upon the bed-rock of democracy.

15. Which of the following scenarios illustrates Hamilton's desired outcome?

    (A) The president vetoes a national security bill, only for the Senate to override the veto and pass the bill into law.

    (B) The House passes a piece of pork-barrel legislation ahead of an election, but the Senate votes the bill down.

    (C) Educated people decide to work in business, as the low pay only tempts less talented people to work for the government.

    (D) The Senate holds hearings on nominees to the president's cabinet and then holds a vote on their appointment.

GO ON TO THE NEXT PAGE

16. Which of the following constitutional reforms weakened the checks that Hamilton called for in the text?

    (A) The Twenty-Sixth Amendment

    (B) The Twenty-Second Amendment

    (C) The Seventeenth Amendment

    (D) The Sixteenth Amendment

17. By using the phrase "a distinct, permanent share," Alexander Hamilton is most likely arguing in favor of which of the following models of democracy?

    (A) The elite model

    (B) The pluralist model

    (C) The participatory model

    (D) The direct democracy model

Questions 18 and 19 refer to the map below.

United States Congressional Reapportionment Based (2010) Census

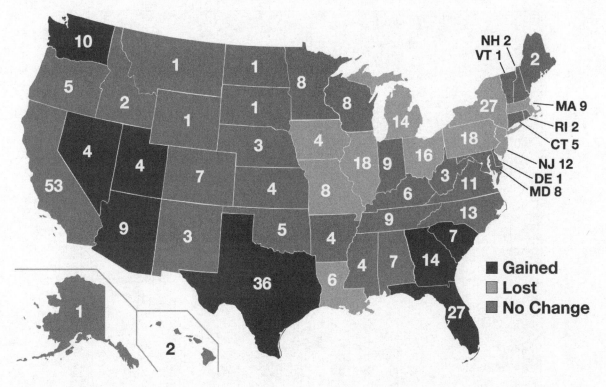

Source: census.gov

18. Which of the following is an accurate statement about the information in the map?

    (A) Texas gained the greatest number of new seats.

    (B) Every state in the Midwest lost seats.

    (C) Most seat gains were in Sunbelt states.

    (D) Most seat gains were in the Northeast.

19. Which of the following statements illustrates the most important limitation of the data presented in the map?

    (A) There is no information about exactly how many seats were gained or lost by the various states.

    (B) There is insufficient information to detect any regional shift in the balance of power in the House in this time period.

    (C) A bar graph would be superior for discerning any regional shift in the balance of power in the House in this time period.

    (D) There is no data concerning the total number of seats in the House of Representatives.

GO ON TO THE NEXT PAGE

 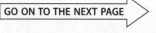

Questions 20 and 21 refer to the political cartoon below.

The Law-Mills Again at Work (1900)

Source: Library of Congress

20. Which of the following best describes the message in the political cartoon?

    (A) The federal government is overwhelming state governments with rules and regulations.

    (B) Although the rule of law clearly requires laws, an overly robust legal code is ineffective.

    (C) Crime can be stamped out with proper rules and regulations, thus encouraging a just society.

    (D) The federal government takes special care in crafting the nation's laws and regulations.

21. Which of the following governmental approaches would the author of this political cartoon most likely prefer?

    (A) The judicial branch should generally defer to the judgment of the legislative and executive branches and avoid striking down laws unless they are clearly unconstitutional.

    (B) The legislative branch can and should pass legislation that lessens the impact of unfavorable Supreme Court decisions.

    (C) The legislative branch's power should be constrained by enumerated constitutional rules, with minimal involvement in the lives of citizens.

    (D) The legislative branch's power should not be restrained by enumerated constitutional rules, as the primary purpose of government is to promote justice and equality.

GO ON TO THE NEXT PAGE

Questions 22 and 23 refer to the infographic below.

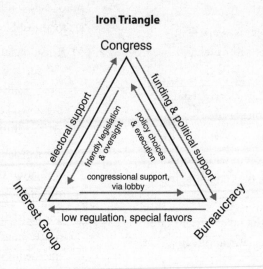

Iron Triangle

Congress

electoral support

funding & political support

friendly legislation & oversight

policy choices & execution

congressional support, via lobby

Interest Group

Bureaucracy

low regulation, special favors

22. Which of the following is true, according to the infographic?

(A) Congress members receive their preferred approach to implementation of their policies in exchange for offering minimal regulation.

(B) Interest groups obtain favorable regulations by funding federal bureaucratic agencies.

(C) Congress receives electoral support from interest groups in exchange for offering jobs to lobbyists.

(D) Interest groups obtain favorable regulations by electioneering, giving them legislative backing for their lobbying aims.

23. Based on the infographic and your knowledge of the topic, which of the following is a common criticism regarding the iron triangle?

(A) These three groups work together to smoothly design many government policies, ensuring that corruption is minimized and American citizens enjoy good government.

(B) Interest groups shape public opinion by engaging media outlets, publishing the findings of research studies, and staging public events such as protests and marches.

(C) The electoral support that interest groups offer enables the wealthiest citizens to have a greater influence over writing government policy than ordinary citizens.

(D) The proliferation of interest groups reflects how citizens have the lawful right to assemble and to directly petition the government.

GO ON TO THE NEXT PAGE

24. Which of the following is a true statement about Title IX of the Education Amendments Act of 1972?

    (A) It prohibits all discrimination on the basis of sex throughout the states and territories of the United States.

    (B) It prohibits discrimination on the basis of sex solely in college sports programs receiving federal financial assistance.

    (C) It prohibits discrimination on the basis of race, color, religion, sex, or national origin at any school receiving federal funding.

    (D) It prohibits discrimination on the basis of sex in any programs or activities that are receiving federal financial assistance.

25. Which of the following would likely violate the exclusionary rule?

    (A) Denying an alleged murderer the right to a speedy, public trial

    (B) Using illegally seized videos in prosecution against an alleged arsonist

    (C) Neglecting to read due process rights prior to the interrogation of an alleged vandal

    (D) Gathering victims of burglaries to act as jury members in a robbery case

26. Which of the following best illustrates the free-rider problem?

    (A) By splitting the vote for the major party candidate she is most similar to ideologically, a third-party candidate unintentionally helps the other major party candidate win an election.

    (B) A citizen believes it is important to protect the environment but does not participate in environmental causes, believing that direct participation will not make a difference in environmental protection.

    (C) A self-perpetuating relationship develops in which a business-related interest group supports certain congressional candidates who, once elected, experience pressure to fund and regulate bureaucratic agencies in ways that benefit that business.

    (D) In order to appeal to many demographics of voters, a major party candidate endorses moderate stances on issues, despite his own more extreme views, to help himself win an election.

27. Which of the following sets of policies would a self-identified liberal most likely support?

    (A) Implementing affirmative action for minority groups and increasing taxes on the wealthy to fund existing entitlements

    (B) Eliminating federal domestic surveillance programs and reducing regulation of the economy beyond policing for fraud

    (C) Expanding spending on national defense and reforming entitlement programs to ensure their long-term solvency

    (D) Sponsoring publicly funded free pre-kindergarten and breaking up large banks into smaller financial institutions

GO ON TO THE NEXT PAGE

28. Which of the following policies would a self-identified libertarian most likely support?

    (A) Criminalizing hate speech directed at members of a protected class

    (B) Decriminalizing narcotics and abolishing the death penalty

    (C) Legalizing "soft" drugs like marijuana while banning "hard" drugs like methamphetamine

    (D) Offering a tax credit to families that have more than two children

29. Which of the following best describes the concept of discretionary and rule-making authority?

    (A) The way in which Congress exercises its oversight power when interacting with the executive branch

    (B) The measures the president takes to ensure that the bureaucracy carries out its responsibilities

    (C) The latitude exercised by bureaucratic agencies in how to implement policy directives from elected officials

    (D) The way in which the branches hold each other accountable despite competing goals and interests

30. In *United States v. Lopez* (1995), the Supreme Court held that

    (A) Congress cannot use its powers under the commerce clause to regulate firearm possession nationwide via federal law

    (B) Congress cannot use its powers under the commerce clause to make firearm possession in school zones a federal offense

    (C) Congress cannot regulate interstate commerce as that power must be reserved to the states

    (D) Congress cannot regulate firearm possession under the commerce clause because the Second Amendment applies to the states

31. Which of the following provides the most accurate explanation for why the southern states agreed to the Three-Fifths Compromise?

    (A) Southern states wanted to lower the amount of federal taxes that they would pay, so if slaves were counted as people, they could not be taxed as property.

    (B) Southern states did not wish to be politically dominated by the North, so they wanted slaves to be counted for the purpose of legislative representation.

    (C) Southern states agreed to count slaves partially as property, thus increasing their taxes, in exchange for constitutionally barring Congress from ever banning slave importation.

    (D) Southern states wanted slaves counted for the purpose of legislative representation, and if each was three-fifths of a person, then no male slave had the right to vote.

GO ON TO THE NEXT PAGE

32. A citizen strongly supports a particular candidate in an upcoming election. She has already made a donation of $2,700 to the candidate's campaign committee, the maximum amount permitted for an individual. Which of the following is another way she may legally support the candidate's campaign monetarily?

    (A) She may donate additional funds to a PAC that supports the candidate.

    (B) She may donate unlimited funds to the candidate's political party committee at the national level.

    (C) She may pay for television ads in the candidate's name without the candidate's direct approval.

    (D) Since she has already donated the maximum individual amount to the candidate, there are no other ways in which she can support the candidate's campaign monetarily.

33. Based on the Supreme Court's ruling in *Gideon v. Wainwright* (1963), which of the following would most likely be considered unconstitutional?

    (A) Allowing private documents seized without a warrant to act as evidence in trial

    (B) Denying a man the right to an attorney because he cannot afford one

    (C) Refusing a citizen the right to trial by jury because of video evidence

    (D) Setting a cap of $2,700 on political donations and other political activities

34. In response to the military being overstretched with an ongoing foreign occupation, Congress reinstates the military draft to bolster the army's manpower. A group of citizens sues the government, arguing that the draft is unconstitutional because it is not an enumerated power. The Supreme Court ultimately sides with Congress. Which of the following Supreme Court precedents could be used to support the ruling in this case?

    (A) *Engel v. Vitale* (1962)

    (B) *Gideon v. Wainwright* (1963)

    (C) *Marbury v. Madison* (1803)

    (D) *McCulloch v. Maryland* (1819)

35. A second-term president has recently decided to require that airline accidents be investigated with a higher level of scrutiny. In which of the following ways can the president ensure that the Department of Transportation is aligned with this priority?

    (A) Add a signing statement to a bill funding the Department of Transportation that was passed back in the president's first term

    (B) Announce that the Department of Transportation will be audited to ensure it is properly enforcing safety regulations

    (C) Exercise authority as Commander-in-Chief to have the Air Force court martial the board of any airline that does not comply with FAA safety regulations

    (D) Issue an executive order that directs the Department of Transportation to more deeply investigate airline accidents

GO ON TO THE NEXT PAGE

 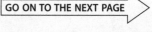

36. Which of the following could be a potential consequence of voting according to the party-line model?

    (A) A party-line voter would analyze the voting records of any candidates running for office.

    (B) A party-line voter would be inclined to vote for a third-party candidate over candidates from the two major parties.

    (C) A party-line voter might vote for a candidate without knowing the specific viewpoints of that candidate.

    (D) A party-line voter would carefully consider which candidates might best serve the interests of other groups of constituents.

37. Which of the following scenarios would most likely be considered a violation of the guidelines established in *New York Times Co. v. United States* (1971) regarding freedom of the press?

    (A) An embedded reporter describing troop movements in the middle of an ongoing battle on live television

    (B) A newspaper publishing photos of the flag-draped coffins of dead soldiers being unloaded from cargo planes in the middle of the night

    (C) The military filtering the Internet on army bases, restricting soldiers from viewing news websites with articles containing leaked classified information

    (D) A newspaper publishing details about American government procedures for wiretapping the leadership of its foreign allies

38. A member of the House of Representatives believes that the president has broken the law by committing criminal actions. However, no one has begun the impeachment process yet. Which of the following is an action that a single House member can take to address the problem?

    (A) The member can petition the Speaker of the House to introduce impeachment charges for a floor vote.

    (B) The member can submit impeachment charges to the House's judiciary committee so they can investigate the president.

    (C) The member can introduce a resolution calling for an inquiry into the president's alleged crimes to be authorized.

    (D) The member can introduce impeachment charges to the full House and, if approved, they will be sent directly to the Senate.

39. A local high school principal organizes a bake sale for a student religious youth group so that its impoverished members can afford an overseas spiritual pilgrimage. However, a local parent sues the school, arguing that the bake sale violates the Constitution. The courts side with the parent. Which of the following Supreme Court precedents could be used to support the ruling in this case?

    (A) *Engel v. Vitale* (1962)

    (B) *Wisconsin v. Yoder* (1972)

    (C) *Tinker v. Des Moines Independent Community School District* (1969)

    (D) *Brown v. Board of Education* (1954)

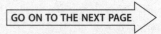
GO ON TO THE NEXT PAGE

40. Which of the following scenarios would most likely be considered a violation of the Twenty-Sixth Amendment?

    (A) Several cities within a state close their polling places at 4 pm, which results in it becoming difficult for working citizens in those cities to vote.

    (B) A state does not prohibit polling places from requiring African American men to provide two forms of identification in order to vote.

    (C) Concerned about disorderly behavior, a state passes a law that young children are not permitted in polling places, which results in it becoming difficult for both male and female caregivers to vote.

    (D) Concerned about potential voter immaturity, a state passes a requirement that voters between ages 19–21 must provide proof of employment or proof of enrollment in post-secondary education in order to vote.

41. During a recent flood, barrels of toxic waste surfaced at a cleanup site the Environmental Protection Agency had previously rated as safe for building a proposed elementary school. It is unclear whether negligence or corruption led to the EPA classifying the site as safe. Which of the following is an action that Congress can take to investigate the EPA?

    (A) Recommend that the president increase funding for the EPA

    (B) Hold committee hearings where EPA officials will submit to public questioning

    (C) Issue fines to the EPA officials who cleared the site for redevelopment

    (D) Enforce existing regulations to ensure that the EPA follows proper guidelines in the future

42. Which of the following best illustrates the concept of low political efficacy?

    (A) A House member running unopposed for reelection still experiences high turnout in her district on election day.

    (B) Republican voters in California choose to stay home rather than vote in a presidential election, as their state is overwhelmingly Democratic.

    (C) A House member in a tightly contested primary race finds that there is moderate turnout by potential voters on election day.

    (D) Democratic voters in Utah choose to vote in a presidential election rather than stay home, even if their state is overwhelmingly Republican.

GO ON TO THE NEXT PAGE

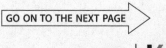

43. Which of the following is an accurate comparison of the activities of linkage institutions?

	Interest Groups	Political Parties
(A)	Organize local election campaigns and raise volunteers	Educate congressional committees about specific voters' interests
(B)	Provide the public with real-time information about actions of government	Provide polling locations for voters on election days
(C)	Persuade policy makers to act on particular voters' concerns	Persuade voters to take specific stances on issues and encourage their participation in elections
(D)	Make appointments to bureaucratic agency leadership positions	Supply structure and leadership to congressional organization

44. Which of the following is an accurate comparison of *Tinker v. Des Moines Independent Community School District* (1969) and *Schenck v. United States* (1919)?

	Tinker v. Des Moines Independent Community School District	*Schenck v. United States*
(A)	Supported the rights of students to wear armbands in opposition to a war	Declared that speech may be restricted if it threatens national security
(B)	Created the "clear and present danger" test to determine if a certain kind of speech is legal	Legalized the freedom of speech to protest a war
(C)	Broadened freedom of speech to include clothing choices	Decided that speech that calls for rebellion can be restricted
(D)	Bolstered the freedom of the press in terms of speech, even in cases of national security	Established the "clear and present danger" test as a means to determine if there is a threat to national security

GO ON TO THE NEXT PAGE

45. Which of the following makes a correct comparison between a political party and its policy platform?

	Political Parties	Policy Platforms
(A)	Democrats	Support maintaining *Citizens United v. FEC* (2010) and unrestricted campaign spending by unions
(B)	Republicans	Favor voter photo identification requirements at polling stations
(C)	Democrats	Believe that government regulations hinder both job growth and the economy
(D)	Libertarians	Believe that same-sex marriage should not be legal under the Constitution

46. Which of the following is an accurate comparison of the powers of the Houses of Congress?

	House of Representatives	Senate
(A)	Initiates articles of impeachment	Creates revenue bills
(B)	Approves major presidential appointments	Consents to treaties
(C)	Initiates revenue bills	Tries impeached officials
(D)	Negotiates treaties	Approves major presidential appointments

47. Which of the following is an accurate comparison of an amendment and the Court case that incorporated it to the states?

	Constitutional Amendment	Incorporation Case
(A)	First Amendment	*Gideon v. Wainwright* (1963)
(B)	Sixth Amendment	*Gideon v. Wainwright* (1963)
(C)	Second Amendment	*United States v. Lopez* (1995)
(D)	Fourth Amendment	*United States v. Lopez* (1995)

GO ON TO THE NEXT PAGE

48. Which of the following accurately explains why the Federalists argued that Article V of their proposed constitution was an improvement over the Articles of Confederation?

    (A) National laws were difficult to enforce without a centralized judiciary and lower courts.

    (B) The Articles of Confederation was too inflexible due to the need for unanimous approval of all states to ratify any amendment.

    (C) The lack of a standing army meant that it was difficult to deal with national security emergencies.

    (D) The central government lacked tax powers, instead relying on states to volunteer "extra funds."

49. Which of the following would likely be considered constitutional based on the Supreme Court's ruling in *McDonald v. Chicago* (2010)?

    (A) A police officer arresting a man for bearing arms

    (B) A man keeping arms in his home as a form of self-defense

    (C) A rifle owner transporting his arms across state lines

    (D) A handgun owner being charged with a felony for bringing her arms onto school grounds

50. The political socialization of someone who has not yet entered high school will be least influenced by

    (A) her peers

    (B) her family

    (C) her school

    (D) the media

51. A democratic socialist response to rising healthcare costs would most likely include

    (A) having Congress issue vouchers to help citizens more easily afford the purchase of private health insurance

    (B) the deregulation of the healthcare industry in order to promote savings that would then be passed on to consumers

    (C) the nationalization of the healthcare industry in order to provide government-financed healthcare for all Americans

    (D) raising the minimum requirements to qualify for Medicare in order to keep the program's costs down

52. Which of the following best describes the concept of selective incorporation?

    (A) A constitutional doctrine that protects the rights of American citizens by applying the Bill of Rights to the states

    (B) A constitutional doctrine that allows the states to limit the federal government's creation of unfunded mandates

    (C) A constitutional doctrine that holds that the equal protection clause applies to the federal government

    (D) A constitutional doctrine that allows the states to selectively uphold certain federal laws while overlooking others

GO ON TO THE NEXT PAGE

53. Based on previous court rulings, which of the following scenarios would most likely violate the Fourth Amendment protection against unreasonable searches and seizures?

    (A) Limited bulk collection of telecommunications metadata by the government

    (B) Disregarding any evidence collected in an accused person's home without a warrant

    (C) A judge allowing the police to search the office, but not the home, of an accused person

    (D) Police searches of cell phone data without a warrant

54. Which of the following best describes a benchmark poll?

    (A) A poll that maps the political landscape ahead of a campaign season by surveying public opinion on a range of issues

    (B) A poll that repeatedly contacts the same participants in order to track any changes in their opinions over time

    (C) A poll that attempts to capture a snapshot of what a particular group or nation thinks at a given moment in time

    (D) A poll that asks voters who they intend to cast their ballot for just as they head into a polling station

55. Despite helping to increase public awareness about politics, the modern media has been criticized as being harmful to democracy. Which of the following is a reason for this criticism?

    (A) The 24-hour news cycle results in the repetition of significant news stories.

    (B) Media consumers have many choices about the medium through which they receive their news: TV, online journalism, mobile apps, etc.

    (C) Media consumers often find political news dull because of the way it is typically presented.

    (D) Ideologically driven news outlets tend to reinforce viewers' preexisting beliefs without objectively portraying opposing views.

IF YOU FINISH BEFORE TIME IS CALLED, YOU MAY CHECK YOUR WORK ON SECTION I ONLY. DO NOT MOVE ON TO SECTION II UNTIL INSTRUCTED TO DO SO.

STOP

END OF SECTION I

SECTION II

100 Minutes

4 Questions

You have 1 hour and 40 minutes to answer all four of the following free-response questions. Craft your responses in full sentences and paragraphs, using specific examples where appropriate. It is suggested that you spend a few minutes planning each of your answers. In total, it is recommended that you spend approximately 20 minutes each on questions 1, 2, and 3 and approximately 40 minutes on question 4.

1. A first-time congresswoman is elected from the minority party to the U.S. Senate. The congresswoman's primary motivation for seeking election is her desire to implement changes toward what she believes will be more equitable spending in public education. In particular, she disagrees with a recent Supreme Court ruling determining that the equal protection clause does not require states to mandate that all school districts receive equal funding. The president, also newly elected, is from the majority party, and he has stated that he supports leaving all education-related decisions to the state governments.

   After reading the scenario, respond to Parts A, B, and C.

   (A) Describe one tactic that this newly elected congresswoman could use to potentially impact the education issue while serving as a U.S. Senator.

   (B) In the context of this scenario, explain how the Senate might interact with another part of the federal government in regard to the education issue. Be sure to clearly identify the part of the federal government being referenced.

   (C) For each government measure mentioned in Parts A and B, explain how the measure reflects either the principle of checks and balances OR the principle of separation of powers.

GO ON TO THE NEXT PAGE

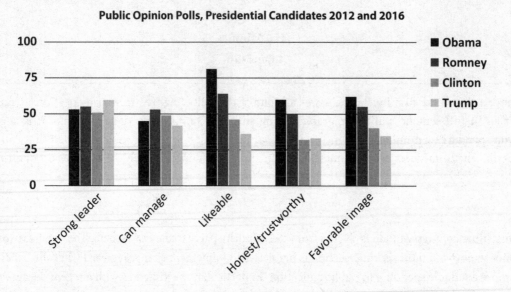

Public Opinion Polls, Presidential Candidates 2012 and 2016

Source: Gallup. Oct 2012, June 2012, May 2016, Nov 2016. Data compiled from public opinion polls conducted via telephone, both landlines and cellular lines, of phone numbers randomly selected, 1,004–1,530 respondents.

2. Use the information graphic to respond to Parts A, B, C, and D.

   (A) Describe a similarity or difference between the trends of the 2012 opinion polls and the trends of the 2016 opinion polls.

   (B) Explain how one characteristic of the polls illustrated in the information graphic makes the polls scientific.

   (C) Explain how another characteristic of polls (other than the one explained in Part B) contributes to their credibility.

   (D) Explain how the media's reporting of opinion polls may impact public opinion, and explain how it may impact voting behavior.

3. Joseph Hurtado was arrested in the state of California and accused of shooting and killing a family friend, José Antonio Estuardo, over a domestic dispute. Hurtado was not indicted by a grand jury; instead, a judge reviewed the information of the case and determined that Hurtado should be tried for murder. This legal process was in line with California's state constitution at the time. At trial, Hurtado was found guilty and sentenced to death. Hurtado appealed the decision, arguing that the Fifth Amendment guaranteed him the right to a grand jury hearing, which he had not been granted.

The Supreme Court determined in *Hurtado v. California* (1884) in a 7–1 decision that the Fifth Amendment right to a grand jury hearing to determine indictment was not applicable to the states, which can each create their own legal proceedings. Justice Matthews explained in the majority opinion that Hurtado's rights had not been violated in the legal process; although Hurtado was not indicted by a grand jury, the judge's review of the information was permissible, as the proceeding was "merely a preliminary proceeding" that could "result in no final judgment." The opinion concluded that Hurtado's ensuing trial was fair.

GO ON TO THE NEXT PAGE

Based on the information given, respond to Parts A, B, and C.

(A) Identify the constitutional clause that is relevant to both *Hurtado v. California* (1884) and *McDonald v. Chicago* (2010).

(B) The majority opinion of *McDonald v. Chicago* describes a guideline for determining whether a right is "fundamental": such a right is either "implicit in the concept of ordered liberty" or "deeply rooted in our nation's history and traditions." Based on this reasoning and your knowledge of constitutional history, explain why the Supreme Court reached a different holding about the constitutional clause identified in Part A in *Hurtado v. California* than in *McDonald v. Chicago*.

(C) Explain how these two cases reflect the tensions inherent in a federal system.

4. The power of the executive branch over matters of war and peace has often gone unchecked by the other branches of government. Although Congress has occasionally sought to limit the president's power, as it did with the War Powers Act of 1973, the modern presidency has much latitude in the use of military force. Some believe the executive branch's control over the military is both necessary and consistent with the intent of the Constitution's framers. Choose a position on this controversy and develop an argument defending your position.

In your essay you must:

- Formulate a defensible thesis that establishes a chain of reasoning

- Provide evidence for your thesis with at least TWO pieces of relevant, accurate information:
    - Take at least ONE of your pieces of evidence from one of the following foundational documents:
        - *Federalist* 70
        - *Brutus* 1
        - U.S. Constitution
    - Take your other piece of evidence from a different foundational document from the list above OR from your own study

- Logically explain why your evidence supports your thesis

- Present and reply to an alternative viewpoint using refutation, concession, or rebuttal

IF YOU FINISH BEFORE TIME IS CALLED, YOU MAY CHECK YOUR WORK ON SECTION II ONLY. DO NOT TURN TO ANY OTHER SECTION OF THE EXAM.

STOP

315 | K

END OF SECTION II

ANSWER KEY

Section I

1. B	12. D	23. C	34. D	45. B
2. A	13. D	24. D	35. D	46. C
3. B	14. C	25. B	36. C	47. B
4. C	15. B	26. B	37. A	48. B
5. D	16. C	27. A	38. C	49. B
6. A	17. A	28. B	39. A	50. A
7. D	18. C	29. C	40. D	51. C
8. C	19. A	30. B	41. B	52. A
9. C	20. B	31. B	42. B	53. D
10. A	21. C	32. A	43. C	54. A
11. A	22. D	33. B	44. A	55. D

Section I Number Correct: _____

Review detailed explanations for Sections I and II at the back of this book. Use the rubrics and sample essays to self-score Section II.

Section II Points Earned: _____

Sign into your online account at kaptest.com and enter your results in the online scoring section to see your 1–5 score.

Haven't registered your book yet? Go to kaptest.com/booksonline to begin.

PRACTICE EXAM 1 BREAKDOWN

Use the following table to determine which topics you are already strong in and which topics you need to review most.

Topic	Exam Question(s)	Number You Got Correct	Chapters to Study
Foundations of American Democracy	3, 4, 14, 15, 16, 17, 30, 31, 34, 38, 48	___ out of 11	3, 8
Interactions Among Branches of Government	11, 12, 13, 20, 21, 22, 23, 29, 35, 41, 46	___ out of 11	4, 9
Civil Liberties and Civil Rights	24, 25, 33, 37, 39, 44, 47, 49, 52, 53	___ out of 10	5, 10
American Political Ideologies and Beliefs	1, 2, 5, 7, 27, 28, 45, 50, 51, 54	___ out of 10	6, 11
Political Participation	6, 8, 9, 10, 18, 19, 26, 32, 36, 40, 42, 43, 55	___ out of 13	7, 12

Practice Exam 2

Practice Exam 2 Answer Grid

1. (A)(B)(C)(D)
2. (A)(B)(C)(D)
3. (A)(B)(C)(D)
4. (A)(B)(C)(D)
5. (A)(B)(C)(D)
6. (A)(B)(C)(D)
7. (A)(B)(C)(D)
8. (A)(B)(C)(D)
9. (A)(B)(C)(D)
10. (A)(B)(C)(D)
11. (A)(B)(C)(D)
12. (A)(B)(C)(D)
13. (A)(B)(C)(D)
14. (A)(B)(C)(D)

15. (A)(B)(C)(D)
16. (A)(B)(C)(D)
17. (A)(B)(C)(D)
18. (A)(B)(C)(D)
19. (A)(B)(C)(D)
20. (A)(B)(C)(D)
21. (A)(B)(C)(D)
22. (A)(B)(C)(D)
23. (A)(B)(C)(D)
24. (A)(B)(C)(D)
25. (A)(B)(C)(D)
26. (A)(B)(C)(D)
27. (A)(B)(C)(D)
28. (A)(B)(C)(D)

29. (A)(B)(C)(D)
30. (A)(B)(C)(D)
31. (A)(B)(C)(D)
32. (A)(B)(C)(D)
33. (A)(B)(C)(D)
34. (A)(B)(C)(D)
35. (A)(B)(C)(D)
36. (A)(B)(C)(D)
37. (A)(B)(C)(D)
38. (A)(B)(C)(D)
39. (A)(B)(C)(D)
40. (A)(B)(C)(D)
41. (A)(B)(C)(D)
42. (A)(B)(C)(D)

43. (A)(B)(C)(D)
44. (A)(B)(C)(D)
45. (A)(B)(C)(D)
46. (A)(B)(C)(D)
47. (A)(B)(C)(D)
48. (A)(B)(C)(D)
49. (A)(B)(C)(D)
50. (A)(B)(C)(D)
51. (A)(B)(C)(D)
52. (A)(B)(C)(D)
53. (A)(B)(C)(D)
54. (A)(B)(C)(D)
55. (A)(B)(C)(D)

SECTION I

80 Minutes

55 Questions

Each of the following 55 multiple-choice questions or incomplete statements is accompanied by four possible answers or completions. Select the answer choice that best answers the question or completes the statement.

Questions 1 and 2 refer to the graph below.

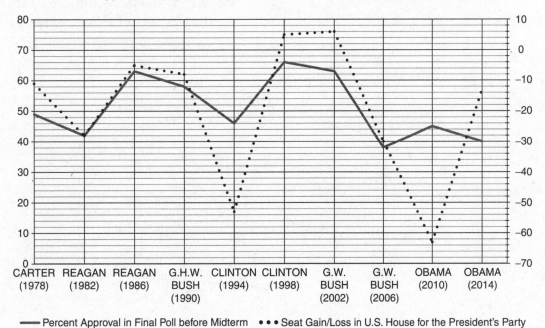

Presidential Approval Ratings and Midterm Seat Changes in the U.S. House of Representatives

—— Percent Approval in Final Poll before Midterm   • • • Seat Gain/Loss in U.S. House for the President's Party

Source: Gallup, 2010 and 2016

GO ON TO THE NEXT PAGE

 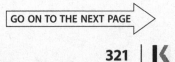

1. Based on the information shown in the table, which two-term president had the smallest difference between their party's midterm election results in the House?

   (A) Bill Clinton

   (B) Barack Obama

   (C) Ronald Reagan

   (D) George W. Bush

2. Based on the data shown in the table, which of the following statements about congressional elections is most likely true?

   (A) Even with a popular president, it is difficult for the president's party to gain more than a few House seats in midterms.

   (B) The power of incumbency protects House legislators even when a president from their own party is wildly unpopular.

   (C) A president whose approval rating is over 50 percent before the midterms will typically see his party gain House seats.

   (D) A president elected with a strong Electoral College mandate is protected against House seat losses in a subsequent midterm.

GO ON TO THE NEXT PAGE

Questions 3 and 4 refer to the graph below.

Distribution of U.S. Households by Size: 1900 and 1940–2000

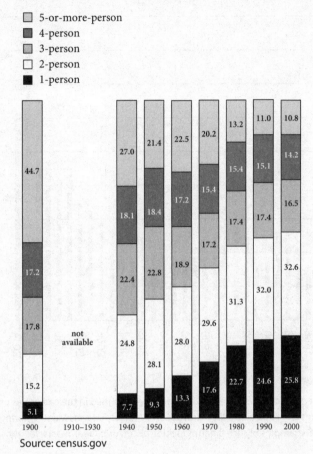

Source: census.gov

3. Which of the following is a potential consequence if the trends illustrated in the bar graph continue into the future?

   (A) Childcare will become a more important issue for most voters.

   (B) Fewer and fewer people will marry or cohabitate.

   (C) Entitlement programs will be increasingly difficult to fund.

   (D) Fewer and fewer women will enter the U.S. workforce.

4. Given the data in the graph, the demographic trends from 1940 to 2000 best reflect a social shift toward

   (A) a focus on individual rights and responsibilities

   (B) a focus on communal obligations and local ties

   (C) a focus on enumerated, constrained constitutional order

   (D) a focus on equal access to opportunity for all persons

GO ON TO THE NEXT PAGE

 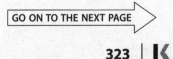

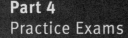
Questions 5 and 6 refer to the graph below.

Net Annual Increases in U.S. Civilian Gun Stock (Firearms in thousands)

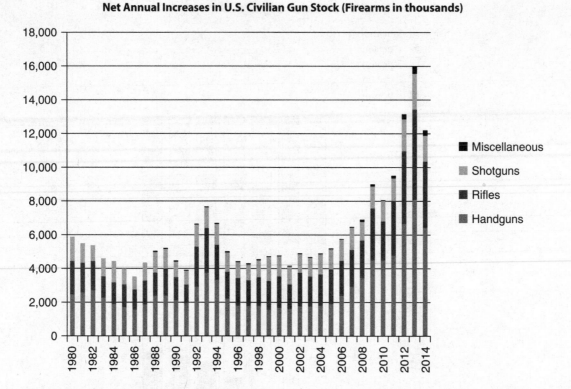

Source: Congressional Research Service, 2017

Note: Miscellaneous firearms include any firearms not specifically defined in the categories on the Bureau of Alcohol, Tobacco, Firearms and Explosives (ATF) form 5300.11 Annual Firearms Manufacturing and Exportation Report. According to ATF, examples of such firearms include piston grip firearms, starter guns, and firearms frames and receivers.

5. Which of the following best describes a trend in the bar graph?

   (A) The net annual increase in handgun ownership declined between 2010 and 2014.

   (B) The net annual increase in handgun ownership spiked between 1990 and 1995.

   (C) The net annual increase in handgun ownership held steady between 1980 and 1985.

   (D) The net annual increase in handgun ownership held steady between 2000 and 2010.

6. Which of the following most likely had an effect on in the net annual increase in handgun, rifle, and shotgun ownership between 1980 and 2014 as shown in the graph?

   (A) *Shaw v. Reno* (1993)

   (B) *United States v. Lopez* (1995)

   (C) *Citizens United v. FEC* (2010)

   (D) *McDonald v. Chicago* (2010)

GO ON TO THE NEXT PAGE

Questions 7 and 8 refer to the graph below.

Composition of Federal Revenue (Selected Years 1946–2021)

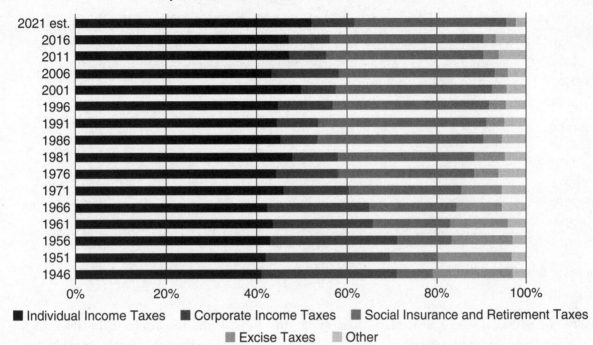

Source: Congressional Research Service, 2017

Note: The composition of revenue for 2021 are projections based on the president's 2017 budget proposal.

7. Which of the following statements illustrates the most important limitation of the data presented in the bar graph?

(A) A table would be superior for discerning the shift in the composition of federal revenue over time.

(B) There is not enough information to precisely determine the shift in revenue sources over time.

(C) There is not enough information to determine any trends in the composition of federal revenue over time.

(D) There is no information about how much money each revenue stream brings in for the federal government.

8. Which of the following is most likely a consequence of the trends depicted in the bar graph?

(A) Corporate income taxes significantly decreased as a share of federal revenue between 1981 and 2011.

(B) Excise taxes have generally decreased as a share of federal revenue between 1946 and 2016.

(C) Individual income taxes have generally decreased as a share of federal revenue between 1946 and 1986.

(D) Individual income taxes have generally increased as a share of federal revenue between 1986 and 2016.

GO ON TO THE NEXT PAGE

Questions 9 and 10 refer to the table below.

Impact on Poverty of Alternative Resource Measures, Age 65 and over

Year	Official Poverty Total	Poverty Total if Social Security Was Not Available	Poverty Total if Food Stamp Users Are Not Included
2007	9.7%	45.1%	9.2%
2008	9.7%	45.2%	9.2%
2009	8.9%	45.1%	8.3%
2010	8.9%	44.3%	8.2%
2011	8.7%	43.6%	7.9%
2012	9.1%	44.4%	8.3%
2013	10.2%	41.2%	9.4%
2014	10.0%	41.5%	9.1%
2015	8.8%	40.5%	8.1%
2016	9.3%	40.3%	8.6%

Source: census.gov

9. Which of the following is an accurate statement about the information in the table?

   (A) The U.S. poverty rate is stable across all age groups, regardless of economic conditions.

   (B) Social Security has been effective in alleviating mass poverty among seniors.

   (C) The poverty rate among seniors is highly dependent on the country's overall economic health.

   (D) Food stamps have a far smaller effect on the overall U.S. poverty rate than Social Security does.

10. Based on the information in the table, which of the following is the most likely implication for the issue of entitlement reform during a presidential election?

   (A) No candidate is likely to call for cuts to entitlement programs that voters age 65 and over are already benefiting from.

   (B) Food stamps are a key voting issue among senior citizens, and most will punish any candidate who threatens that program.

   (C) No presidential hopeful can hope to win over voters without outlining a plan to immediately restrict entitlements.

   (D) A candidate could advocate for eliminating food stamps without major risk of alienating the majority of all voters.

GO ON TO THE NEXT PAGE

Questions 11–14 refer to the passage below.

In summary, it is the judgment of the Court that the 18-year-old vote provisions of the Voting Rights Act Amendments of 1970 are constitutional and enforceable insofar as they pertain to federal elections and unconstitutional and unenforceable insofar as they pertain to state and local elections.

In the very beginning the responsibility of the States for setting the qualifications of voters in [national] congressional elections was made subject to the power of Congress to make or alter such regulations if it deemed it advisable to do so. . . . In short, the Constitution allotted to the States the power to make laws regarding national elections, but provided that if Congress became dissatisfied with the state laws, Congress could alter them. . . . On the other hand, the Constitution was also intended to preserve to the States the power that even the Colonies had to establish and maintain their own separate and independent governments, except insofar as the Constitution itself commands otherwise.

—Justice Hugo Black, announcing the judgments of the Court in an opinion expressing his own view of the cases, *Oregon v. Mitchell* (1970)

11. Which of the following statements is most consistent with the reasoning in the excerpt of the court opinion written by Justice Black?

    (A) The Constitution only grants states the power to structure state and local elections.

    (B) Congress can require a state to change its laws about how it structures federal elections.

    (C) The writers of the Constitution were only concerned with federal elections.

    (D) The Voting Rights Act's provision allowing 18-year-olds to vote is not enforceable.

12. The scenario in the court opinion best illustrates which of the following debates?

    (A) The interpretation of the federal government's implied powers under the necessary and proper clause

    (B) The application of the federal government's system of checks and balances among its branches

    (C) The application of the concurrent powers of the national and state governments in a federalist system

    (D) The interpretation of the states' obligations under the full faith and credit clause

13. Which of the following scenarios is most similar to the reasoning of the court opinion?

    (A) Congress has the power to make laws that regulate commerce between states and can therefore regulate standards on automobiles.

    (B) The president's appointment of Supreme Court justices must be approved by the legislative branch.

    (C) Each state has the authority to establish its own county and state court systems.

    (D) State and local governments manage public education, but the federal government may intervene to promote constitutional protections of student rights.

14. Which of the following makes the qualifications of voters in congressional elections subject to the power of Congress?

    (A) The Civil Rights Act of 1964

    (B) The Voting Rights Act of 1965

    (C) Enumerated powers in Article I

    (D) Time, place, and manner of holding in Article I

GO ON TO THE NEXT PAGE

Questions 15–17 refer to the passage below.

Much has been said of the impropriety of representing men who have no will of their own. Whether this be reasoning or declamation, I will not presume to say. It is the unfortunate situation of the Southern States to have a great part of their population as well as property in blacks. The regulation complained of was one result of the spirit of accommodation which governed the convention; and without this indulgence no Union could possibly have been formed. But, sir, considering some peculiar advantages which we derive from them, it is entirely just that they should be gratified. The Southern States possess certain staples—tobacco, rice, indigo, etc.—which must be capital objects in treaties of commerce with foreign nations; and the advantage which they necessarily procure in these treaties will be felt throughout all the States. But the justice of this plan will appear in another view. The best writers on government have held that representation should be compounded of persons and property. This rule has been adopted, as far as it could be, in the Constitution of New York. It will, however, be by no means admitted that the slaves are considered altogether as property. They are men, though degraded to the condition of slavery. They are persons known to the municipal laws of the States which they inhabit, as well as to the laws of nature. But representation and taxation go together, and one uniform rule ought to apply to both. Would it be just to compute these slaves in the assessment of taxes, and discard them from the estimate in the apportionment of representatives? Would it be just to impose a singular burden without conferring some adequate advantage?

—Alexander Hamilton, *The Debates in the Several State Conventions on the Adoption of the Federal Constitution*

15. Which of the following statements best summarizes Hamilton's argument?

    (A) Slaves do not represent a legal entity and are only subject to the laws of nature. Thus, they should not be counted when determining a state's congressional representation.

    (B) The amount that a state is taxed by the federal government should be proportional to the number of slaves that reside in that state.

    (C) Even though slaves do not pay taxes, they should still be counted when determining a state's congressional representation.

    (D) Though they are not free, slaves are human beings. It would be unfair to count them for determining a state's taxation without counting them for determining a state's congressional representation as well.

16. Which of the following provisions was the direct result of the debate reflected in Hamilton's argument?

    (A) The Thirteenth Amendment

    (B) The Three-Fifths Compromise

    (C) The compromise about ending the importation of slaves

    (D) The Great Compromise

17. Supporters of Hamilton's view that "without this indulgence no Union could possibly have been formed" could point to which of the following texts to best justify their position?

    (A) *Federalist* 10

    (B) *Federalist* 51

    (C) *Federalist* 70

    (D) *Federalist* 78

GO ON TO THE NEXT PAGE

Questions 18 and 19 refer to the map below.

Illinois Senate Election Results by County, 2016

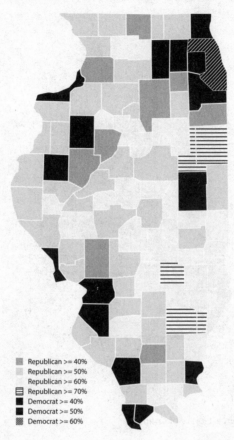

Legend:
- Republican >= 40%
- Republican >= 50%
- Republican >= 60%
- Republican >= 70%
- Democrat >= 40%
- Democrat >= 50%
- Democrat >= 60%

18. Which of the following statements best describes the information in the map?

    (A) Over half the counties registered more votes for the Democratic candidate than for the Republican one.

    (B) Only four counties registered more votes for the Republican candidate than for the Democratic one.

    (C) Most counties in the far northeastern portion of Illinois backed the Democratic candidate.

    (D) No counties in the eastern portion of the state overwhelmingly backed the Republican candidate.

19. The Democratic candidate for Senate won this race. Which of the following statements best explains how that is possible given the information depicted on the map?

    (A) Overall turnout was low due to it being a midterm election, leaving seniors over-represented in many counties.

    (B) The electoral map has been gerrymandered to unfairly favor one party in the election.

    (C) The Republican Party is more popular in rural areas, and poll taxes act as a barrier to entry for the working class.

    (D) The Democratic Party is more popular in urban areas, meaning a few counties will have far more voters than most.

GO ON TO THE NEXT PAGE

Questions 20 and 21 refer to the illustration below.

In memoriam—Our civil service as it was (1877)

Source: Library of Congress

20. Which of the following best describes the message of the political cartoon?

   (A) A critique of the patronage system used to grant duties based on relationship rather than merit

   (B) A celebration of the spoils system that began with Andrew Jackson's victory

   (C) A criticism of the way in which Andrew Jackson was elected president

   (D) A commemoration of the spoils system, which was used to grant duties based on merit

21. Which of the following government bodies is most relevant to the topic of the cartoon?

   (A) State governments

   (B) Congress

   (C) Supreme Court

   (D) Federal bureaucracy

GO ON TO THE NEXT PAGE

Questions 22 and 23 refer to the following infographic.

Contribution Limits for 2017–2018 Federal Elections

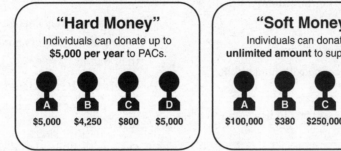
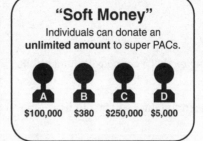

22. Based on the infographic, which of the following claims would a proponent of campaign finance reform most likely make?

(A) Individuals without the means to monetarily support a political party, candidate, or cause can make an equally important political contribution by volunteering their time.

(B) Unlimited campaign contributions to super PACs allow outside organizations to effectively coordinate openly with a specific candidate's campaign for office.

(C) Unlimited campaign contributions to super PACs give unions, corporations, and wealthy individuals too much power in the political process.

(D) Unlimited campaign contributions to super PACs are not a fundamentally different form of speech from "hard money" donations made directly to a candidate or a party.

23. Based on the infographic, which of the following strategies would a candidate seeking to raise campaign funds most likely pursue?

(A) Publicly refuse to accept support from super PACs and denounce any of their efforts

(B) Call for Congress to remove the current cap on hard money donations

(C) Encourage wealthy donors to contribute to super PACs friendly to the candidate's campaign

(D) Coordinate with friendly super PACs to launch a unified TV ad campaign

GO ON TO THE NEXT PAGE

24. From which of the following would a U.S. citizen be protected according to due process rights?

    (A) Being required to register for military service

    (B) Being libeled in a newspaper

    (C) Being convicted of a crime without a public trial

    (D) Being forced to house soldiers in her home

25. The two-party system has dominated most of American history. Which of the following is among the reasons for this?

    (A) The rigid and unchanging political ideologies of both major parties offer voters a stark contrast at the ballot box.

    (B) The Electoral College system requires parties to win the plurality of the national popular vote to win any electors, which is difficult for third parties.

    (C) Most states have rules allowing the two major parties an automatic place on the ballot. Third parties must raise a large number of petition signatures to gain access to the ballot.

    (D) Third parties are unable to win any local and state elections; therefore, they have no platform for nationwide elections.

26. Which of the following most likely accounts for the difference sometimes seen between exit polling and election results?

    (A) Swing voters may change their minds after talking with pollsters but before filling out their ballots.

    (B) Voters may be reluctant to reveal whom they voted for since a ballot is meant to be secret.

    (C) Once the polling places have closed, the results of exit polling may influence potential voters to stay home.

    (D) Pollsters can ask an unrepresentative sample of voters, and the limited sample size can skew the poll.

27. The president of the United States has the constitutional power to negotiate treaties with other nations. Which of the following actions must be taken for a treaty to be legally binding on the United States government and its citizens?

    (A) Congress votes to accept it by a simple majority of both houses.

    (B) The Senate votes to accept it by a two-thirds majority.

    (C) The House of Representatives votes to accept it by a two-thirds majority.

    (D) The Senate votes to accept it by a simple majority, and the Supreme Court declares it constitutional.

GO ON TO THE NEXT PAGE

28. Which of the following would most likely be considered unconstitutional based on the Supreme Court's ruling in *Marbury v. Madison* (1803)?

    (A) A president citing national security concerns in order to withhold information from a criminal trial

    (B) Congress granting itself the power to declare an action of the president to be unconstitutional

    (C) A president seizing private property

    (D) The states regulating interstate commerce

29. Which of the following policies is most likely to cause tension between the competing values of social order and individualism?

    (A) Federal laws prohibiting defamatory speech

    (B) Federal laws regulating child labor

    (C) Federal laws banning discrimination on the basis of race

    (D) Federal laws establishing a nationwide minimum wage

30. In *Federalist* 51, James Madison states that "Ambition must be made to counteract ambition." In that statement, Madison summarizes the argument for

    (A) the necessity of lifetime appointments for judges in order to elevate them above the political fray

    (B) the critical failings of the Articles of Confederation and the need for them to be wholly replaced

    (C) the election of senators by state legislatures rather than direct election by citizens

    (D) a system of checks and balances in government to take into account the failings of human nature

31. Which of the following most accurately describes the Speaker of the House of Representatives?

    (A) The Speaker is nominated by the president and confirmed by the Senate.

    (B) The Speaker is elected by members of the majority party in the House of Representatives.

    (C) The Speaker only votes when a House vote has ended in a tie.

    (D) The Speaker must be at least 35 years of age.

32. A president who supports supply-side economics is faced with an economic recession. Given a supportive Congress, which of the following measures would this president most likely advocate?

    (A) Deregulation of the economy and cutting taxes in order to spur an increase in the number of goods and supplies available

    (B) Increased government spending in order to pick up the slack in consumer demand, thus stimulating economic growth

    (C) An end to government regulation of the economy beyond what is necessary to protect voluntary trade and property

    (D) Nationalization of various industries and the strengthening of a cradle-to-grave social safety net

GO ON TO THE NEXT PAGE

 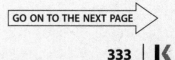

33. Which of the following scenarios would most likely be considered a violation of the Fifth Amendment?

    (A) The government seizes a dilapidated church to build a new airport runway on its land, without paying the landowner.

    (B) A suspect's medical records are taken from his doctor's office before a warrant has been issued.

    (C) A defendant's lawyer is not allowed to cross-examine a witness testifying for the prosecution.

    (D) A suspect is tried again for the same crime after a judge declares a mistrial.

34. The shift from indirect to direct election of U.S. senators best reflects a shift from

    (A) participatory democracy to elite democracy

    (B) elite democracy to pluralist democracy

    (C) elite democracy to participatory democracy

    (D) pluralist democracy to participatory democracy

35. During a presidential election when the incumbent is running for reelection, an undecided voter considers how four years ago there was a recession and now the economy is booming. Which behavioral model of voting decisions does this voter embody?

    (A) Prospective voting

    (B) Retrospective voting

    (C) Rational-choice voting

    (D) Party-line voting

36. Laws requiring photo identification for voting are often contentious for which of the following reasons?

    (A) Opponents argue that the photo identification requirement is burdensome for lower-income residents and that voter fraud itself is very rare.

    (B) Proponents argue that tying voter registration to the application process for driver's licenses increases overall turnout.

    (C) Opponents grant that the photo requirement affords greater public confidence to the election process but argue that it is a costly barrier for lower-income residents.

    (D) Proponents argue that photo identification prevents in-person voter fraud but agree with opponents that the requirement undermines public confidence in the election process.

37. The Supreme Court's decision in *Brown v. Board of Education* in 1954 led to

    (A) an immediate end to segregation in schools

    (B) the passage of a constitutional amendment to strengthen the ruling

    (C) states and individuals trying to circumvent desegregation laws by opening segregated private schools

    (D) a national show of support for desegregation

GO ON TO THE NEXT PAGE

38. Historically, bureaucracies in the United States have grown significantly during which of the following times?

    (A) Periods of economic stability

    (B) Periods of war

    (C) Periods of prosperity

    (D) Periods of conservative government

39. Senator Anderson cannot persuade enough of her colleagues to support funding a new hydroelectric dam on its own merits. Senator Smith cannot get enough of his colleagues to authorize funding a firefighter memorial on the National Mall. Which of the following scenarios is an example of these senators using logrolling to secure funding for their respective projects?

    (A) Senators Anderson and Smith add amendments to an upcoming omnibus bill that will give their opponents tangible benefits to their home states if they vote for their bills.

    (B) Senators Anderson and Smith help each other out by agreeing to vote for each other's amendments to an upcoming omnibus bill, even if they really only care about their own amendment.

    (C) Senators Anderson and Smith quietly offer their opponents large campaign donations in cash if they will support their respective amendments to an upcoming omnibus bill.

    (D) Senators Anderson and Smith go to the media to try and marshal public opinion in support of their respective amendments to an upcoming omnibus bill.

40. Which of the following statements best describes the difficulty a plaintiff faces in winning a libel case against a newspaper company?

    (A) The Supreme Court has established a "heavy presumption against prior restraint" even with defamatory statements.

    (B) A plaintiff must prove the publication knowingly ignored a "clear and present danger" to the plaintiff in what it published.

    (C) The publication must prove that it did not knowingly publish any direct incitement to violence against the plaintiff.

    (D) The publication must be shown to have knowingly published something false or showcased a total disregard for the truth.

41. The Supreme Court's ruling in *Engel v. Vitale* (1962) was based upon which of the following constitutional clauses?

    (A) The commerce clause

    (B) The necessary and proper clause

    (C) The free exercise clause

    (D) The establishment clause

42. Which of the following is the primary function of a congressional whip?

    (A) Effectively enforcing inter-party discipline

    (B) Organizing fellow party members to vote uniformly

    (C) Making committee assignments

    (D) Breaking a vote in the event of a tie

 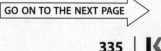

43. Which of the following is an accurate comparison of the two foundational documents?

	Constitution	Articles of Confederation
(A)	Bicameral legislature	Unicameral legislature
(B)	Assigns war powers entirely to the President	Lacked centralized military power
(C)	Enforcement powers do not exist for taxes	Federal government had to request money from the states
(D)	Allows for the admission of new states	Did not allow for the admission of new states

44. Which of the following is an accurate comparison of judicial philosophies?

	Judicial Restraint	Judicial Activism
(A)	Courts are not constrained by political popularity and must act as a safeguard against the whims of the electoral process	Courts should defer to the judgment of the legislative and executive branches unless laws are clearly unconstitutional
(B)	Courts must be limited to the Constitution's text and read it as commonly understood at its adoption	Courts must consider contemporary notions of fairness and equality to inform their decisions
(C)	The court system is best positioned to safeguard liberty and equality	The democratically elected branches of government can best safeguard liberty and equality
(D)	Generally associated with the political philosophy of liberalism	Generally associated with the political philosophy of conservatism

45. Which of the following is an accurate comparison of Democrat and Republican views on fiscal policy?

	Democrats	Republicans
(A)	During a bull market, interest rates should be raised to keep the economy from growing too rapidly and creating a bubble	During a bull market, interest rates should be lowered to keep the economy growing
(B)	During recessions, the government should spend to stimulate the demand for goods	During recessions, the government should cut taxes to stimulate the supply of goods
(C)	During a bear market, interest rates should be lowered to encourage a recovery	During a bear market, interest rates should be frozen to provide stability
(D)	During recessions, the government should tax the wealthy to fund public programs	During recessions, the government should eliminate entitlement programs to cut the deficit

GO ON TO THE NEXT PAGE

46. Which of the following is an accurate comparison of the two Supreme Court cases?

	Wisconsin v. Yoder	*Engel v. Vitale*
(A)	Compelling Amish students to participate in school-sponsored prayer violates the Constitution	Violated the free exercise clause of the First Amendment
(B)	Compelling Amish students to participate in school-sponsored prayer does not violate the Constitution	Dealt with state-sponsored prayer in public schools
(C)	Compelling Amish students to attend school past the 8th grade does not violate the Constitution	Students cannot be forced to salute the flag if they have a religious or political objection
(D)	Compelling Amish students to attend school past the 8th grade violates the Constitution	Public schools cannot open each day with a voluntary prayer

47. Which of the following is an accurate comparison of these two aspects of the executive branch?

	Cabinet Departments	Independent Regulatory Agencies
(A)	Oversee national security	Oversee key sectors of the economy
(B)	The president can fire their heads at his discretion	The president can fire their commissioners only with cause
(C)	Presidential advisory bodies	Congressional advisory bodies
(D)	Leaders are nominated by the president and appointed by the Senate	Leaders are appointed by the president without need for Senate confirmation

GO ON TO THE NEXT PAGE

48. A state government bans abortion during the first trimester, with a narrow exemption to protect the life of the mother in medical emergencies. If that ban is challenged in the courts, a judge is likely to

    (A) uphold the ban because states have the right to regulate abortion during that particular trimester

    (B) uphold the ban because the Constitution does not protect the right to abortion in any instance

    (C) strike down the ban because states cannot prohibit abortion during that particular trimester

    (D) strike down the ban because all regulation of abortion is prohibited at the state level

49. De facto segregation is best defined as

    (A) a type of segregation that took place in the South prior to the Civil War

    (B) a type of segregation created by laws, such as Jim Crow laws

    (C) a type of segregation based on social custom or economic factors

    (D) a type of segregation affecting only economic opportunities, not social equality

50. The allocation of tax powers to the House reflects the intent of the framers to

    (A) balance the interests of the Senate, where small northern states dominated, with a House dominated by southern states

    (B) force Congress to rely on money requested from the governments of its member states

    (C) see that any income tax is written by the people who would be subject to it

    (D) ensure that taxation power is most closely subjected to the will of the people voting for elected officials

51. Which of the following scenarios best illustrates the principle of separation of powers?

    (A) The president may be removed from office after a trial in the Senate.

    (B) The federal bureaucracy is under the authority of the president.

    (C) The vice president is the President of the Senate.

    (D) The executive branch implements laws that were drafted by Congress.

52. A citizen is concerned about the state of public education, and she wants to make her viewpoints about education reform known to her political representatives. Which of the following is an example of a way she can express her concerns through a linkage institution?

    (A) Registering to vote and then patiently waiting for election day to make her opinion known through the ballot box

    (B) Writing a letter to her state representatives to persuade them to vote in accordance with her views on education reform

    (C) Attending her local school board meetings and asking the school board members how they will implement education reform policies

    (D) Volunteering with a political party whose platform and candidates mirror her views on education reform

GO ON TO THE NEXT PAGE

53. Senator Doe has stuck with public opinion on major and minor bills, but now the country is on the verge of a new war. The war polls well with Doe's voters. The leadership of Doe's own party supports the war. However, Senator Doe feels that the war is unwinnable and is against long-term U.S. interests. So, he votes against the declaration of war. What model of representation do his actions embody?

    (A) Conscience model

    (B) Delegate model

    (C) Politico model

    (D) Trustee model

54. In the House of Representatives, a discharge petition is rarely issued for which of the following reasons?

    (A) They can only be requested by members of the minority party, and it is difficult to convince members of the majority party to break ranks and vote with their opposition.

    (B) They harden the House leadership's resolve to oppose a bill, so even a potentially successful discharge petition can kill a bill.

    (C) They require an absolute majority, and it is difficult to get members of the majority party to undermine the House leadership they themselves elected.

    (D) They require plurality support, and it is difficult to get members of the majority party to undermine the House leadership they themselves elected.

55. Political socialization is best described as

    (A) the framework people use to evaluate the government, society, and public policy

    (B) how the public decides which issues merit attention and action

    (C) the process by which a person comes to favor rapid change in the socioeconomic order

    (D) how people acquire their political beliefs, identity, and values

IF YOU FINISH BEFORE TIME IS CALLED, YOU MAY CHECK YOUR WORK ON SECTION I ONLY. DO NOT MOVE ON TO SECTION II UNTIL INSTRUCTED TO DO SO.

STOP

END OF SECTION I

SECTION II
100 Minutes
4 Questions

You have 1 hour and 40 minutes to answer all four of the following free-response questions. Craft your responses in full sentences and paragraphs, using specific examples where appropriate. It is suggested that you spend a few minutes planning each of your answers. In total, it is recommended that you spend approximately 20 minutes each on questions 1, 2, and 3 and approximately 40 minutes on question 4.

1. For most of the twentieth century the authority of the executive branch expanded in various ways, such that scholars now identify this as the period of the "Imperial Presidency." Scholars have identified the ability of the president to wage war without congressional approval, the growing number of executive orders enacting policy without the involvement of Congress, and the president's influence over the federal bureaucracy and judiciary as concerns with relation to executive overreach.

   After reading the scenario, respond to Parts A, B, and C.

   (A) Identify one specific power exercised by the president that is not explicitly identified in the Constitution.

   (B) Describe an action Congress could take to limit the presidential power identified in Part A.

   (C) Explain how two different linkage institutions have responded to the expansion of presidential authority.

GO ON TO THE NEXT PAGE

Constitutional Amendments: Time Spans from Congressional Passage to Ratification

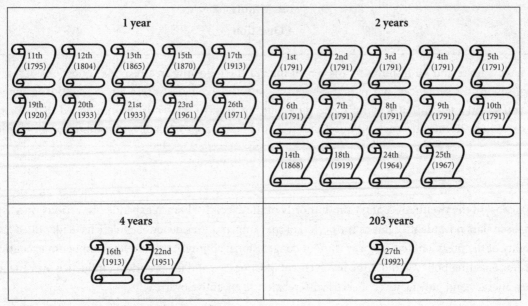

Total amendments sent to the states for approval: 33
Total amendments proposed by U.S. Congress: over 11,000

2. Use the information graphic to respond to Parts A, B, C, and D.

   (A) Identify a trend, as illustrated in the information graphic, about the ratification of constitutional amendments.

   (B) Describe the process of amending the Constitution, and explain how the trend described in Part A reflects the design of the founders in regard to the amendment process.

   (C) Considering the number of proposed versus ratified amendments, explain why amendments are not an effective way to address immediate matters of public policy.

   (D) Describe one example of the Constitution being adapted in response to changing societal norms.

3. In the 2013 case of *Shelby County v. Holder*, the Supreme Court struck down Section 4(b) of the Voting Rights Act of 1965. This section included a "coverage formula" based on states' past histories of discriminatory voting practices that determined which states were required to obtain federal approval before changing their voting laws. This process of obtaining federal approval for state voting laws is called the "preclearance requirement," and it was explained in Section 5 of the Voting Rights Act. Officials in Shelby County, Alabama, sued and argued that the Voting Rights Act was unconstitutional because the coverage formula in Section 4(b) was outdated.

   Chief Justice Roberts, writing for a narrow majority, argued that since the data used to create the coverage formula in Section 4(b) was over 40 years old, the section was no longer valid and impermissibly punished individual states for past wrongs. Section 4(b) was therefore ruled unconstitutional. The holding concluded that a new formula to determine which states would be subject to the preclearance requirement would have

GO ON TO THE NEXT PAGE

to be created by Congress, which has yet to act on the issue. This renders the Voting Rights Act's Section 5 preclearance requirement unenforceable until Congress acts to create a new formula, so while the Court did not explicitly declare Section 5 unconstitutional, it effectively removed any preclearance requirement as a check on the states. After the ruling, several states that had been subject to the preclearance requirement based on the old coverage formula passed new laws regulating elections in their states.

Based on the information given, respond to Parts A, B, and C.

(A) *Shelby County v. Holder* (2013) concerned the Voting Rights Act of 1965 and the Act's intention to uphold the Fifteenth Amendment. Identify the constitutional clause that is relevant to *Shaw v. Reno* (1993), which is another Supreme Court case that involved voting rights.

(B) Though both *Shelby* and *Shaw* concern voting rights, explain how the holding in *Shelby County v. Holder* differs from the holding in *Shaw v. Reno*.

(C) Describe an action that civil rights groups could take to respond to *Shelby County v. Holder* if they disagreed with the decision.

4. The struggle for equality has historically been and continues to be a significant influence on U.S. political life. While some contend that the founders institutionalized inequality by allowing racial and sexual discrimination in the Constitution, others argue that the United States is founded on universal principles that, if followed consistently, would forbid discrimination on the basis of demographic categories. Choose a side and argue for or against the claim that human equality is a founding principle of the United States.

In your essay you must:

- Formulate a defensible thesis that establishes a chain of reasoning
- Provide evidence for your thesis with at least TWO pieces of relevant, accurate information
  - Take at least ONE of your pieces of evidence from one of the following foundational documents:
    - The Declaration of Independence
    - U.S. Constitution and Amendments
    - Letter from a Birmingham Jail
  - Take your other piece of evidence from a different foundational document from the list above OR from your own study
- Logically explain why your evidence supports your thesis
- Present and reply to an alternative viewpoint using refutation, concession, or rebuttal

END OF SECTION II

ANSWER KEY

Section I

1. C	12. C	23. C	34. C	45. B
2. A	13. D	24. C	35. B	46. D
3. C	14. D	25. C	36. A	47. B
4. A	15. D	26. D	37. C	48. C
5. B	16. B	27. B	38. B	49. C
6. D	17. A	28. B	39. B	50. D
7. D	18. C	29. A	40. D	51. D
8. B	19. D	30. D	41. D	52. D
9. B	20. A	31. B	42. B	53. A
10. A	21. D	32. A	43. A	54. C
11. B	22. C	33. A	44. B	55. D

Section I Number Correct: _____

Review detailed explanations for Sections I and II at the back of this book. Use the rubrics and sample essays to self-score Section II.

Section II Points Earned: _____

Sign into your online account at kaptest.com and enter your results in the online scoring section to see your 1–5 score.

Haven't registered your book yet? Go to kaptest.com/booksonline to begin.

PRACTICE EXAM 2 BREAKDOWN

Use the following table to determine which topics you are already strong in and which topics you need to review most.

Topic	Exam Question(s)	Number You Got Correct	Chapters to Study
Foundations of American Democracy	11, 12, 13, 14, 15, 16, 17, 30, 34, 43, 46, 51	___ out of 12	3, 8
Interactions Among Branches of Government	3, 21, 27, 28, 31, 38, 39, 41, 42, 47, 50, 53, 54	___ out of 13	4, 9
Civil Liberties and Civil Rights	5, 6, 24, 29, 33, 37, 40, 44, 48, 49	___ out of 10	5, 10
American Political Ideologies and Beliefs	4, 7, 8, 18, 19, 25, 26, 32, 45, 55	___ out of 10	6, 11
Political Participation	1, 2, 9, 10, 20, 22, 23, 35, 36, 52	___ out of 10	7, 12

Practice Exam 3

Practice Exam 3 Answer Grid

1. Ⓐ Ⓑ Ⓒ Ⓓ
2. Ⓐ Ⓑ Ⓒ Ⓓ
3. Ⓐ Ⓑ Ⓒ Ⓓ
4. Ⓐ Ⓑ Ⓒ Ⓓ
5. Ⓐ Ⓑ Ⓒ Ⓓ
6. Ⓐ Ⓑ Ⓒ Ⓓ
7. Ⓐ Ⓑ Ⓒ Ⓓ
8. Ⓐ Ⓑ Ⓒ Ⓓ
9. Ⓐ Ⓑ Ⓒ Ⓓ
10. Ⓐ Ⓑ Ⓒ Ⓓ
11. Ⓐ Ⓑ Ⓒ Ⓓ
12. Ⓐ Ⓑ Ⓒ Ⓓ
13. Ⓐ Ⓑ Ⓒ Ⓓ
14. Ⓐ Ⓑ Ⓒ Ⓓ

15. Ⓐ Ⓑ Ⓒ Ⓓ
16. Ⓐ Ⓑ Ⓒ Ⓓ
17. Ⓐ Ⓑ Ⓒ Ⓓ
18. Ⓐ Ⓑ Ⓒ Ⓓ
19. Ⓐ Ⓑ Ⓒ Ⓓ
20. Ⓐ Ⓑ Ⓒ Ⓓ
21. Ⓐ Ⓑ Ⓒ Ⓓ
22. Ⓐ Ⓑ Ⓒ Ⓓ
23. Ⓐ Ⓑ Ⓒ Ⓓ
24. Ⓐ Ⓑ Ⓒ Ⓓ
25. Ⓐ Ⓑ Ⓒ Ⓓ
26. Ⓐ Ⓑ Ⓒ Ⓓ
27. Ⓐ Ⓑ Ⓒ Ⓓ
28. Ⓐ Ⓑ Ⓒ Ⓓ

29. Ⓐ Ⓑ Ⓒ Ⓓ
30. Ⓐ Ⓑ Ⓒ Ⓓ
31. Ⓐ Ⓑ Ⓒ Ⓓ
32. Ⓐ Ⓑ Ⓒ Ⓓ
33. Ⓐ Ⓑ Ⓒ Ⓓ
34. Ⓐ Ⓑ Ⓒ Ⓓ
35. Ⓐ Ⓑ Ⓒ Ⓓ
36. Ⓐ Ⓑ Ⓒ Ⓓ
37. Ⓐ Ⓑ Ⓒ Ⓓ
38. Ⓐ Ⓑ Ⓒ Ⓓ
39. Ⓐ Ⓑ Ⓒ Ⓓ
40. Ⓐ Ⓑ Ⓒ Ⓓ
41. Ⓐ Ⓑ Ⓒ Ⓓ
42. Ⓐ Ⓑ Ⓒ Ⓓ

43. Ⓐ Ⓑ Ⓒ Ⓓ
44. Ⓐ Ⓑ Ⓒ Ⓓ
45. Ⓐ Ⓑ Ⓒ Ⓓ
46. Ⓐ Ⓑ Ⓒ Ⓓ
47. Ⓐ Ⓑ Ⓒ Ⓓ
48. Ⓐ Ⓑ Ⓒ Ⓓ
49. Ⓐ Ⓑ Ⓒ Ⓓ
50. Ⓐ Ⓑ Ⓒ Ⓓ
51. Ⓐ Ⓑ Ⓒ Ⓓ
52. Ⓐ Ⓑ Ⓒ Ⓓ
53. Ⓐ Ⓑ Ⓒ Ⓓ
54. Ⓐ Ⓑ Ⓒ Ⓓ
55. Ⓐ Ⓑ Ⓒ Ⓓ

SECTION I
80 Minutes
55 Questions

Each of the following 55 multiple-choice questions or incomplete statements is accompanied by four possible answers or completions. Select the answer choice that best answers the question or completes the statement.

Questions 1 and 2 refer to the bar graph below.

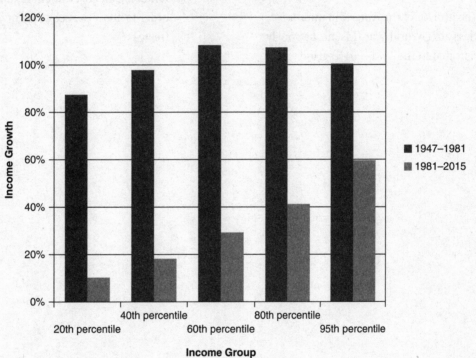

Income Growth Before and After 1981

GO ON TO THE NEXT PAGE

1. Which of the following is an accurate statement about the information presented in the bar graph?

   (A) Between 1981 and 2015, the 95th and 20th percentiles saw approximately equal increases in their income growth.

   (B) The 95th percentile consistently saw the greatest income growth over the entire timespan depicted.

   (C) Growth was more evenly distributed across all income groups in the 1947–1981 time period.

   (D) The growth of the American middle class after World War II is most strongly reflected in the 1981–2015 period.

2. A liberal response to the data from the 1981–2015 period most likely would include

   (A) increasing taxes on at least the 95th percentile paired with increasing the national minimum wage

   (B) redistributing wealth across society through the nationalization of major industries

   (C) cutting taxes in order to increase the income of all groups across the socioeconomic spectrum

   (D) removing all government regulations in order to allow the economy to develop freely

GO ON TO THE NEXT PAGE

Questions 3 and 4 refer to the graph below.

U.S. Popular Vote for President as Percentage of Total Population

Source: CircleAdrian (compiled from U.S. Census and U.S. Election Atlas)

3. Which of the following is an accurate statement about the information in the line graph?

   (A) The percentage of the total population that voted in presidential elections consistently increased over the twentieth century.

   (B) The percentage of the total population that voted in presidential elections more than tripled over the course of the nineteenth century.

   (C) The percentage of the total population that voted in presidential elections never rose above 15 percent in the nineteenth century.

   (D) The percentage of the total population that voted in presidential elections increased all throughout the first decade of the twentieth century.

4. Which of the following best explains the difference in voter turnout between 1900 and 2000?

   (A) The Twenty-Sixth Amendment

   (B) The Voting Rights Act of 1965

   (C) The Nineteenth Amendment

   (D) The Seventeenth Amendment

GO ON TO THE NEXT PAGE

Questions 5 and 6 refer to the graph below.

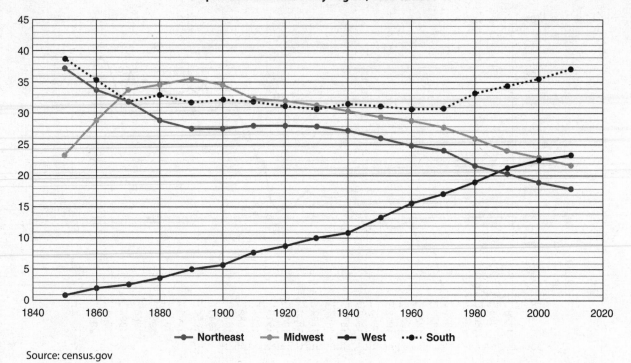

Population Distribution by Region, 1850 to 2010

Legend: —●— Northeast —●— Midwest —●— West ••●•• South

Source: census.gov

5. Which of the following would make it easier to interpret the results or implications of the data presented in the graph?

   (A) Knowing which states belonged to which regions

   (B) Having the information presented in a data table

   (C) Having more data points to better discern the regional trends

   (D) Knowing the regional population distribution by decade

6. Which of the following is an accurate conclusion based on a comparison of the trends in the line graph above and your knowledge of the two major political parties?

   (A) The Republican Party gained a greater share of House seats in the Northeast due to that region's population trend after 1960.

   (B) The Democratic Party gained a greater share of House seats in the South due to that region's population trend after 1960.

   (C) The Democratic Party lost a greater share of House seats in the South due to that region's population trend between 1900 and 1950.

   (D) The Republican Party gained a greater share of House seats in the South due to that region's population trend after 1980.

GO ON TO THE NEXT PAGE

Questions 7 and 8 refer to the graph below.

Distribution of School Enrollment of the U.S. Population 3 Years and Older, by Level, 1955 to 2016

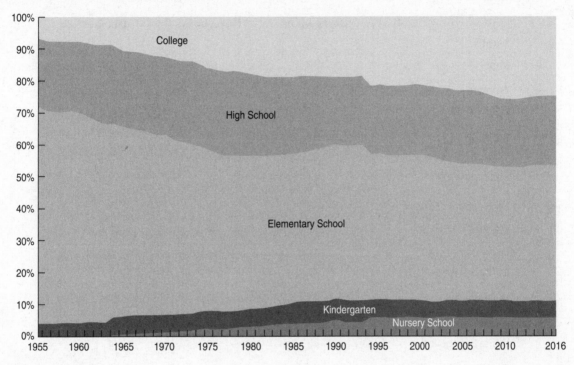

Source: census.gov

Note: Data on nursery school enrollment not available from 1955 to 1963.

7. Based on the data shown in the graph, which of the following statements is true about school enrollment in the United States?

(A) The share of the elementary school population overall is growing.

(B) The share of the college-educated population is growing.

(C) The share of the high school population is declining.

(D) The share of the kindergarten population is declining.

8. Which of the following is most likely an implication of the graph?

(A) The Democratic Party's voter base is likely to grow due to the increase of youth in elementary school and high school.

(B) The Democratic Party's voter base is likely to decline due to an increase in college-educated voters.

(C) The Republican Party's voter base is likely to grow due to an increase in college-educated voters.

(D) The Democratic Party's voter base is likely to grow due to an increase in college-educated voters.

GO ON TO THE NEXT PAGE

 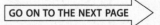

Questions 9 and 10 refer to the table below.

Public Opinion on Overturning *Roe v. Wade*, 2017

	In Favor %	Oppose %	DK %
Total	28	69	3
Men	30	67	3
Women	26	72	2
Ages 18–49	24	73	3
Ages 50+	33	64	3
College graduate	23	74	3
Some college	27	70	3
High school or less	35	62	3
Republican / Lean R.	44	53	3
Democrat / Lean D.	14	84	2
Conservative	57	41	2
Liberal	11	87	2
Protestant	35	63	2
White Evangelical	47	49	4
Catholic	34	61	5
Unaffiliated	9	89	2

Source: Pew Research Center

9. Which of the following statements concerning the data in the table is accurate?

   (A) A 21-year-old would more likely support the overturn of *Roe v. Wade* than a 65-year-old.

   (B) A person who has only completed some college would be more opposed to overturning *Roe v. Wade* than a college graduate.

   (C) A majority of men favor overturning *Roe v. Wade* while a majority of women oppose overturning it.

   (D) White Evangelicals are more in favor of overturning *Roe v. Wade* than Catholics.

10. Which of the following conclusions can be drawn based on the data?

    (A) Generational demographic shifts are unlikely to dramatically influence public opinion on *Roe v. Wade*.

    (B) As citizens get older, they will tend to become far more in favor of overturning *Roe v. Wade*.

    (C) The next generation will likely identify as Democrats and will likely be less in favor of overturning *Roe v. Wade*.

    (D) Religious affiliation impacts how much education citizens will complete.

GO ON TO THE NEXT PAGE

Questions 11–14 refer to the passage below.

Few things were better known, than the immediate causes which led to the adoption of the present constitution . . . that the prevailing motive was *to regulate commerce*; to rescue it from the embarrassing and destructive consequences, resulting from the legislation of so many different States, and to place it under the protection of a uniform law. . .

The entire purpose for which the delegates assembled at Annapolis, was to devise means for the uniform regulation of trade. They found no means, but in a general government.

We do not find, in the history of the formation and adoption of the constitution, that any man speaks of a general *concurrent power*, in the regulation of foreign and domestic trade, as still residing in the States. The very object intended, more than any other, was to take away such power. If it had not so provided, the constitution would not have been worth accepting. . .

—Chief Justice John Marshall, *Gibbons v. Ogden* (1824)

11. Which of the following statements best summarizes Justice Marshall's argument?

    (A) The Constitution is unclear with regard to the power to regulate interstate commerce.

    (B) The Constitution leaves it to state governments to collaborate with one another to regulate foreign and domestic trade.

    (C) The Constitution aimed to take all power away from state governments, including regulation of commerce.

    (D) The Constitution delegated the regulation of interstate and foreign commerce to Congress alone.

12. Which of the following perspectives is most consistent with the passage?

    (A) Congress's power to regulate depends on whether the activity is related to commerce and whether it is local or interstate.

    (B) Congress's power to regulate commerce is absolute, regardless of whether the trade is foreign, interstate, or local in nature.

    (C) Congress has ample power to regulate all sectors of commercial intercourse between states, including navigation.

    (D) Congress does not have the power to regulate manufacturing at a local level because it is not an act of interstate commerce.

GO ON TO THE NEXT PAGE

13. Which of the following would supporters of Marshall's view most likely support?

    (A) The federal government regulating any activity occurring in a single state

    (B) The federal government regulating trade between Florida and Alabama

    (C) A state government choosing to reject a federal regulation on trade within that state

    (D) A state government regulating trade between Maine and a British outpost just across the border in Canada

14. Which of the following is a power delegated to state legislatures?

    (A) States may redraw the boundaries of their federal congressional districts following a national census.

    (B) States can impose taxes on goods coming into their territory from other states or from foreign countries.

    (C) States may choose to ignore federal laws that violate their state constitution.

    (D) States can freely enter into compacts with one another without federal approval.

GO ON TO THE NEXT PAGE

Questions 15–17 refer to the passage below.

Chicago and Oak Park (municipal respondents) maintain that a right set out in the Bill of Rights applies to the States only when it is an indispensable attribute of any "civilized" legal system. If it is possible to imagine a civilized country that does not recognize the right, municipal respondents assert, that right is not protected by due process. And since there are civilized countries that ban or strictly regulate the private possession of handguns, they maintain that due process does not preclude such measures.

The Bill of Rights, including the Second Amendment, originally applied only to the Federal Government, not to the States, but the constitutional Amendments adopted in the Civil War's aftermath fundamentally altered the federal system. Four years after the adoption of the Fourteenth Amendment, this Court held in the *Slaughter-House Cases*, that the Privileges or Immunities Clause protects only those rights "which owe their existence to the Federal government, its National character, its Constitution, or its laws," and that the fundamental rights predating the creation of the Federal Government were not protected by the Clause…Under this narrow reading, the Court held that the Privileges or Immunities Clause protects only very limited rights…Subsequently, the Court held that the Second Amendment applies only to the Federal Government in *Cruikshank*, *Presser*, and *Miller*, the decisions on which the Seventh Circuit relied in this case.

—Justice Alito, *McDonald v. Chicago* (2010)

15. Which of the following statements best summarizes Justice Alito's argument?

    (A) The Bill of Rights applies to states.

    (B) The Second Amendment applies only to the federal government.

    (C) This case should have the same outcome as *Cruikshank*, *Presser*, and *Miller*.

    (D) This case violates the Fourteenth Amendment.

16. With the phrase "under this narrow reading," Justice Alito is most likely referring to which of the following philosophies?

    (A) Judicial activism

    (B) Judicial restraint

    (C) Originalism

    (D) Strict scrutiny

17. In what respect did the Amendments adopted in the Civil War's aftermath "fundamentally" alter the federal system?

    (A) The Bill of Rights was no longer applicable only to the federal government but to the states as well.

    (B) The Fourteenth Amendment resulted in the total incorporation of the Bill of Rights to the states.

    (C) The privileges and immunities clause of the Constitution was overturned by the Fourteenth Amendment.

    (D) Nullification was no longer considered a legally plausible approach for state governments.

 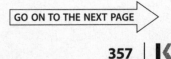

Questions 18 and 19 refer to the map below.

Geographic Boundaries of United States Courts of Appeals and United States District Courts

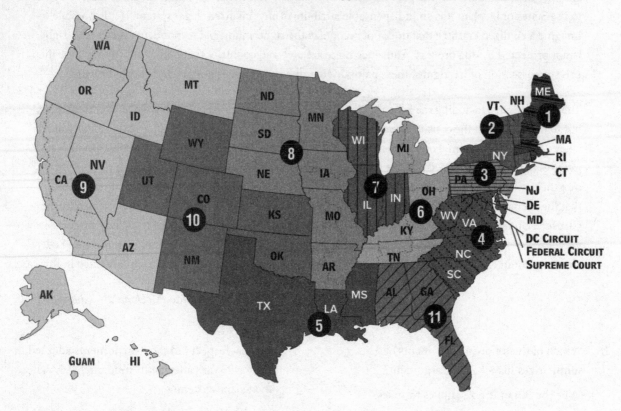

18. The map shows the outlines of the United States courts of appeals. Which of the following statements best explains the reason behind the way in which it is drawn?

(A) Article I of the Constitution authorizes Congress to create "inferior" courts at its discretion.

(B) Article III of the Constitution authorizes Congress to create "inferior" courts at its discretion.

(C) Article III of the Constitution authorizes the Supreme Court to create "inferior" courts at its discretion.

(D) Article II of the Constitution authorizes the president to create "inferior" courts at his discretion.

19. Which of the following best describes the information in the map?

(A) Kansas and Oklahoma are covered by the United States court of appeals for the Tenth Circuit.

(B) California is covered by the United States court of appeals for the Seventh Circuit.

(C) Florida, Georgia, and Mississippi constitute the United States court of appeals for the Eleventh Circuit.

(D) The United States court of appeals for the First Circuit can be found in the Midwest.

GO ON TO THE NEXT PAGE →

Questions 20 and 21 refer to the political cartoon below.

The big type war of the yellow kids (1898)

Source: Library of Congress

Note: Newspaper publishers Pulitzer and Hearst both wearing yellow and pushing blocks that spell "WAR."

20. Which of the following statements pertaining to the media is both reflected in the political cartoon and still relevant in politics today?

(A) Extensive media coverage tends to turn elections into personality contests between candidates.

(B) Public perceptions of bias in the media influence both public opinion and government action.

(C) Average voters would be unlikely to be influenced by political information they learn through the media.

(D) Most voters seek out media with a viewpoint that differs from their own ideology to better understand other perspectives on current issues.

21. Which of the following policies would the artist most likely support?

(A) Stripping Congress of its enumerated power to declare war

(B) Varying one's choice of news outlets so as to be fully informed

(C) Protecting and vigorously enforcing the FCC's equal-time rule

(D) Amending the Bill of Rights to remove freedom of the press

GO ON TO THE NEXT PAGE

Questions 22 and 23 refer to the infographic below.

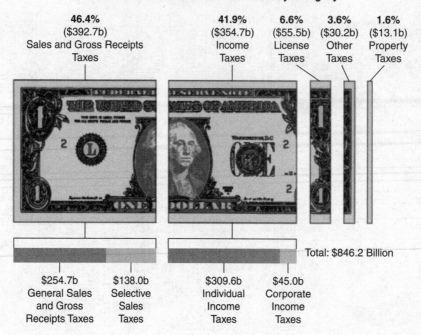

Total State Government Tax Collection by Category

| **46.4%** ($392.7b) Sales and Gross Receipts Taxes | **41.9%** ($354.7b) Income Taxes | **6.6%** ($55.5b) License Taxes | **3.6%** ($30.2b) Other Taxes | **1.6%** ($13.1b) Property Taxes |

| $254.7b General Sales and Gross Receipts Taxes | $138.0b Selective Sales Taxes | $309.6b Individual Income Taxes | $45.0b Corporate Income Taxes |

Total: $846.2 Billion

Source: census.gov

Note: Details may not add to the total due to independent rounding.

22. Which of the following is true of the information graphic?

   (A) Property taxes brought in approximately 13.1 billion dollars for state governments.

   (B) At just under 41.9 percent of total tax revenue, sales and gross receipts taxes constitute the single largest source of revenue for state governments.

   (C) License taxes are the smallest source of revenue listed for state governments.

   (D) Corporate income taxes constituted over 309 billion dollars of revenue for state governments.

23. Which of the following would a state government likely spend some of the collected revenue on?

   (A) Contributing to the national defense

   (B) Running post offices

   (C) Regulating trade with neighboring states

   (D) Funding school systems

GO ON TO THE NEXT PAGE

24. Based on the Supreme Court's ruling in *Shaw v. Reno* (1993), which of the following would be considered constitutional?

    (A) A university desegregating its student housing

    (B) A local government censoring local newspapers to avoid any potential lawsuits

    (C) A college professor publicly protesting against the university's board

    (D) An area being conscious of race while redistricting in order to maintain compliance with the Voting Rights Act of 1965

25. In *Brutus* 1, the author states that "In the business therefore of laying and collecting taxes, the idea of confederation is totally lost." In other words, the author makes the case that

    (A) the Articles of Confederation were not strong enough to deal with the problems facing the United States

    (B) the Necessary and Proper Clause of the proposed Constitution will allow the central government to pass any laws it wishes

    (C) the sovereignty of the states is ultimately rooted in their taxation powers, so the Constitution undermines them

    (D) a large, diverse republic will be unable to function as its various parts will be at odds with themselves

26. Which of the following scenarios would most likely be considered an unconstitutional abuse of the separation of powers?

    (A) A court ordering the president to turn over information protected by executive privilege to a criminal investigation

    (B) The Senate not consenting by two-thirds vote to a treaty that the president negotiated with a foreign nation

    (C) A president vetoing sections of a bill without rejecting the bill as a whole

    (D) A president delivering the State of the Union by written statement rather than by addressing Congress in person

27. Title IX of the Education Amendments Act of 1972 made it federal law that no person can be discriminated against on the basis of their sex in any federally funded activity. What constitutional clause most directly provided the basis for this law?

    (A) The banning of sex-specific laws on the grounds that they are cruel and unusual punishments

    (B) Birthright citizenship affording men and women equivalent rights and protections

    (C) The prohibition that any person be denied the equal protection of the law

    (D) The constitutional right to free expression through sports

GO ON TO THE NEXT PAGE

 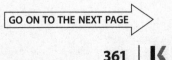

28. An unfunded mandate is best defined as

    (A) the federal government passing a law without raising the revenue necessary to support that law

    (B) the federal government only recommending certain policies, with no funding needed to be appropriated for them

    (C) the federal government creating policies without allocating specific funds to implement the policies

    (D) a form of nullification in which a state government passes a law that requires certain actions on the federal government's part

29. Which of the following statements most accurately characterizes the Supreme Court's decision in *McCulloch v. Maryland*?

    (A) It created the constitutional concept of eminent domain.

    (B) It denied states the right to form treaties with other nations.

    (C) It expanded Congress's ability to exercise its implied powers.

    (D) It established Supreme Court decisions as the supreme law of the land.

30. From which of the following would a U.S. citizen be protected according to due process rights?

    (A) Being required to register for military service

    (B) Becoming libeled in a newspaper

    (C) Being imprisoned without a public trial

    (D) Being forced to house soldiers in her home

31. A deficit watchdog group protests a new fighter jet project. Which of the following describes an application of an iron triangle to this situation?

    (A) The watchdog is a key interest group for the Armed Services Committee, meaning that their lobbying may kill the project.

    (B) Testimony by the watchdog group and Pentagon officials will be given equal weight, despite the watchdog group not being military experts.

    (C) The Appropriations Committee will be pulled into the debate over the project thanks to the watchdog group's lobbying.

    (D) The Pentagon and aerospace lobbying groups will have greater influence over the Armed Services Committee than a non-military lobby.

32. Which of the following statements describes a difficulty the framers had with electing the president by a direct popular vote?

    (A) They feared it would be too contentious and the entire process would be subject to corruption.

    (B) They feared it would undermine presidential federal authority.

    (C) They feared it would lead to lower-class voters raising taxes on planters and merchants.

    (D) They feared it would lead to uninformed voters making a decision without proper consideration.

GO ON TO THE NEXT PAGE

33. A political realignment refers to

(A) when voters must be registered with a political party to vote for one of its candidates

(B) a retroactive change of the law that criminalizes conduct that was legal when originally performed

(C) any association of individuals or organizations that is trying to influence public policy in its favor

(D) when the electoral base of a party changes, as does the political agenda of that party

34. Which of the following best describes the media's influence on public opinion?

(A) It helps establish the policy-making agenda for the public by deciding the priority of various issues.

(B) It devotes equal time to discussing both sides of issues vital to the public interest.

(C) It affects the public by centering elections on the qualifications and platforms of candidates.

(D) It provides reliable, unbiased information for its consumers.

35. Which of the following is an example of how *stare decisis* creates friction between the judicial branch and interest groups with respect to overturning precedent?

(A) It undermines the court system's legitimacy through inconsistent rulings and unpredictable results.

(B) It makes judges unconcerned with political popularity, leading interest groups to lobby against the judicial system itself.

(C) It instills a slow pace of change in court opinion that can take decades of coordinated effort to change.

(D) It limits liberal interest groups by reading a constitutional provision strictly as the text was understood at adoption.

36. Which of the following polls would have the largest sampling error?

(A) A public opinion survey that exclusively contacts thousands of randomized landlines

(B) An exit poll conducted at a thousand randomized polling places across the country

(C) A benchmark poll of a thousand people conducted by a new candidate for Senate

(D) An opinion poll conducted through live interviews with thousands of people nationwide

GO ON TO THE NEXT PAGE

37. A self-identified libertarian would describe a laissez-faire economic system as promoting which of the following core values?

    (A) Equality of outcome

    (B) Equality of opportunity

    (C) Rule of law

    (D) Individual freedom

38. Which of the following changes would most likely result in reducing a barrier that third-party candidates currently face in winning elections?

    (A) Major political parties adding more platform items that reflect the preferences of third-party members

    (B) Rewriting campaign finance law to permit public financing for parties based on their performance in the last election cycle

    (C) Implementing a federal provision that requires all states to permit write-in candidates on presidential ballots

    (D) Converting more winner-take-all districts into proportional voting districts

39. The National Organization for Women (NOW) advocates for women's rights and was initially run by second-wave feminist leaders when it was founded in 1966. Which model of democracy does this group play a key role in?

    (A) The participatory model

    (B) The pluralist model

    (C) The elite model

    (D) The direct democracy model

40. Which of the following Supreme Court decisions allows parents to pull their children out of public schools and homeschool them for religious reasons?

    (A) *Tinker v. Des Moines Independent Community School District* (1969)

    (B) *Wisconsin v. Yoder* (1972)

    (C) *Engel v. Vitale* (1962)

    (D) *Shaw v. Reno* (1993)

41. One month before the 2018 U.S. Senate election, a major business corporation purchases TV airtime to broadcast a film, which it spent $15 million to produce, that negatively portrays an incumbent senator's policies and directly opposes her reelection. Supporters of the criticized senator claim the film will unfairly impact the election. Which of the following is most relevant in determining whether the corporation's actions were legal?

    (A) *New York Times Co. v. United States* (1971), which determined that, due to the First Amendment's protection of freedom of speech, the government has a "heavy burden" for justifying its use of prior restraint

    (B) *Citizens United v. Federal Election Commission* (2010), which determined that the right of groups, such as corporations and labor unions, to spend money on political messages is protected by the First Amendment

    (C) Article I of the Constitution, which specifies that the states have the power to determine most of the logistics of federal congressional elections

    (D) The Bipartisan Campaign Reform Act of 2002, which implemented the regulation of soft money contributions in federal elections

GO ON TO THE NEXT PAGE

42. Which of the following best illustrates the free-rider problem?

    (A) An advocacy group unable to sway Congress to its side turns to the judicial system in order to achieve its goal.

    (B) A politician supported by an interest group lets that group take on the financial burden of electioneering for him.

    (C) Recently retired members of Congress use their connections to boost centrist interest groups over more ideological ones.

    (D) An interest group cannot attract enough contributors because beneficiaries receive privileges of membership without joining.

43. Which of the following is an accurate comparison of the two amendments?

	Fifteenth Amendment	Twenty-Sixth Amendment
(A)	The right to vote cannot be limited due to a person's sex	The right to vote can be limited due to a person's citizenship status
(B)	Religious affiliation or creed cannot be used as criteria to prohibit political participation	Members of the House of Representatives are selected through direct election
(C)	The right to vote cannot be limited due to a person's race	The right to vote is extended to those who are at least 18 years old
(D)	If over 18, a person's right to vote cannot be limited by requiring them to pay a poll tax	U.S. senators are selected through direct election

44. Which of the following is an accurate comparison of rationales for voting according to the rational-choice and prospective voting behavior models?

	Rational-Choice Voting	Prospective Voting
(A)	"I'm voting for candidate Wu because she supports lowering taxes for small businesses, which will increase profits for my small business"	"I'm voting for candidate Lee because he supports education reform, which I believe is the most critical issue that faces our community"
(B)	"I'm voting for candidate Wu because she is a Republican, and I always vote Republican"	"I'm voting for candidate Lee because he is a Democrat, and I think the Republicans have done a poor job of managing the state legislature in recent years"
(C)	"I'm voting to elect candidate Wu because I think her opponent did a poor job as a state legislator for the past two years"	"I'm voting to reelect candidate Lee because the local economy has been thriving for the past year"
(D)	"I'm voting for candidate Wu because I think she will be an effective leader in the legislature"	"I'm voting to reelect candidate Lee because he has many years of experience in both business and in the state legislature"

GO ON TO THE NEXT PAGE

45. Which of the following is an accurate comparison of the two court cases?

	Shaw v. Reno	*Baker v. Carr*
(A)	Established that the federal government is supreme over the states	Public school students have the right to free speech on school grounds
(B)	Legislative redistricting must be conscious of race and ensure compliance with the Voting Rights Act of 1965	Although creation of congressional districts is a state responsibility, allegations of inappropriate redistricting can be heard in federal court
(C)	Bolstered the freedom of the press, establishing a "heavy presumption against prior restraint" even in cases involving national security	Public school students have the right to free speech on school grounds
(D)	Although creation of congressional districts is a state responsibility, allegations of inappropriate redistricting can be heard in federal court	Legislative redistricting must be conscious of race and ensure compliance with the Voting Rights Act of 1965

46. Which of the following is an accurate comparison of the powers of the executive and legislative branches?

	President	Congress
(A)	Passes bills	Declares states of emergency
(B)	Exercises judicial review	Has the power to impeach a president
(C)	Has the power to veto bills	Declares war and funds the military
(D)	Acts as the commander-in-chief of the armed forces	Decides how laws should be interpreted

47. Which of the following is an accurate comparison between a core value and a Supreme Court case that embodies it?

	Core Value	Case
(A)	Equality of opportunity	*New York Times Co. v. United States* (1971)
(B)	Individualism	*Gideon v. Wainwright (1963)*
(C)	Limited government	*Schenck v. United States* (1919)
(D)	Free enterprise	*McDonald v. Chicago* (2010)

GO ON TO THE NEXT PAGE

48. Only the House can pass articles of impeachment, while only the Senate can convict the president on those charges. This division reflects the intent of the framers of the Constitution that

(A) popularly elected officials in both the House and Senate have a say in determining the president's guilt

(B) if the president in office had been appointed by the House after not winning enough electoral votes, the House would not be impartial enough to stand in judgment of the president

(C) the Supreme Court was not to be trusted, as the judges were not yet lifetime appointments during the lifetime of the founders

(D) the accusers and the judges should be from different bodies, just as is the case in the setup of the judicial branch

49. In a public opinion poll, a survey company took the results of everyone who participated in their telephone poll and weighted each response by the user's demographic characteristics, assigning some poll participants more importance than others. Which of the following best explains this decision?

(A) The company was running a tracking poll, and those give importance to previous participants.

(B) The company wanted to separate likely voters out from registered voters.

(C) The company was trying to ensure a representative random sample of the population.

(D) The company tried to maximize the sample size of their poll to minimize the margin of error.

50. Which of the following most likely accounts for the rejection of the Virginia Plan at the Constitutional Convention?

(A) Smaller, less populous states were afraid of being dominated by the larger, more populous states in a system based on population.

(B) Its bicameral legislature provided equal representation to the states in the upper house but proportional representation based on population in the lower house.

(C) Larger, more populous states were afraid of being dominated by the smaller, less populous states in its unicameral legislature.

(D) The lack of a Bill of Rights in the Virginia Plan upset the Anti-Federalists.

51. Which of the following laws would most likely be an unconstitutional violation of the commerce clause based on the precedent established by *United States v. Lopez* (1995)?

(A) Federalizing the crime of kidnapping if a victim is taken across state lines

(B) A congressional law banning the local cultivation, use, and sale of marijuana within a state

(C) Federalizing the crime of battery

(D) A congressional law imposing tariffs on foreign electronics

GO ON TO THE NEXT PAGE

52. Which of the following is an action Congress can take if the Supreme Court declares a federal law unconstitutional?

    (A) Congress can override Supreme Court decisions with a two-thirds vote.

    (B) Congress can request that the executive branch veto the court decision with a simple majority vote.

    (C) Congress can vote to have the federal appeals court restart the case for reconsideration.

    (D) Congress can propose a constitutional amendment with a two-thirds supermajority vote.

53. The wide-ranging regulatory powers of the federal bureaucracy are often contentious for which of the following reasons?

    (A) Their rules are created without input by the public, but the public still has to abide by them.

    (B) Their regulations affect American businesses and consumers, but their officials are not democratically elected.

    (C) The federal bureaucracy has vast sums of money at its disposal to duplicate results already achieved by the private sector.

    (D) The federal bureaucracy's critics are biased toward a vigorous federal government that provides extensive social services.

54. According to supply-side economic theory, the concentration of wealth at the top of the socioeconomic spectrum should result in which of the following consequences?

    (A) The wealthy will reinvest their income, stimulating broad economic growth.

    (B) Increased government spending will encourage economic growth for the lower classes.

    (C) The government will cut taxes and loosen regulations on the economy.

    (D) The wealth at the top of society will be redistributed by the government to all levels of society.

55. Which of the following statements best reflects an Anti-Federalist view about the ratification of the U.S. Constitution?

    (A) The role of the president is fundamentally different from the authoritarian monarch of Great Britain and is necessary to a well-functioning federal republic.

    (B) A powerful central government will threaten the sovereignty of the state governments.

    (C) A bill of rights is unnecessary since the practice of listing protected rights may result in the limitation of rights that are not listed.

    (D) A bill of rights is necessary since the failure to enact one would threaten the sovereignty of the central government.

IF YOU FINISH BEFORE TIME IS CALLED, YOU MAY CHECK YOUR WORK ON SECTION I ONLY. DO NOT MOVE ON TO SECTION II UNTIL INSTRUCTED TO DO SO.

STOP

END OF SECTION I

SECTION II
100 Minutes
4 Questions

You have 1 hour and 40 minutes to answer all four of the following free-response questions. Craft your responses in full sentences and paragraphs, using specific examples where appropriate. It is suggested that you spend a few minutes planning each of your answers. In total, it is recommended that you spend approximately 20 minutes each on questions 1, 2, and 3 and approximately 40 minutes on question 4.

1. The victors of U.S. presidential elections commonly win the popular vote as well. However, there have been five occasions in U.S. history when the elected president did not win the popular vote. This occurred in 1824 with John Quincy Adams, 1876 with Rutherford B. Hayes, 1888 with Benjamin Harrison, 2000 with George W. Bush, and 2016 with Donald Trump.

   After reading the scenario, respond to Parts A, B, and C.

   (A) Describe how votes in the Electoral College are assigned and how individual electors are chosen.

   (B) Explain one way that the Electoral College has changed since the Constitution was drafted.

   (C) Explain one impact of the Electoral College's winner-take-all system on the outcome of presidential elections in the United States.

GO ON TO THE NEXT PAGE

 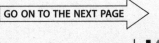

U.S. House of Representatives Members from California and New Hampshire, Selected Years 1790–2010

Year	Total Reps in House	CA Reps	CA % of Total Reps	NH Reps	NH % of Total Reps
1790	67	—	—	5	7.46%
1800	106	—	—	7	6.60%
1810	143	—	—	7	4.90%
1820	187	—	—	7	3.74%
1830	213	—	—	6	2.82%
1840	242	—	—	6	2.48%
1850	233	2	0.86%	4	1.72%
1860	183	2	1.09%	4	2.19%
1870	243	3	1.23%	4	1.65%
1880	293	4	1.37%	4	1.37%
1890	232	6	2.59%	4	1.72%
1900	357	7	1.96%	4	1.12%
1910	394	8	2.03%	5	1.27%
1920	435	11	2.53%	5	1.15%
1930	435	11	2.53%	5	1.15%
1940	435	20	4.60%	6	1.38%
1950	435	23	5.29%	6	1.38%
1960	435	30	6.90%	6	1.38%
1970	435	38	8.74%	6	1.38%
1980	435	43	9.89%	6	1.38%
1990	435	45	10.34%	6	1.38%
2000	435	52	11.95%	5	1.15%
2010	435	53	12.18%	5	1.15%

2. Use the information graphic to respond to Parts A, B, and C.

   (A) Compare the changes in representation over time for California and New Hampshire, and discuss an implication of these changes.

   (B) Explain how the trends in the information graphic reflect the intentions of the Constitution's writers regarding representation in the U.S. Congress. In your response, describe how representation is determined in both the House of Representatives and the Senate.

   (C) Discuss one possible advantage OR one possible disadvantage of this two-house system of representation in the U.S. Congress. Use data from the information graphic to support your response.

GO ON TO THE NEXT PAGE

3. At Hazelwood East High School, students enrolled in a journalism class oversaw the writing and editing of their school newspaper. Two articles attracted their principal's attention. The first article, on divorce, featured an interview in which a girl blamed her father for the breakup of their family. The second, on teen pregnancy, featured interviews with several anonymous students. The principal felt that the father in the divorce story should be allowed to offer comment, as is standard journalistic practice, and that the topic of teen pregnancy was not appropriate for younger students. Thus, the principal refused to allow the publication of either article.

The student journalists brought suit, arguing that their constitutional rights had been violated. Disagreeing with the students, the Supreme Court sided with the principal in *Hazelwood School District v. Kuhlmeier*. The Court ruled that because the school sponsored the newspaper, it had a legitimate interest in preventing the publication of articles that it felt were inappropriate. The newspaper was the product of students in a journalism class, bore the school's name in its title, and thus it was subject to editorial approval by the school.

Based on the information given, respond to Parts A, B, and C.

(A) Identify the constitutional provision that pertains to both *Hazelwood School District v. Kuhlmeier* (1988) and *Tinker v. Des Moines Independent Community School District* (1969).

(B) Based on the constitutional provision identified in Part A, explain why the facts of *Tinker v. Des Moines Independent Community School District* led to a different holding than in *Hazelwood School District v. Kuhlmeier*.

(C) Describe an action that members of the public could take to mitigate the *Hazelwood* ruling if they disagreed with the decision.

GO ON TO THE NEXT PAGE

4. The balance of power between state governments and the federal government has shifted throughout the course of U.S. history. Choose either state governments or the federal government and construct an argument to justify why your choice is more responsible for safeguarding individual liberty.

In your essay you must:

- Formulate a defensible thesis that establishes a chain of reasoning

- Provide evidence for your thesis with at least TWO pieces of relevant, accurate information

  ○ Take at least ONE of your pieces of evidence from one of the following foundational documents:

    - *Federalist* 51

    - *Brutus* 1

    - Letter from a Birmingham Jail

  ○ Take your other piece of evidence from a different foundational document from the list above OR from your own study

- Logically explain why your evidence supports your thesis

- Present and reply to an alternative viewpoint using refutation, concession, or rebuttal

IF YOU FINISH BEFORE TIME IS CALLED, YOU MAY CHECK YOUR WORK ON SECTION II ONLY. DO NOT TURN TO ANY OTHER SECTION OF THE EXAM.

STOP

K | 374

END OF SECTION II

ANSWER KEY

Section I

1. C	12. C	23. D	34. A	45. B
2. A	13. B	24. D	35. C	46. C
3. B	14. A	25. C	36. A	47. B
4. C	15. A	26. C	37. D	48. D
5. A	16. B	27. C	38. D	49. C
6. D	17. A	28. C	39. B	50. A
7. B	18. B	29. C	40. B	51. C
8. D	19. A	30. C	41. B	52. D
9. D	20. B	31. D	42. D	53. B
10. A	21. B	32. D	43. C	54. A
11. D	22. A	33. D	44. A	55. B

Section I Number Correct: _____

Review detailed explanations for Sections I and II at the back of this book. Use the rubrics and sample essays to self-score Section II.

Section II Points Earned: _____

Sign into your online account at kaptest.com and enter your results in the online scoring section to see your 1–5 score.

Haven't registered your book yet? Go to kaptest.com/booksonline to begin.

PRACTICE EXAM 3 BREAKDOWN

Use the following table to determine which topics you are already strong in and which topics you need to review most.

Topic	Exam Question(s)	Number You Got Correct	Chapters to Study
Foundations of American Democracy	22, 23, 25, 26, 28, 32, 39, 48, 50, 51, 55	___ out of 11	3, 8
Interactions Among Branches of Government	11, 12, 13, 14, 18, 19, 29, 31, 35, 46, 52, 53	___ out of 12	4, 9
Civil Liberties and Civil Rights	9, 10, 15, 16, 17, 24, 27, 30, 40, 45	___ out of 10	5, 10
American Political Ideologies and Beliefs	1, 2, 7, 8, 34, 36, 37, 47, 49, 54	___ out of 10	6, 11
Political Participation	3, 4, 5, 6, 20, 21, 33, 38, 41, 42, 43, 44	___ out of 12	7, 12

Practice Exam
Answers
and Explanations

PRACTICE EXAM 1 ANSWERS AND EXPLANATIONS

Section I

1. B

Socialism generally has a more negative than positive image among those polled, save for the 18–29-year-old demographic where it has 55 percent positive approval; **(B)** is correct. While people 30–49 years old have a more negative image of the federal government than 18–29-year-olds, those 65+ have a slightly more positive image of it than those 50–64 years old, making (A) incorrect. (C) is incorrect because it reverses the trend displayed in the graph; capitalism has a less positive image than free enterprise does across all age demographics. (D) is incorrect because those 65+ do not hold the most positive views in all categories polled (for example, toward socialism).

2. A

The nearly 80% positive image of free enterprise among those 18–29 years old, compared to the lower mid-50s approval for capitalism, would most likely motivate the Republican Party to appeal to that age demographic by enabling them to more easily start their own businesses. A tax credit would accomplish that goal, and it would be in line with the traditional conservative platform of reducing taxes. Thus, **(A)** is correct. While socialism evokes more positive than negative responses among 18–29 year-olds, socialist policies are generally antithetical to the Republican Party platform of limited government. It is unlikely that the GOP would change its platform to appeal to young voters, especially when older voters, a key voting bloc for the party, have a very negative image of socialist ideas. Therefore, (B) and (C) are incorrect. (D) is incorrect because it suffers from the aforementioned ideological conflict, as well as the additional problem of alienating senior voters, a core GOP demographic, through cuts to Medicare.

3. B

Transportation grants nearly doubled in terms of dollars spent between 2000 (32.2 billion) and 2015 (60.8 billion). Thus, **(B)** is correct. While grants for income security shrank as a percentage of all grants to the states, in terms of overall dollars, income security grants actually increased between 2000 and 2015; (A) is incorrect. Healthcare grants did indeed triple between 2000 and 2015, but they did not shrink as a percentage of all grants. On the contrary, over half of all federal grants to state and local governments were allocated to healthcare in 2015, making (C) incorrect. More money was spent on federal grants in 2015 than in 2000. For example, healthcare in 2015 consumed more money than all federal grants combined in 2000; (D) is incorrect.

4. C

Given the historic trend of the federal government increasing its power over state and local governments, it is likely that the federal government will continue to increase its power over state and local governments as a result of the trends depicted on the pie graph. One particular highlight is the increasing importance of federal healthcare spending, which would be a burdensome financial responsibility for state and local officials. Thus, **(C)** is correct and (B) is incorrect. The graph depicts the continued allocation of federal grants by specific policy area, which does not indicate any federal deference to state and local governments; (A) is incorrect. Given that federal grants typically come with strings attached, it is unlikely that state and local governments will gain more power on spending decisions; (D) is incorrect.

5. D

Florida's urban population increased by over four million citizens between 2000 and 2010. North Carolina's total population increased by less than four million during that same time period. Thus, **(D)** is correct and (B) is incorrect. Urban population growth outstripped rural population growth in both states; (A) is incorrect. The rural population in both states stayed approximately the same during the 2000 to 2010 time period; (C) is incorrect.

6. A

North Carolina is traditionally a Republican state, while Florida is a swing state. The Democratic Party generally performs more strongly in urban areas like cities, while the Republican Party generally does not. Thus, a likely consequence of the urbanizing trends depicted in the bar graph is that both North Carolina and Florida will shift into the Democratic Party column in the Electoral College. **(A)** is correct while (D) is incorrect. As urban areas grow in population, the relative importance of votes from rural areas will decrease, because the concerns of urban voters will become of greater importance to politicians. Thus, (B) is incorrect. The trend of urbanization favoring the Democratic Party typically does not have exceptions, so it is unlikely that the Republican Party would reliably keep North Carolina in its column in the Electoral College while at the same time losing Florida; (C) is incorrect.

7. D

Turnout by 25–44-year-olds in presidential elections hovers at approximately 50 percent of the voting-eligible population, which is comparable to the midterm turnout by 45–64-year-olds; **(D)** is correct. Although those 65 and older demonstrate the highest turnout percentage among the voting-eligible population, (A) is incorrect because there has been a modest dip in their turnout during midterm elections since 2006. (B) is incorrect because turnout by 25–44-year-olds surpassed 50 percent in the 2004 election. While turnout by 18–24-year-olds in presidential elections has generally beaten midterm turnout by 25–44-year-olds, the weak turnout by 18–24-year-olds in the 2000 election bucks the trend. So, (C) is incorrect.

8. C

Approximately 20 percent of voting-eligible 18–24-year-olds turn out in the midterms, while around 40 percent of 18–24-year-olds voted in presidential elections after 2000. Thus, policies important to the youth vote will likely only receive major attention every four years, since 18–24-year-olds are not a major factor in midterm elections. **(C)** is correct. Major events like 9/11 do not necessarily drive an increase in voter turnout. For example, the 2002 midterms had almost no change in the turnout of any age group compared to the 1998 midterms. Thus, (A) is incorrect. Although seniors are a reliable voting bloc that turns out at the highest level of all age groups, seniors are not traditionally associated with the Democratic Party. Instead, senior voters tend to skew toward the Republican Party; (B) is incorrect. There is no overall general decline in voter turnout, making (D) incorrect.

9. C

Some overall trends from the table are that Clinton had a higher total number of posts and a higher average number of posts per day overall than Trump, and that both candidates peaked in posts in October. **(C)** is correct; comparing the "Average Posts Per Day" columns shows a higher number for Clinton each month. (A) is incorrect because both candidates' numbers show fluctuation up and down from month to month; for instance, Trump has 11 posts per day in August, but only 10 per day in September. Although Trump had his fewest posts in September (290), Clinton had her fewest in June (385), so (B) is incorrect. (D) is incorrect because Trump had 89 posts *overall* during the first week of November, not 89 posts *per day*.

10. A

Clinton had more total posts, a higher average number of posts per day, and she won the popular vote, while Trump won the electoral vote and thus the election. Even if the data did suggest that Clinton's high number of posts earned her votes, these conclusions are based on data from just one election.

(A) correctly summarizes the use of social media and its impact on voters. (B) incorrectly assumes a causal relationship between posts and votes; although the table shows a correlation, it is incorrect to assume a causal relationship and to generalize this data to all elections. While Clinton did make many posts and ultimately lost the election, (C) once again draws a conclusion that cannot be supported based on the data alone; further, Clinton actually won the popular vote, which does not suggest voter disenchantment. Finally, (D) is incorrect because the data from one election cannot predict future candidate behavior.

11. A

The excerpt states that "In all cases affecting ambassadors...the Supreme Court shall have original jurisdiction. In all the other cases before mentioned, the Supreme Court shall have appellate jurisdiction" and that all criminal cases (except impeachment) must be tried by a jury; **(A)** is correct and (D) is incorrect. (B) is incorrect because Congress only decides where trials take place if the crime was not committed within any state. (C) is incorrect because the Supreme Court holds both original and appellate jurisdiction.

12. D

According to the excerpt, "such trial shall be held in the state where the said crimes shall have been committed." Because Orlando and Tampa are both in Florida, **(D)** is correct. (A) is incorrect because "the Supreme Court shall have original jurisdiction" for any cases involving a state. When a crime is not committed in any state, Congress, not the Supreme Court, decides where the case will be tried; (B) is incorrect. Based on the excerpt, "The trial of all crimes, except in cases of impeachment, shall be by jury"; (C) is incorrect.

13. D

The Constitution's use of the phrase "shall hold their Offices during good Behaviour" establishes that Supreme Court justices can only be removed by impeachment or, implicitly, by resignation. Unlike representatives, senators, and presidents, there is no term length for a Supreme Court appointment. Thus, **(D)** is correct. Although the Constitution does outline the appointment process for Supreme Court justices by the president with the advice and consent of Congress, it does so in Article II, not Article III; (A) and (C) are incorrect. While Article III does establish the Supreme Court as being vested with all judicial power, with Congress establishing inferior courts as they so desire, it does so in the opening line of Article III, not the quoted excerpt in the question stem; (B) is incorrect.

14. C

In the passage, Hamilton argues that the great majority of people cannot be trusted to judge things correctly, and that their opinions shift so frequently that they cannot provide stable rule. So, the rich and well-born must check the will of the masses by being given a larger share of power in government. Thus, **(C)** is correct. Although Hamilton argues that the rich make for better rulers, he does not say that wealth itself is a sign of divine favor or morality, so (A) is incorrect. (B) is incorrect because Hamilton discusses government in general, not the judicial branch in any specific detail. (D) is incorrect because Hamilton argues against the merits of pure democracy.

15. B

Hamilton's desired outcome is for the aristocratic element of society to temper the ever-shifting popular will. This desire is reflected in the original structure of Congress, where a popularly elected House was balanced against a Senate whose members were selected by the legislatures of their home state. **(B)** is correct because it describes the Senate elites checking the House membership, who tried to 'buy' votes in an upcoming election with pork-barrel spending in their districts. Although (A) illustrates one branch of government checking the other, Hamilton's concern was with the legislative branch and the need to make democracy and republicanism work together. The president is not popularly elected but indirectly elected through the Electoral College, which would be another check in the Hamiltonian fashion. (C) is incorrect because it describes a concern of Hamilton's, not a desired outcome. (D) is incorrect because it does not involve a check on the popular will.

16. C

Hamilton described the masses as unwise and constantly changing their collective mind on various matters. Strong, steady government required influence by wealthy elites, as they had demonstrated good judgment. The direct election of senators, rather than their indirect election through state legislatures, weakened the check on participatory democracy that Hamilton called for. Thus, **(C)** is correct. Although the Twenty-Sixth Amendment increased the total amount of potential voters, Hamilton would not necessarily object to the voting age being lowered from 21 to 18 if the property requirement for voting, poll taxes, and various indirect methods of election were still in place, as the result would only be wealthy elites voting at a slightly younger age. Thus, (A) is incorrect. (B) and (D) are incorrect because Hamilton was concerned in the text with the makeup of the voters, not restrictions on the elected offices themselves or the scope of how Congress might levy taxes.

17. A

Hamilton's use of the phrase "distinct, permanent share" is part of his case for a government where wealthy elites serve as a check on the desires of the masses. In other words, Hamilton is arguing in favor of the elite model of democracy, which emphasizes limited participation in politics and civil society for all but a select number of the wealthy and powerful. Thus, **(A)** is correct. The pluralist model emphasizes the need for different organized groups to compete against each other in order to influence policy. Although Hamilton is arguing that elites need to band together in service of the new republic, he does not view the masses as any kind of organized

opposition; (B) is incorrect. The participatory model of democracy emphasizes broad citizen participation in government and politics, not group-based interests; Hamilton is expressly arguing for the group-based interests of the elite, so (C) is incorrect. Direct democracy involves citizens directly controlling the government and decision-making process, and is thus based on raw majorities rather than group-based interests. Hamilton is arguing against this model, as evidenced by his description of the masses. (D) is incorrect.

18. C

The majority of states that gained new seats after the 2010 census reapportionment were in the Sunbelt region. The exception to this was Washington state, in the Pacific Northwest, which also gained seats. Thus, **(C)** is correct. Although Texas did gain seats, and has the greatest number of House seats among the states that gained seats, there is nothing in the map to indicate exactly how many seats Texas gained. The map merely shows the states that changed or maintained their number of House seats after the 2010 census. Therefore, (A) is incorrect. While several Midwest states lost seats, not all of them did. For example, Wisconsin and Indiana saw no change in their number of seats; (B) is incorrect. While the Northeast states saw a change in seats, it was a loss in seats rather than a gain, making (D) incorrect.

19. A

The reapportionment map does not detail how many seats were specifically gained or lost by the various states. For example, after the 2010 census, Illinois lost one seat but New York lost two, while Arizona gained one seat and Texas gained four. Thus, **(A)** is correct. The advantage of presenting shifts in House apportionment with a map is that regional shifts are obvious at a glance. So, it is not a limitation in terms of presentation. Likewise, a bar graph would not display regional trends as clearly as a map. (B) and (C) are incorrect. Although the map does not list the total number of seats in the House of Representatives, that number is fixed at 435 seats and can be assumed to be common background knowledge for the viewer. (D) is incorrect.

20. B

The political cartoon depicts Justice, with her scales, being swamped by a tidal wave of laws issued by Congress. The cartoon's caption refers to "law-mills," which in this case means the industrial-scale production of laws. There are too many laws on the books to enforce, meaning that the rule of law, or Justice, is undermined. Thus, **(B)** is correct and (C) is incorrect. Although the cartoon depicts the federal government overwhelming a figure with rules and regulations, that figure represents Justice rather than state governments; (A) is incorrect. In the scenario depicted here, the federal government is being careless with the overwhelming number of laws it is cranking out; (D) describes the opposite of such a scenario and is therefore incorrect.

21. C

Given the poor image that the author presents of the legislative branch in relation to the judiciary, it is most likely that the author would prefer a system of limited government, in which the government's power is enumerated and constrained by constitutional rules. Proponents of this system believe that the government should have minimal involvement in the lives of citizens. Such an approach would avoid the industrial-scale production of laws as seen in the "law-mills" depicted in the political cartoon, so **(C)** is correct. As the focus of the political cartoon is squarely on how the legislative branch is harming the judiciary, (A) is incorrect; the author would more likely hold that the judicial branch should be deferred to than the other way around. Given the negative depiction of the legislative branch in the cartoon, it is unlikely that the author would prefer a proactive legislative branch; thus, (B) and (D) are incorrect.

22. D

The close relationship that interest groups develop with Congress and the executive bureaucracy is referred to as the iron triangle. The interest groups obtain favorable regulations by electioneering for members of Congress, who then help the groups achieve their goals by giving lobbyists special access to legislators or allowing them to help write new laws that will be executed by the executive branch. Thus, **(D)** is correct. While (A) does describe aspects of the iron triangle, it ignores the involvement of interest groups, which receive preferred regulations in exchange for electioneering for members of Congress, who prefer a certain implementation of the laws they write in order to satisfy their supporters in that interest group. (B) is incorrect because interest groups do not fund federal agencies; Congress does. (C) is incorrect because it is interest groups, not Congress, that trade special favors with the bureaucracy. Former members of the bureaucracy often join interest groups to become lobbyists themselves. Likewise, former members of Congress often become lobbyists, while the reverse is not the case.

23. C

A common criticism of the iron triangle is that the money required to support an interest group often means that the wealthiest citizens have the greatest influence over writing policy. Thus, **(C)** is correct. Another common criticism of the iron triangle is that it leads to wasted money and political corruption. For example, a bureaucrat may write favorable air pollution regulations for a coal company and later be hired by that company as a lobbyist with deep connections to the federal bureaucracy. Rather than writing rules in the interest of all citizens, the lobbyist is mainly serving the interests of a potential employer. Thus, (A) is incorrect. (B) is incorrect because it provides a neutral description of interest groups, not a common criticism of them. (D) is incorrect because it describes a positive aspect of interest groups, as they are an expression of democratic participation in a free republic.

24. D

While Title IX is commonly associated with college sports for women, its scope is even larger. Title IX of the Education Amendments Act of 1972 prohibits discrimination on the basis of sex in any program or activity receiving federal financial assistance. Thus, **(D)** is correct and (B) is incorrect. (A) is incorrect because Title IX only applies to federally funded programs and activities. While Title IX does ban sex discrimination at schools receiving federal funding, it does not cover discrimination on the basis of skin color, religion, or national origin; (C) is incorrect.

25. B

The exclusionary rule protects citizens from having illegally seized evidence used against them in court; **(B)** is correct. The Fourteenth Amendment, not the exclusionary rule, guarantees citizens the right to a speedy, public trial and an impartial jury; (A) and (D) are incorrect. (C) is incorrect because this refers to the Miranda rule, not the exclusionary rule.

26. B

Interest groups often experience the free-rider problem, which refers in this case to the tendency of people to assume that others will do the work of supporting an interest group, resulting in those individuals enjoying the benefits of the interest group's efforts without contributing any effort themselves. This description matches the scenario in **(B)**. None of the other scenarios relates to the free-rider problem. (A) describes a challenge that third-party candidates face. While (C) does involve interest groups, it describes an example of an iron triangle. (D) describes a typical campaigning strategy in modern elections.

27. A

Liberal ideology supports the government taking a central role in promoting social welfare. Thus, it would support affirmative action as well as increased taxation on wealthy individuals in order to safeguard existing entitlements like Social Security and Medicare; **(A)** is correct. The other answers are incorrect because they describe ideas influenced by other ideologies: libertarian, conservative, and democratic socialist, respectively.

28. B

Libertarians advocate broad economic and social freedoms and believe that government power should be limited to preventing fraud in the marketplace. As such, ending any government regulation over narcotics, as well as ending the state's power to kill criminals, would most likely find support with a self-identified libertarian. Thus, **(B)** is correct. (A) is incorrect because a libertarian would not approve of government regulating speech. While the legalization of cannabis is commonly associated with libertarianism, a self-identified libertarian would also support the legalization of "hard" drugs, believing that the use of such drugs is a matter of individual choice; (C) is incorrect. Although (D) deals with lowering taxes, which a libertarian would typically support, it is more of a traditionally conservative policy. A libertarian would likely not support this specific form of tax cut because it endorses one lifestyle choice (having a large family) over alternatives, making it an attempt by government to influence individual choice. (D) is incorrect.

29. C

Discretionary and rule-making authority is given to the federal bureaucracy to implement policy; **(C)** is correct. (A) and (B) are incorrect because they describe congressional oversight and presidential supervision, respectively, instead of the bureaucracy's power to implement policy. (D) is incorrect because it describes the concept of checks and balances.

30. B

In the *Lopez* ruling, Chief Justice Rehnquist explained that "the [Gun-Free School Zones Act of 1990] neither regulates a commercial activity nor contains a requirement that the possession be connected in any way to interstate commerce," meaning that it cannot plausibly be viewed as a regulation of interstate commerce. Thus, this situation exceeds Congress's powers under the commerce clause; **(B)** is correct. (A) is incorrect because the *Lopez* ruling dealt with firearm possession in a limited area: schools. Although *Lopez* does place limits on Congress, it still holds that regulation of interstate commerce is a power of the federal government; (C) is incorrect. (D) is incorrect because it merges together the *Lopez* and *McDonald v. Chicago* (2010) rulings, which selectively incorporated the Second Amendment to the states.

31. B

During the Constitutional Convention, taxes and representation were proposed to be based on a state's total population. Southern states wished for slaves to be counted as people for the sake of House seats, but as property for the sake of taxation. The northern states would not agree to this, as it greatly empowered the southern states at their expense. By agreeing to count slaves as three-fifths of a person for both taxation and representation, the southern states gained seats in the legislative branch while also not paying as much in taxes. Thus, **(B)** is correct. Taxation was not to be based on the amount of property owned, but rather on a state's population; (A) is incorrect. While the Constitution did ban the federal government from regulating slave importation, it only did so until 1808, when the practice was promptly banned; (C) is incorrect. Male slaves would not gain the right to vote even if counted as full persons. White women, for example, were considered full persons for the sake of tallying a state's population, but they did not have the right to vote. Thus, (D) is incorrect.

32. A

Campaign contributions are highly regulated, but there are many ways an individual or group may support a campaign monetarily. **(A)** is correct because it represents an appropriate way to make an additional contribution. Financial contributions

to a political committee are always limited, making (B) incorrect. (C) is incorrect because doing so would violate the "stand by your ad" requirement of the Bipartisan Campaign Reform Act of 2002. (D) is incorrect because a citizen may contribute to many organizations, such as PACs and political party committees, to support a candidate.

33. B

In *Gideon v. Wainwright*, the Supreme Court decided that citizens are guaranteed the right to an attorney according to the Sixth Amendment, regardless of whether they are poor or indigent; **(B)** is correct. (A), (C), and (D) are incorrect because these would likely be ruled unconstitutional based on other cases: *Mapp v. Ohio* (1961), *Duncan v. Louisiana* (1968), and *Buckley v. Valeo* (1976), respectively.

34. D

The question describes a scenario in which Congress has an implied power, a power that is not explicitly stated in the Constitution but is considered necessary to carry out an enumerated power. *McCulloch v. Maryland*, in addition to reinforcing the supremacy of federal law over state actions, determined that the Necessary and Proper Clause gave Congress implied powers. Therefore, **(D)** is correct. (A) and (B) are incorrect because they concern the interpretation of constitutional individual rights: *Engel v. Vitale* addressed the establishment clause, while *Gideon v. Wainwright* addressed the right to an attorney. *Marbury v. Madison* established the principle of judicial review, which refers to the Supreme Court's ability to declare laws of Congress unconstitutional; (C) is incorrect.

35. D

The president can influence the federal bureaucracy by issuing executive orders, which determine how (and to what extent) federal law will be implemented, providing an additional opportunity for the president to shape public policy. Thus, **(D)** is correct. Although the president can use signing statements to more clearly direct executive resources, they may not be added to bills after the fact. They are made when the bill is signed into law; (A) is incorrect. (B) is incorrect because conducting audits is within Congress's, not the president's, power. (C) is incorrect because the president's military authority does not apply to commercial airline companies, which fall under civilian authority.

36. C

The party-line voting model entails voting for candidates from one political party for every position on a ballot, regardless of other factors. Therefore, only **(C)** is a likely consequence of party-line voting, as voters would only look for candidates' party affiliations and would not necessarily learn each candidate's own views. (A) is incorrect because it reflects the retrospective voting model. (B) is an unlikely consequence; there are rarely candidates from the same third party for multiple positions across a ballot, making party-line third-party voting an unlikely possibility. Widespread party-line voting would cause people to vote for major party candidates across a ballot rather than voting for third-party candidates for select positions. (D) represents a distortion of rational-choice voting, which entails people voting for candidates they believe will best serve their own interests.

37. A

New York Times Co. v. United States established that the First Amendment offers broad protections for freedom of the press, including the publication of classified intelligence leaked to them. The only exception was for reporting that would cause "grave and irreparable" harm to the United States. An embedded reporter publicly announcing troop movements in the middle of an ongoing battle would potentially endanger the lives of soldiers. This would most likely not be protected under the First Amendment; **(A)** is correct. Publishing photos of coffins that are being moved under cover of night may embarrass the government, but it will not cause "grave and irreparable" harm; (B) is incorrect. (C) is

incorrect because members of the military voluntarily allow their constitutional rights to be restricted in some ways when they join the military. For example, civilians can openly insult the president, but active-duty soldiers cannot because the president is technically their superior officer. (D) is incorrect because it is comparable to the leaked Pentagon Papers at the heart of the *New York Times Co. v. United States* ruling; because there is no "grave and irreparable" harm threatened, a news story about the wire tapping program would be constitutionally protected under the First Amendment.

38. C

Impeachment is a multistep process in the House of Representatives. First, a House member must call for an inquiry into possible crimes by the president. Second, the House must authorize an inquiry by the judiciary committee. Third, the committee must explore the charges. Fourth, the committee must vote on whether or not to draft articles of impeachment. Fifth, the articles are brought to the full House for approval. Sixth, if approved, the articles are forwarded to the Senate. Thus, **(C)** is correct. The Speaker does not have to be the one to introduce the charges or the inquiry, so (A) is incorrect. The judiciary committee can do nothing before the House authorizes an inquiry, making (B) and (D) incorrect.

39. A

In *Engel v. Vitale*, the Supreme Court ruled that a public school sponsoring any religious activity is in violation of the establishment clause. Since the bake sale in this scenario involves the school administration raising funds for a school-based religious club, **(A)** is correct. *Wisconsin v. Yoder* dealt with the free exercise clause of the First Amendment, not state-sponsored religious activity; (B) is incorrect. Although the *Tinker* decision also dealt with the First Amendment, it involved freedom of speech rather than freedom of religion, so (C) is incorrect. The *Brown* case involved race-based school segregation, not religious activity; (D) is incorrect.

40. D

The Twenty-Sixth Amendment prohibits denying someone older than 18 the right to vote based on age. Therefore, **(D)** correctly identifies a violation of the amendment, as it places a voting restriction based on age. The other choices could be considered violations based on other reasons, but they do not deny or suppress the right to vote on the basis of age requirements.

41. B

The two methods Congress can use to ensure that policy is implemented as intended are committee hearings and power of the purse. Thus, **(B)** is correct. (A) is incorrect because Congress directs funding to the executive agencies, not the president. (C) and (D) are incorrect because issuing fines and enforcing regulations are responsibilities that fall under the umbrella of the federal bureaucracy.

42. B

Political efficacy refers to voters' belief that they can understand and influence political affairs. If voters have low political efficacy, then they do not believe their vote makes any difference. Thus, **(B)** is correct. As California is an overwhelmingly Democratic-aligned state, a Republican voter may likely believe he has little influence at the ballot box. (A) is incorrect because, although the representative runs unopposed, high turnout suggests that the member is popular with her constituents. (C) is incorrect because moderate turnout suggests that many voters believe they can influence the tightly contested primary race. While its political efficacy is not as high as in (B) and (D), this election cannot be said to best showcase low political efficacy, thanks to the still-respectable turnout. (D) is incorrect because a voter who turns out will typically believe voting is important to making his voice heard, even if a given election may be unwinnable for his preferred party, such as in a deeply Republican state like Utah.

43. C

Interest groups serve as linkage institutions because they represent special interests of the public to the government, engaging in activities such as lobbying politicians, testifying at congressional hearings, pursuing legislation and litigation, and supporting candidates who endorse their special interests. Political parties serve as linkage institutions because they connect the public to the election process, collaborating with like-minded citizens and institutions, educating the public, supplying candidates, and structuring campaigns. Only **(C)** accurately reflects these roles. (A) incorrectly flips the activities of interest groups and political parties. (B) is incorrect because the item in the first column applies to another linkage institution, the media, while the item in the second column is not a role of political parties. (D) is incorrect because the item in the first column describes a role of the president; the item in the second column is a role of political parties, but not in their capacity as linkage institutions.

44. A

In *Tinker v. Des Moines Independent Community School District*, the Supreme Court decided that public school students had the right to wear black armbands in school to protest the Vietnam War. In *Schenck v. United States,* the Court stated that speech may be restricted if it presents a "clear and present danger" to national security. Thus, **(A)** is correct. (B) is incorrect because it mixes up the two cases. The Court decided that speech that calls for rebellion can be restricted in *Gitlow v. New York* (1925), not *Schenck v. United States*; (C) is incorrect. (D) is incorrect because it was the Court's decision in *New York Times Co. v. United States* (1971) that bolstered the freedom of the press in cases of national security, not *Tinker*.

45. B

The Republican Party's platform favors photo identification requirements at polling stations, and several Republican-controlled state legislatures have enacted laws requiring photo IDs to vote. Thus, **(B)** is correct. (A) is incorrect because the Democratic Party favors overturning *Citizens United*, which also allows unrestricted campaign spending by corporations. Democrats are generally opposed to real and perceived corporate influence over government. (C) is incorrect because it attributes a Republican policy to the Democrats. (D) is incorrect because Libertarians support same-sex marriage, believing that the government should not regulate marriage.

46. C

The House of Representatives initiates revenue bills and articles of impeachment, while the Senate tries impeached officials and approves major presidential appointments and treaties; **(C)** is correct. (A) and (B) are incorrect because these confuse the roles of the House of Representatives and the Senate. It is the executive branch, not the House of Representatives, that is responsible for negotiating treaties, making (D) incorrect.

47. B

The ruling in *Gideon v. Wainwright* required that the state provide counsel upon request for those who cannot afford a lawyer in criminal cases; this is the selective incorporation of the Sixth Amendment right to counsel. Thus, **(B)** is correct and (A) is incorrect. While *United States v. Lopez* involved the issue of firearms on school grounds, the heart of the case dealt with the commerce clause, not the Second Amendment. So, (C) and (D) are incorrect.

48. B

The Articles of Confederation required the unanimous approval of all member states to ratify amendments. As a result, there were no amendments to the Articles of Confederation, despite several major problems. Article V of the Constitution corrected this issue; it required only three-fourths of state legislatures to ratify proposed amendments. Thus, **(B)** is correct. (A) is incorrect because the judiciary is outlined in Article III. (C) and (D) are incorrect because those problems were addressed with the enumerated powers of Congress in Article I.

49. B

In *McDonald v. Chicago,* the Supreme Court decided that the Second Amendment protects citizens' rights to keep and bear arms in their homes in self-defense; **(B)** is correct. (A) and (C) are incorrect because this court ruling only touched on bearing arms in one's own home. (D) is incorrect because the scenario described was ruled unconstitutional in the *Lopez* case.

50. A

During high school, most teenagers will probably have at least some friends who hold vocal political beliefs. As with the other decisions they make, teenagers can be influenced by their friends' political opinions. However, prior to entering high school, younger children aren't likely to discuss politics in a meaningful way. Thus, **(A)** is correct. The strongest influence on the political socialization of young people is their family. Young people will often base their initial political beliefs on what their parents believe, and parents will sometimes directly instruct their children about politics. So, (B) is incorrect. Most primary and secondary schools in the United States offer some form of civics instruction that teaches students about American political values; (C) is incorrect. The influence of media can be indirect, such as when someone watches a television show primarily for entertainment value but absorbs its subtle political themes. People of nearly all ages consume media, so it will influence the political socialization of even young children.

51. C

Democratic socialism typically favors some form of universal healthcare, as its ideology supports increased government regulation and involvement in the economy. Thus, **(C)** is correct. (A) is incorrect because it describes the moderate liberal approach to rising healthcare costs, where the existing healthcare industry is maintained while the government aids the poor. (B) is incorrect because it describes a conservative approach to the issue. (D) is incorrect because it describes entitlement reform, which is associated with elements of both the Democratic and Republican parties.

52. A

Selective incorporation is a constitutional doctrine that protects citizens from laws enacted by the states that are meant to remove constitutional rights; **(A)** is correct. While unfunded mandates have been limited since 1995, that is due to the Unfunded Mandates Reform Act, an act of Congress and not the states; thus, (B) is incorrect. Reverse incorporation, not selective incorporation, holds that the equal protection clause applies to the federal government; (C) is incorrect. (D) is incorrect because it describes nullification, a legal theory positing that states can pick and choose which federal laws to ignore.

53. D

Warrantless searches of cell phone data are prohibited under the Fourth Amendment; **(D)** is correct. Limited bulk collection of telecommunications metadata by the federal government is legal under the Fourth Amendment; (A) is incorrect. Evidence collected in a warrantless search of someone's home will be thrown out because it is a violation of a suspect's Fourth Amendment rights, and warrants can be issued for specific locations that limit the scope of police searches. (B) and (C) are incorrect.

54. A

A benchmark poll is a poll used by candidates or political groups at the start of campaign season to gauge public opinion on various issues. In other words, the benchmark is an attempt to map the political landscape ahead. Thus, **(A)** is correct. The other answer choices are incorrect because they describe other types of polls: a tracking poll, a standard opinion poll, and an entrance poll, respectively.

55. D

The media has several potentially negative impacts on the political process, including the influence of biased reporting, the near-constant coverage of candidates that can turn elections into personality contests, the commercial motivation of networks to dramatize political news, and the cumulative result of a growing public mistrust of media reporting. Depicting this trend toward subjective, sensationalized news catered to viewers who already share the same views, **(D)** correctly identifies a possible reason for criticism. (A) is a characteristic of the media's political coverage, but the repetition of stories, especially "significant" ones, does not necessarily have a negative impact on the democratic process. (B), which entails increased media access, is not in itself a criticism of media's impact on the democratic process. (C) is incorrect because the trend is for news to be presented *less* objectively in order to draw in viewers.

ANSWERS AND EXPLANATIONS

Section II

The following are general rubrics an AP reader might use to grade these free-response questions. Use both this scoring information and the sample responses to assess your own writing.

Rubric for Question 1: 4 points (1 + 1 + 2)

Part A (1 point)

One point for describing a tactic that a senator could use to impact education policy. To earn the point, the response must not only identify but also describe the tactic.

- Example measures: drafting/proposing a bill that impacts education policy or funding; persuading other senators to support education bill; serving on committees that concern education issues (Senate Health, Education, Labor, and Pensions Committee) to draft bills or engage in oversight of Education Department; appropriating different funding for Education Department; confirming/not confirming president's appointments to Education Department and/or Supreme Court justices based on individuals' views on education policy; potential use of filibuster on legislation that is not favorable to education refinancing mandate, particularly since she is a member of the minority party; working with Minority Leader/Whip to prioritize education policy; collaborating with education-related interest groups; utilizing media to gain public support for education reform

Part B (1 point)

One point for explaining an interaction of the Senate with another part of the federal government. To earn the point, the response must clearly identify the part of the federal government.

- Example interactions with executive branch: president vetoing education legislation, Congress overriding vetoes; formal and informal meetings with president about education policy; congressional oversight of Education Department through committee investigations and hearings; passing legislation that impacts Education Department regulations or authority; using the budget to impact Education Department (power of the purse); holding confirmation hearings for agency appointments

- Example interactions with judicial branch: Congress passing legislation that would override or work around the Supreme Court decision about school district funding; holding confirmation hearings for new Supreme Court justices; Supreme Court could make new ruling on education issue that impacts Congress's decisions about education legislation/budget

- Example interactions with House of Representatives: persuading House members to support education bill if passed by Senate; serving on conference committee to reconcile different versions of education bill passed by both houses

Part C (2 points)

Two points (one point each) for explaining how the measure from Part A and the measure from Part B each reflect a principle.

- Separation of powers: measures that entail powers that are unique to a particular branch, such as Congress passing legislation

- Checks and balances: measures that entail interactions between branches or houses with the intent of putting a check on a power of another branch, such as the Senate's confirmation hearings of presidential appointments

Sample High-Scoring Response

As a senator, the congresswoman could impact education policy by serving on the committee that addresses education. On this committee, she could research the financing of education to learn about its possible inequities and the impacts of these inequities. The committee could hear testimony from experts, such as school district administrators and child psychologists, to analyze education financing. Then, the committee could provide recommendations and draft appropriate legislation that could positively impact education.

Despite the committee's work, the Education Department has the most significant impact on public education. Still, though they are part of the executive branch, Congress has ways of impacting bureaucratic agencies. For instance, a new president will make new appointments to the executive agencies. These appointments must be approved in confirmation hearings that are held in the Senate. Therefore, the congresswoman in particular and Congress in general can consider the appointees to the Education Department in regard to where they stand on addressing the issue of disproportionate funding in schools, or whether the appointees have other plans to address inequality in public schools.

Both of these measures reflect the principle of checks and balances, which refers to a power that one branch has that serves as a check on a power of another branch, with the goal of limiting abuses in power by any one branch. Congressional committees are a check on the executive branch, namely the bureaucratic agencies. Committees hear testimony from those with positions in the bureaucracy, not only to learn from experts in the field to help draft legislation, but also to investigate agencies and hold them accountable for how they are functioning. Confirmation hearings are also a check; the legislative branch is checking the power of the executive branch, and in particular, the president's power to make appointments to government positions. If the president appoints someone who is inexperienced, corrupt, or unsuitable for the position, the Senate could prevent the appointment from happening.

Sample Low-Scoring Response

One way that the congresswoman could impact the education issue is by attempting to force Congress to vote on legislation that is related to education. Perhaps, since she is in the minority party, the education financing issue is not one that is supported by the majority party. If this is the case, it could be difficult for the legislation to pass. It can also be difficult for a bill that is drafted by a committee to move to the floor and even be voted upon at all. If this happens, the congresswoman could initiate a discharge petition, which would force the bill to move to the floor for voting. The bill would still have a difficult road ahead, since a simple majority is needed in order for a bill to pass and move to the other house of Congress, where it would also require a simple majority of votes in order to pass. If the bill passes both houses, it would go to the president. After that step, the congresswoman could then encourage her fellow congress members to still vote for the bill, though this time a 2/3 vote would be required in both houses.

Once both houses of Congress pass a bill about education finance reform, the president and the Supreme Court might both disagree with it. If so, they have the power to veto the legislation.

Employing a discharge petition is related to Congress's power to create legislation. This is an example of separation of powers because it is an ability that is unique to the legislative branch. With the branches having separate powers, this helps ensure that authority is spread out over different parts of government in order to limit abuses, allow for checks, and clearly define each branch's specific governing responsibilities.

Explanation of Sample Responses

For Part A, the writer of the high-scoring response correctly identifies the senator's possible tactic, and then effectively describes both what serving on a committee would entail and how this could impact policy. The low-scoring response has two main issues. First, the writer incorrectly focuses on discharge petitions, which are a measure used in the House of Representatives, not in the Senate as directed by the prompt. Second, the writer unnecessarily goes into extensive detail about the process of voting on bills. This is not only irrelevant to the prompt but also gives the writer inadequate time to address the other parts of the prompt.

For Part B, the writer of the high-scoring response not only identifies but also explains an interaction between Congress and another part of the federal government that could impact policy. The writer of the low-scoring response unnecessarily addresses two parts of the federal government. The writer also gives misinformation about the judiciary, which cannot veto legislation. However, the most significant issue is that the low-scoring response merely *identifies* rather than *explains* how the parts of government can interact; the writer hints at vetoing in Part A, but never explains the process.

The high-scoring response effectively addresses all aspects of the prompt in the answer to Part C. The writer correctly identifies both measures as examples of checks and balances and explains the term. Then, the writer of the high-scoring response provides detailed explanations of why each measure is an example of checks and balances. By thoroughly explaining the concept, the writer of the low-scoring response provides a great explanation of how law-making illustrates an example of separation of powers. However, this writer fails to address the government measures for *both* A and B, and would thus not earn full credit for Part C.

Rubric for Question 2: 5 Points (1 + 1 + 1 + 2)

Part A (1 point)

One point for describing a similarity OR difference between the 2012 and 2016 poll trends.

- Example similarities: "strong leader" and "can manage government" results hover around 50% both years; both election winners did not have the highest results in all categories

- Example differences: 2012 candidates had significantly higher results than 2016 candidates in several categories ("likable," "honest/trustworthy," and "favorable image"); 2012 election winner (Obama) scored higher than opponent in three categories, while 2016 winner (Trump) scored higher than opponent in two categories; 2012 candidates had highest numbers in "likable," "honest/trustworthy," and "favorable image," while 2016 candidates had highest numbers in "strong leader" and "can manage government"

Part B (1 point)

One point for explaining how a characteristic of the polls makes them scientific. To earn the point, the response must not only identify a characteristic but also *explain* how the characteristic makes the polls scientific.

- Example poll characteristics and explanations:
  - scientific sampling procedures help ensure that the sample group is actually representative of the target population (random phone number selection, inclusion of both landlines and cell phone lines, large sample size)

  - scientific question wording helps ensure unbiased, comparable results (asking same categories for all candidates)

Part C (1 point)

One point for explaining how another characteristic lends credibility to polls. To earn the point, the response must not only identify a characteristic but also *explain* how the characteristic makes polls more credible.

- Example characteristics:
  - Sampling procedures that help ensure a representational sample: random sampling in which each person has an equal chance of being selected, representative sampling that represents demographic groups in proportion to U.S. population
  - Polling procedures and question wording that help ensure objectivity and fair representation: interviewer's clear and fair delivery of questions, interviewer's ability to deliver poll in different languages, unbiased wording of questions
  - Low margin of error signals a poll was conducted fairly and representationally, resulting in valid data

Part D (2 points)

One point for explaining a way in which the media's reporting of polls can impact public opinion. To earn the point, responses must not only identify but also *explain* the impact.

- Example impacts: reporting could create "bandwagon effect," where the media, and thus the public, pay more attention to early leaders in polls; reporting can create "horse race coverage" in which the public hears more about opinion polls than about candidates' stances on issues; reporting could reinforce public's preexisting beliefs; reporting could change public's opinions about candidate; reporting could cause public to view a politician more/less favorably

One point for explaining a way in which the media's reporting of polls can impact voter behavior. To earn the point, responses must not only identify but also *explain* the impact.

- Example impacts: reporting could cause voters to ignore candidates who don't perform as strongly in opinion polls; reporting could influence which candidates receive the most financial contributions; reporting could discourage voting participation if public thinks a particular candidate will definitely win/lose based on poll results; reporting could motivate voters who strongly agree/disagree with poll results

Sample High-Scoring Response

One difference in the poll trends is that the 2012 poll had one category in which one candidate scored much higher than his opponent, with Obama scoring about 20% higher in the "likable" category than Romney. The 2016 candidates did not have any one category in which there was such a sizable difference.

One feature that makes these polls scientific is that they attempted to create a random sampling of participants, as they used random number selection for phone interviews. Also, the polls reflected the growing prevalence of cell phones by including both landlines and cell phone lines in the sampling. Together, these measures helped randomize the sample and thus made the poll more scientific. Another factor that can make a poll more credible is the use of a sampling that is not only random but also representative of the overall population. For instance, the use of landlines and cell phone lines to obtain the sample group could lead to disproportionate results: the elderly may be more likely to have landlines today, while in general people tend to do higher screening of cell phone calls. A resulting over-reliance on landline responses could lead to a sample that over-represents the elderly.

However polls are conducted, the media's coverage of them can impact public opinion and elections. There exists a bandwagon effect in which those candidates who perform best in early opinion polls receive the bulk of the media's attention; thus, the public assumes that only those particular candidates are significant. For instance, even if a voter initially supports a candidate who performs poorly in opinion polls, that voter might shift his own views based on the media reporting and withdraw his support for the candidate. Poll reporting also impacts voting behavior. In the previous example, the voter would likely have voted for the original candidate, but based on opinion poll reporting, he decides that his vote will count more if he casts it for one of the reported front runners. Thus, he changes who he votes for, as do many other voters, thus greatly impacting the outcome of elections.

Sample Low-Scoring Response

The categories in which the 2012 candidates scored highest were different than the categories in which the 2016 candidates scored highest. Apparently, the qualities that voters value in a president changed over time.

Public opinion polls are more credible when they have a low margin of error. For instance, a public opinion poll would not be very credible if it were attempting to represent the whole national population, but it only interviewed people from one particular neighborhood. Although such a poll might be useful for understanding the views of the citizens in that particular area, it would not likely represent the nation as a whole. It might include people of, for instance, only one socioeconomic class, and thus would not be representative of a diverse nation. Still, based on these opinion polls, voters might decide to vote for a different candidate than they had originally supported.

Explanation of Sample Responses

The writer of the high-scoring response accurately describes a difference between the 2012 and 2016 opinion poll trends for Part A. The writer of the low-scoring response correctly identifies that the categories in which the candidates scored highest were different in the two election years, but does not provide any *description* of the trends, as required by the prompt.

The writer of the high-scoring response carefully addresses each prompt requirement for Part B, first identifying relevant characteristics of the polls and then explaining how these characteristics make the polls more randomized, and thus scientific. The writer of the low-scoring response fails to identify any scientific characteristic of the polls from the information graphic.

For Part C, the writer of the high-scoring response accurately explains another factor that makes polls credible. The writer's use of a specific example of how a poll could be disproportionate contributes to the effective explanation. Although the writer of the low-scoring response identifies a quality that makes polls more credible (low margin of error), the explanation that follows addresses a quality (representative sampling) that the writer never mentions by name. Thus, the explanation is not sufficient.

The writer of the high-scoring response carefully addresses each requirement for Part D with a relevant example, resulting in effective explanations. The writer of the low-scoring response superficially addresses Part D; the writer only *identifies* a possible impact on voting behavior, without providing any *explanation* of the behavior change, and fails to explain an impact on public opinion.

Rubric for Question 3: 4 Points (1 + 2 + 1)

Part A (1 point)

One point for identifying the due process clause (of the Fourteenth Amendment).

Part B (2 points)

One point for describing facts and/or constitutional history relevant to *McDonald v. Chicago*.

- Example facts/constitutional history include: McDonald argued that the city of Chicago's prohibiting his purchase of a handgun for self-defense purposes violated his Second Amendment rights; Court determined that the due process clause of the Fourteenth Amendment incorporated the Second Amendment against the states

One point for explaining why the Court's reasoning/history led to different holdings in the two cases.

- Example explanations include:

  - The *Hurtado* case (1884) was before the Supreme Court began using the due process clause of the Fourteenth Amendment in the twentieth century to selectively incorporate constitutional rights against the states, while the holding for *McDonald* (2010) came after a decades-long history of the Supreme Court's selective incorporation of constitutional rights against the states

  - The scenario in *Hurtado v. California* was determined to not violate due process because: 1) Hurtado still had a fair legal proceeding and 2) the ultimate judgement is not based on a grand jury indictment, so therefore the use of grand juries is not necessary for "ordered liberty"

  - In *McDonald v. Chicago*, the right to bear arms was considered a fundamental right of self-defense with a "historic tradition" and was thus incorporated against the states

Part C (1 point)

One point for explaining how such court cases relate to federalism.

- Federalism: a system of government in which different levels of government each have separate responsibilities; in the United States, the federal government handles national matters, and the states handle regional matters (optional: federal powers are enumerated in the Constitution, and the Tenth Amendment reserves all other, non-prohibited powers to the states; powers have become more concurrent over time)

- Examples of how such cases reflect federalism:

  - cases about selective incorporation reflect the debate about the balance of separate and concurrent powers between federal and state governments; for example, states can structure their legal systems (*Hurtado v. California*) and can enact gun regulation (*McDonald v. Chicago*), but the federal government can override those powers if they violate the Constitution

  - cases about selective incorporation involve rights/liberties that were originally guaranteed from the federal government, and now the Fourteenth Amendment's due process clause is used to apply some of those rights/liberties to state governments

  - the Supreme Court's ultimate authority to adjudicate cases reflects the shift over time from more equal state and federal powers to a stronger national government

Sample High-Scoring Response

The due process clause of the Fourteenth Amendment is relevant in both cases. The Supreme Court uses this clause, which declares that no state can deprive citizens of rights without due process of the law, to apply constitutional rights to the states. The right involved in McDonald v. Chicago, gun ownership, was incorporated to the states, while the right involved in

Hurtado v. California, grand jury indictment before trial, was not incorporated. The Court used the evaluation of whether a right is "fundamental" as a litmus test to determine if it should be incorporated using the due process clause. In Hurtado, the Court determined that using a grand jury to determine whether someone should go to trial was not a "fundamental" right, as there are other possible, fair ways to determine if a case should be tried. However, in McDonald, the Court determined that the Second Amendment's protection of the right to bear arms, specifically for self-defense purposes, is necessary for "ordered liberty." The Court also likely considered this right "deeply rooted in our nation's history and traditions" since the framers so intentionally included the amendment after their recent use of militias to defeat Britain. Thus, the right in McDonald was found to be "fundamental," while the right in Hurtado was not, leading to different holdings.

Cases concerning the selective incorporation of rights reflect the continual balance needed under a federalist system. Federalism entails having different levels of government, each with its own individual powers, together creating a country's ruling structure. The Constitution specifies that powers that are not specifically delegated to the federal government are reserved for the states. However, this seemingly straightforward system leads to debates, as the interpretation of delegated/reserved powers might be unclear, and some powers of federal and state governments actually overlap. Cases about incorporation therefore reflect these debates because they concern applying provisions from the federal constitution to the states, including powers that are reserved to the states. For instance, the ruling in McDonald creates a federal override on states' authority to create certain regulations on gun ownership. Balancing powers that are supposed to be separate, yet in practice are concurrent, is an ongoing process in a federalist system.

Sample Low-Scoring Response

The due process clause is relevant. In Hurtado v. California, the Supreme Court decided that a grand jury hearing is not a fundamental right, while in McDonald v. Chicago, the court determined that having a gun is a fundamental right. These cases show how federalism works. There are both state governments and the federal government. However, the federal government has the highest authority because the Supreme Court is the highest court.

Explanation of Sample Responses

The writer of the high-scoring response correctly identifies the relevant clause for Part A, providing just enough explanation to demonstrate understanding. Note that the low-scoring response is only one paragraph in total. While this is not necessarily inappropriate, addressing all parts of a prompt with a one-paragraph response can make the organization unclear and make it difficult for the reader to assess whether each part of the prompt has been addressed. The writer of the low-scoring response correctly identifies the constitutional clause but does not use it to effectively begin an organized response with transitions.

The writer of the high-scoring response effectively uses one paragraph to combine the responses for Parts A and B, transitioning from the identification of the due process clause to an explanation of what the clause is and how it applies to selective incorporation cases. Then, using the definition of "fundamental" rights as used by the Court, the writer adequately explains how each case would lead to a different holding. The writer of the low-scoring response does correctly identify the main consideration about whether rights are "fundamental," but the response is not nuanced and fails to provide any explanation about the facts of the cases or the legal reasoning that led to the decisions.

Finally, for Part C, the writer of the high-scoring response creates a logical paragraph relating the court cases to federalism by defining federalism, discussing how applying federalism can be debatable, and explaining how incorporation cases reflect this tension. The writer of the low-scoring response attempts to describe federalism, but fails to mention the essential fact that the levels of government have separate powers in such a system.

Rubric for Question 4: 6 Points (1 + 3 + 1 + 1)

Category	Appropriate Responses	Notes
A: Thesis (**1 pt** for stating a thesis that can be defended, is responsive to the issue posed, and sets up a line of reasoning)	"Granting extensive military authority to the executive branch is [contrary to/consistent with] U.S. foundational principles because…"	You cannot earn a point by simply pointing out that the executive branch has unchecked military authority; this would be essentially repeating the prompt.
B: Support (**1 pt** for presenting a piece of evidence relevant to the topic)	A statement or piece of evidence about the executive branch that does not provide specific support for your thesis.	Example: you make a reasonable statement about the executive branch's powers, but neglect to address its military authority specifically.
OR B: Support (**2 pts** for using a single piece of evidence appropriately supporting your thesis)	• *Federalist* 70: argument for the president as unitary executive • *Brutus* 1: wariness of standing armies and of concentrating power in executive hands • U.S. Constitution: Article I, which grants Congress the power to declare war; and/or Article II, which invests the president as Commander-in-Chief	Including a relevant reference from one of the listed founding documents is essential. Clearly state the document you are using and present the relevant information contained in it.

(Continued)

(Continued)

OR B: Support (**3 pts** for using two pieces of evidence appropriately supporting your thesis)	• "The Vietnam War and its aftermath is a tragic example of presidents exercising haphazard overreach and Congress not stepping up to do its job." • "If Congress stuck its nose into the everyday conduct of the military, Osama bin Laden would be alive today. President Obama's ability to order the strike could've been fatally compromised by dithering politicians." • "The president's ability to order nuclear strikes causes many to wonder whether one person should have the power to destroy civilization."	Your second piece of evidence can come from your reading or general knowledge. Be sure that it is relevant and supports your thesis.
C: Reasoning (**1 pt** for explaining why or how your evidence supports your thesis)	• "Executive authority over the military is theoretically limitless, because the Constitution draws no explicit exception or provision to suggest the president is answerable in her military decisions to anything except the people or the impeachment process." • "Since 1945, the president has had one finger on the nuclear button and one eye on the public mood. But even centuries before, the founders saw wisdom in putting barriers between hasty executive decisions and Armageddon, and today those barriers are even more needed." • "The successful arguments in *Federalist* 70 for a unitary executive have helped the U.S. weather many emergencies, from Washington's unilateral declaration of neutrality with Britain and France down to G.W. Bush's actions to rein in the chaos after 9/11."	Don't assume that the AP reader will understand that the evidence you presented supports a particular point that you are making. Be sure to state explicitly how the evidence demonstrates your point.
D: Reply to Alternative Viewpoint (**1 pt** for offering a point of view different from yours and going on to rebut, refute, or concede it)	You present a point in favor of the other opinion—pro-executive if you have been arguing anti-executive, or vice versa—and either show it to be false, argue that it is not valid, or concede it may have some validity.	Don't just assert that the other side is wrong. Provide a reason why it is wrong (rebut it) or grant their point (concede it), while not backing away from your own view. Example: admitting some past excesses while affirming that, in general, military power is well placed in the executive.

Sample High-Scoring Response

The wording of foundational documents, as well as subsequent actions of Congress, leads to the conclusion that granting the president broad authority as Commander-in-Chief was meant to be a founding principle.

Article II of the Constitution names the president Commander-in-Chief, while the legislative branch participates in funding and oversight (according to Article I). That means they declare war, supply it, and punish violations during it but are not assigned direction over deployment or tactics in times of distress or immediate need. The Articles of Confederation granted Congress power to both regulate the army and navy and direct their operations. But the later document retained the former condition almost word for word, while the latter was pointedly removed. Also, Hamilton in Federalist 70 is emphatic on the importance of a "unitary" executive, a single individual who can provide consistent leadership.

With the exception of 1973's War Powers Act (WPA), Congress has generally granted presidents great leeway in deciding when to commit troops and for what length. Passed because of frustration over the lack of purpose and clarity in U.S. involvement in Vietnam, the WPA has been politely ignored since. All presidents have behaved as if they were abiding by the Act out of courtesy rather than compulsion. In the tragic aftermath of 9/11, the passage of the Authorization for Use of Military Force (AUMF) granted the executive so much leeway in fighting terrorism, the WPA might as well have never existed.

The omission, in the Constitution, of any language unambiguously charging Congress with decision-making power in military operations speaks strongly to the founders' intent in keeping meddling legislators out of the important business of waging war. Additional support is provided by the deliberate removal of such language from the previous governing document, the Articles, when drafting the final one. Meanwhile, Congress's back and forth efforts to rein in presidential power have been based on passions of the moment. Surely Hamilton was not the only founder who would dread it if emotion and politics raised any doubts at home or abroad about who is running our military. With all this support from the country's founding documents, there can be no doubt that the founders wanted the president to have broad military authority.

Concerns about a rogue executive rashly taking us to war are understandable given the stakes involved. In theory, an irresponsible president with broad authority as Commander-in-Chief could engage in destructive and counterproductive military conflicts that undermined national security. But the carefully crafted checks and balances woven into the Constitution are reliable. With the power of the purse and the ability to strengthen the WPA or lobby the courts to uphold it, Congress has plenty of opportunity to steer the general flow of U.S. military might, even short of declaring war.

Sample Low-Scoring Response

The stance which I hold in regards to the strong executive branch authority over the armed forces is the one against it. There is too much risk in letting a Commander-in-Chief who might never have served in the military have free power to send our people into harm's way or worse.

That said, the Constitution definitely does make the president the one and only Commander-in-Chief and tells Congress it can declare a war and come up with the funding or withhold the funding, but not more than that. This shows the founders thinking on strong military control.

I support the idea that the Commander-in-Chief's ability to put our forces in harm's way should be checked and balanced by getting congressional approval, but I can see why someone might disagree. When 9/11 happened and we had to go after the Taliban that backed Al Qaeda, we had to present a strong face to our enemies and friends alike and President Bush was right in going right in there (Afghanistan). After that, President Obama needed to launch air strikes at many countries in the Middle East and also introduced drones which helped to keep our people safer, and I don't believe he got Congress to agree to those acts in every case. Still, both presidents would have gotten more public support and endured less criticisms if they had gotten Congress to go along at the get go. Our government is a government of checks and balances and overall, the president needs strong oversight and should get it.

Explanation of Sample Responses

Both writers provide an argument, each earning the 1 Thesis point, although the writer of the high-scoring response is more careful to stick to the prompt, which asks specifically for a stance on whether "the executive branch's control over the military is both necessary and consistent with the intent of the Constitution's framers." The high-scoring response claims that the framers intended for the president to have broad military authority. The low-scoring response does eventually address the issue of the founders' intent, but does not include it as part of the thesis in the first paragraph, instead only claiming that broad military authority is undesirable because of the risk posed by inexperienced presidents.

With respect to Support, the high-scoring response cites and elaborates upon Articles I and II of the Constitution, the Articles of Confederation, and *Federalist* 70, which is more than enough to earn all 3 of the points for evidence. In contrast, the low-scoring response would only earn 1 point for a vague piece of evidence that is from one of the required documents, but which doesn't adequately support the thesis.

The high-scoring response would earn 1 point for Reasoning, with a detailed discussion of how the contrast between the Articles of Confederation and the Constitution shows that the framers evolved on the position of military authority to support a stronger executive. The low-scoring response, however, would earn 0 points for no significant attempt at explaining how its evidence supports its thesis.

Finally, both responses would earn 1 point for Reply to Alternative Viewpoint. The high-scoring writer brings up the possibility of an irresponsible executive, but concedes that there are checks and balances built into the Constitution that provide enough limits on the president's military authority. The low-scoring response provides a lot of evidence in favor of the view it opposes, but counters that popular support for some military actions would have been higher had past presidents gotten more involvement from Congress.

Overall, the high-scoring response would earn all 6 points, while the low-scoring response would earn only 3 out of 6, missing potential points in Support and Reasoning. The low-scoring response provides so much evidence for the opposing view in the last paragraph that it probably would have been better to argue for that view instead. This goes to show that you should be strategic when choosing a side to take in an argumentative essay. Always defend the position that you can more easily support with the foundational documents and other evidence, even if it may not be the view that you personally believe.

PRACTICE EXAM 2 ANSWERS AND EXPLANATIONS

Section I

1. C

President Reagan's party lost 28 seats in the 1982 midterms and another 5 seats in 1986, a difference of only 23 seats in the two results. According to the chart, this is the most consistent outcome among the two-term presidents listed. **(C)** is correct. President Clinton's results differed by 58 seats, President Obama's by 50, and President Bush's by 36. All are greater differences than in Reagan's two results, so (A), (B), and (D) are incorrect.

2. A

As shown by Bill Clinton in 1998 and George W. Bush in 2002, strong approval ratings mainly shield the president's party from the loss of seats rather than earn them many new seats. Thus, **(A)** is correct. (B) is incorrect because the power of incumbency does not protect House legislators from an unpopular president, as indicated in the table by the significant seat losses that typically occurred for presidents with low approval ratings. (C) is incorrect because a popular president can still lose seats, as Ronald Reagan and George H. W. Bush did in 1988 and 1990, respectively. (D) is incorrect because the table provides no information on Electoral College results (and, in fact, a strong Electoral College showing by Ronald Reagan in 1984 and Barack Obama in 2008 did not protect their respective parties from losses in the subsequent midterms).

3. C

Entitlement programs like Social Security will be increasingly difficult to fund if the trends on the graph continue, as fewer and fewer young people will enter the U.S. workforce while more and more people will become senior citizens without having more than one child, if they have children at all. Thus, **(C)** is correct. Given the shrinking sizes of families and the increase in people not getting married, it is unlikely that childcare will become a major issue for most voters; (A) is incorrect.

Although family sizes have been declining over the decades, two-person households are on an upward trend, so (B) is incorrect. A decline in the size of families, combined with a rise in people apparently putting off marriage, suggests that the trends more likely reflect that more and more women are entering the workforce rather than the opposite, as laws protecting the rights of women allow them the equality of opportunity to compete with men that they lacked previously. (D) is incorrect.

4. A

The percentage of one-person households in the United States grew from 7.7 percent in 1940 to 25.8 percent by 2000; therefore, the demographic trends in the graph best reflect an increasing focus on individualism in the United States rather than any sort of communal social order. Therefore, **(A)** is correct and (B) is incorrect. There is nothing in the trends to support an increasing emphasis on limited government, so (C) is incorrect. Although the data in the graph is suggestive of growing equality of opportunity for women, as the growth in single- and two-person households reflects the declining size of families likely influenced by women entering the workforce, the data is insufficient to judge the graph when it comes to racial equality of opportunity. Thus, (D) is incorrect.

5. B

From 1990 to 1995, the net annual increase in handgun ownership increased from approximately two million to three million per year. Therefore, **(B)** is correct. (A) is incorrect because the net annual increase in handgun ownership grew substantially between 2010 and 2014, from approximately four million to over six million. (C) is incorrect because the net annual increase in handgun ownership moderately declined between 1980 and 1985. (D) is incorrect because handgun ownership visibly spiked toward the end of the 2010s.

6. D

McDonald v. Chicago resulted in the application of the Second Amendment to the states, invalidating many gun control laws and contributing to the growth seen in the graph; **(D)** is correct. *Shaw v. Reno* dealt with legislative redistricting, and *Citizens United v. FEC* dealt with how the First Amendment applied to campaign financing law. Neither involved gun control laws, making (A) and (B) incorrect. While the *Lopez* ruling did involve handgun possession in a school zone, the underlying issue was that of the commerce clause. *Lopez* did not substantially contribute to a growth in handgun, rifle, and shotgun ownership rates. As the graph illustrates, there was actually a slight dip in the net annual increase of firearm ownership after 1995; (C) is incorrect.

7. D

While the bar graph illustrates at a glance the proportion of each revenue stream, it does not provide any information about how much each source brings in. For example, the corporate income tax has declined from contributing roughly 15 percent of federal revenue in 1946 to contributing roughly 5 percent in 2016, but there is no data about how much money those percentages actually represent. Thus, **(D)** is correct. A table would not be a superior means of visualizing the shift in the composition of federal revenue over time, as a bar graph is informative at a glance; (A) is incorrect. With data points for every 5 years over a 70-year time span, there is enough information to determine the shift in revenue sources as well as the composition of federal revenue at a given time. (B) and (C) are incorrect.

8. B

Excise taxes have generally decreased as a share of federal revenue between 1946 and 2016, going from just shy of 20 percent of federal revenue in 1946 to less than 5 percent in 2016. **(B)** is correct. Although corporate income taxes have significantly decreased as a share of federal revenue over the whole period of time represented on the graph, between 1981 and 2011 they basically held steady at a little over 10 percent of federal revenue; (A) is incorrect. Between 1946 and 1986, and again

between 1986 and 2016, individual income taxes slightly increased as a share of federal revenue. So, (C) and (D) are incorrect.

9. B

As the table demonstrates, poverty among seniors 65 years or older would be approximately four times as high if those seniors did not receive Social Security payments; **(B)** is correct. (A) is incorrect because it refers to the overall U.S. poverty rate, while the table is limited to discussing poverty among seniors 65 years or older. (C) is incorrect because the level of senior poverty is fairly stable despite the financial crisis of 2007/2008 or the resulting Great Recession and eventual recovery. While food stamps do have a smaller effect on the poverty rate than does Social Security, the table only shows poverty rates among seniors, not the overall U.S. population, making (D) incorrect.

10. A

Given the high voter turnout rate among seniors, it is unlikely that any presidential hopeful would risk losing their votes by advocating for cuts to entitlement programs like Social Security. **(A)** is correct. While food stamps are vital to some seniors near the poverty line, Social Security is far more important to far more seniors. Thus, (B) is incorrect, as is (C). The table only offers information about food stamp usage among seniors, not among the general population. Therefore, there is not enough information to support the conclusion that cutting food stamps will not alienate the majority of voters; (D) is incorrect.

11. B

The excerpt from the court opinion begins with a summary of the decision: the 18-year-old voting provision of the Voting Rights Act is constitutional for national elections, but not for state elections. The opinion then declares that the states, according to Article I of the Constitution, can structure federal elections in their state, but Congress can "alter" these laws if it is "dissatisfied" with them. Still, the excerpt ends by acknowledging the constitutional importance of states maintaining their own governments. Only **(B)** accurately reflects part of the court opinion. (A) is incorrect because the excerpt asserts that "the Constitution allotted to the States the power to make laws regarding national elections." (C) is incorrect because the last sentence of the excerpt asserts that the Constitution "was also intended to preserve to the States the power . . . to establish and maintain their own separate and independent governments." (The first sentence states that the court decided the 18-year-old voting provision was only unenforceable for state and local elections. Note that the Twenty-Sixth Amendment later superseded this court decision; (D) is incorrect.

12. C

The court opinion concerns the federal and state governments' powers to regulate federal and state/local elections. Among the conclusions in the opinion are: 1) states can organize federal elections, 2) the federal government has the power to cause states to change these policies, and 3) a particular provision of a law made about elections by the federal government cannot be enforced upon state elections. Therefore, the scenario has to do with the concurrent power of federal and state governments to organize elections, which matches **(C)**. (A) is incorrect because it concerns the federal government's implied powers to carry out its enumerated constitutional powers; the clause is not applicable in this case because the opinion references a power of Congress that is specifically articulated in Article I, Section 4, and is thus not an implied power. (B) is incorrect because nothing about the scenario reflects the checks and balances among the three branches of the federal government; rather, the scenario reflects the separation of powers among levels of government in a federal system. Finally, (D), the full faith and credit clause, refers to the states' obligation to honor the legal matters of other states, and has nothing to do with this scenario.

13. D

The court opinion describes a concurrent power of the state and federal governments: both establish regulations for organizing elections. While the court determined that the federal government cannot impose some regulations, such as the 18-year-old voting provision, on state and local elections, it can put qualifications on states' systems for federal elections. **(D)** best represents a similar scenario: state and local governments can structure public education, just as they can structure federal elections in their states, but the federal government can intervene in both public education and federal elections in certain situations, such as preventing segregation after the *Brown v. Board* decision. (A) is incorrect because it only describes a power of the federal government, rather than a concurrent power of the federal and state governments. (B) is incorrect because it represents a check among the three branches of federal government. (C) is incorrect because it only describes a power of state and local governments, rather than any aspect of the federal government.

14. D

The qualifications of voters in congressional elections are subject to the power of Congress due to the time, place, and manner of holding rules outlined in Article I. So, **(D)** is correct. As Justice Black states in his opinion, "the Constitution allotted to the States the power to make laws regarding national elections, but provided that if Congress became dissatisfied with the state laws, Congress could alter them." Thus, the qualifications of voters in congressional elections being subject to the power of Congress is the result of a constitutional provision, not a mere legislative act of Congress; (A) and (B) are incorrect. The enumerated powers in Article I do not include any discussion of organizing elections; (C) is incorrect.

15. D

This passage is from debates about the adoption of the Constitution, which resulted in several constitutional compromises. Hamilton begins by arguing against the idea that it would be inappropriate to have congressional representatives for slaves, since slaves are still considered "persons" by local laws and natural law. He then concludes that it would only be "just" to include slave populations for calculating *both* representation and taxation. This summary matches **(D)**. (A) is incorrect because it states the opposite of Hamilton's argument on two points: he claims that slaves *are* a legal entity and that they *should* count in determining representation. (B) is incorrect because it only reflects a part of Hamilton's argument, as he claims slaves should count for representation as well. On the other hand, (C) is incorrect because it fails to account for Hamilton's claim that slaves should be counted for taxation purposes, and it also creates a logical relationship between taxation and representation that Hamilton does not make.

16. B

Hamilton's argument reflects the controversy about state slave populations, specifically the issue of whether the populations would count towards the amount of taxation on the state (favored by non-slave states), the number of congressional representatives from the state (favored by slave states), or both. **(B)** is correct, as it connects this debate to the Three-Fifths Compromise; the ultimate decision was that slaves would count as three-fifths of a person for both taxation and representation purposes. The Thirteenth Amendment later prohibited slavery, but it does not reflect Hamilton's argument, which assumes the existence of slavery; (A) is incorrect. While (C) represents a constitutional compromise about slavery, it incorrectly refers to the eventual termination of slave imports, rather than to the taxation and representation of existing slave populations. (D) refers to the compromise about Congress's bicameral structure, which determined that representation in one house would be proportional to population, and representation in the other house would be equal for each state; (D) is incorrect.

17. A

Federalist 10 discusses partisan politics in a republic, or "mischief of faction" as it was then termed. Its author, James Madison, argued that a large republic is desirable for its homogeneous nature, as any action the republican government undertakes will need broad cooperation rather than rule by a vigorous minority. This philosophy would support Hamilton's view that the Three-Fifths Compromise was an "indulgence" of Southern interests in order to reach a broad agreement. Thus, **(A)** is correct. While (B) deals with the inner workings of the federal government, it is mainly focused on the legalistic system of checks and balances rather than the more political aspects of organizing a republican government. (C) is incorrect because *Federalist* 70 concerns the mechanics

of the executive branch rather than the legislative one. (D) is incorrect because *Federalist* 78 deals with the judicial branch.

18. C

While the Democratic Party won a scattering of counties throughout Illinois, the largest cluster was in the far northeastern portion of the state, where most counties went for the Democratic candidate; **(C)** is correct. The GOP won more raw counties than the Democratic Party did; (A) is incorrect. While four counties favored the GOP by more than 70 percent of their vote total, those were not the only four counties that the GOP won in Illinois. In fact, they won most counties, just at a smaller vote share than 70 percent. So, (B) is incorrect. Two counties in the eastern part of Illinois backed the GOP by over 70 percent of the vote; (D) is incorrect.

19. D

The Democratic Party is more popular in urban areas, which are densely populated, meaning that a few counties will have far more voters than most other counties. So, the GOP can win many more counties but still, in terms of raw vote total, finish behind the Democrats. Thus, **(D)** is correct. Although (A) accurately describes seniors as a key voting bloc during midterm elections, 2016 was not a midterm; it was a presidential election year. (B) is incorrect because gerrymandering affects House races, not Senate races; the map key indicates that this is a Senate race. While (C) accurately describes the Republican Party as being more popular in rural areas, poll taxes have been unconstitutional since the ratification of the Twenty-Fourth Amendment back in 1964, so (C) is incorrect.

20. A

The cartoon depicts a gravestone for "our civil service as it was" and represents Andrew Jackson as a proponent of bribery, fraud, spoils, and plunder; this offers a critique of the patronage system used by incoming presidents to grant civil service jobs to friends rather than basing appointments on merit. Thus, **(A)** is correct and (D) is incorrect. (B) is incorrect because the cartoon is criticizing, not celebrating, the spoils system. The cartoon is critical of how those who work in the federal bureaucracy are appointed, not the way in which Andrew Jackson was elected president, making (C) incorrect.

21. D

The inscription in the cartoon reads, "To the victors belong the spoils," which refers to the patronage system that a new president could use to give government civil service jobs within the federal bureaucracy to supporters, friends, and relatives. **(D)** is correct. (A), (B), and (C) are incorrect because these do not operate under the spoils system.

22. C

A proponent of campaign finance reform would most likely claim that unlimited campaign contributions to super PACs give unions, corporations, and wealthy individuals too large of a role in the political process. Critics of unlimited money in politics often point to the large influence that one wealthy individual can have. For example, Person "A" in the "Soft Money" infographic box donated $100,000. Twenty donors would need to give the maximum possible "Hard Money" donation to equal this amount. Vast sums of money can then be spent on hiring more staff and buying ads, which can itself outweigh the volunteer efforts of lone citizens. Therefore, **(C)** is correct, and (A) is incorrect. Super PACs are not allowed to directly coordinate with a candidate or party; (B) is incorrect. Although (D) is an argument associated with the debate over campaign finance, it is one made by opponents of campaign finance reform, not its proponents.

23. C

While direct coordination with super PACs is forbidden by law, indirect coordination is acceptable. This can take many forms, one of which is directing potential donors to several super PACs friendly to a candidate's campaign. This allows the candidate to raise campaign funds in a roundabout way without violating federal law. Thus, **(C)** is correct and (A) is incorrect. Although removing the cap on hard money would allow a candidate to more directly raise money, it would not immediately help the candidate in the current election since there is no guarantee that the cap on hard money would be

removed; (B) is incorrect. Again, campaigns and political parties may not directly coordinate with super PACs, so (D) is incorrect.

24. C

Due process rights guarantee a citizen's basic rights to life, liberty, and property, protecting a U.S. citizen from being imprisoned without a public trial; **(C)** is correct. All men in the United States are required to register for military service within 30 days of their 18th birthday, making (A) incorrect. Defamation and libel laws protect citizens from newspapers publishing falsehoods about them; (B) is incorrect. (D) is incorrect since the Third Amendment, not due process, protects citizens from being forced to house soldiers in their homes.

25. C

The structure of American elections supports the two-party system. State laws often allow the two major parties automatic ballot access in an election, while third parties must collect signatures and reapply each election cycle in order to appear on a ballot. Thus, **(C)** is correct. (A) is incorrect because the two major parties change over time; for example, segregationists once formed a major faction of the Democratic Party, but since the mid-1960s, the party has been associated with civil rights for African Americans. (B) is incorrect because it states that electors are won through the national popular vote. In fact, votes in the Electoral College are allotted based on the popular votes in each individual state. A president can thus win the Electoral College while losing the popular vote. (D) is incorrect because third parties sometimes do win local and state elections.

26. D

Voter enthusiasm can skew exit polls by creating an unrepresentative sample. For example, voters who are very enthusiastic about their candidate will be more likely to volunteer their time to talk with a pollster. Additionally, pollsters may assume the wrong demographics for their poll, and weigh the responses of voters improperly. Thus, **(D)** is incorrect. (A) is incorrect because it describes a potential issue with entrance polls, not exit polls. (B) is incorrect because, while voters may be reluctant to share their choice of candidate out of general principle, this would not explain a difference between exit polling and election results. (C) is incorrect because exit polls can only dissuade potential voters before polling places close (i.e., while people can still vote).

27. B

The Senate must ratify treaties negotiated by the president with other nations by a two-thirds vote; **(B)** is correct. This is part of the system of checks and balances. (A) and (C) are incorrect because the Senate, not the House of Representatives, must vote to accept the treaty for it to become final. The Supreme Court cannot declare a treaty constitutional or unconstitutional unless a legal case is presented; (D) is incorrect.

28. B

In *Marbury v. Madison*, the Supreme Court established judicial review and declared that the Supreme Court is the main interpreter of the Constitution; **(B)** is correct. (A), (C), and (D) are incorrect because these would be unconstitutional based on other Supreme Court decisions. The decision in *United States v. Nixon* (1974) prohibits presidents from withholding information from a criminal trial; the ruling for *Youngstown Sheet & Tube Co. v. Sawyer* (1952) limited the power of the president to take control of private property; and the decision in *Gibbons v. Ogden* (1824) confirmed that the federal government, not the states, should regulate interstate commerce.

29. A

Efforts to balance social order and individual freedom are reflected in interpretations of the First Amendment that limit speech, including regulations about defamatory, offensive, and obscene statements and gestures; **(A)** is correct. Regulation of child labor is allowable under the commerce clause. While the regulation of child labor promotes a healthier social order, it has little to do with individualism. Instead, regulating child labor deals with economic values, such as free enterprise and limited government. Thus, (B) is incorrect. Anti-discrimination efforts often balance the American core value of limited government with the value of equality of opportunity; (C) is incorrect. Minimum wage laws balance social order with economic values but do not involve individualism; (D) is incorrect.

30. D

In *Federalist* 51, James Madison states that "Ambition must be made to counteract ambition." This is, in brief, the argument for a system of checks and balances in government. Madison argues that human nature is imperfect, but the ambition of one man can check another man's ambition if federal power is dispersed. No one person could grow to become an all-powerful tyrant. Ambitious men might rise to prominence in one branch, but their aims would be checked by ambitious men safeguarding their power in another branch. Therefore, **(D)** is correct. The lifetime appointment of judges is elaborated on in *Federalist* 78, not *Federalist* 51, making (A) incorrect. The failing of the Articles of Confederation was not the concentration of power in one branch, but the lack of power in the federal government itself, so Madison's argument in *Federalist* 51 would not apply; (B) is incorrect. Likewise, the election of senators is not discussed in *Federalist* 51, making (C) incorrect.

31. B

The Speaker of the House is chosen by the members of the majority party in the House of Representatives; **(B)** is correct and (A) is incorrect. The Speaker has the right to vote, but rarely participates in debate or votes except when a House vote has ended in a tie; (C) is incorrect. Any member of the House of Representatives must have been a citizen for at least seven years, must be 25 years of age or older, and must be a resident of the state she is representing, but there are no separate age requirements for the Speaker of the House, making (D) incorrect.

32. A

"Trickle-down economics" is a common nickname for supply-side economics, which is the economic theory that the government can spur growth through deregulation and tax cuts. Thus, **(A)** is correct. (B) is incorrect because it describes Keynesian economics.

(C) is incorrect because it describes libertarian attitudes towards economics. (D) is incorrect because it describes democratic socialism.

33. A

The Fifth Amendment outlines the basis for eminent domain, which is the right of the government to take private property for public use as long as the government provides just compensation for that property. Taking the church land without compensating the owner would be a violation of the owner's Fifth Amendment rights. **(A)** is correct. (B) is incorrect because it describes a violation of the Fourth Amendment protection against warrantless searches. (C) is incorrect because it describes a violation of the Sixth Amendment right to confront one's accusers in a court of law. (D) is incorrect because the Fifth Amendment protection against double jeopardy does not apply to mistrials, as no verdict is reached in mistrials.

34. C

The Constitution originally provided for indirect election of senators; senators were not elected directly by the people, but by state legislatures. The Seventeenth Amendment changed this process so that senators are now elected by popular vote. This corresponds with **(C)**: since elite democracy entails limited participation and participatory democracy entails more broad popular participation in government, these models best reflect the shift from indirect to direct election of senators. (A) incorrectly flips the two models. (B) and (D) are incorrect because they include pluralist democracy, which emphasizes the influence of groups on politics.

35. B

When a voter's judgment is based on the past performance of political parties and elected officials, it is known as retrospective voting. This behavior model is often seen in periods of strong economic growth, as voters will be more inclined to reward the party in power. **(B)** is correct. Prospective voting is based on how a candidate might improve the life of a voter in the years ahead. In this scenario, the voter is already doing well, making (A) incorrect. Likewise, rational-choice voting is focused on what the current candidates can offer the voter on an individual level, with less focus on large-scale past performance; (C) is incorrect. Party-line voting is a strictly partisan approach. A party-line voter would not consider her own circumstances, past or present, but would simply vote for the party she identified with. (D) is incorrect.

36. A

The opponents of photo identification laws for voting argue that such laws create an entry barrier for lower-income voters, who may not have a driver's license or may not be easily able to afford another form of ID. Opponents also argue that voter fraud itself is very rare. Thus, **(A)** is correct. (B) is incorrect because it describes the motor-voter law, not photo identification laws. (C) is incorrect because opponents do not necessarily believe the laws increase public confidence, given that they also state that voter fraud is rare. (D) is incorrect because proponents of photo ID laws do not believe such laws undermine public confidence.

37. C

Immediately following the decision in *Brown v. Board of Education* in 1954, there was a rapid growth of segregated private schools in the South; **(C)** is correct and (D) is incorrect. Many schools did not desegregate until the mid-1960s or later, making (A) incorrect. In its ruling, the Supreme Court decided that state-sanctioned segregation of public schools was in violation of the Fourteenth Amendment. Because segregation in public schools was deemed unconstitutional, no additional amendment was necessary to strengthen the ruling; (B) is incorrect.

38. B

Bureaucracies tend to grow in the United States when the government is facing a crisis situation, such as military conflicts or an economic depression; **(B)** is correct. (A), (C), and (D) are incorrect since these periods do not describe any crises that would cause bureaucracies to grow significantly.

39. B

In politics, logrolling is the one-for-one trading of votes. A politician agrees to vote a certain way in order to secure a fellow politician's vote on another issue, even if they have no actual opinion about what they are voting for. Thus, **(B)** is correct. (A) is incorrect because it describes pork barrel legislation. (C) is incorrect because it describes bribery. (D) is incorrect because it describes the use of political office as a platform to draw attention to one's views.

40. D

In a departure from common law standards, the burden of proof in libel charges is placed on the plaintiff rather than the defendant. The plaintiff must prove that a publication knowingly published something false, or that it showcased a total disregard of the truth or falsity of its statements. Therefore, **(D)** is correct. (A) is incorrect because prior restraint refers to stopping something from being published in the first place, while libel deals with statements that have already been published. (B) is incorrect because the "clear and present danger" test deals with free speech, not freedom of the press. Also, as stated earlier, the burden of proof in libel cases is on the plaintiff and not the defendant. (C) is incorrect, as libel is damaging to a person's reputation, not their physical safety. Libel is written defamation, a kind of character assassination.

41. D

In *Engel v. Vitale*, the Supreme Court ruled that a public school sponsoring any religious activity is in violation of the establishment clause of the First Amendment; **(D)** is correct. While the commerce clause gives Congress wide-ranging powers, the *Engel* case dealt with a school issue, and education is an area reserved to the states. Likewise, while the necessary and proper clause, also known as the elastic clause, gives Congress wide latitude in terms of lawmaking, education is ultimately a state-level power, not a federal one. So, (A) and (B) are incorrect. Although the free exercise clause is an important aspect of religious rights under the First Amendment, that clause deals specifically with people being prevented by the government from exercising their religious freedom. The *Engel*

case dealt with the government trying to foster a particular religion through state-sponsored prayer. (C) is incorrect.

42. B

Majority whips are responsible for getting their fellow party members to vote in accordance with the majority party's legislative priorities; **(B)** is correct. (A) is incorrect because a whip only coordinates votes within his or her own party (intra-party discipline), not between parties (inter-party discipline). (C) and (D) are incorrect because they describe different roles: the Speaker of the House and the vice president in the Senate, respectively.

43. A

The Articles of Confederation favored the states over the federal government. As such, it featured a unicameral legislature where every state, regardless of population, had a single vote. The Constitution replaced this with a bicameral legislature that balanced representation based on population and on state. Thus, **(A)** is correct. While the Articles lacked centralized military power, the Constitution does not assign war powers entirely to the President. Congress must still declare war, for example. So, (B) is incorrect. The federal government had to request money from the states under the Articles, but it does have tax enforcement powers under the Constitution. (C) is incorrect. Both the Articles and Constitution allowed for the admission of new states. The Articles did so under the Northwest Ordinance. So, (D) is incorrect.

44. B

Judicial activism is a philosophy that holds that judges are not bound by the original text or intent of a constitutional provision when engaging in judicial review. Typically associated with political liberalism, its tendency is to find laws unconstitutional and to hold less deference to the popularly elected branches. Judicial restraint is a philosophy which holds that judges are required to adhere to the original text or intent of a constitutional provision when engaging in judicial review. Typically associated with political conservatism, its tendency is to uphold laws and to defer to the popularly elected branches. Thus, **(B)** is correct while (A), (C), and (D) are incorrect.

45. B

During recessions, Democrats traditionally favor Keynesian economic policies, which entail the government spending more money in order to compensate for the overall decline in the demand for goods. Republicans, on the other hand, generally oppose direct economic stimulus from the government, and instead favor cutting taxes during recessions to inspire greater spending by individuals and businesses. In reality, both parties have been open to a mix of tax cuts and spending boots during recessions, but Republicans have consistently argued for more of the former and Democrats for more of the latter. **(B)** is correct. (A) and (C) are incorrect because they describe monetary policy, not fiscal policy. Fiscal policy collectively refers to the taxing and spending actions of the U.S. government. Monetary policy is mainly concerned with managing interest rates and the money supply, which are handled through the Federal Reserve. (D) is incorrect because it is too extreme in defining the policies of both parties. While Democrats generally advocate for higher taxes on the wealthy, they generally do so during normal economic times and not recessions, and while Republicans generally advocate for entitlement reform, describing this as "elimination" of these programs is extreme.

46. D

Engel v. Vitale stated that schools cannot open each day with a voluntary prayer, as this violates the free exercise clause. *Wisconsin v. Yoder* dealt with the right of Amish parents to remove their children from compulsory education for religious reasons, which falls under the free exercise clause. Only *Engel* dealt with school prayer. Thus, **(D)** is correct while (A) and (B) are incorrect. The ruling on students saluting the flag refers to *West Virginia v. Barnette*, not *Engel*; (C) is incorrect.

47. B

Cabinet officials serve at the pleasure of the president, meaning that they can be fired by the president without cause. Commissioners of independent regulatory agencies, such as the FCC, cannot be fired in the middle of their term except for cause,

like criminal wrongdoing. Thus, **(B)** is correct. (A) is incorrect because the cabinet departments oversee more areas than just national security, such as the Department of Agriculture. (C) is incorrect because independent regulatory agencies do not act as advisory bodies for Congress; they serve the public interest. (D) is incorrect because the Senate must confirm the appointment of regulatory agency officials.

48. C

As established in *Roe v. Wade*, states cannot ban abortion in the first trimester, may regulate it in the second, and may ban it in the third. Thus, **(C)** is correct, and (A) and (D) are incorrect. (B) is incorrect because while the right to an abortion is not explicitly enumerated in the Constitution, the Supreme Court has determined that the due process clause protects an individual's right to privacy from state infringement; this is a major factor in the *Roe v. Wade* holding.

49. C

De facto segregation is segregation based on social patterns and forces rather than on laws; **(C)** is correct and (B) is incorrect. De facto segregation took place after the Civil War ended. For example, although U.S. schools were legally desegregated in 1954, racial segregation continued into 1960s, which is an example of de facto segregation; (A) is incorrect. (D) is incorrect because this type of segregation limited African Americans' social equality by preventing them from interacting in shared facilities with other races.

50. D

Tax powers were delegated to the House of Representatives because the framers had just participated in a war over "no taxation without representation." The House represented all voters, while senators were at that time selected by their state governments. Thus, **(D)** is correct. (A) is incorrect because the House was not dominated by representatives from southern states. When agreeing to the Connecticut Compromise, the southern states were growing faster than the northern states, and they expected to eventually dominate the House. However, industrialization in the northern states unexpectedly boosted their growth throughout the nineteenth century. (B) is incorrect because it describes the tax situation under the Articles of the Confederation, where the central government could not lay and collect taxes itself. (C) is incorrect because, while an income tax was first proposed during the War of 1812, Congress did not impose any until the Civil War and only began regularly collecting it after the adoption of the Sixteenth Amendment in 1913. Tax powers initially centered on such measures as tariffs.

51. D

Separation of powers refers to the principle that the U.S. federal government is structured in three branches, each with distinct powers and responsibilities, in order to avoid concentrating too much authority in any one branch. Though checks and balances is a closely related concept, it refers specifically to the abilities of the branches or levels of government (or houses of Congress) to place checks on the powers of the other parts of government. Only **(D)** correctly identifies an example of separation of powers, as it describes the distinct roles of two branches regarding law creation and implementation. (A) describes an example of checks and balances. (B) describes a characteristic of the executive branch. (C) describes a special role of the vice president, which actually represents more of an intermingling of the executive and legislative branches' powers rather than a separation.

52. D

Recall the role and types of linkage institutions. These are entities that serve to "link" the public and the government by providing a means of communication between the two, especially helping the public voice their views to government. The main types of linkage institutions are political parties, the media, interest groups, and elections; look for an answer choice that accurately reflects both the role and one of these types. **(D)** correctly identifies a linkage institution—political parties—and describes how someone might support a party in a way that conveys that person's views about an issue. Although (A) and (B) describe ways to try to influence policy makers, they are incorrect because they do not make use of a linkage institution. Rather, they are ways that an individual might express personal views independently. (C) is certainly an example of political participation at the local level, but it is incorrect because it does not incorporate the use of a linkage institution.

53. A

When legislators adhere to the will of the people except in instances when they believe it is in the best interests of the country to do otherwise, they are following the conscience model of representation. So, **(A)** is correct, while the other choices are incorrect. The delegate model, (B), would see Senator Doe voting for the war because the public favors it. The politico model, (C), sees legislators make their own decisions on votes for minor bills. The trustee model, (D), would see Senator Doe regularly vote in the national interest regardless of the desires of his constituents, not just on special occasions like this war vote.

54. C

A discharge petition is a means to force a bill out of committee and onto the House floor for a vote. Discharge petitions are rarely issued because they require an absolute majority. For example, if 217 House members voted in favor of such a petition, 215 voted against, and 3 abstained, then the petition would fall short of the 218 minimum votes needed for an absolute majority. This process is further complicated because it is difficult to get members of the majority party to undermine the House leadership, as they themselves elected the leadership from members of their own party. Thus, **(C)** is correct and (D) is incorrect. A discharge petition can be requested by any representative; (A) is incorrect. The threat of such petitions usually spurs the House leadership to move forward on a stalled bill, not dig in their heels. (B) is incorrect.

55. D

Political socialization refers to the process by which people acquire their political beliefs, identity, and values. This can be through indoctrination in schools, received wisdom from parents, debate among same-aged peers, and news coverage in the media, among other sources. Thus, **(D)** is correct. (A) incorrectly offers a description of political ideology, not political socialization. (B) is incorrect because it describes setting a political agenda. (C) is incorrect because it is overly narrow. A person may acquire a political belief that favors rapid socioeconomic change, but that is only one form of political socialization. One might just as easily come to favor tradition and maintaining the status quo.

ANSWERS AND EXPLANATIONS

Section II

The following are general rubrics an AP reader might use to grade these free-response questions. Use both this scoring information and the sample responses to assess your own writing.

Rubric for Question 1: 4 Points (1 + 1 + 2)

Part A (1 point)

One point for identifying a specific example of an executive power that is not explicitly stated in the Constitution. Note: Powers explicitly stated in the Constitution, such as the presidential veto, will not earn the point.

- Example powers:
  - creating advisory bureaus, committees, and commissions that are not subject to congressional oversight, such as the National Security Council
  - issuing executive orders or proclamations, such as Lincoln's Emancipation Proclamation, Franklin D. Roosevelt's Executive Order 9066 (internment of Japanese Americans), Truman's Executive Order 9981 (desegregating the military), and Trump's travel bans
  - making executive agreements with other heads of state, such as the Paris Agreement on climate change under Obama
  - claiming emergency powers during times of war/conflict, such as Truman's nationalizing steel mills during the Korean War (which was eventually declared unconstitutional by the Supreme Court)
  - claiming executive privilege, such as Nixon's (failed) attempt to block the release of subpoenaed information related to Watergate
  - using the "bully pulpit"—employing the influence of position as president to persuade the public, force attention on particular issues, and pressure lawmakers

Part B (1 point)

One point for describing an action of Congress that limits the presidential power identified in Part A. Note: To earn the point, responses must directly link the action of Congress to the presidential power from Part A, and must not just *identify* but also *describe* the action of Congress.

- Example actions of Congress:
  - congressional oversight: creating investigative committees to determine potential presidential wrongdoing, or impacting the president's actions over the bureaucracy through committee hearings and Congress's power of the purse

- constitutional checks and balances: the Senate refusing to confirm presidential appointments, or the House initiating impeachment procedures against the president

- legislation: passing laws that regulate the bureaucracy, impact the bureaucracy through the budget (the "power of the purse"), or override executive actions (for example, the War Powers Act of 1973 to limit the president's power to commit troops without congressional approval)

Part C (2 points)

Two points for explaining how TWO different linkage institutions have responded to expanded presidential authority (one point per linkage institution).

- Example linkage institutions and responses:

  - Campaigns: development of candidate-centered campaigns, campaigns as "personality contests," increased importance of candidate's campaign promises, increased appeal of platforms/slogans about president working with other branches/party rather than acting unilaterally

  - Elections: serve as way for voters to voice opinion about presidential authority as indicated by candidates' past performance (if seeking reelection) or campaign promises

  - Interest groups: increased necessity of gaining presidential support for issues in addition to congressional support

  - Media: increased coverage of president's actions and words, increased polarization of coverage since presidential actions are so influential

  - Political parties: development of candidate-centered campaigns, high stakes of winning the presidency due to increased impact of presidential authority, protests of presidential actions by opposition party and even the president's own party if the president acts unilaterally, partisan or even bipartisan support of congressional actions to overturn presidential actions

Sample High-Scoring Response

The presidency has become more powerful over time, especially as it has used powers that may be implied, but not directly stated, in Article II. Executive orders have been considered an implied power since the president has authority to execute the laws. For instance, during WWII FDR claimed that he had special emergency powers in his role as Commander-in-Chief and therefore issued an executive order that authorized the internment of Americans of Japanese descent, claiming national security reasons.

No matter how much the president's power may expand, Congress still has checks on it. For instance, in response to FDR interning Japanese Americans, Congress could have attempted to pass a bill to make the internments illegal, such as a law specifically prohibiting the detaining of individuals due to only their race or ethnicity. Or Congress could have made a law to make the internments essentially unenforceable, such as defunding the agencies or military departments that would carry out the internments. Although FDR would likely have vetoed such a bill, both houses of Congress could still make the bill a law with a 2/3 approval vote.

Linkage institutions have changed how they function as a result of increased presidential power. The media has increased its coverage of modern presidents' actions, given that these actions can have such a significant impact on policy. Media coverage especially increases if the actions are controversial, with the effect of polarizing both the coverage and the viewers. For instance, President Trump's executive orders that instituted travel bans on persons from majority-Muslim countries were controversial and potentially entailed significant impacts on families, and thus were highly reported on. Likewise, campaigns place an increased emphasis on the priorities and promises of presidential candidates. If an elected president has such a potential to act unilaterally, the speeches of a candidate take on even more weight; if elected, the president might be able to enact campaign promises without congressional support or action.

Sample Low-Scoring Response

One executive action that is not in the Constitution is claiming executive privilege based on the president's high position. This power means that the president might not have to provide requested information related to the executive branch. This clearly is an abuse of presidential power. President Nixon, for instance, attempted to withhold information from the courts about the Watergate scandal.

Fortunately, the president's power is still limited. For instance, Congress can decide to not confirm presidential appointments of Supreme Court justices.

Two linkage institutions, the media and the courts, have responded to expanded executive authority. For instance, the media devotes a significant amount of coverage to President Trump's social media postings. Also, the courts have responded to increased executive authority by declaring actions unconstitutional. For instance, the Supreme Court considered whether executive orders by both President Trump and President Obama were constitutional.

Explanation of Sample Responses

Overall, the high-scoring response contains transitions and a clear organization, which helps the writer ensure that the response addresses each part of the prompt. For Part A, the writer identifies a relevant, specific example of a presidential power, demonstrating full understanding by briefly explaining the constitutional rationale for the implicit power of executive orders. The low-scoring response also correctly identifies a presidential power that is not in the Constitution. However, although it would not result in the loss of the point, this writer introduces unnecessary opinion about executive privilege, which is not required by the prompt and thus wastes the writer's time.

For Part B, the writer of the high-scoring response does not merely *identify* an action of Congress that can limit the impact of executive orders, but also fully *describes* the process of passing a new law, including examples of laws that could have limited FDR's executive order. On the other hand, the writer of the low-scoring response fails to respond to the task of Part B, describing an action of Congress that is neither a response to the power identified in Part A (executive privilege) nor a response to any implied presidential power (since appointment of Supreme Court justices is an explicit constitutional power).

Finally, for Part C, the high-scoring response fully addresses the prompt: the writer identifies two linkage institutions and fully explains how they have responded to expanded presidential power, using the relevant example of media coverage of President Trump's executive orders. The writer of the low-scoring response correctly identifies the media as a linkage institution and states that the media has given high coverage to President Trump's social media posts, but the explanation is insufficient because the writer never explains how social media posts represent an expansion of presidential authority. Additionally, the low-scoring response incorrectly identifies the courts as a linkage institution.

Rubric for Question 2: 5 Points (1 + 2 + 1 + 1)

Part A (1 point)

One point for identifying a trend from the information graphic.

- Example trends:
  - 1–2 years is the most common time span between amendments being sent to the states and being ratified
  - the ratification of amendments is a relatively rare occurrence (for instance, no amendments were ratified in 1804–1865 or 1971–1992)
  - some amendments were passed together or within a relatively short time span, for example:
    - 1st–10th Amendments (Bill of Rights)
    - 13th–15th Amendments (Reconstruction Amendments)
    - 16th–19th Amendments (Progressive Era Amendments)
    - 20th and 21st Amendments

Part B (2 points)

One point for describing the amendment process.

- Responses MUST include the two-step process:
  - 2/3 passage by both houses of Congress
  - approval by 3/4 of the states for ratification

- Responses MAY include: alternately, the first step may be passage by national convention called by 2/3 of states

One point for explaining how the trend identified in Part A reflects the design of the founders. Note: To earn the point, the response must relate the trend from Part A to the founders' design of the amendment process.

- Example explanations:
  - 1–2 year most common time span: founders intended the Constitution to be a living document that could be altered with proper intention; the relatively short time frame reflects the general national consensus (2/3 of Congress and 3/4 of states) that founders desired for ratified amendments
  - relatively rare: founders intended the Constitution to be changeable over time, but designed the process to be multi-step (involving both Congress and state approval) and require widespread support to help ensure permanent changes to the Constitution would not be made rashly or only reflect the interests of one group(s)
  - sometimes ratified in groups: at times of high national consensus, amendments (sometimes related in nature, such as the Bill of Rights) have been able to pass through the 2-step process in relatively quick periods of time

Part C (1 point)

One point for explaining why amendments are not effective for addressing public policy.

- Example explanations: due to their very low rate of ratification, amendments are not a practical way to address immediate matters of public policy, which are most likely better addressed by legislation; amendments are intended to address permanent principles about U.S. governance rather than short-term policies; amendments require very widespread, bipartisan support (2/3 of Congress and 3/4 of states), which may be unlikely for matters of immediate policy concerns

Part D (1 point)

One point for describing an example of a constitutional amendment reflecting a change in societal norms.

- The response can use any amendment to earn the point, as long as the student describes a way that the amendment's ratification reflected changing societal norms.

- Example amendments and descriptions:

    ◦ Thirteenth Amendment: the federal prohibition of slavery reflected the abolitionist movement that had grown over time and the Union's victory in the Civil War

    ◦ Seventeenth Amendment: the direct election of U.S. senators reflected the progressive political ideals of the early twentieth century and the shift towards more participatory democracy over time

    ◦ Nineteenth Amendment: women's suffrage reflected the women's suffrage movement, progressive political ideals, cultural shifts in perceptions of citizenship/gender roles, and the overall shift towards more participatory democracy

Sample High-Scoring Response

Most commonly, amendments passed by Congress were ratified by the states in 2 years. This relatively short time frame suggests that amendments that are actually ratified must enjoy widespread popular support: they were not only first passed by 2/3 of each house of Congress, but also then ratified by 3/4 of the state legislatures. The fact that the founders created an amendment process that requires so much agreement was intentional. They wanted the Constitution to be both constant and changeable: a reliable foundation for government that could still adapt to the country's evolving needs in ways the founders knew they could not fully anticipate. So the amendment process was intended to be doable, but only in cases of widespread national support on the most important governing principles of the country.

Amendments were not intended to address immediate public policy matters. Although Congress members have proposed thousands of amendments, the process is structured so that only 27 of these proposals have actually become amendments. This indicates that amendments are intended to address long-lasting governing principles rather than short-term policy concerns, which Congress instead addresses by passing new laws.

Ratified amendments often reflect that national consensus about a fundamental issue has changed over time. For instance, at the time of the writing of the Constitution, political leaders' ideas about who could participate in our representative democracy were generally limited to white male citizens, and some states still had property-ownership requirements. Over time, the culture has become more inclusive about who should be able to participate. The 26th Amendment lowered the voting age from 21 to 18, reflecting student social movements of the time period and the growing national sentiment that 18-year-olds were responsible enough to vote, especially given their service in the Vietnam War.

Sample Low-Scoring Response

Amendments to the Constitution are rare. 27 out of 33 amendments that have been proposed by Congress have been ratified by the states, which indicates that most amendments that are proposed are successful; therefore, they serve as an effective way to address matters of public policy since they have a high rate of success.

Therefore, people must support ratified amendments a lot, which reflects the intent of the founders, who likely wanted only highly supported amendments to pass. For instance, many people must have supported women's right to vote by the time the Nineteenth Amendment passed.

Explanation of Sample Responses

For Part A, the writer of the high-scoring response uses specific data to identify a trend from the information graphic. The writer of the low-scoring response, however, only states that ratified amendments are "rare" and does not provide data. The next statement about "27 out of 33 amendments" is inaccurate, as 33 represents the number of amendments sent to the states for approval, not the number of proposed amendments (11,000+). Overall, the low-scoring response is difficult to follow as it addresses the parts of the prompt out of order.

For Part B, the writer of the high-scoring response concisely describes the amendment process, and then logically relates the trend from Part A (the two-year time span) to the founders' intentions for the amendment process (the high national consensus required). The writer of the low-scoring response forgets to address the first task of Part B, failing to describe the amendment process. For the second task, although the writer mentions "the intent of the founders," the low-scoring response is insufficient because it does not relate this intent to a trend from the information graphic.

For Part C, the writer of the high-scoring response provides an effective explanation by accurately describing the ratio of proposed to ratified amendments and logically explaining why this ratio implies that amendments are not an effective way to address short-term public policy. The writer of the low-scoring response considers the wrong ratio for Part C (passed:ratified amendments instead of proposed:ratified amendments), which renders the resulting conclusion about using amendments for public policy inaccurate.

Finally, for Part D, the writer of the high-scoring response thoroughly describes how the Twenty-Sixth Amendment reflected changing societal norms, stating that the norms for voting have become more inclusive over time, and identifying social factors that impacted the ratification of the amendment at the time of its passage. The writer of the low-scoring response correctly identifies an amendment, but the description about how its ratification reflected changing societal norms ("many people must have supported women's right to vote") is too vague to earn the point.

Rubric for Question 3: 4 Points (1 + 2 + 1)

Part A (1 point)

One point for identifying the equal protection clause (of the Fourteenth Amendment) as relevant.

Part B (2 points)

One point for describing the holding in *Shaw v. Reno*.

- Description MUST include: *Shaw v. Reno* held that redistricting by race is generally prohibited

- Description MAY include: given the Fourteenth Amendment's equal protection clause, redistricting by race is to be held under strict scrutiny; still, redistricting must also take race into account to ensure redistricting does not violate the Voting Rights Act's prohibition against using gerrymandering to weaken the significance of the votes of minority groups

One point for explaining how the holding in *Shelby County v. Holder* contrasts with the holding in *Shaw v. Reno*.

- Example contrasts:

  ○ Constitutional amendments involved: the holding from *Shelby* concerns the application of the Fifteenth Amendment/Voting Rights Act of 1965, while the holding from *Shaw* concerns the Fourteenth Amendment's equal protection clause

  ○ Types of voting rights laws involved: *Shelby* concerns a preclearance requirement on states that they must obtain federal approval before passing any new voting laws and ruled that the formula for determining preclearance was outdated and thus unconstitutional, while *Shaw* specifically concerns redistricting laws and how redistricting must generally not be based on race

  ○ Relation to Voting Rights Act of 1965: *Shelby* concerns the preclearance requirement of the Voting Rights Act, while *Shaw* concerns the necessity of being conscious of race to ensure compliance with the Voting Rights Act in not intentionally weakening minority votes

  ○ Restrictions on state voting laws: *Shelby* places a restriction on how states can carry out their voting laws, while *Shaw* indirectly, though effectively in practice, removes a previous restriction on states' voting laws, the federal preclearance requirement

Part C (1 point)

One point for describing a possible action of a civil rights group that disagreed with the decision in *Shelby v. Holder*.

- Example actions:
    - Influencing representatives: writing/calling national congressional representatives to pass legislation with new coverage formula so that the preclearance requirement is reinstated; persuading state legislators to pass equitable voting laws and create fair voting districts

    - Voting/campaigning: voting/campaigning for representatives, at both the state and national level, who favor broad voting rights; voting/campaigning for national congressional representatives who support passing a new coverage formula

    - Impacting public opinion: organizing protest marches in response to *Shelby* case; organizing rallies in favor of voting rights; utilizing social media to influence public opinion and gain supporters; utilizing media coverage to raise awareness about the *Shelby* ruling and voting rights issues

Sample High-Scoring Response

The equal protection clause of the 14th Amendment is relevant to Shaw v. Reno. This clause mandates that the states must provide all people "equal protection under the law," which the Court has determined includes protection of the right to vote.

In Shaw v. Reno, the Court determined that redistricting according to race likely violates the Constitution's equal protection clause. At the same time, however, states should be aware of race when redistricting to make sure they do not create districts that violate the anti-discriminatory requirements of the Voting Rights Act. This differs from the holding in Shelby County v. Holder, which also concerned the Voting Rights Act. However, this ruling did not concern compliance with the Act, as Shaw did, but rather concerned the Act itself. While only the formula for determining which states were subject to the preclearance requirement was found unconstitutional, the holding effectively makes preclearance unenforceable. Therefore, while Shelby places a restriction on how states can carry out their voting laws, Shelby effectively removes a previous restriction (federal preclearance for state voting laws).

Since Shelby makes it so that no state voting laws must be approved by the federal government, civil rights groups would likely be concerned that states could more easily pass discriminatory voting laws. To help prevent this, civil rights groups could focus on influencing and electing state legislators who would not support discriminatory voting laws in the first place. Groups could write their state legislators, encouraging them to support practices like fair redistricting. They could campaign for state legislators with a record of supporting fair voting legislation. While this would not reinstate preclearance, it would help reduce the need for federal oversight.

Sample Low-Scoring Response

The supremacy clause is relevant to *Shelby County v. Holder* since the Voting Rights Act is an example of federal authority because it dictates how the states must regulate their elections.

The holding in *Shaw v. Reno* was that racial gerrymandering is not allowed. The holding in *Shelby County v. Holder* found the coverage formula for the Voting Rights Act's preclearance requirement unconstitutional.

A civil rights group that disagrees with the decision in *Shelby* could have protests.

Explanation of Sample Responses

For Part A, the writer of the high-scoring response correctly identifies the equal protection clause. The writer of the low-scoring response misreads the prompt and attempts to provide a constitutional clause that is relevant to *Shelby County v. Holder* rather than *Shaw v. Reno*. Also, although the supremacy clause is somewhat implied in that the court did not find the federal preclearance requirement over the states unconstitutional, the clause is not the primary legal reasoning in the case.

The writer of the high-scoring response carefully addresses each requirement for Part B. The writer first summarizes the holdings in both cases and then explains a contrast between the two cases: one case concerns a restriction on state voting laws, and the other case essentially removes a restriction. The writer of the low-scoring response correctly summaries both cases, but since the response never explains how the holdings contrast, it would not earn full points.

For Part C, the writer of the high-scoring response fully describes a potential response of civil rights groups. The writer begins the final paragraph with a brief explanation of why a civil rights group might be concerned about the *Shelby* decision, which, while not necessary, helps demonstrate the writer's deep understanding of the political scenario. The writer of the low-scoring response vaguely *identifies* a possible reaction of a civil rights group, but the response is insufficient because it provides no *description* of the action "have protests."

Rubric for Question 4: 6 Points (1 + 3 + 1 + 1)

Category	Appropriate Responses	Notes
A: Thesis (**1 pt** for stating a thesis that can be defended, is responsive to the issue posed, and sets up a line of reasoning)	"Human equality [is/is not] a founding principle of the United States because…"	You cannot earn a point by simply pointing out that the equality struggle is an ongoing U.S. concern—that is, by essentially repeating the prompt. You must "choose a side," to quote the prompt, and will gain a sure 1 pt by announcing that side up front.
B: Support (**1 pt** for presenting a piece of evidence relevant to the topic)	A statement or piece of evidence on the topic of equality that does not provide specific support for your thesis.	Example: you make a reasonable statement about a historical group's activities in advancing or resisting equality but neglect to relate those activities to the notion of U.S. founding principles.
OR B: Support (**2 pts** for using a single piece of evidence appropriately supporting your thesis)	• Declaration of Independence: "All men are created equal" • U.S. Constitution: equality is reflected in the Fourteenth, Fifteenth, and/or Nineteenth Amendments • Letter From a Birmingham Jail: Dr. King's detailing of how discrimination in practice contradicts the Declaration's and the Constitution's aspirational language.	Including a relevant reference from one of the listed founding documents is essential. Clearly state the document you are using and present the relevant information contained in it. (They don't expect direct quotes other than the briefest or most famous, but they do want to see that you've absorbed what you read.)
OR B: Support (**3 pts** for using two pieces of evidence appropriately supporting your thesis)	• "Patrick Henry didn't announce 'Give me equality or give me death.' He believed liberty is paramount because it creates the possibility of people's being treated equally." • "Chief Justice Taney, in the *Dred Scott* decision, left no ambiguity that African Americans at that time were not considered 'people' as the Declaration of Independence saw them." • "The defeat of the Equal Rights Amendment reflects the ongoing opposition in this country to confirming people's equality in hard-and-fast law."	Your second piece of evidence can come from your reading or general knowledge. Be sure that it is relevant and supports your thesis.

(Continued)

(Continued)

Category	Appropriate Responses	Notes
C: Reasoning (**1 pt** for explaining why or how your evidence supports your thesis)	• "The Declaration of Independence was one of the first attempts by any nation to enshrine equality as a foundational principle. That means that its signers must have known how extraordinary and difficult it would be to make that equality a reality for everyone." • "The very fact that women's suffrage was not made universal until 1920 indicates the huge gap between the rhetoric and the reality." • "Despite his careful politeness and humility throughout the Birmingham letter, you can feel Dr. King's exasperation that fellow clergymen could be so obtuse. How could they not see that the struggle to end discrimination through committed nonviolent activism was a reflection of foundational values like equality?"	Don't assume that the AP reader will understand that the evidence you presented supports a particular point that you are making. Be sure to state explicitly how the evidence demonstrates your point.
D: Reply to Alternative Viewpoint (**1 pt** for offering a point of view different from yours and going on to rebut, refute, or concede it)	You present a point in favor of the other opinion—in favor of equality as a foundational value if you have been arguing against it, or vice versa—and either show it to be false, argue that it is not valid, or concede it may have some validity.	Don't just assert that the other side is wrong. Provide a reason (rebut it) or grant their point (concede it), while not backing away from your own view. Example: admitting your opponent could assert that the U.S. has made considerable progress on the equality front, but rebutting that view by claiming that the legacy of the founding documents has made that progress slower than it ought to have been.

Sample High-Scoring Response

Our founding documents state or imply a belief in equality for everyone, if the term is understood to mean moral equality, or equality under God. They provide an inspiring goal for the U.S. nation, even though equality under the law and equality in each person's eyes have been a long time coming and still are far from becoming a reality.

The Declaration of Independence, the first real attempt at a statement of American aspirational principles, states clearly and unambiguously that "all men are created equal." At the time that Thomas Jefferson wrote the Declaration, the words "men" and "mankind" were widely understood and used as collective nouns for all human beings. Reading Jefferson's words conveys no sense of deliberate exclusion—quite the reverse. It would be an insult to the Declaration's ringing rhetoric about the uniqueness of America to assume that buried within it is some sinister patriarchal power play. After all, the founders rejected the institution of monarchy, the ultimate expression of patriarchy. Moreover, attitudes and norms change, something the founders had to know. They had to anticipate that at some point the rhetoric would be applied to everyone.

The Constitution is in some ways even more clear about this lack of exclusion. The Preamble begins, "We the People of the United States"—not "We the land-owning white males of the United States"—and sets forth a series of objectives like "the common defense" and "the general Welfare," which are clearly meant to benefit all people living in the US. It took constitutional amendments such as the Fifteenth and Nineteenth (which removed constraints on race and gender, respectively, to the right to vote) to realize this founding principle of equality fully, but the aspirational language is unmistakably present in the original document.

Some may contend that the fact that these amendments were necessary shows that equality was not a founding principle, but one which only emerged later in the history of the United States. Indeed, many of the framers, including Jefferson himself, owned slaves, and the original Constitution even suggested that a slave was only 3/5 of a person—a clear contradiction to the principle of equality. But to say that equality was a founding principle is not the same thing as saying it was the only founding principle. For example, the principle of liberty, which included the notion that states have some rights to self-determination, also played a role in the compromises that forged the Constitution. So even though the founders did not always apply the principle of equality consistently, there can be no question that a group of people who rejected the divine right of kings to rule truly believed that "all men are created equal."

Sample Low-Scoring Response

There are many pretty words about equality in the Declaration and Constitution and other founding documents. But there really is not a commitment to equality woven into the American "tapestry." Just empty words that 200+ years of life in this country have failed to live up to.

Dr. Martin Luther King Jr. put it best in his Letter from a Birmingham Jail when he said that justice delayed is justice denied, and that the word "wait" always means "never." Wait and wait and wait, and it took forever for local or state or federal governments to throw the descendants of slavery a few crumbs of equal treatment. If America was founded, as the prompt says, on the concept of equality for everyone, then what took so long? Talk is cheap, like they say.

People who take that inspiring language as foundational are patriots but they have blinders on. They fail to see that all that fancy language doesn't mean anything to ordinary people on the ground who are treated like 3/5 of a person. "All men are created equal" is a nice thought but the country hasn't lived up to that.

Explanation of Sample Responses

Both essays would earn 1 point for Thesis. The high-scoring response clearly advocates for equality as a founding principle, while the low-scoring response rejects that idea. Both essays do a decent job of sticking to the prompt and asserting a clear stance.

With respect to Support, the high-scoring response would earn all 3 points while the low-scoring response would earn 2 at most. The high-scoring response cites both the Declaration of Independence and the Preamble to the Constitution, along with some of the amendments, and elaborates on the language these documents contain. The low-scoring response only references King's Letter for support, but some other evidence would be necessary to earn all 3 points.

The high-scoring response would earn 1 point for Reasoning, because the writer goes on at length about how each of the documents provides support to the idea that equality was a founding principle, something that the framers aspired to. In contrast, the low-scoring response would probably earn no points, because there is not sufficient explanation of how King's Letter challenges the idea that equality is a founding principle. The second paragraph is too vague to establish the connection adequately. Don't just assume that the grader will understand references that lack specificity.

Finally, for Reply to Alternative Viewpoint, the high-scoring response would earn 1 point, but the low-scoring response would not. The first essay elaborates on the idea that the principle of equality was contradicted by support for slavery, but answers that this only shows that there were other founding principles, in addition to equality, which also played a role in the creation of the nation. The low-scoring response not only fails to elaborate upon the opposing view, but treats it dismissively and almost disrespectfully. Dismissal of an opposing view is not sufficient to earn the point here.

Overall, the high-scoring response would earn a perfect 6 out of 6, while the low-scoring response would only earn 3 points, losing out in Support, Reasoning, and Reply to Alternative Viewpoint. The low-scoring response would have done better to include at least one other source of evidence, to go into more specific details about the evidence and how it supports the thesis, and to offer a more respectful and rigorous treatment of the opposing view.

PRACTICE EXAM 3 ANSWERS AND EXPLANATIONS

Section I

1. C

The graph shows an even distribution of income growth in the 1947–1981 period, with all income groups seeing roughly between 80 and 110 percent growth. In contrast, the 1981–2015 period sees the distribution of income growth skewed left, with gains increasingly concentrated in the high-percentile earners. Thus, **(C)** is correct. (A) incorrectly states that lower-income groups saw the same major gains as higher-income groups during the 1981–2015 period. (B) is incorrect because the 60th and 80th percentile income groups saw the greatest gains in the 1947–1981 period. (D) is incorrect because the growth of the post-World War II middle class can most strongly be seen in the 1947–1981 period, when income growth was both large and evenly distributed across income groups.

2. A

The data from the 1981–2015 period shows minimal gains for the lower classes while the wealthy enjoyed far greater income growth. In response to this trend, liberals would generally favor redistributive policies, such as progressive taxation on the wealthy and raising the minimum wage to boost the working class. **(A)** is correct. While liberals do favor a degree of wealth redistribution through economic policy, they do not typically favor the nationalization of industries; (B) is incorrect. (C) is incorrect because it describes a more characteristically conservative approach, and (D) is incorrect because it describes a libertarian approach.

3. B

The percentage of the total population that voted in presidential elections more than tripled over the course of the nineteenth century, from under 5 percent to roughly 20 percent, so **(B)** is correct. While the percentage basically doubled over the course of the twentieth century, the increase has not been a constant one; there were dips in the 1900s, 1940s, and 1990s. (A) and (D) are incorrect. In the nineteenth century, the percentage of the total population that voted in presidential elections was consistently above 15 percent starting in roughly 1868; (C) is incorrect.

4. C

The Nineteenth Amendment extended suffrage to women, which caused the U.S. presidential voter turnout to nearly double between 1900 and 1940; **(C)** is correct. The Twenty-Sixth Amendment lowered the voting age from 21 to 18, which resulted in a modest increase in turnout; it does not serve as the best explanation for the vast difference between 1900 and 2000, making (A) incorrect. The Voting Rights Act of 1965 safeguarded the constitutional right of African Americans to vote. However, as with the Twenty-Sixth Amendment, it only resulted in a modest rise in overall turnout throughout the whole country, so (B) is incorrect. The Seventeenth Amendment reformed the Senate so that its members were directly elected by the citizens of their respective states. This reform did not extend suffrage to anyone new, and thus is not relevant for presidential elections; (D) is incorrect.

5. A

Knowing which states belonged to which regions would make it easier to interpret the results or implications of the data presented in the graph. For example, while the South and Northeast are well-defined regions, the graph does not make it clear where the Midwest ends and the West begins, and how the Great Plains and Rocky Mountain states are divided between them. Even the makeup of the Midwest could be a matter of debate, as there is some overlap with the Northeast and the South. Therefore, **(A)** is correct. While a data table would more cleanly present the individual data points, a graph is preferable for visualizing the trends and implications of such a volume of data points; (B) is incorrect. There are sufficient data points to discern the regional trends, such as the growth and relative decline of the Midwest region. Also, while the x-axis is set in twenty-year increments, the decade by decade nature of the data points is clearly discernible on the graph. (C) and (D) are incorrect.

6. D

Based on the trends in the line graph, it is accurate to conclude that the Republican Party gained a greater share of House seats in the South due to that region's population growth relative to the rest of the country after 1980. **(D)** is correct. The Republican Party's presence has been declining in the Northeast in recent decades, making (A) incorrect. Likewise, the Democratic Party has declined in the South since the 1960s, so (B) is incorrect. While the Democratic Party traditionally had a lock on the South until the mid-1960s, between 1900 and 1950 the population of the South relative to the rest of the country held steady, meaning the Democrats would have neither gained nor lost seats; (C) is incorrect.

7. B

The share of the college-educated population is growing, increasing from under 10 percent in 1955 to roughly 25 percent in 2016. Thus, **(B)** is correct. Given the decline of the elementary school population from about 65 percent in 1955 to about 40 percent in 2016, it follows that the youngest generation is not gaining a greater share of the overall population; (A) is incorrect. The share of the high school population has held steady at approximately 20 percent between 1955 and 2016, with a brief increase between 1975 and 1985; (C) is incorrect. (D) is incorrect because the share of the population that is in kindergarten has held steady at a little under 5 percent of the population.

8. D

The implication of the trends illustrated in the graph is that the Democratic Party's voter base is likely to grow due to the increasing numbers of college-educated voters, as higher levels of education are associated with a tendency to vote for Democratic candidates. The Republican Party draws less support from college-educated voters and more support from voters who do not have a college education. Thus, **(D)** is correct while (B) and (C) are incorrect. Although the youth vote is strongly associated with

the Democratic Party, there is no recent swelling of the elementary and high school share of the population. The swell associated with the Baby Boomers is apparent circa 1955 on the graph, but there is nothing comparable in the twenty-first century; (A) is incorrect.

9. D

According to the table, 47 percent of white Evangelicals are in favor of overturning *Roe v. Wade* while only 34 percent of Catholics are in favor of overturning it. Thus, **(D)** is correct. (A) is incorrect because 33 percent of those ages 50+ are in favor of overturning *Roe*, while only 24 percent of those ages 18–49 are in favor. (B) is incorrect because 74 percent of college graduates oppose overturning *Roe* while only 70 percent of people who have completed some college oppose overturning it. (C) is incorrect because 67 percent of men and 72 percent of women oppose overturning *Roe*.

10. A

The data shows that both support for and opposition to *Roe v. Wade* are largely consistent regardless of gender or age group. **(A)** is correct, as there does not seem to be a major change in public opinion approaching despite ongoing demographic change in the United States. The table does not indicate that the views of those who are older have changed over time, making (B) incorrect. The data does not illustrate the age breakdown of those who identify as Democrats or Republicans; (C) is incorrect because it infers too much from limited data. While those who identify as white Evangelicals and those who complete a high school education or less are more likely to agree on whether to overturn *Roe v. Wade*, it is not evident from the data that a person's religion dictates their level of education; (D) is incorrect.

11. D

The Supreme Court's decision in *Gibbons v. Ogden* affirms congressional power over interstate commerce because Marshall explains that the delegates in Annapolis "found no means, but in a general government" to form a "uniform regulation of trade"; **(D)** is correct. Marshall states, "If it had not so provided, the constitution would not have been worth accepting," which clarifies that the Constitution originally defined the federal government as the regulator of interstate commerce; (A) and (B) are incorrect. (C) is incorrect because it overstates the case being made. When Marshall speaks of the mistaken belief about commerce regulation "as still residing in the States," he means that while the states still possess their own powers distinct from the federal government, those state powers no longer include the regulation of interstate commerce.

12. C

In *Gibbons v. Ogden*, the Supreme Court found that Congress has ample power to regulate commerce; this is the "uniform regulation of trade" that Marshall references in the excerpt. **(C)** is correct. The excerpt does not suggest limits to Congress's ability to regulate interstate commerce or how Congress interacts with local activity, making (A), (B), and (D) incorrect.

13. B

The quoted excerpt suggests that the federal government should regulate trade between states; **(B)** is correct. While Marshall's opinion gives the federal government broad authority in regulating commerce, it does not extend to every activity. For example, education is still a state-level matter. Thus, (A) is incorrect. (C) is incorrect because it describes the concept of nullification, which goes against the federal power inherent in Marshall's opinion. Marshall states that Congress, not state governments, should regulate "foreign and domestic trade," which would naturally cover trade between a state like Maine and another country like Canada; (D) is incorrect.

14. A

While the specific mechanism varies by state, legislatures at the state level have the right to determine how federal congressional districts are redrawn following each national census. Thus, **(A)** is correct. *Gibbons v. Ogden* affirms congressional power over interstate commerce; (B) is incorrect. Even though *McCulloch v. Maryland* established the supremacy of the federal government over the states, nullification has been functionally untenable since the Civil War; (C) is incorrect. While states may

freely enter into a compact with one another if the compact does not increase the power of the states at the expense of the federal government, all other such compacts require the consent of Congress. (D) is incorrect.

15. A

In the excerpt, Alito explains that the Bill of Rights "originally applied only to the Federal Government, not to the States, but the constitutional Amendments adopted in the Civil War's aftermath fundamentally altered the federal system," meaning that the Bill of Rights now applies to states; thus, **(A)** is correct and (B) is incorrect. In *Cruikshank*, *Presser*, and *Miller*, "the Court held that the Second Amendment applies only to the Federal Government," which would be the opposite of what Alito is arguing; (C) is incorrect. (D) is incorrect since the excerpt suggests that the Court had previously read the Fourteenth Amendment in a "narrow" way, not that this case violated it.

16. B

Judicial activism holds that the primary purpose of government is to promote justice and equality. Judicial restraint advocates for limited government and stresses the need for caution when changing the status quo. Selective incorporation of the Bill of Rights on a case-by-case basis is an expression of judicial restraint, while the proposed idea of total incorporation of the Bill of Rights to the states would be the judicial activist approach. Therefore, **(B)** is correct while (A) is incorrect. Although originalism is closely tied to judicial restraint, it is a more strident and reactive expression of it, holding that the Constitution must be interpreted using the commonly understood definitions of its terms at the time it was adopted. As such, an originalist would likely not incorporate the Bill of Rights to any degree. (C) is incorrect. Strict scrutiny is the most rigorous standard for reviewing the constitutionality of law. As Justice Alito is discussing the Supreme Court's general approach to the Fourteenth Amendment rather than any specific law, that review process does not apply here. So, (D) is incorrect.

17. A

Passed after the Civil War, the Fourteenth Amendment altered the federal system through its equal protection clause, which applied the Bill of Rights to the states and not just the federal government. *McDonald v. Chicago* resulted in a ruling that applied the Second Amendment to the states. Thus, **(A)** is correct. Although (B) generally outlines the role of the Fourteenth Amendment, it incorrectly overstates events, as the Bill of Rights has only been selectively incorporated at the state level on a case-by-case basis over time. Total incorporation would require the application of the entire Bill of Rights to the state level, including rights not yet incorporated, as the Second Amendment was not by 2010. The privileges and immunities clause of the Constitution was not overturned by the Fourteenth Amendment; (C) is incorrect. While nullification is no longer considered legally plausible in the aftermath of the Civil War, that is the result of the war itself rather than the post-war amendments; (D) is incorrect.

18. B

Article III of the Constitution establishes the Supreme Court of the United States (SCOTUS) and authorizes Congress to create "inferior" courts at its discretion. Today, the federal court system consists of 94 trial courts (known as district courts) and 13 appellate courts (known as courts of appeals), in addition to the Supreme Court. Thus, **(B)** is correct while (A), (C), and (D) are incorrect.

19. A

Kansas and Oklahoma are indeed covered by the United States court of appeals for the Tenth Circuit. Thus, **(A)** is correct. California is covered by the Ninth Circuit, not the Seventh; (B) is incorrect. Although Florida and Georgia are covered by the Eleventh Circuit, Mississippi is not. Rather, the third slot is filled by Alabama. (C) is incorrect. The First Circuit is in the Northeast and consists of Maine, New Hampshire, Massachusetts, and Rhode Island; (D) is incorrect.

20. B

The cartoon shows two newspaper editors arguing about which of them most influenced America's entry into war; the artist of the cartoon is trying to persuade viewers that the sensationalism of newspapers has negatively affected American politics. Today, potential bias in the media continues to be a subject of debate, and media discourse continues to influence political decision making; **(B)** is correct. Although (A) identifies an area of controversy concerning media and politics, political "personalities" are not portrayed in the political cartoon, which contains news editors, not politicians. (C) incorrectly downplays the influence of media. Finally, (D) is neither depicted in the cartoon nor accurately reflecting typical voter behavior; voters tend to seek media that affirms preexisting views.

21. B

The artist of the cartoon is trying to persuade viewers that the newspapers exhibit strong viewpoints that can ultimately influence America's political decisions, including entry into wars. Thus, varying one's consumption of news by seeking out many different outlets would allow an informed citizen to avoid undue bias in the media. So, **(B)** is correct. (A) is incorrect because it goes too far; the media can influence congressional decisions indirectly, but cannot strip Congress of enumerated powers. (C) is incorrect because the equal-time rule dictates that television and radio broadcast stations must provide an equal opportunity to any opposing political candidates who request it. This rule should not be confused with the now-defunct Fairness Doctrine, which dealt with presenting balanced points of view on matters of public importance. Although the artist is critical of certain newspaper publishers, there is nothing in the cartoon to suggest that artist favors abolishing the freedom of the press; (D) is incorrect.

22. A

Property taxes brought in approximately 13.1 billion dollars for state governments; **(A)** is correct. Although sales and gross receipts taxes are the single largest source of revenue for state governments, they constitute 46.4 percent of revenue, not 41.9 percent of revenue, which is actually the amount provided by income taxes. So, (B) is incorrect. Property taxes, not license taxes, are the smallest revenue source for state government, making (C) incorrect. Individual income taxes brought in 309.6 billion dollars, while corporate income taxes brought in 45 billion dollars; (D) is incorrect.

23. D

Education is a power reserved for state governments. Therefore, school systems would likely receive state revenue to continue operating; **(D)** is correct. Organizing the national defense, operating post offices, and regulating interstate commerce are all enumerated powers reserved to the federal government. They would not receive funding from the states, making (A), (B), and (C) incorrect.

24. D

The Supreme Court decision in *Shaw v. Reno* dealt with making sure that areas continue to comply with the Voting Rights Act of 1965 when redistricting; **(D)** is correct. (A), (B), and (C) are incorrect because none of these relate to redistricting or ensuring that voting rights and the equal protection clause are not violated.

25. C

In *Brutus* 1, when the author discusses how the idea of confederation will be totally lost as the central government assumes the responsibility to lay and collect taxes, he is making the case that the sovereignty of the states is ultimately rooted in their taxation powers, so the Constitution undermines them. Thus, **(C)** is correct. While Brutus does state that the Articles document was insufficient to the challenges facing the United States, that is not the core of his argument when discussing taxes; (A) is incorrect. Although Brutus draws attention to the Necessary and Proper Clause as a danger to state sovereignty, that is a separate and broader concern for Brutus than taxation powers. So, (B) is incorrect. While Brutus does argue that a large, diverse, centralized republic is unworkable on a practical level, that complaint is likewise not rooted in concerns over the federal government assuming the power to lay and collect taxes. (D) is incorrect.

26. C

The line-item veto has been deemed an unconstitutional abuse of the separation of powers, as it functionally gives the executive branch the ability to write legislation by picking and choosing what parts of a bill to accept; **(C)** is correct. (A) is incorrect because the separation of powers does not

allow for absolute executive privilege in withholding potentially relevant information from a criminal investigation. (B) is incorrect because it is, in fact, a proper expression of the separation of powers. The Senate must confirm any treaty by a two-thirds vote to make it legally binding. While Article II, Section 3 requires the president to make policy proposals to Congress "from time to time," it does not dictate how the president should do so; (D) is incorrect.

27. C

The equal protection clause provides the constitutional basis for Title IX, ensuring that men and women are treated equally in any federally funded activity. Thus, **(C)** is correct. Sex-specific laws are not considered a form of cruel and unusual punishment; (A) is incorrect. Birthright citizenship does, in a roundabout way, offer all Americans rights under the Constitution, including the equal protection clause, but it is not the direct constitutional basis for Title IX. (B) is incorrect. The First Amendment does not provide the basis for Title IX. While it is most famously associated with sports, Title IX covers all federally funded activities; (D) is incorrect.

28. C

Unfunded mandates occur when the federal government creates policies without allocating specific funds that local and state governments can use to implement those policies. Thus, **(C)** is correct. (A) is incorrect because it describes deficit spending. (B) is incorrect because federal government mandates require compliance; an example of this would be the Americans with Disabilities Act, which requires all private businesses to be accessible to disabled citizens but does not assist business owners with the cost of conforming to the act. (D) is incorrect because an unfunded mandate is a federal policy, not a state one.

29. C

The landmark decision *McCulloch v. Maryland* expanded Congress's ability to exercise its implied powers by interpreting the scope of the elastic clause; **(C)** is correct. Eminent domain is the power of a government to take private property for public use provided that the former owner is justly compensated. The U.S. Constitution, not the *McCulloch v. Maryland* decision, gives national and state governments this power; (A) is incorrect. The doctrine of preemption, not the *McCulloch v. Maryland* decision, restricts states' powers in areas reserved for the federal government in the Constitution, such as forming treaties with other nations, making (B) incorrect. *Marbury v. Madison* established the Supreme Court as the ultimate interpreter of the Constitution and stated that Supreme Court decisions are to become the supreme law of the land; (D) is incorrect.

30. C

Due process rights guarantee a citizen's basic rights to life, liberty, and property, protecting a U.S. citizen from being imprisoned without a public trial; **(C)** is correct. All men in the United States are required to register for military service within 30 days of their 18th birthday, making (A) incorrect. Defamation and libel laws protect citizens from newspapers publishing falsehoods about them; (B) is incorrect. (D) is incorrect since the Third Amendment, not due process, protects citizens from being forced to house soldiers in their homes.

31. D

An iron triangle is an alliance between interest groups, bureaucratic agencies, and legislative committees for the sake of a particular agenda. A deficit watchdog group would not share the agenda of the iron triangle members in this scenario, meaning it will have lesser influence over the Armed Services Committee. Thus, **(D)** is correct while (A) and (B) are incorrect. The Armed Services Committee has, as its name implies, oversight on military matters in Congress. This would naturally include reviewing a new fighter jet project. Thus, a different committee would not likely be pulled into a domain outside their area of concern, making (C) incorrect.

32. D

At the Constitutional Convention, one of the main arguments against electing the president by direct popular vote was that it would lead to uninformed voters making a decision without proper consideration of the candidates. **(D)** is correct. (A) is incorrect because it describes a fear about a proposal in which Congress would select the president. (B) is incorrect

because it describes a fear about a proposal in which the state legislatures would choose the president. (C) is incorrect because universal suffrage for white men was not yet a factor in American politics; most states limited voting rights to the wealthy, as they needed to own enough property to qualify to vote.

33. D

A political realignment is when the electoral base of a party changes, as does the political agenda of that party; **(D)** is correct. The other choices are incorrect because they describe other terms: a closed primary, an ex post facto law, and an interest group, respectively.

34. A

The media primarily influences public opinion through its choices about what news stories to cover or not cover. For example, continuing coverage of an overpass collapse that resulted in mass fatalities would help foment and sustain public outrage over infrastructure issues, possibly influencing the public and officials to embrace reform policies. **(A)** is correct. (B) is incorrect because it describes the now-defunct Fairness Doctrine, which was eliminated by the FCC in 1987. The news media generally turns elections into "horse races" and does not center its coverage on the platforms of the candidates; (C) is incorrect. While being an unbaised source may be an aspirational role of the media, there are many outlets that do not match this description and so it is not a fair statement to make of the media as a whole; (D) is incorrect.

35. C

Stare decisis holds that judicial precedent, once established, should not be reversed except in the most extraordinary circumstances. This provides for consistent and predictable results in court cases, which grants the judicial system legitimacy, but it also means that overturning precedent is a slow, often piecemeal process. Therefore, **(C)** is correct and (A) is incorrect. (B) is incorrect for two reasons. First, judges are unconcerned with political popularity mainly due to having lifetime appointments to the bench. Second, few interest groups go so far as to lobby against the judicial branch existing at all. Although (D) describes a tension between the judicial branch and liberal interest groups, that tension is based on originalism, also known as a strict-construction reading of the Constitution; (D) is incorrect.

36. A

A major problem for modern polling is the widespread decline of landlines, as many people in younger, more diverse demographics only own cell phones. This introduces a sampling error in many polls that must be accounted for through various means, such as by weighting the responses of poll participants by age, gender, race, and class. Therefore, **(A)** is correct. Both (B) and (D) are incorrect because they include large, randomized samples of the population, which would minimize any potential polling error. (C) is incorrect because benchmark polling specifically targets potential voters, allowing a candidate to calibrate their messaging early in a campaign. This typically involves a representative sample of voters, which would produce a low margin of error with a thousand participants.

37. D

For libertarians, a laissez-faire economic system promotes individual freedom by allowing people to have maximum control over their own economic choices; **(D)** is correct. (A) is incorrect because equality of outcome is where individuals within a society experience similar or equal material wealth and income. This typically requires a great deal of state intervention in the economy, which is against libertarian ideals. (B) is incorrect because ensuring equality of opportunity often requires governmental and legal protections, which go against the individual freedom emphasized at the heart of libertarianism. While libertarians do believe the rule of law, (C), should exist to the extent that the government can ensure fair dealing between individuals, it is not the core value promoted by a laissez-faire economic system.

38. D

Third-party candidates face multiple difficulties, including the structure of the election system (e.g., the Electoral College and other winner-take-all elections) and the tendency of voters to align with the major parties because they assume other candidates will not win. **(D)** is correct because it addresses a current challenge third parties face. In winner-take-all

systems, whichever candidate receives a plurality of the votes—or in other words, more votes than any other candidate—wins the entire district; using more proportional systems would likely increase the election of third-party candidates. (A) is incorrect because major parties adopting platforms that third-party voters support would likely cause more of those voters to vote for the major parties instead of third-party candidates. (B) is incorrect because, although some third-party candidates might benefit from such a system by receiving more funding from some individuals, overall this change would likely further benefit major party candidates, who already receive a greater share of overall contributions. Finally, prohibitions on write-in candidates in presidential elections, (C), is not a major difficulty that third-party candidates face. Most states already permit write-in candidates in some fashion; the difficulty lies in any one write-in candidate receiving enough votes to win a plurality of votes in the state.

39. B

The pluralist model emphasizes the need for different organized groups to compete against each other in order to influence policy. Interest groups such as the National Organization of Women (NOW) are an example of such organized groups. Thus, **(B)** is correct. The participatory model of democracy emphasizes broad citizen participation in government and politics, not group-based interests, making (A) incorrect. The elite model emphasizes limited participation in politics and civil society except by a select number of the wealthy and powerful. Again, this is not a group-based approach, so (C) is incorrect. Direct democracy involves citizens directly controlling the government and decision-making process and is thus based on raw majorities rather than group-based interests; (D) is incorrect.

40. B

The ruling in *Wisconsin v. Yoder* stated that compelling Amish students to attend school past the eighth grade violated the free exercise clause. This ruling provides part of the rationale for homeschooling; **(B)** is correct. (A) is incorrect because *Tinker* involved freedom of speech, not freedom of religion. Although the *Engel v. Vitale* decision, (C), involved public schools and religion, its focus was on state-sponsored religious activity. (D) is incorrect because *Shaw* did not involve the free exercise clause at all, but instead dealt with legislative redistricting.

41. B

The scenario describes a situation in which a private corporation spends money in a way that results in it broadcasting a political message, in this case opposing a particular candidate. **(B)** is the relevant consideration in this scenario, as this case determined that money spent by groups on political messages is protected speech under the First Amendment. (A) is incorrect because it does not refer to political spending, but rather to the application of the government's power to prohibit the publication of certain information in the press, which the Supreme Court determined can only be done if the publication would cause "grave and irreparable danger." (C) is incorrect because it is not relevant to determining the legality of political spending by a private corporation. The act identified in (D) *was* relevant to this scenario in the past, as it actually stated that corporations could *not* spend money on political messages; however, this provision was replaced by the ruling in *Citizens United v. FEC*. The 2002 act's restrictions on "hard money" contributions still stand, but soft money refers to contributions made to political parties or committees and is thus not relevant in this case. Thus, (D) is incorrect.

42. D

The free-rider problem refers to an interest group being unable to attract greater support among its potential base because everyone in that base is inherently represented in that interest group by default. Thus, outsiders don't need to join the group to enjoy its successes. **(D)** is correct. (A) is incorrect because it defines the political practice of litigating. (B) describes electioneering, but does so incorrectly. Interest groups intentionally electioneer for politicians in order to gain influence over them, as campaigning is intensive in time, money, and labor for politicians. (C) incorrectly describes lobbying. Former Congress members will use their connections to boost some interest groups, but not because they are centrists. Instead, they often do so because the groups are aligned with their party; for example, Democrats might more commonly lobby on behalf of unions than Republicans would.

43. C

The Fifteenth Amendment bans denying someone the right to vote due to the person's "race, color, or previous condition of servitude," while the Twenty-Sixth Amendment lowers the minimum voting age to 18. Thus, **(C)** is correct. (A) is incorrect because the first column refers to the Nineteenth Amendment and the second column does not reflect any amendment, though it does reflect current federal election law. Likewise, the content of (B) does not reflect any amendments. Finally, while the first column of (D) refers to a voting restriction associated with racism, the second column is incorrect. Direct election of senators was established early in the twentieth century, which implies it is not likely to be one of the last few amendments; (D) is incorrect.

44. A

Voters make decisions in the rational-choice model based on who they think will benefit them personally, while voters make decisions in the prospective model based on who they think will perform well in the near future. **(A)** is correct because it provides a rationale based on personal benefit in the first column and based on future performance in the second column. (B) is incorrect because it reflects the party-line model (voting by party) in the first column and a mix of party-line and retrospective models in the second column. Both columns in (C) reflect the retrospective model (voting based on past performance), so (C) is incorrect. The first column of (D) reflects the prospective model, while the second column of (D) reflects the retrospective model; (D) is incorrect.

45. B

Shaw v. Reno established that legislative redistricting must be conscious of race and ensure compliance with the Voting Rights Act of 1965. *Baker v. Carr* established that, although the creation of congressional districts is a state responsibility, allegations of inappropriate redistricting can be heard in federal court. Thus, **(B)** is correct and (D) is incorrect. (A) is incorrect because it describes the *McCulloch* and

Tinker decisions, respectively. (C) is incorrect because it describes the *New York Times v. United States* and *Tinker* cases, respectively.

46. C

Two examples of the United States' checks and balances are the president's ability to veto any bill passed by Congress and Congress's unique ability to declare war and fund the U.S. military; **(C)** is correct. The president can declare a state of emergency, and Congress passes bills, making (A) incorrect. (B) is incorrect since the Supreme Court, not the president, exercises judicial review. The Supreme Court, not Congress, decides how laws should be interpreted; (D) is incorrect.

47. B

Individualism is the focus on individual rights and responsibilities. *Gideon v. Wainwright* dealt with the Sixth Amendment's guarantee of the right to an attorney, an individual right, so **(B)** is correct. Equality of opportunity is the notion that all people, when treated equally, will be able to succeed or fail based on their own personal merits. *New York Times v. United States* does not deal with that core value, but rather with the rule of law; (A) is incorrect. Limited government is the idea that the government's power is enumerated and constrained by constitutional rules. *Schenck v. United States* (1919) dealt with the ability of the government to regulate speech and was based on a wartime crackdown of anti-draft activism, so it does not embody the core value of limited government. (C) is incorrect. Free enterprise is the economic practice of private business competing with as little government regulation as possible. However, *McDonald* deals primarily with the Second Amendment, part of the Bill of Rights, so it is better associated with individualism or the rule of law. (D) is incorrect.

48. D

The division of responsibilities in the impeachment process reflects the standard setup of the judicial system, in which the accusers and the judges are not the same body. So, **(D)** is correct. At the time the Constitution was written, senators were not popularly elected; (A) is incorrect. The House members

judge the president when they vote on articles of impeachment, so (B) is incorrect. It is the Senate that agrees to or dismisses the House's accusations of the president. Supreme Court justices have enjoyed lifetime appointments since the creation of the Constitution; (C) is incorrect.

49. C

In order to ensure that a randomized poll is representative of the general population, polling companies will often weight the responses they collect by their demographic qualities. For example, if a telephone poll only contacted landlines, that poll would need to account for the low ownership of landlines among young people in order to avoid older people being over-represented in the result. Thus, **(C)** is correct. (A) is incorrect because tracking polls contact the same participants each time data is collected. In other words, the opinions of the same people are being "tracked." (B) is incorrect because separating out likely voters from registered voters is only done after a randomized poll has been properly weighted demographically. While demographic weighting does minimize the errors in a poll, (D) is incorrect because sample size refers to the raw number of participants polled. The survey company did not aim to poll as many people as it could. Rather, it tried to compensate for the number of people polled through demographic weighting.

50. A

The Virginia Plan proposed a bicameral legislature elected on the basis of population. This would have given the larger, more populous states like Virginia greater political power compared to the smaller, less populous states like New Jersey; **(A)** is correct. (B) is incorrect because it describes our current constitutional arrangement for the legislative branch, which was proposed in the Connecticut Compromise. (C) is incorrect because it describes the New Jersey Plan, which had a unicameral legislature with seats allotted by state rather than by population. While the Anti-Federalists were concerned with the lack of a Bill of Rights in the Constitution, they did not care about the details of the Virginia Plan. (D) is incorrect.

51. C

United States v. Lopez was important because it held that the commerce clause had to be related to interstate commerce of some sort. For example, the *Lopez* precedent would hold that the crime of battery could not be federalized under the commerce clause because the activity involved did not cross state lines and did not involve commerce. Thus, **(C)** is correct. That same reasoning allows for a federal crime to be made out of a kidnapping victim being transported across state lines; (A) is incorrect. Marijuana cultivation can be regulated by the federal government because local commerce can affect interstate commerce. The same is true of international commerce, so (B) and (D) are incorrect.

52. D

If Congress disagrees with a Supreme Court ruling, it may attempt to propose an amendment to the Constitution by a two-thirds vote from the House and the Senate; **(D)** is correct. Congress does not have the power to veto a ruling, ask the executive branch to veto a decision, or vote to restart a case through the judicial system, making (A), (B), and (C) incorrect.

53. B

The wide-ranging regulatory powers of the federal bureaucracy are often contentious because, while their regulations affect American businesses and consumers, their officials are not democratically elected, which some critics charge as representing a lack of political legitimacy. Therefore, **(B)** is correct. While the public has to abide by the rules they create, federal bureaucratic agencies do hold hearings to allow the public and businesses to offer input during the drafting of new or revised rules; (A) is incorrect. Conservative-leaning critics often charge that the private sector can take on many roles of the federal bureaucracy and do those tasks more efficiently. They propose this as an alternative, not a description of the current state of affairs. (C) is incorrect. (D) is incorrect because the federal bureaucracy's critics typically favor a small federal government that provides limited social services, not the opposite.

54. A

According to supply-side economic theory, once the wealthy have more money at their disposal, they will reinvest it, thus stimulating the production of goods. This increase in supply would then drive demand and reinvigorate the economy for everyone. Thus, **(A)** is correct. (B) is incorrect because it describes Keynesian economic theory. (C) is incorrect because, even though it presents a policy that is consistent with supply-side economic theory, it does not present an expected consequence of wealth concentration at the top (instead offering a way to increase this concentration further). (D) is incorrect because it describes a redistributive approach to economics, which is explicitly opposed by supply-side theory.

55. B

Anti-Federalists were wary of a strong central government and wanted to ensure the sovereignty of the states and preserve individual rights. Therefore, they favored a weaker central government and supported a bill of rights for the Constitution. **(B)** correctly reflects these positions. (A) is incorrect because the Anti-Federalists were suspicious of the role of president, fearing it would concentrate too much power in the executive and lead to similar abuses as under British monarchical rule. Likewise, (C) is incorrect because it is an argument used by Federalists, who also considered a bill of rights redundant due to Article X's provision that powers not delegated to the central government were reserved for the states or people. Finally, (D) is incorrect because, while it correctly identifies that Anti-Federalists supported a bill of rights, it gives an incorrect reason for their support.

ANSWERS AND EXPLANATIONS

Section II

The following are general rubrics an AP reader might use to grade these free-response questions. Use both this scoring information and the sample responses to assess your own writing.

Rubric for Question 1: 4 Points (2 + 1 + 1)

Part A (2 points)

One point for correctly describing how votes in the Electoral College are assigned.

- Responses MUST include: The number of electoral votes is based on a state's population; the greater a state's population, the more electoral votes it has.
- Responses MAY include: The concepts of winner-take-all and faithless electors.

One point for correctly describing how individual electors are chosen.

- Responses MUST include: U.S. citizens indirectly select a party's electors to vote for the next president.
- Responses MAY include: Citizens do not directly vote for a president or vice president; instead, the selected electors do.

Part B (1 point)

One point for explaining how the Electoral College has changed since the Constitution was drafted.

- Responses MUST include: Explanation of a change with before and after details (for example, when the Constitution was originally drafted, the candidate receiving the most votes became president and the candidate receiving the second-most votes became vice president; today, a candidate must receive an absolute majority of electoral votes, and electors vote for a joint ticket).
- Responses MAY include: Historical details about the creation of the Electoral College at the time the Constitution was drafted.

Part C (1 point)

One point for accurately explaining one effect of the Electoral College's winner-take-all system on the outcome of U.S. presidential elections.

- Responses MUST include: The winner-take-all system means that all of a state's electoral votes will go to a single candidate; this system makes it hard for a third-party candidate to gain enough electoral votes to become president.
- Responses MAY include: The winner-take-all rule applies in 48 states plus Washington, D.C.; the rule encourages candidates to campaign heavily in swing states.

Sample High-Scoring Response

Once the U.S. population casts its votes on Election Day, these votes are counted; however, the people do not directly elect a vice president or a president. Instead, popular votes determine which party's electors will join the Electoral College; this is the group that elects the president and the vice president. Each state has a certain number of electoral votes based on its population. The greater a state's population, the more electoral votes it has. It's very rare for an elector to defect against the popular vote, so if the popular vote within a state goes toward a certain candidate, this candidate will more than likely win all of that state's electoral votes.

The Founding Fathers originally set up the Electoral College as a compromise that allowed the people to have a voice in deciding who voted for the nation's next leader while also continuing Congress's role in the election. When the Constitution was drafted, a state chose its electors based on the number of senators and representatives it had, and the electors then voted for two candidates each. The candidate receiving the most votes would become president, and the one who received the second-most votes would become vice president. If no candidate received a majority, the House of Representatives would choose from the leading three candidates. Today, while the selection process for electors is the same, a candidate must receive an absolute majority of at least 270 electoral votes to become president, and the Electoral College is made up of 538 electors. In addition, electors today vote with a joint ticket, which is a ticket containing sets of presidential/vice presidential candidates, in order to ensure that the president and vice president will be part of the same political party.

The winner-take-all system in the Electoral College makes it very difficult for any third-party candidate to become president or vice president. This is the case because 48 states (excluding Maine and Nebraska) plus Washington, D.C., have a winner-take-all rule that dictates that whoever wins the popular vote in that state or district will win all of that state's electoral votes. In addition, this winner-take-all system encourages modern presidential candidates from the two major parties to spend more time campaigning in states where the vote is more evenly split, and, thus, all of the state's electoral votes could go either way.

Sample Low-Scoring Response

The Electoral College is a group of people who elect the president and vice president. With the exception of five presidents, the candidate who wins the popular vote typically becomes the next U.S. president. However, because five presidents have missed out on the popular vote while winning the majority of electoral votes, they became president. Each election year, U.S. citizens vote for new electors, who are responsible for submitting the aforementioned electoral votes. Every state has a specific number of electoral votes, the distribution of which is dependent on numerous factors. But overall, the selection of those who submit electoral votes is very significant since these votes carry much more weight in terms of presidential elections than the popular votes submitted by U.S. citizens.

Over time, the Electoral College has become a bit stricter in terms of how it votes. When the Constitution was drafted, the electors had more freedom to vote for whomever they thought would make the best president. Today, they tend to vote how the population voted. Additionally, the president today must win a majority of the electoral votes. This was not the case in previous years.

The Electoral College has a winner-take-all rule in which state electors vote the way the population did. This makes it very clear-cut in terms of who eventually wins the election and also minimizes the number of times the victor ends up winning the election but losing the popular vote.

Explanation of Sample Responses

The high-scoring response covers the basics of the Electoral College, as required for Part A, including how votes for the Electoral College are assigned and how individual electors are chosen. This writer also explains how this factors into the election itself. The low-scoring response, on the other hand, only covers superficial aspects of the Electoral College, such as how the popular vote and electoral votes are different, and only explains how electors are selected and how votes are assigned in general terms. Note that the writer of the low-scoring response also repeats the stimulus wording without additional analysis.

The high-scoring response communicates how the Electoral College was created, how it originally functioned after the Constitution was drafted, and how it now functions, which answers Part B. On the contrary, the low-scoring response includes vague statements, such as "a bit stricter in terms of how it votes," and doesn't adequately explain how the Electoral College has changed since the Constitution was drafted.

In accordance with Part C, the writer of the high-scoring response explains the main impact of the winner-take-all system on the outcome of U.S. presidential elections: the decreased chance that a third-party candidate will become president. In addition, this writer correctly states that 48 states and Washington, D.C., all uphold the winner-take-all system and that a candidate is likely to campaign more heavily in states that are split. The low-scoring sample, however, does not adequately explain the impact of the winner-take-all system for Part C; the response fails to even define what the system is, only stating that "the state electors vote the way the population did." The writer also does not fully develop any supporting points.

Rubric for Question 2: 5 Points (2 + 1 + 2)

Part A (2 points)

One point for comparing the changes in representation over time for California and New Hampshire. Note: To earn the point, the response must describe changes in representation in BOTH states.

- Example changes: CA's percentage of total representatives increased over time, while NH's percentage decreased; CA's number of representatives increased significantly over time, while NH's number remained relatively constant.

One point for discussing an implication based on the changes.

- Example implications: CA's population has increased significantly over time; NH's population may have increased over time, but constitutes a smaller percentage of the total U.S. population than it did in the late 1700s; the number of total representatives in the House likely increased over time as more states were added and total U.S. population grew, but was capped in the 1900s.

Part B (1 point)

One point for explaining how the structure of Congress reflects the writers' intentions.

- Responses MUST include: two senators from each state; writers intended to have two-house (bicameral) structure with representation in one house based on population and one house with equal representation from each state.

- Responses MAY include: Great (Connecticut) Compromise.

Part C (2 points)

One point for discussing a possible advantage OR a possible disadvantage of the two-house structure of Congress.

- Example advantages: bicameral structure allows representation to be based on both proportional population and by each state individually; bicameral structure reflects the compromise reached by the writers of the Constitution, particularly those from large versus small states; bicameral structure helps address the issue of legislative gridlock that was a problem under the Articles of Confederation; bicameral structure helps maintain checks and balances by limiting the power of each house.

- Example disadvantages: representation still potentially unfair, as states with large populations could be considered underrepresented in the Senate; bicameral structure slows the legislative process.

One point for including relevant evidence from the table to support the advantage or disadvantage.

Sample High-Scoring Response

Overall, the number of representatives from California steadily increased over time, while New Hampshire's number of representatives remained relatively constant. Another change is in the percentage of total representatives in Congress: CA steadily increased, growing from less than 1% to over 12% of total representatives, while NH decreased from about 7.5% to only about 1% today. Because representation in the House is determined by population, these trends indicate that CA has steadily increased in population since becoming a state, experiencing large jumps in population, and thus representation, from 1930 onward. With NH's relatively steady number of representatives but declining percentage, the data suggests that NH started with a larger proportion of the country's overall population compared to its proportion today.

The fluctuating numbers of representatives shown in the table reflect part of the Great Compromise that was made in order to secure ratification of the Constitution. Large and small states disagreed about how to determine representation in Congress. While delegates from small states balked at a system of representation that was based purely on population, delegates from large states felt that a system in which each state had equal representation (as under the Articles of Confederation) did not fairly represent their states' larger populations. To appease both sides, the Great Compromise structured the legislative branch in its current form, with representation in the House of Representatives based on relative populations, while each state would send two senators to the Senate. Since the approval of both houses is needed to pass laws, representation in Congress is thus based on both each state's population and individual state status. In relation to the data, CA thus has a much higher number of representatives in the House than NH based on their populations, though both states have equal representation in the Senate.

A possible disadvantage of the structure of Congress is that it still gives disproportionate representation to smaller states, since each state has equal standing in the Senate. Also, the Senate is considered the upper house, possessing some powers that the House lacks, such as holding confirmation and impeachment hearings. As indicated by the percentages of total representatives in the table, CA must have approximately 12% of the country's population, while NH has only about 1%. Despite this discrepancy, both have equal standing in the Senate; thus, CA could be said to have too small and NH too great an influence in the decisions the Senate makes, despite the states' very different populations.

Sample Low-Scoring Response

The table shows that the total number of representatives from California has increased over time, while the number of representatives from New Hampshire has decreased. The data indicates that California's population has been increasing over time, but that New Hampshire's state population has been steady, since its number of representatives has remained relatively constant.

Representation in the Senate is equal for each state: each state sends two senators. Each state has a different number of representatives in the House, the number of which is proportional to each state's population as determined by censuses. This system is still the same as the one the writers of the Constitution developed in Article I.

One advantage of this structure is that Congress is bicameral. The table demonstrates that the number of representatives in the House can be different from state to state, as California has many more representatives than New Hampshire does today, 53 compared to 5.

Explanation of Sample Responses

The writers of both responses attempt to address the two requirements of Part A, comparing the changes in both states and discussing an implication. The writer of the high-scoring response effectively includes specific data, describes two changes in trends, and discusses a relevant implication of the changes. The writer of the low-scoring response confuses New Hampshire's raw numbers of representatives with its percentages of total representatives, incorrectly stating that NH's *number* of representatives, rather than its *percentage* of representatives, has decreased over time. The low-scoring response also distorts the implication: NH's relatively steady number of representatives does not indicate that its population has remained steady; rather, it has had a relatively constant number of representatives, based on its percentage of the total U.S. population, even as the number of total representatives in the House increased over time. Since the late 1800s, New Hampshire has had less than 2 percent of the total U.S. population.

The writer of the high-scoring response carefully addresses all the requirements of Part B, not only describing how representation is determined in both houses of Congress, but also specifically explaining how this structure reflects the framers' intentions and is illustrated by the table data. While the writer of the low-scoring response accurately describes representation in Congress and explains how it reflects the framers' intentions, the writer fails to relate this description to the table data.

Part C asks the writer to discuss an advantage *or* a disadvantage, as long as data from the table is incorporated as support. The writer of the high-scoring response fully discusses a possible disadvantage, explaining why representation in the Senate might be unfair based on its structure of equal representation from each state, regardless of state population. The response includes the effective use of data from the table to support its argument. In contrast, the writer of the low-scoring response attempts to identify an advantage, but fails to explain *why* Congress's bicameral structure is an advantage. The response contains data from the table, but the writer does not use the data in support of any statements.

Rubric for Question 3: 4 Points (1 + 2 + 1)

Part A (1 point)

One point for correctly identifying the First Amendment as the common constitutional provision.

- Responses MUST include: a summation OR quotation of the First Amendment.
- Responses MAY include: a definition of freedom of expression, freedom of speech, and freedom of the press; an explanation that the Fourteenth Amendment applies the First Amendment to the states, and that education is a state responsibility.

Part B (2 points)

One point for describing relevant facts about the *Tinker* case.

- Responses MAY include: the student protesters were not participating in a school-sponsored activity or using a school-sponsored platform, and they were ruled not to be disrupting student discipline; the protests did not reflect on the character of the school itself; the topic and method of their protest were not seen as "indecent"; the Supreme Court ruled that the student protesters did not lose their free speech rights when they were inside a school; the Warren Court was known for its more liberal rulings.

One point for explaining how the facts of the cases led to different holdings.

- Responses MUST include: unlike the student protests in the *Tinker* case, the newspaper at the heart of the *Hazelwood* case was a school-sponsored platform provided to students in a journalism class and not a purely individual act of self-expression by the students, leading to different interpretations of the students' First Amendment freedom of speech/press rights.
- Responses MAY include: in the *Hazelwood* case, the topic of teen pregnancy was considered "indecent" for younger students; the newspaper in the *Hazelwood* case would carry the stamp of authority of the school itself, so the articles would potentially affect the school's reputation; the Rehnquist Court skewed more conservative in its rulings.

Part C (1 point)

One point for discussing a measure that a student reporter could take to work around the *Hazelwood* ruling. (Saying that there are no ways to work around the ruling is not a point-earning option.)

- Responses MAY include at least one (1) of the following: a student could start an alternate newspaper or newsletter, taking the lessons learned in their journalism class and applying them outside of a school-sponsored platform; both students and non-students could lobby state governments to establish legal protections for fellow student journalists, such as what happened in Illinois in 2016 with the "Speech Rights of Student Journalists

Act"; the student could raise awareness of censorship incidents through alternate channels, such as at a local community newspaper; professional journalists could conduct community outreach to students interested in their profession, educating them on their rights and helping them network as a profession ahead of any future censorship.

Sample High-Scoring Response

The First Amendment provides for the protection of several rights, including freedom of speech (Tinker) and freedom of the press (Hazelwood). These rights may not be abridged except in very narrow circumstances, and even then not for things like hate speech or even most national security concerns. These rights apply to students in schools, despite the U.S. education system being a state rather than a federal responsibility, due to the establishment clause of the Fourteenth Amendment, which applied the Bill of Rights to the states.

The core issue at the heart of both these cases is the "who." Who is speaking? In Tinker, the students chose to wear black armbands to school to protest the Vietnam War. Their own bodies were their free speech platform. In Hazelwood, the students were expressing themselves in those two censored articles, but they were doing so via a school newspaper. The school owned the newspaper and also ran the journalism class the students writing those articles were taking. Thus, the school had a vested interest in that these articles might negatively reflect on the school itself. The students were not their own free speech platform. The school was providing that platform. The school was speaking too.

There are several ways members of the public might be able to work around the censorship made possible by the Hazelwood ruling. For example, a student journalist could post a suppressed story on Instagram or Twitter, or even just alert people that the administration banned the publication of an article, which would attract interest in what the banned story was. Social media makes it easy to share links, text friends, and generally get the word out. This is a short-term local solution. Adults and students alike could lobby their state government for greater protections for the First Amendment rights of student journalists, because states run the education system; similarly, a free-speech lobbying group could reach out and educate high schoolers about their rights.

Sample Low-Scoring Response

The First Amendment of the U.S. Constitution explicitly forbids the government from abridging the freedom of the press. For example, in New York Times v. United States, the Supreme Court even let the press publish classified information from the Pentagon Papers about the Vietnam War, ruling that the First Amendment trumped executive privilege and national security.

There are multiple reasons why the facts of Hazelwood (1988) led to a different ruling than in Tinker (1969). One is the makeup of the court. By 1988, the Supreme Court was run by Chief Justice Rehnquist, a far more conservative judge of a mold far different than the historically liberal Warren Court. For example, United States v. Lopez (1995) saw the Supreme Court issue an absolutist ruling on guns that barred Congress from using the commerce clause to enforce gun control measures. This is in stark contrast to the liberalism of the likes of the Brown v. Board ruling of the 1950s under Chief Justice Warren or the later Miranda ruling. Also, there had been a societal shift towards more conservative values in the 1980s with the Reagan Revolution and rise of the Christian Right. This is reflected in how teen pregnancy was seen as too controversial an issue to discuss in a school paper despite many girls in that school obviously being publicly pregnant in the hallways for all to see.

Thanks to Hazelwood, student journalists can only hope that their school administration believes in freedom of the press and supports their right to publish whatever stories they see fit.

Explanation of Sample Responses

Both responses rightly discuss the First Amendment, which applies to both cases, satisfying the requirement of Part A. However, the low-scoring response has an overly narrow focus on the *Hazelwood* case and freedom of the press. *Tinker* dealt with freedom of speech, which the high-scoring response points out. The high-scoring response also discusses the Fourteenth Amendment, which is a second constitutional provision that applies to both cases, as the federal government does not run the U.S. education system.

The high-scoring response discusses the specifics of both cases, as required by Part B, and why those facts led to a different holding in *Hazelwood* as compared with *Tinker*. In the low-scoring response, the writer demonstrates a broad knowledge of the post-World War II Supreme Court, but name-dropping landmark cases and the names of chief justices does not compensate for the fact that the author doesn't discuss the facts of *Tinker* in detail as the prompt requires.

When it comes to Part C, the low-scoring response does not engage with the *Hazelwood* case. Its author is working off a definition of student journalism that is limited to what is laid out in the case's description: a top-down system where the school newspaper itself is the only platform for student journalists to express themselves. The high-scoring response expands upon the individual liberty of the *Tinker* decision, where a student can be their own platform for their First Amendment rights. The writer of the high-scoring response also acknowledges that political activism can be collective.

Rubric for Question 4: 6 Points (1 + 3 + 1 + 1)

Category	Appropriate Responses	Notes
A: Thesis (**1 pt** for stating a thesis that can be defended, is responsive to the issue posed, and sets up a line of reasoning)	"The greater responsibility for protecting individual liberty belongs to [state governments/ the federal government] because…"	You cannot earn a point by simply pointing out the give-and-take between the state and federal governments—that is, by essentially repeating the prompt. You will gain 1 pt by choosing one of the two up front.
B: Support (**1 pt** for presenting a piece of evidence relevant to the topic)	A statement or piece of evidence on the topic of state and federal governments that does not provide specific support for your thesis.	Example: you make a reasonable statement about state or federal government operations, but fail to relate your evidence to the specific issue of safeguarding individual freedom.
OR B: Support (**2 pts** for using a single piece of evidence appropriately supporting your thesis)	• *Federalist* 51: Assertion that liberty is safeguarded by dividing administration between state and national authorities; argues that U.S. Constitution is superior to state constitutions. • *Brutus* 1: Conviction that a large central government threatens liberty. • Letter From a Birmingham Jail: Advocates' use of the Fourteenth Amendment to nullify discriminatory state laws to protect civil rights, as in *Brown v. Board of Education*.	Including a relevant reference from one of the listed founding documents is essential. Clearly state the document you are using and present the relevant information contained in it.
OR B: Support (**3 pts** for using two pieces of evidence appropriately supporting your thesis)	• "Notwithstanding the Tenth Amendment insistence on granting unexpressly listed powers to the states or the people, the federal government has assumed for itself many such powers over the years." • "Following the Civil War, many states passed social welfare legislation regulating hours and working conditions—laws the Supreme Court tended to strike down as violations of personal liberty." • "Multiple amendments to the Constitution have imposed behavior—from the income tax to 18-year-olds' voting—which individual states had voted to prohibit."	Your second piece of evidence can come from your reading or general knowledge. Be sure that it is relevant and supports your thesis.

(Continued)

(Continued)

Category	Appropriate Responses	Notes
C: Reasoning (**1 pt** for explaining why or how your evidence supports your thesis)	• "The freedom of the people to grow, smoke, and sell cannabis is permitted by many states, but the supremacy clause means the federal government's ban has to prevail." • "For over a century, Americans have had to deal with the Sixteenth Amendment, which grants a faceless central authority the right to enforce a tax on the income that the state has already taxed." • "If, as Dr. King so memorably argued, injustice anywhere is a threat to justice everywhere, then residents of every state must have a duty to defend liberty in every other state."	Don't assume that the AP reader will understand that the evidence you presented supports a particular point that you are making. Be sure to state explicitly how the evidence demonstrates your point.
D: Reply to Alternative Viewpoint (**1 pt** for offering a point of view different from yours and going on to rebut, refute, or concede it)	You present a point in favor of the other opinion—in favor of state governments if you have been arguing for the federal government, or vice versa—and either show it to be false, argue that it is not valid, or concede it may have some validity.	Don't just assert that the other side is wrong. Provide a reason (rebut it) or grant their point (concede it), while not backing away from your own view. Example: admitting that some states may protect liberty better than the federal government in some limited contexts, but countering that many states have historically been poor at protecting civil rights, as was seen in the Jim Crow era.

Sample High-Scoring Response

To truly protect individual liberty, a government must ensure that all people have the freedom to determine the course of their own lives. In the United States, several state governments have a history of impeding the civil rights of some of their citizens, only changing their ways after a federal mandate. Thus, it is clear that the federal government is most responsible for safeguarding liberty in the United States.

The clearest indication of this can be found in Dr. Martin Luther King Jr.'s "Letter from a Birmingham Jail," in which he argues that "injustice anywhere is a threat to justice everywhere." Though talking about the principle of justice, King would no doubt agree that the same point applies to liberty: if even just a few individuals are wrongly denied their liberty, then the United States is not truly a free country. And, indeed, King discusses in the Letter how the denial of civil rights by Southern states required citizens from other states to go there to take direct action against these injustices. While the federal government was willing to take a stand in favor of civil rights through Supreme Court rulings like Brown v. Board of Education and legislation like the Civil Rights Act of 1964, some states were reluctant to see such rulings and legislation enforced, which is why the efforts of King and other leaders in the civil rights movement were so essential.

Further support for this idea that the federal government is the best safeguard of liberty can be found in Federalist 51. James Madison argues there that the best protections against oppression by a government or a majority faction are the separation of powers and the checks and balances built into the federal Constitution. Dividing the government into separate departments that can check the power of other departments, as in the Constitution, ensures that no one portion of the government gains too much power. By preventing government from becoming tyrannical, individual liberty, including the liberty of minority groups, is better protected. Madison even makes the point that, if the federal Constitution is not adequate to the job of protecting liberty with its extensive system of checks and balances, then surely state constitutions with their less extensive systems would not be up to the task either. In short, the federal government best protects liberty because it best implements the freedom-promoting principles of separation of powers and checks and balances.

Some might take the position articulated in Brutus 1, which suggests that the federal government is intrinsically more tyrannical in claiming to govern over a larger entity. The author of Brutus contends that a unitary federal republic would violate the rights of states for self-determination. Indeed, one might argue that changes implemented as a result of the Civil War and the later civil rights movement were violations of the rights of Southern states. But this would be a misunderstanding of what liberty truly is. The freedom to oppress is a "freedom" in name only. True freedom is found only in individuals, not in collections of people like states. Because the federal government has shown a more active willingness to protect the civil rights and civil liberties of all U.S. citizens, it is the entity most responsible for safeguarding individual liberty in this country.

Sample Low-Scoring Response

The federal government in Washington runs roughshod over the states in terms of all sorts of their rights, in violation of the Constitution, and that hurts everyone equally. A famous response to The Federalist Papers was Brutus 1. Brutus saw exactly what was to come when he predicted the states' laws would be ignored whenever the national government decided to do so. A federal government destroys liberty, said Brutus, and he was dead right.

One way the federal government clashes with the states has to do with illegal immigration. A state has the right, and I would say the duty, to protect its citizens on its portion of a border. But if the federal government decides not to act or to act in violation of the expressed will of that state's people, the feds will prevail and injustice will result.

Another way the federal government clashes with the states is in the area of health care. Health care in the U.S. falls under both federal and state jurisdiction. If a health care practitioner was paid kickbacks to affect the referral of Medicare patients, both governments could prosecute for the same transactions. I feel that that is wrong.

No one is saying that the states should have total authority. It would be foolish to go back to the old way of states printing their own money. It would be bad if Florida negotiated its own treaty with Cuba. But the Constitution recognized that the 13 states, born of the 13 colonies, had equal rights and those rights should be respected.

Explanation of Sample Responses

Both essays earn the 1 point for Thesis. The high-scoring response contends that the federal government is the best protector of individual freedom because it respects civil rights more consistently than the states have. The low-scoring response claims instead that the federal government actually destroys liberty and that the states are the better protectors of freedom. Remember that multiple positions can earn you the Thesis point as long as you present a clear statement of your stance.

For Support, the high-scoring response earns all 3 points. There are extensive discussions both of King's Letter and *Federalist* 51. The writer makes references to specific arguments made in the documents, which is essential for getting all the Support points. On the other hand, the low-scoring response would likely earn only 1 point for mentioning a claim made in Brutus 1 without much specific elaboration.

The high-scoring response also earns 1 point for Reasoning. The writer takes pains to explain how each of the documents specifically supports the idea that the federal government safeguards liberty better than state governments. The low-scoring response claims that Brutus was right about the federal government destroying liberty, but does not explain why. The examples provided about immigration and health care are cases in which federal law seems to trump state laws, but it's not clear how this connects to the concept of individual liberty. Thus, the low-scoring response earns 0 points for Reasoning.

For the Reply to Alternative Viewpoint, the high-scoring response lays out an argument made in *Brutus* 1 that the federal government violates states' rights, but refutes it by arguing that it misunderstands what individual liberty truly is. This would earn 1 point. In contrast, the low-scoring response would earn 0 points because it does not present an opposing view about who protects liberty better, but instead focuses on the issue of whether state or federal governments should have more power.

All told, the high-scoring response would earn all 6 points, while the low-scoring response would likely only receive 2 out of 6. The major fault of the latter is its divergence from the question at hand. By focusing on the question of whether state or federal governments should have more power, it ignores the issue of individual liberty that is central to the prompt, thereby losing points in Support, Reasoning, and Reply to Alternative Viewpoint.

AP U.S. Government and Politics Resources

REQUIRED FOUNDATIONAL DOCUMENTS

Foundational Document	Author(s)	Historical Context	Major Arguments
The Declaration of Independence	Thomas Jefferson, with revisions by the Second Continental Congress	Ratified July 4, 1776. Announced American independence from Britain, while laying out the political and practical justifications for that move.	• Human beings have certain natural rights, and the British King had trespassed upon those rights. • As peaceful diplomacy had been exhausted, the Thirteen Colonies were forced to resort to violence and break away from British control, forming a new government. • **Themes:** natural law, civil liberties, social contract, revolution, taxation, representative government, popular sovereignty
The Articles of Confederation	John Dickinson, with revisions by a committee of the Second Continental Congress	Published 1777, ratified 1781. First constitution. Written and adopted during the American Revolutionary War, it reflected the broad concerns about infringements on state sovereignty by a distant government.	• Established a confederal republic where state governments were supreme. • Contained no executive or judicial branch. • The federal government had no power to lay or collect taxes, declare war, or easily negotiate treaties. • **Themes:** popular sovereignty, confederal government, states' rights, dual federalism, state vs. federal governments

(Continued)

Foundational Document	Author(s)	Historical Context	Major Arguments
The Constitution of the United States	The delegates of the Constitutional Convention	Published 1787, ratified 1788. Second constitution. After Shays' Rebellion and several years of federal dysfunction, the Articles were widely seen as needing alteration or replacement.	• Established a strong federal government that was supreme over the states. • A system of checks and balances distributed power across three branches. • Bills and amendments no longer required unanimous approval. • **Themes:** federalism, state vs. federal governments, elite democracy, separation of powers, checks and balances
Brutus 1	Author unknown; published under the pseudonym "Brutus"	Published 1787. An Anti-Federalist argument against the ratification of the then-proposed Constitution.	• A federal government would inevitably grow despotic and corrupt, dominating state governments. • The United States was too large for a truly representative government to be practical. • **Themes:** ambition, corruption, state vs. federal governments, judicial jurisdiction, taxation, representation, large vs. small republics, militias vs. standing armies
Federalist 10	James Madison, under the pseudonym "Publius"	Published 1787. Part of a series of papers promoting the ratification of the then-proposed Constitution.	• Political factions cannot be prevented, but their influence can be mitigated in a large republic. • **Themes:** factionalism, class conflict, democracy vs. republic, large vs. small republics
Federalist 51	James Madison, under the pseudonym "Publius"	Published 1788. Part of a series of papers promoting the ratification of the then-proposed Constitution.	• Tyranny in a government cannot be prevented by external controls but must be achieved internally through a genuine separation of powers; this is easier in a large federal republic. • **Themes:** internal vs. external controls, executive vs. legislative, state vs. federal governments, factionalism, large vs. small republics, human nature

(Continued)

Foundational Document	Author(s)	Historical Context	Major Arguments
Federalist 70	Alexander Hamilton, under the pseudonym "Publius"	Published 1788. Part of a series of papers promoting the ratification of the then-proposed Constitution.	• A powerful unified executive is necessary in a republican government. • An energetic executive provides counterbalance against the slow, deliberative legislative branch. • **Themes:** characteristics and limits of a powerful executive, unitary vs. divided executives, executive councils, monarchical vs. republican executives
Federalist 78	Alexander Hamilton, under the pseudonym "Publius"	Published 1788. Part of a series of papers promoting the ratification of the then-proposed Constitution.	• As the weakest branch of government, the federal judiciary needs special protections, such as lifetime tenure, independence, and the ability to nullify unconstitutional laws. • **Themes:** separation of powers, judicial tenure, judicial review, constitutional sovereignty (as an expression of popular sovereignty), legal interpretation, constitutional amendments, precedents
"Letter from a Birmingham Jail"	Rev. Dr. Martin Luther King Jr.	An open letter published in 1963, during the Birmingham civil rights campaign.	• Nonviolent resistance must be used to combat injustice, regardless of time, place, or the law itself. • **Themes:** civil disobedience, nonviolence, protest as a means of achieving policy outcomes, racial justice, just vs. unjust laws, the pernicious effects of moderates, order vs. justice, nonviolent vs. violent protest

Note: The AP exam will test students on these foundational documents in both the multiple-choice and free-response sections. The same documents may show up in different contexts. For more information on question types, see Chapter 2. For more information on the Argument Essay, which will require specific citation and discussion of foundational documents, see Chapter 13.

REQUIRED SUPREME COURT CASES

Theme	Supreme Court Case	Holding
Federalism	*McCulloch v. Maryland* (1819)	• The states cannot tax federal government institutions because Constitutional authority usurps state taxation authority (via the Necessary and Proper clause). ○ Institution in question: Second Bank of the United States • These powers do not need to be enumerated.
Federalism	*United States v. Lopez* (1995)	• Congress cannot create blanket federal criminal regulations on guns because that would exceed the powers reserved to Congress (via the commerce clause). Congress's authority under the commerce clause is limited. • Congress may make regulations related to guns physically transported between states pursuant to their power to regulate interstate commerce.
Bill of Rights (Religion), Individual Liberty vs. Social Order	*Engel v. Vitale* (1962)	• School officials cannot compose prayer or encourage students to recite it, even if the prayer is nondenominational. • Prayer does not have to be coercive to violate the establishment clause.
Bill of Rights (Religion), Individual Liberty vs. Social Order	*Wisconsin v. Yoder* (1972)	• States cannot force parents to send their children to secondary school if that violates their religious beliefs. • This case dealt with Amish parents who did not want to have their children go to school past the 8th grade.
Bill of Rights (Speech), Individual Liberty vs. Social Order	*Tinker v. Des Moines Independent Community School District* (1969)	• Students have free speech rights in public schools as long as the speech is not obscene or disruptive. • This case dealt with students wearing black armbands to protest the Vietnam War.
Bill of Rights (Press), Individual Liberty vs. Social Order	*New York Times Co. v. United States* (1971)	• The government may not prevent the publication of news unless there is a compelling national security reason. • This case was about whether the *New York Times* and *Washington Post* could publish the Pentagon Papers. It effectively banned prior restraint.

(Continued)

Theme	Supreme Court Case	Holding
Bill of Rights (Speech), Individual Liberty vs. Social Order	*Schenck v. United States* (1919)	• Speech that creates a "clear and present danger" is not protected by the First Amendment. • This case pertained to political dissidents speaking in protest about the First World War, specifically encouraging people to dodge the draft.
Selective Incorporation, Bill of Rights (Counsel)	*Gideon v. Wainwright* (1963)	• Defendants in a criminal case are guaranteed the right to counsel by the Sixth Amendment. • This case originated from Florida and was filed pro se (on their own behalf) by Clarence Earl Gideon, an indigent Florida inmate who had not had counsel at his trial because he could not pay a lawyer and the state refused to appoint one.
Selective Incorporation, Bill of Rights (Privacy)	*Roe v. Wade* (1973)	• The government may only restrict access to abortion in limited circumstances and may not ban it outright. • This decision expanded an unenumerated right to privacy (Fourth Amendment).
Selective Incorporation, Bill of Rights (Bear Arms)	*McDonald v. Chicago* (2010)	• The Second Amendment right to keep and bear arms applies to the states. • This case built upon *District of Columbia v. Heller* (2008).
Equal Protection Clause	*Brown v. Board of Education* (1954)	• Invalidated the doctrine of "separate but equal" that had controlled access to public facilities since *Plessy v. Ferguson* (1896). • Race-based segregation of public facilities violates the equal protection clause of the Fourteenth Amendment. • This case consolidated several cases challenging unequal school facilities for African American children and was brought by the NAACP.
Elections	*Citizens United v. Federal Election Commission* (2010)	• Political spending by corporations and other groups (like political action committees, or PACs) is protected speech under the First Amendment. • This case increased the ability of interest groups to spend money to influence elections.

(Continued)

Theme	Supreme Court Case	Holding
Elections, Equal Protection Clause	*Baker v. Carr* (1961)	• States must apportion districts equitably, with the standard of "one man, one vote." • Questions of districting are justiciable and are not purely political questions, which means the Court can consider them rather than having to leave them to electoral results. • This case changed the balance of power in state legislatures which favored rural districts and disfavored urban districts, the latter of which had grown substantially but were not equitably represented.
Elections	*Shaw v. Reno* (1993)	• Race-based districting may violate the equal protection clause and must only be done for a compelling government interest. • This case addressed majority-minority districts in North Carolina after the 1990 census, based on what looked like race-based gerrymandering.
Separation of Powers, Judicial Review	*Marbury v. Madison* (1803)	• The Supreme Court has the power of judicial review, which means it is the ultimate arbiter of what is constitutional, including actions by the other branches of the federal government. • This case dealt with bureaucratic appointments by President Adams, who was trying to pack the government with his supporters before President Jefferson took office. • This case is the foundational case for the Supreme Court and established its authority to decide questions of constitutionality.

Note: The AP exam will test students on these SCOTUS cases in both the multiple-choice and free-response sections. The same cases may show up in different contexts. For more information on question types, see Chapter 2. For more information on the SCOTUS Comparison free-response question, see Chapter 13.

THE CONSTITUTION OF THE UNITED STATES

WE THE PEOPLE of the United States, in Order to form a more perfect Union, establish justice, insure domestic Tranquility, provide for the common defence, promote the general Welfare, and secure the Blessings of Liberty to ourselves and our Posterity, do ordain and establish this Constitution for the United States of America.

Article I

Section 1.   All legislative Powers herein granted shall be vested in a Congress of the United States, which shall consist of a Senate and House of Representatives.

Section 2.   The House of Representatives shall be composed of Members chosen every second Year by the People of the several States, and the Electors in each State shall have the Qualifications requisite for Electors of the most numerous Branch of the State Legislature.

No Person shall be a Representative who shall not have attained to the Age of twenty five Years, and been seven Years a Citizen of the United States, and who shall not, when elected, be an Inhabitant of that State in which he shall be chosen.

[Representatives and [direct Taxes] shall be apportioned among the several States [which may be included within this Union,] according to their respective Numbers, which shall be determined by adding to the whole Number of free Persons, including those bound to Service for a Term of Years, and excluding Indians not taxed, three fifths of all other Persons. (This clause was changed by section 2 of the Fourteenth Amendment.)] The actual Enumeration shall be made within three Years after the first Meeting of the Congress of the United States, and within every subsequent Term of ten Years, in such Manner as they shall by Law direct. The Number of Representatives shall not exceed one for every thirty Thousand, but each State shall have at Least one Representative; and until such enumeration shall be made, the State of New Hampshire shall be entitled to chuse three, Massachusetts eight, Rhode Island and Providence Plantations one, Connecticut five, New York six, New Jersey four, Pennsylvania eight, Delaware one, Maryland six, Virginia ten, North Carolina five, South Carolina five, and Georgia three.

When vacancies happen in the Representation from any State, the Executive Authority thereof shall issue Writs of Election to fill such Vacancies.

The House of Representatives shall chuse their Speaker and other Officers; and shall have the sole Power of Impeachment.

Section 3.   The Senate of the United States shall be composed of two Senators from each State, [chosen by the Legislature thereof, (This provision was changed by section 1 of the Seventeenth Amendment.)] for six Years; and each Senator shall have one Vote.

Immediately after they shall be assembled in Consequence of the first Election, they shall be divided as equally as may be into three Classes. The Seats of the Senators of the first Class shall be vacated at the Expiration of the second Year, of the second Class at the Expiration of the fourth Year, and of the third Class at the Expiration of the sixth Year, so that one third may be chosen every second Year; [and if Vacancies happen by Resignation, or otherwise, during the Recess of the Legislature of any State, the Executive thereof may make temporary Appointments until the next Meeting of the Legislature, which shall then fill such Vacancies. (This clause was changed by section 2 of the Seventeenth Amendment.)]

No Person shall be a Senator who shall not have attained to the Age of thirty Years, and been nine Years a Citizen of the United States, and who shall not, when elected, be an Inhabitant of that State for which he shall be chosen.

The Vice President of the United States shall be President of the Senate, but shall have no Vote, unless they be equally divided.

The Senate shall chuse their other Officers, and also a President *pro tempore*, in the Absence of the Vice President, or when he shall exercise the Office of President of the United States.

The Senate shall have the sole Power to try all Impeachments. When sitting for that Purpose, they shall be on Oath or Affirmation. When the President of the United States is tried, the Chief justice shall preside: And no Person shall be convicted without the Concurrence of two thirds of the Members present.

Judgment in Cases of Impeachment shall not extend further than to removal from Office, and disqualification to hold and enjoy any Office of honor, Trust or Profit under the United States: but the Party convicted shall nevertheless be liable and subject to Indictment, Trial, Judgment and Punishment, according to Law.

Section 4.   The Times, Places and Manner of holding Elections for Senators and Representatives, shall be prescribed in each State by the Legislature thereof; but the Congress may at any time by Law make or alter such Regulations, except as to the Places of chusing Senators.

The Congress shall assemble at least once in every Year, and such Meeting shall be [on the first Monday in December, (This provision was changed by section 2 of the Twentieth Amendment.)] unless they shall by Law appoint a different Day.

Section 5.   Each House shall be the judge of the Elections, Returns and Qualifications of its own Members, and a Majority of each shall constitute a Quorum to do Business; but a smaller Number may adjourn from day to day, and may be authorized to compel the Attendance of absent Members, in such Manner, and under such Penalties as each House may provide.

Each House may determine the Rules of its Proceedings, punish its Members for disorderly Behaviour, and, with the Concurrence of two thirds, expel a Member.

Each House shall keep a journal of its Proceedings, and from time to time publish the same, excepting such Parts as may in their judgment require Secrecy; and the Yeas and Nays of the Members of either House on any question shall, at the Desire of one fifth of those Present, be entered on the journal.

Neither House, during the Session of Congress, shall, without the Consent of the other, adjourn for more than three days, nor to any other Place than that in which the two Houses shall be sitting.

Section 6. The Senators and Representatives shall receive a Compensation for their Services, to be ascertained by Law, and paid out of the Treasury of the United States. They shall in all Cases, except Treason, Felony and Breach of the Peace, be privileged from Arrest during their Attendance at the Session of their respective Houses, and in going to and returning from the same; and for any Speech or Debate in either House, they shall not be questioned in any other Place.

No Senator or Representative shall, during the Time for which he was elected, be appointed to any civil Office under the Authority of the United States, which shall have been created, or the Emoluments whereof shall have been encreased during such time; and no Person holding any Office under the United States, shall be a Member of either House during his Continuance in Office.

Section 7. All Bills for raising Revenue shall originate in the House of Representatives; but the Senate may propose or concur with Amendments as on other Bills.

Every Bill which shall have passed the House of Representatives and the Senate, shall, before it become a Law, be presented to the President of the United States; If he approve he shall sign it, but if not he shall return it, with his Objections to that House in which it shall have originated, who shall enter the Objections at large on their Journal, and proceed to reconsider it. If after such Reconsideration two thirds of that House shall agree to pass the Bill, it shall be sent, together with the Objections, to the other House, by which it shall likewise be reconsidered, and if approved by two thirds of that House, it shall become a Law. But in all such Cases the Votes of both Houses shall be determined by Yeas and Nays, and the Names of the Persons voting for and against the Bill shall be entered on the journal of each House respectively. If any bill shall not be returned by the President within ten Days (Sundays excepted) after it shall have been presented to him, the Same shall be a Law, in like Manner as if he had signed it, unless the Congress by their Adjournment prevent its Return, in which Case it shall not be a Law.

Every Order, Resolution, or Vote to which the Concurrence of the Senate and House of Representatives may be necessary (except on a question of Adjournment) shall be presented to the President of the United States; and before the Same shall take Effect, shall be approved by him, or being disapproved by him, shall be repassed by two thirds of the Senate and House of Representatives, according to the Rules and Limitations prescribed in the Case of a Bill.

Section 8. The Congress shall have Power To lay and collect Taxes, Duties, Imposts and Excises, to pay the Debts and provide for the common Defence and general Welfare of the United States; but all Duties, Imposts and Excises shall be uniform throughout the United States;

To borrow Money on the credit of the United States;

To regulate Commerce with Foreign Nations, and among the several States, and with the Indian tribes;

To establish an uniform Rule of Naturalization, and uniform Laws on the subject of Bankruptcies throughout the United States;

To coin Money, regulate the Value thereof, and of foreign Coin, and fix the Standard of Weights and Measures;

To provide for the Punishment of counterfeiting the Securities and current Coin of the United States;

To establish Post Offices and post Roads;

To promote the Progress of Science and useful Arts, by securing for limited Times to Authors and Inventors the exclusive Right to their respective Writings and Discoveries;

To constitute Tribunals inferior to the supreme Court;

To define and punish Piracies and Felonies committed on the high Seas, and Offences against the Law of Nations;

To declare War, grant Letters of Marque and Reprisal, and make Rules concerning Captures on Land and Water;

To raise and support Armies, but no Appropriation of Money to that Use shall be for a longer Term than two Years;

To provide and maintain a Navy;

To make Rules for the Government and Regulation of the land and naval Forces;

To provide for calling forth the Militia to execute the Laws of the Union, suppress Insurrections and repel Invasions;

To provide for organizing, arming, and disciplining, the Militia and for governing such Part of them as may be employed in the Service of the United States, reserving to the States respectively, the Appointment of the Officers, and the Authority of training the Militia according to the discipline prescribed by Congress;

To exercise exclusive Legislation in all Cases whatsoever, over such District (not exceeding ten Miles square) as may, by Cession of particular States, and the Acceptance of Congress, become the Seat of the Government of the United States, and to exercise like Authority over all Places purchased by the Consent of the Legislature of the State in which the Same shall be, for the Erection of Forts, Magazines, Arsenals, Dockyards, and other needful Buildings; And

To make all Laws which shall be necessary and proper for carrying into Execution the foregoing Powers, and all other Powers vested by this Constitution in the Government of the United States, or in any Department or Officer thereof.

Section 9. The Migration or Importation of such Persons any of the States now existing shall think proper to admit, shall not be prohibited by the Congress prior to the Year one thousand eight hundred and eight, but a Tax or duty may be imposed on such Importation, not exceeding ten dollars for each Person.

The Privilege of the Writ of Habeas Corpus shall not be suspended, unless when in Cases of Rebellion or Invasion the public Safety may require it.

No Bill of Attainder or *ex post facto* Law shall be passed.

No Capitation, or other direct, Tax shall be laid, unless in Proportion to the Census or Enumeration herein before directed to be taken.

No Tax or Duty shall be laid on Articles exported from any State.

No Preference shall be given by any Regulation of Commerce or Revenue to the Ports of one State over those of another: nor shall Vessels bound to, or from, one State, be obliged to enter, clear, or pay Duties in another.

No Money shall be drawn from the Treasury, but in Consequence of Appropriations made by Law; and a regular Statement and Account of the Receipts and Expenditures of all public Money shall be published from time to time.

No Title of Nobility shall be granted by the United States: And no Person holding any Office of Profit or Trust under them, shall, without the Consent of the Congress, accept of any present, Emolument, Office, or Tide, of any kind whatever, from any King, Prince, or foreign State.

Section 10. No State shall enter into any Treaty, Alliance, or Confederation; grant Letters of Marque and Reprisal; coin Money; emit Bills of Credit; make any Thing but gold and silver Coin a Tender in Payment of Debts; pass any Bill of Attainder, *ex post facto* Law, or Law impairing the Obligation of Contracts, or grant any Title of Nobility.

No State shall, without the Consent of the Congress, lay any Imposts or Duties on Imports or Exports, except what may be absolutely necessary for executing its inspection Laws: and the net Produce of all Duties and Imposts, laid by any State on Imports or Exports, shall be for the Use of the Treasury of the United States; and all such Laws shall be subject to the Revision and Controul of the Congress.

No State shall, without the Consent of Congress, lay any Duty of Tonnage, keep Troops, or Ships of War in time of Peace, enter into any Agreement or Compact with another State, or with a foreign Power, or engage in War, unless actually invaded, or in such imminent Danger as will not admit of delay.

Article II

Section 1.   The executive Power shall be vested in a President of the United States of America. He shall hold his Office during the Term of four Years, and, together with the Vice President, chosen for the same Term, be elected, as follows.

Each State shall appoint, in such Manner as the Legislature thereof may direct, a Number of Electors, equal to the whole Number of Senators and Representatives to which the State may be entitled in the Congress: but no Senator or Representative, or Person holding an Office of Trust or Profit under the United States, shall be appointed an Elector.

[The Electors shall meet in their respective States, and vote by Ballot for two Persons, of whom one at least shall not be an inhabitant of the same State with themselves. And they shall make a List of all the Persons voted for, and of the Number of Votes for each; which List they shall sign and certify, and transmit sealed to the Seat of the Government of the United States, directed to the President of the Senate. The President of the Senate shall, in the Presence of the Senate and House of Representatives, open all the Certificates, and the Votes shall then be counted. The Person having the greatest Number of Votes shall be the President, if such Number be a Majority of the whole Number of Electors appointed; and if there be more than one who have such Majority, and have an equal Number of Votes, then the House of Representatives shall immediately chuse by Ballot one of them for President; and if no Person have a Majority, then from the five highest on the List the said House shall in like Manner chuse the President. But in chusing the President, the Votes shall be taken by States, the Representation from each State having one Vote; A quorum for this purpose shall consist of a Member or Members from two thirds of the States, and a Majority of all the States shall be necessary to a Choice. In every Case, after the Choice of the President, the Person having the greatest Number of Votes of the Electors shall be the Vice President. But if there should remain two or more who have equal Votes, the Senate shall chuse from them by Ballot the Vice President. (This clause was superseded by the Twelfth Amendment.)]

The Congress may determine the Time of chusing the Electors, and the Day on which they shall give their Votes; which Day shall be the same throughout the United States.

No Person except a natural born Citizen, or a Citizen of the United States, at the time of the Adoption of this Constitution, shall be eligible to the Office of President; neither shall any Person be eligible to that Office who shall not have attained to the Age of thirty five Years, and been fourteen Years a Resident within the United States.

[In Case of the Removal of the President from Office, or of his Death, Resignation, or Inability to discharge the Powers and Duties of the said Office, the Same shall devolve on the Vice President, and the Congress may by Law provide for the Case of Removal, Death, Resignation or Inability, both of the President and Vice President, declaring what Officer shall then act as President, and such Officer shall act accordingly, until the Disability be removed, or a President shall be elected. (This clause was modified by the Twenty-Fifth Amendment.)]

The President shall, at stated Times, receive for his Services, a Compensation, which shall neither be increased nor diminished during the Period for which he shall have been elected, and he shall not receive within that Period any other Emolument from the United States, or any of them.

Before he enter on the Execution of his Office, he shall take the following Oath or Affirmation: "I do solemnly swear (or affirm) that I will faithfully execute the Office of President of the United States, and will to the best of my Ability, preserve, protect and defend the Constitution of the United States."

Section 2.   The President shall be Commander in Chief of the Army and Navy of the United States, and of the Militia of the several States, when called into the actual Service of the United States; he may require the Opinion, in writing, of the principal Officer in each of the executive Departments, upon any Subject relating to the Duties of their respective Offices, and he shall have Power to grant Reprieves and Pardons for Offences against the United States, except in Cases of Impeachment.

He shall have Power, by and with the Advice and Consent of the Senate, to make Treaties, provided two thirds of the Senators present concur; and he shall nominate, and by and with the Advice and Consent of the Senate, shall appoint Ambassadors, other public Ministers and Consuls, judges of the supreme Court, and all other Officers of the United States, whose Appointments are not herein otherwise provided for, and which shall be established by Law: but the Congress may by Law vest the Appointment of such inferior Officers, as they think proper, in the President alone, in the Courts of Law, or in the Heads of Departments.

The President shall have Power to fill up all Vacancies that may happen during the Recess of the Senate, by granting Commissions which shall expire at the End of their next Session.

Section 3.   He shall from time to time give to the Congress Information of the State of the Union, and recommend to their Consideration such Measures as he shall judge necessary and expedient; he may, on extraordinary Occasions, convene both Houses, or either of them, and in Case of Disagreement between them, with Respect to the Time of Adjournment, he may adjourn them to such Time as he shall think proper; he shall receive Ambassadors and other public Ministers; he shall take Care that the Laws be faithfully executed, and shall Commission all the Officers of the United States.

Section 4.   The President, Vice President and all civil Officers of the United States, shall be removed from Office on Impeachment for, and Conviction of, Treason, Bribery, or other high Crimes and Misdemeanors.

Article III

Section 1. The judicial Power of the United States, shall be vested in one supreme Court, and in such inferior Courts as the Congress may from time to time ordain and establish. The judges, both of the supreme and inferior Courts, shall hold their Offices during good Behaviour, and shall, at stated Times receive for their Services, a Compensation, which shall not be diminished during their Continuance in Office.

Section 2. The judicial Power shall extend to all Cases, in Law and Equity, arising under this Constitution, the Laws of the United States, and Treaties made, or which shall be made, under their Authority; to all Cases affecting Ambassadors, other public Ministers and Consuls; to all Cases of admiralty and maritime jurisdiction; to Controversies to which the United States shall be a Party; to Controversies between two or more States; between a State and Citizens of another State; between Citizens of different States, between Citizens of the same State claiming Lands under Grants of different States, and between a State, or the Citizens thereof, and foreign States, Citizens or Subjects.

In all Cases affecting Ambassadors, other public Ministers and Consuls, and those in which a State shall be Party, the supreme Court shall have original jurisdiction. In all the other Cases before mentioned, the supreme Court shall have appellate jurisdiction, both as to Law and Fact, with such Exceptions, and under such Regulations as the Congress shall make.

The Trial of all Crimes, except in Cases of Impeachment, shall be by jury; and such Trial shall be held in the State where the said Crimes shall have been committed; but when not committed within any State, the Trial shall be at such Place or Places as the Congress may by Law have directed.

Section 3. Treason against the United States, shall consist only in levying War against them, or in adhering to their Enemies, giving them Aid and Comfort. No Person shall be convicted of Treason unless on the Testimony of two Witnesses to the same overt Act, or on Confession in open Court.

The Congress shall have Power to declare the Punishment of Treason, but no Attainder of Treason shall work Corruption of Blood, or Forfeiture except during the Life of the Person attainted.

Article IV

Section 1. Full Faith and Credit shall be given in each State to the public Acts, Records, and judicial Proceedings of every other State; And the Congress may by general Laws prescribe the Manner in which such Acts, Records and Proceedings shall be proved, and the Effect thereof.

Section 2. The Citizens of each State shall be entitled to all Privileges and Immunities of Citizens in the several States.

A Person charged in any State with Treason, Felony, or other Crime, who shall flee from justice, and be found in another State, shall on Demand of the executive Authority of the State from which he fled, be delivered up, to be removed to the State having jurisdiction of the Crime.

[No Person held to Service or Labour in one State, under the Laws thereof, escaping into another, shall, in Consequence of any Law or Regulation therein, be discharged from such Service or Labour, but shall be delivered up on Claim of the Party to whom such Service or Labour may be due. (This clause was superseded by the Thirteenth Amendment.)]

Section 3. New States may be admitted by the Congress into this Union; but no new State shall be formed or erected within the jurisdiction of any other State; nor any State be formed by the junction of two or more States, or Parts of States, without the Consent of the Legislatures of the States concerned as well as of the Congress.

The Congress shall have Power to dispose of and make all needful Rules and Regulations respecting the Territory or other Property belonging to the United States; and nothing in this Constitution shall be so construed as to Prejudice any Claims of the United States, or of any particular State.

Section 4. The United States shall guarantee to every State in this Union a Republican Form of Government, and shall protect each of them against Invasion; and on Application of the Legislature, or of the Executive (when the Legislature cannot be convened) against domestic Violence.

Article V

The Congress, whenever two thirds of both Houses shall deem it necessary, shall propose Amendments to this Constitution, or, on the Application of the Legislatures of two thirds of the several States, shall call a Convention for proposing Amendments, which, in either Case, shall be valid to all Intents and Purposes, as Part of this Constitution, when ratified by the legislatures of three fourths of the several States, or by Conventions in three fourths thereof, as the one or the other Mode of Ratification may be proposed by the Congress; Provided that no Amendment which may be made prior to the Year One thousand eight hundred and eight shall in any Manner affect the first and fourth Clauses in the Ninth Section of the first Article; and that no State, without its Consent, shall be deprived of its equal Suffrage in the Senate.

Article VI

All Debts contracted and Engagements entered into, before the Adoption of this Constitution, shall be as valid against the United States under this Constitution, as under the Confederation.

This Constitution, and the Laws of the United States which shall be made in Pursuance thereof; and all Treaties made, or which shall be made, under the Authority of the United States, shall be the supreme Law of the Land; and the judges in every State shall be bound thereby, any Thing in the Constitution or Laws of any State to the Contrary notwithstanding.

The Senators and Representatives before mentioned, and the Members of the several State Legislatures, and all executive and judicial Officers, both of the United States and of the several States, shall be bound by Oath or Affirmation, to support this Constitution; but no religious Test shall ever be required as a Qualification to any Office or public Trust under the United States.

Article VII

The Ratification of the Conventions of nine States, shall be sufficient for the Establishment of this Constitution between the States so ratifying the Same.

DONE in Convention by the Unanimous Consent of the States present the Seventeenth Day of September in the Year of our Lord one thousand seven hundred and Eighty seven and of the Independance of the United States of America the Twelfth.

IN WITNESS whereof We have hereunto subscribed our Names.

Amendment I (Ratified December 15, 1791)

Congress shall make no law respecting an establishment of religion, or prohibiting the free exercise thereof; or abridging the freedom of speech, or of the press, or the right of the people peaceably to assemble, and to petition the Government for a redress of grievances.

Amendment II (Ratified December 15, 1791)

A well regulated Militia, being necessary to the security of a free State, the right of the people to keep and bear Arms, shall not be infringed.

Amendment III (Ratified December 15, 1791)

No Soldier shall, in time of peace be quartered in any house, without the consent of the Owner, nor in time of war, but in a manner to be prescribed by law.

Amendment IV (Ratified December 15, 1791)

The right of the people to be secure in their persons, houses, papers, and effects, against unreasonable searches and seizures, shall not be violated, and no Warrants shall issue, but upon probable cause, supported by Oath or affirmation, and particularly describing the place to be searched, and the persons or things to be seized.

Amendment V (Ratified December 15, 1791)

No person shall be held to answer for a capital, or otherwise infamous crime, unless on a presentment or indictment of a Grand jury, except in cases arising in the land or naval forces, or in the Militia, when in actual service in time of War or public danger; nor shall any person be subject for the same offence to be twice put in jeopardy of life or limb, nor shall be compelled in any criminal case to be a witness against himself, nor be deprived of life, liberty, or property, without due process of law; nor shall private property be taken for public use, without just compensation.

Amendment VI (Ratified December 15, 1791)

In all criminal prosecutions, the accused shall enjoy the right to a speedy and public trial, by an impartial jury of the State and district wherein the crime shall have been committed; which district shall have been previously ascertained by law, and to be informed of the nature and cause of the accusation; to be confronted with the witnesses against him; to have compulsory process for obtaining witnesses in his favor, and to have the Assistance of Counsel for his defence.

Amendment VII (Ratified December 15, 1791)

In Suits at common law, where the value in controversy shall exceed twenty dollars, the right of trial by jury shall be preserved, and no fact tried by a jury, shall be otherwise reexamined in any Court of the United States, than according to the rules of the common law.

Amendment VIII (Ratified December 15, 1791)

Excessive bail shall not be required, nor excessive fines imposed, nor cruel and unusual punishments inflicted.

Amendment IX (Ratified December 15, 1791)

The enumeration in the Constitution, of certain rights, shall not be construed to deny or disparage others retained by the people.

Amendment X (Ratified December 15, 1791)

The powers not delegated to the United States by the Constitution, nor prohibited by it to the States, are reserved to the States respectively, or to the people.

Amendment XI (Ratified February 7, 1795)

The judicial power of the United States shall not be construed to extend to any suit in law or equity, commenced or prosecuted against one of the United States by Citizens of another State, or by Citizens or Subjects of any Foreign State.

Amendment XII (Ratified June 15, 1804)

The Electors shall meet in their respective states, and vote by ballot for President and Vice President, one of whom, at least, shall not be an inhabitant of the same state with themselves; they shall name in their ballots the person voted for as President, and in distinct ballots the person voted for as Vice President, and they shall make distinct lists of all persons voted for as President, and of all persons voted for as Vice President, and of the number of votes for each, which lists they shall sign and certify, and transmit sealed to the seat of the government of the United States, directed to the President of the Senate; The President of the Senate shall, in the presence of the Senate and House of Representatives, open all the certificates and the votes shall then be counted; The person having the greatest number of votes for President, shall be the President, if such number be a majority of the whole number of Electors appointed; and if no person have such majority, then from the persons having the highest numbers not exceeding three on the list of those voted for as President, the House of Representatives shall choose immediately, by ballot, the President. But in choosing the President, the votes shall be taken by states, the representation from each state having one vote; a quorum for this purpose shall consist of a member or members from two-thirds of the states, and a majority of all the states shall be necessary to a choice. [And if the House of Representatives shall not choose a President whenever the right of choice shall devolve upon them, before the fourth day of March next following, then the Vice-President shall act as President, as in the case of the death or other constitutional disability of the President (This clause was superseded by section 3 of the Twentieth Amendment.)]. The person having the greatest number of votes as Vice President, shall be the Vice President, if such number be a majority of the whole number of Electors appointed, and if no person have a majority, then from the two highest numbers on the list, the Senate shall choose the Vice President; a quorum for the purpose shall consist of two-thirds of the whole number of Senators, and a majority of the whole number shall be necessary to a choice. But no person constitutionally ineligible to the office of President shall be eligible to that of Vice President of the United States.

Amendment XIII (Ratified December 6, 1865)

Section 1.   Neither slavery nor involuntary servitude, except as a punishment for crime whereof the party shall have been duly convicted, shall exist within the United States, or any place subject to their jurisdiction.

Section 2.   Congress shall have power to enforce this article by appropriate legislation.

Amendment XIV (Ratified July 9, 1868)

Section 1.   All persons born or naturalized in the United States, and subject to the jurisdiction thereof, are citizens of the United States and of the State wherein they reside. No State shall make or enforce any law which shall abridge the privileges or immunities of citizens of the United States; nor shall any State deprive any person of life, liberty, or property, without due process of law; nor deny to any person within its jurisdiction the equal protection of the laws.

Section 2. Representatives shall be apportioned among the several States according to their respective numbers, counting the whole number of persons in each State, excluding Indians not taxed. But when the right to vote at any election for the choice of electors for President and Vice President of the United States, Representatives in Congress, the Executive and judicial officers of a State, or the members of the Legislature thereof, is denied to any of the male inhabitants of such State, being twenty-one years of age, and citizens of the United States, or in any way abridged, except for participation in rebellion, or other crime, the basis of representation therein shall be reduced in the proportion which the number of such male citizens shall bear to the whole number of male citizens twenty-one years of age in such State.

Section 3. No person shall be a Senator or Representative in Congress, or elector of President and Vice President, or hold any office, civil or military, under the United States, or under any State, who, having previously taken an oath, as a member of Congress, or as an officer of the United States, or as a member of any State legislature, or as an executive or judicial officer of any State, to support the Constitution of the United States, shall have engaged in insurrection or rebellion against the same, or given aid or comfort to the enemies thereof. But Congress may by a vote of two-thirds of each House, remove such disability.

Section 4. The validity of the public debt of the United States, authorized by law, including debts incurred for payment of pensions and bounties for services in suppressing insurrection or rebellion, shall not be questioned. But neither the United States nor any State shall assume or pay any debt or obligation incurred in aid of insurrection or rebellion against the United States, or any claim for the loss of emancipation of any slave; but all such debts, obligations and claims shall be held illegal and void.

Section 5. The Congress shall have power to enforce, by appropriate legislation, the provisions of this article.

Amendment XV (Ratified February 3, 1870)

Section 1. The right of citizens of the United States to vote shall not be denied or abridged by the United States or by any State on account of race, color, or previous condition of servitude.

Section 2. The Congress shall have power to enforce this article by appropriate legislation.

Amendment XVI (Ratified February 3, 1913)

The Congress shall have power to lay and collect taxes on incomes, from whatever source derived, without apportionment among the several States, and without regard to any census or enumeration.

Amendment XVII (Ratified April 8, 1913)

The Senate of the United States shall be composed of two Senators from each State, elected by the people thereof, for six years; and each Senator shall have one vote. The electors in each State shall have the qualifications requisite for electors of the most numerous branch of the State legislatures.

When vacancies happen in the representation of any State in the Senate, the executive authority of such State shall issue writs of election to fill such vacancies: Provided, That the legislature of any State may empower the executive thereof to make temporary appointments until the people fill the vacancies by election as the legislature may direct.

This amendment shall not be so construed as to affect the election or term of any Senator chosen before it becomes valid as part of the Constitution.

Amendment XVIII (Ratified January 16, 1919)

Section 1. After one year from the ratification of this article the manufacture, sale, or transportation of intoxicating liquors within, the importation thereof into, or the exportation thereof from the United States and all territory subject to the jurisdiction thereof for beverage purposes is hereby prohibited.

Section 2. The Congress and the several States shall have concurrent power to enforce this article by appropriate legislation.

Section 3. This article shall be inoperative unless it shall have been ratified as an amendment to the Constitution by the legislatures of the several States, as provided in the Constitution, within seven years from the date of the submission hereof to the States by the Congress.

Amendment XIX (Ratified August 18, 1920)

The right of citizens of the United States to vote shall not be denied or abridged by the United States or by any State on account of sex.

Congress shall have power to enforce this article by appropriate legislation.

Amendment XX (Ratified January 23, 1933)

Section 1. The terms of the President and Vice President shall end at noon on the 20th day of January, and the terms of Senators and Representatives at noon on the 3d day of January, of the years in which such terms would have ended if this article had not been ratified; and the terms of their successors shall then begin.

Section 2. The Congress shall assemble at least once in every year, and such meeting shall begin at noon on the 3d day of January, unless they shall by law appoint a different day.

Section 3. If, at the time fixed for the beginning of the term of the President, the President elect shall have died, the Vice President elect shall become President. If a President shall not have been chosen before the time fixed for the beginning of his term, or if the President elect shall have failed to qualify, then the Vice President elect shall act as President until a President shall have qualified; and the Congress may by law provide for the case wherein neither a President elect nor a Vice President elect shall have qualified, declaring who shall then act as President, or the manner in which one who is to act shall be selected, and such person shall act accordingly until a President or Vice President shall have qualified.

Section 4. The Congress may by law provide for the case of the death of any of the persons from whom the House of Representatives may choose a President whenever the right of choice shall have devolved upon them, and for the case of the death of any of the persons from whom the Senate may choose a Vice President whenever the right of choice shall have devolved upon them.

Section 5. Sections 1 and 2 shall take effect on the 15th day of October following the ratification of this article.

Section 6. This article shall be inoperative unless it shall have been ratified as an amendment to the Constitution by the legislatures of three-fourths of the several States within seven years from the date of its submission.

Amendment XXI (Ratified December 3, 1933)

Section 1. The eighteenth article of amendment to the Constitution of the United States is hereby repealed.

Section 2. The transportation or importation into any State, Territory, or possession of the United States for delivery or use therein of intoxicating liquors, in violation of the laws thereof, is hereby prohibited.

Section 3. This article shall be inoperative unless it shall have been ratified as an amendment to the Constitution by conventions in the several States, as provided in the Constitution, within seven years from the date of the submission hereof to the States by the Congress.

Amendment XXII (Ratified February 27, 1951)

Section 1. No person shall be elected to the office of the President more than twice, and no person who has held the office of President, or acted as President, for more than two years of a term to which some other person was elected President shall be elected to the office of the President more than once. But this Article shall not apply to any person holding the office of President when this Article was proposed by the Congress, and shall not prevent any person who may be holding the office of President, or acting as President, during the term within which this Article becomes operative from holding the office of President or acting as President during the remainder of such term.

Section 2. This article shall be inoperative unless it shall have been ratified as an amendment to the Constitution by the legislatures of three-fourths of the several States within seven years from the date of its submission to the States by the Congress.

Amendment XXIII (Ratified March 29, 1961)

Section 1. The District constituting the seat of Government of the United States shall appoint in such manner as the Congress may direct:

A number of electors of President and Vice President equal to the whole number of Senators and Representatives in Congress to which the District would be entitled if it were a State, but in no event more than the least populous State; they shall be in addition to those appointed by the States, but they shall be considered, for the purposes of the election of President and Vice President, to be electors appointed by a State; and they shall meet in the District and perform such duties as provided by the twelfth article of amendment.

Section 2. The Congress shall have power to enforce this article by appropriate legislation.

Amendment XXIV (Ratified January 23, 1964)

Section 1. The right of citizens of the United States to vote in any primary or other election for President or Vice President, for electors for President or Vice President, or for Senator or Representatives in Congress, shall not be denied or abridged by the United States or any State by reason of failure to pay any poll tax or other tax.

Section 2. The Congress shall have power to enforce this article by appropriate legislation.

Amendment XXV (Ratified February 10, 1967)

Section 1.   In case of the removal of the President from office or of his death or resignation, the Vice President shall become President.

Section 2.   Whenever there is a vacancy in the office of the Vice President, the President shall nominate a Vice President who shall take office upon confirmation by a majority vote of both Houses of Congress.

Section 3.   Whenever the President transmits to the President *pro tempore* of the Senate and the Speaker of the House of Representatives his written declaration that he is unable to discharge the powers and duties of his office, and until he transmits to them a written declaration to the contrary, such powers and duties shall be discharged by the Vice President as Acting President.

Section 4.   Whenever the Vice President and a majority of either the principal officers of the executive departments or of such other body as Congress may by law provide, transmit to the President *pro tempore* of the Senate and the Speaker of the House of Representatives their written declaration that the President is unable to discharge the powers and duties of his office, the Vice President shall immediately assume the powers and duties of the office as Acting President.

Thereafter, when the President transmits to the President *pro tempore* of the Senate and the Speaker of the House of Representatives his written declaration that no inability exists, he shall resume the powers and duties of his office unless the Vice President and a majority of either the principal officers of the executive department or of such other body as Congress may by law provide, transmit within four days to the President *pro tempore* of the Senate and the Speaker of the House of Representatives their written declaration that the President is unable to discharge the powers and duties of his office. Thereupon Congress shall decide the issue, assembling within forty-eight hours for that purpose if not in session. If the Congress, within twenty-one days after receipt of the latter written declaration, or, if Congress is not in session, within twenty-one days after Congress is required to assemble, determines by two-thirds vote of both Houses that the President is unable to discharge the powers and duties of his office, the Vice President shall continue to discharge the same as Acting President; otherwise, the President shall resume the powers and duties of his office.

Amendment XXVI (Ratified July 1, 1971)

Section 1.   The right of citizens of the United States, who are eighteen years of age or older, to vote shall not be denied or abridged by the United States or by any State on account of age.

Section 2.   The Congress shall have power to enforce this article by appropriate legislation.

Amendment XXVII (Ratified May 7, 1992)

No law varying the compensation for the services of Senators and Representatives shall take effect until an election of Representatives shall have intervened.